Repentance for the Holocaust

signale
modern german letters, cultures, and thought

Series editor: Peter Uwe Hohendahl, Cornell University

Signale: Modern German Letters, Cultures, and Thought publishes new English-language books in literary studies, criticism, cultural studies, and intellectual history pertaining to the German-speaking world, as well as translations of important German-language works. *Signale* construes "modern" in the broadest terms: the series covers topics ranging from the early modern period to the present. *Signale* books are published under a joint imprint of Cornell University Press and Cornell University Library in electronic and print formats. Please see http://signale.cornell.edu/.

REPENTANCE FOR THE HOLOCAUST

*Lessons from Jewish Thought
for Confronting the German Past*

C. K. MARTIN CHUNG

A Signale Book

CORNELL UNIVERSITY PRESS AND CORNELL UNIVERSITY LIBRARY
ITHACA AND LONDON

Cornell University Press and Cornell University Library gratefully acknowledge the College of Arts & Sciences, Cornell University, for support of the Signale series.

First published 2017 by Cornell University Press and Cornell University Library

Printed in the United States of America

Library of Congress Cataloging-in-Publication Data

Names: Chung, C. K. Martin, author.
Title: Repentance for the Holocaust : lessons from Jewish thought for confronting the German past / C.K. Martin Chung.
Description: Ithaca : Cornell University Press : Cornell University Library, 2017. | Series: Signale : modern German letters, cultures, and thought | Includes bibliographical references and index.
Identifiers: LCCN 2017020179 (print) | LCCN 2017023970 (ebook) | ISBN 9781501712531 (pdf) | ISBN 9781501712524 (epub/mobi) | ISBN 9781501707612 (cloth : alk. paper) | ISBN 9781501707629 (pbk. : alk. paper)
Subjects: LCSH: Holocaust, Jewish (1939–1945)—Moral and ethical aspects. | Holocaust, Jewish (1939–1945)—Influence. | Repentance—Judaism. | Memory—Religious aspects—Judaism. | Historiography—Moral and ethical aspects—Germany. | Holocaust, Jewish (1939–1945)—Public opinion, German. | Public opinion—Germany.
Classification: LCC D804.7.M67 (ebook) | LCC D804.7.M67 C47 2017 (print) | DDC 940.53/18—dc23
LC record available at https://lccn.loc.gov/2017020179

Cornell University Press strives to use environmentally responsible suppliers and materials to the fullest extent possible in the publishing of its books. Such materials include vegetable-based, low-VOC inks and acid-free papers that are recycled, totally chlorine-free, or partly composed of nonwood fibers. For further information, visit our website at www.cornellpress.cornell.edu.

Cloth printing   10 9 8 7 6 5 4 3 2 1
Paperback printing   10 9 8 7 6 5 4 3 2 1

For Queenie, Natalie, and Tin Yu

Die große Schuld des Menschen sind nicht die Sünden,
die er begeht—die Versuchung ist mächtig und seine Kraft
gering! Die große Schuld des Menschen ist, daß er in jedem
Augenblick die Umkehr tun kann und nicht tut.*

Rabbi Bunam

Christen wünschen nicht, der Buße oder dem Chaos zu
entgehen, wenn Gottes Wille es über uns bringen will. Wir
müssen dieses Gericht als Christen annehmen.**

Dietrich Bonhoeffer

---

* "The major guilt of human beings is not the sins they have committed—for
the temptation is powerful and their power little! The major guilt of human beings is that in every moment they can repent but do not." Quoted in "Die große
Schuld," *Freiburger Rundbrief* 15, no. 57/60 (1963/1964): 32.

** "Christians ask not to escape from repentance or chaos if it is what the will
of God has in store for us. We must accept this proceeding as Christians." Quoted
in George K. A. Bell, "Die Ökumene und die innerdeutsche Opposition," *Vierteljahrshefte für Zeitgeschichte* 5, no. 4 (1957): 369.

CONTENTS

ACKNOWLEDGMENTS

This book would not have come into being without the support of many. First and foremost, I would like to thank Wayne Cristaudo and C. Roland Vogt, for their enduring mentorship and friendship—even after my graduation from the University of Hong Kong. At Hong Kong Baptist University, I am indebted to Jean-Pierre Cabestan and H. Werner Hess, who gave me the opportunity to work at the European Union Academic Programme Hong Kong, where I finished the revision of the manuscript of this book.

The improvement of this work has benefited tremendously from the recommendations of the editorial board of Signale, Peter Uwe Hohendahl, the series editor, and the two anonymous readers. I am grateful for their thoughtful suggestions, and also for the encouragement of Kizer Walker, the managing editor of the series. To Marian Rogers, my copyeditor, I want to say a special word of thanks and admiration: her professionalism and dedication were humbling and heartening at the same time. I felt truly privileged to have worked with her on this project.

Previously, I profited greatly from the critiques of Christopher Hutton, Stefan Auer, and Dan Diner, former director of the Simon Dubnow Institute (SDI) at Leipzig University. I am particularly pleased that an article version of this book is included in the SDI Yearbook for 2015. Without the perseverance of Petra Klara Gamke-Breitschopf, the manuscript editor, I don't think I would have come this far.

For my wider intellectual and professional development, I am irreparably indebted to Sid Ching, Alberto Rossa CMF, Marcelino Fonts CMF, Peter Chung, Beatrice Leung SPB, Chan Wai Chi and Tam Yik Fai, Laureen Velasco, Milette Zamora and Victor Gojocco, José Luís de Sales Marques, Ivo Carneiro de Sousa and Thomas Meyer, Keith Morrison, Éric Sautedé, Émilie Tran, Dominique Tyl SJ and Yves Camus SJ, Dixon Wong, Kendall Johnson, Louise Edwards and Andreas Leutzsch, Matthias Christian SVD, Anton Weber SVD, Ludger Feldkämper SVD and Heinz-Gerhard Justenhoven, Manfred Henningsen, Sander Gilman, Paul Bacon, Yang Daqing, Annika Frieberg, Pesach Schindler, Ephraim and Steffie Kaye, Irene Eber, Lauren Pfister, John Paul Lederach, Edward Kaplan and Glenn Timmermans.

Above all, I thank my wife, Queenie, for her unfailing love and support. It has not been easy to have a husband who is regularly away "doing research" year after year, especially when with two daughters at home to take care of in addition to a full-time job. Had her yes been less unswerving at any point in the last ten years or so, I might have stopped somewhere midway. For this reason, my final thank-you goes to my mother-in-law, Vanessa, for stepping in when we most needed an extra pair of hands at home.

ABBREVIATIONS

ASF   Aktion Sühnezeichen Friedensdienste (Action Reconciliation Service for Peace)

BRD   Bundesrepublik Deutschland (Federal Republic of Germany)

CDU   Christlich Demokratische Union Deutschlands (Christian Democratic Union of Germany)

DDR   Deutsche Demokratische Republik (German Democratic Republic)

EKD   Evangelische Kirche in Deutschland (Evangelical Church in Germany)

GEI   Georg-Eckert-Institut

JNF   Jewish National Fund

PRIME Peace Research Institute in the Middle East

SPD   Sozialdemokratische Partei Deutschlands (Social Democratic Party of Germany)

TRC   South African Truth and Reconciliation Commission

VgB   A convenient shorthand for *Vergangenheitsbewältigung* (coming to terms with the past); not generally used in the literature

ZdJ   Zentralrat der Juden in Deutschland (Central Council of Jews in Germany)

REPENTANCE FOR THE HOLOCAUST

INTRODUCTION

The German Problem of Vergangenheitsbewältigung

A national catastrophe, a physical and psychic collapse without parallel.[1]

THOMAS MANN, 1945

Here then is a whole people in a state of spiritual ruin such as has never been known, perhaps, in the history of the world.[2]

VICTOR GOLLANCZ, 1946

I

This book develops the biblical idea of "turning" (*tshuvah* in Hebrew) into a conceptual framework to analyze a particular area of contemporary German history, often loosely referred to as "coming to terms with the past" (*Vergangenheitsbewältigung* in German, or VgB for short). It examines a selection of German responses to the

---

1. Thomas Mann, "Germany and the Germans," in *Thomas Mann's Addresses Delivered at the Library of Congress, 1942–1949* (Rockville, MD: Wildside Press, 2008), 64. See the use of this speech by Jean Améry to encourage the German youth in **P14**.

2. Victor Gollancz, *Our Threatened Values* (London: Victor Gollancz, 1946), 84.

Nazi past, their interaction with the victims' responses, such as those of Jewish individuals,[3] and their correspondence with biblical "repentance." In demonstrating the victims' influence on German responses, I argue that the latter can be better analyzed and understood as a "model for coping with the past" in a relational rather than national paradigm. By establishing the conformity between such responses and the idea of *Umkehr/Buße tun*, as *tshuvah* is invariably translated into German,[4] the book asserts that the religious texts from the "Old Testament" encapsulating this idea are viable intellectual resources for dialogues among victims, perpetrators, bystanders, and their later generations in the discussion of guilt and responsibility, justice and reparation, remembrance and reconciliation. It thus is perhaps one of the greatest ironies of the twentieth century, in which Nazi Germany had sought to eliminate each and every single Jew within its reach, that postwar Germans have relied on the Jewish device of repentance as a feasible way out of their unparalleled "national catastrophe" (Mann), their unprecedented "spiritual ruin" (Gollancz).

The controversial nature of the research materials in question necessitates a further clarification of the aims and limits of this study before we venture into the relevant literature, methodology, and structure of the book. First and foremost, this is neither

---

3. It does not belong to the scope of this study to delve into what constitutes "Jewishness." When a certain idea is labeled or a certain personality is referred to as "Jewish" in this book, it is meant only to convey the fact that it is or can be *perceived* as Jewish (or to have perceived Jewish familial roots)—whether the basis of such perception is valid or not belongs to another inquiry. I would like to thank Sander Gilman for pointing me to this qualification. Nevertheless, given the overlapping meanings (i.e., ethnic, religious, cultural, etc.) of the term, and the Nazi perversion of it, a less-than-precise use of the word "Jewish" is bound to be problematic. My starting point for using it is the identity-legitimacy of the victim's claim arising from Nazi German crimes, and my intention is to give credit (when extraordinary expressions of "turning" are recorded, for instance) where credit is due, rather than arriving at the bizarre situation where somebody was persecuted as a "Jew," and then subsequently honored as a "Christian."

4. In general, the Einheitsübersetzung (1980) tends to use *Umkehr* (*umkehren*) throughout the Bible, whereas the Lutherbibel (1984) shifts between it and *Buße* (*tun*) in the New Testament and *Bekehrung* (*bekehren*) in the "Old Testament." Compare Jeremiah 31:19, 2 Kings 17:13, and Matthew 3:2.

affirmation nor negation of *moral realities* in postwar Germany; whether the responses analyzed bespeak *real* repentance or not exceeds the analytical purview of the researcher. Rather, this book recognizes its judgmental limits and bases its conclusions solely and consciously on what is "on the surface": forms of expression and ways of argumentation that are—themselves belonging to observable realities nonetheless—open to interpretation by all.[5] Likewise, in documenting Jewish efforts of "turning" in correspondence with the biblical idea of "assisted" repentance (i.e., God helping the sinner repent, who is unable to transform himself if left alone), there is no intention—explicit or implicit—to suggest that Jewish victims were themselves guilty, hence "in need" of repentance vis-à-vis the Germans; "co-repentance" in this sense is categorically rejected by the author. Rather, when "mutual-turning" is spoken of in this study, it is meant to describe the process in which the victims, who did not need "turning," turned nonetheless in aid of the turning of the wrongdoers, who needed it. It is to the explication of the multiple senses of turning (both biblical and historical) that this research dedicates itself. Neither a German nor a Jew, I do not see it as my "duty" to defend one or the other in their responses to the Shoah, or to "idealize" particular individuals, significant as their turning contributions might be. If there is something to defend in this book, it is the biblical notion of repentance, which is its core and organizing principle, as a viable blueprint for international reconciliation.

---

5. In this sense, my approach differs from that of Klaus Briegleb, who looks at the postwar German literary scene (Gruppe 47 in particular) and finds "contempt and taboo" when it comes to the encounter with Jews and Judaism after the Shoah. Making judgment on whether or how much a particular individual, group, or epoch has come to terms with the past is far from what this book is about. The existence of observable expression—rather than the lack of expected expression—is also important for my investigation, without which there is no correspondence to prove. See Klaus Briegleb, *Mißachtung und Tabu: Eine Streitschrift zur Frage: 'Wie antisemitisch war die Gruppe 47?'* (Berlin/Vienna: Philo, 2003).

II

While there is no lack of in-depth studies on German VgB, most of which were published in the last two decades or so,[6] relatively little has been done to explore the religious roots of this phenomenon, and nothing, so far as I could gather in the English and German languages, on the direct link between it and biblical repentance.[7] Among the most prolific scholars on the phenomenon are Norbert Frei, Peter Reichel, and Constantin Goschler, whose works lay the basis for subsequent research on VgB in its political, juridical, and institutional dimensions, as well as with respect to reparation and artistic representation.[8] There are also specific studies on key "episodes" or policy areas of coming to terms with the past, such as the Historikerstreit, in which the question and meaning of the singularity of the Holocaust were at stake.[9] The phenomenon

---

6. There are also VgB-dedicated monographs published before the 1990s, for example, Armin Mohler's *Vergangenheitsbewältigung: Von der Läuterung zur Manipulation* (Stuttgart-Degerloch: Seewald, 1968); and *Der Nasenring: Im Dickicht der Vergangenheitsbewältigung* (Essen: Heitz & Höffkes, 1989). These, however, are in fact polemics *against* rather than factual analyses *of* VgB.

7. Though Konrad Jarausch ostensibly uses "repentance/turning" as the title for his narrative of German "transformations," an idea he borrowed from Gustav Radbruch's "Umkehr zur Humanität," the religious contents of the concept are not explored, and hence no attempt is made to connect these to postwar "transformations." See Konrad Jarausch, *Die Umkehr: Deutsche Wandlungen 1945–1995* (Munich: Deutsche Verlags-Anstalt, 2004); Gustav Radbruch, "Die Erneuerung des Rechts," in *Rechtsphilosophie*, ed. Arthur Kaufmann (Heidelberg: C. F. Müller Juristischer Verlag, 1990), 112. Likewise, *Umkehr* also appears throughout Werner Wertgen's monograph on VgB, but it is not employed as the overarching analytical and organizational concept. See Werner Wertgen, *Vergangenheitsbewältigung: Interpretation und Verantwortung* (Paderborn: Ferdinand Schöningh, 2001).

8. Norbert Frei, *Vergangenheitspolitik: Die Anfänge der Bundesrepublik und die NS-Vergangenheit* (Munich: Deutscher Taschenbuch, 2003); Constantin Goschler, *Schuld und Schulden: Die Politik der Wiedergutmachung für NS-Verfolgte seit 1945* (Göttingen: Wallstein, 2005); Peter Reichel, *Vergangenheitsbewältigung in Deutschland: Die Auseinandersetzung mit der NS-Diktatur von 1945 bis heute* (Munich: C.H. Beck, 2001); Reichel, *Erfundene Erinnerung: Weltkrieg und Judenmord in Film und Theater* (Munich: Hanser, 2004).

9. Charles Maier, *The Unmasterable Past: History, Holocaust, and German National Identity* (Cambridge, MA: Harvard University Press, 1988); Lily Gardner

has attracted so much scholarly attention that it can already boast of having its own "dictionaries" and "lexicons."[10] Added to these are numerous comparative studies addressing the issues of disparity and transference in the intra-German, European, and interregional contexts.[11]

In the existing works where religion takes center stage, focus tends to be restricted to how the German churches have or have not dealt with the Nazi legacy—or more precisely, the question of Christian guilt in the Nazi era—while at times offering "theological reflection" as a means of coming to terms with this past.[12] In other words, these works present VgB in the domain of theology and religion as an institution, rather than analyzing the wider history of VgB through theological concepts. Aleida Assmann's earlier intervention in tracing certain catchwords in VgB discourse to their biblical roots proves a rarity in the literature.[13] Yet even she would later agree with Ulrike Jureit—who criticizes the religious intrusion into the "secular system" of coming to terms with the past[14]—that

Feldman, *Germany's Foreign Policy of Reconciliation: From Enmity to Amity* (Lanham, MD: Rowman & Littlefield, 2012).

10. Torben Fischer and Matthias N. Lorenz, eds., *Lexikon der 'Vergangenheitsbewältigung' in Deutschland: Debatten- und Diskursgeschichte des Nationalsozialismus nach 1945* (Bielefeld: transcript, 2007); Thorsten Eitz and Georg Stötzel, *Wörterbuch der 'Vergangenheitsbewältigung': Die NS-Vergangenheit im öffentlichen Sprachgebrauch*, vols. 1–2 (Hildesheim: Georg Olms, 2007 and 2009).

11. See, among others, Annette Weinke, *Die Verfolgung von NS-Tätern im geteilten Deutschland: Vergangenheitsbewältigungen 1949–1969 oder: Eine deutsch-deutsche Beziehungsgeschichte im Kalten Krieg* (Paderborn: Ferdinand Schöningh, 2002); Christoph Cornelißen, Lutz Klinkhammer, and Wolfgang Schwentker, eds., *Erinnerungskulturen: Deutschland, Italien und Japan seit 1945* (Frankfurt a.M.: Fischer Taschenbuch, 2004); and Elazar Barkan, *The Guilt of Nations: Restitution and Negotiating Historical Injustices* (New York: Norton, 2000).

12. Lucia Scherzberg, ed., *Theologie und Vergangenheitsbewältigung: Eine kritische Bestandsaufnahme im interdisziplinären Vergleich* (Paderborn: Ferdinand Schöningh, 2005); and Matthew Hockenos, *A Church Divided: German Protestants Confront the Nazi Past* (Bloomington: Indiana University Press, 2004).

13. Aleida Assmann and Ute Frevert, *Geschichtsvergessenheit, Geschichtsversessenheit: Vom Umgang mit deutschen Vergangenheiten nach 1945* (Stuttgart: Deutsche Verlags-Anstalt, 1999), 54, 59–60, 80–81.

14. Ulrike Jureit and Christian Schneider, *Gefühlte Opfer: Illusionen der Vergangenheitsbewältigung* (Bonn: Bundeszentrale für politische Bildung, 2010), 42.

religious concepts, having no reference in the "secular-speaking area," have no place in the vocabulary of remembrance culture (*Erinnerungskultur*).[15]

Yet, as we shall see later and throughout the historical chapters in part 2 of this book, the religious vocabulary of sin and guilt, of atonement and repentance, has accompanied VgB as a historical process[16] from the very beginning. It is therefore questionable as a research practice and historiographical principle that certain materials and expressions are excluded at the outset from the subject matter simply because they don't conform to a certain view of secularity and its relationship with the phenomenon.[17] As Assmann herself concluded early on, "The entire concept of reconciliation (*Versöhnung*) through repentance (*Buße*) is only thinkable on the ground of a guilt culture (*Schuldkultur*)."[18] It is argued here that the concept of repentance from the Hebrew Bible has indeed had a significant influence on the German process of facing the Nazi past. The historical records show that the notions of "turning" are

15. Aleida Assmann, *Das neue Unbehagen an der Erinnerungskultur* (Munich: C. H. Beck, 2013), 116. The point on which she disagrees with Jureit, though, is the latter's conflation of victim-identification and victim-orientation, an objection also raised by Werner Konitzer, "Opferorientierung und Opferidentifizierung: Überlegungen zu einer begrifflichen Unterscheidung," in *Das Unbehagen an der Erinnerung: Wandlungsprozesse im Gedenken an den Holocaust*, ed. Ulrike Jureit, Christian Schneider, and Margrit Fröhlich (Frankfurt a. M.: Brandes & Apsel, 2012).

16. As it is a heavily contested coinage, there have been no doubt various attempts at defining and periodizing *Vergangenheitsbewältigung* by its proponents and opponents alike. On the conceptual history of the term, see Helmut König, Michael Kohlstruck, and Andreas Wöll, "Einleitung," in *Vergangenheitsbewältigung am Ende des zwanzigsten Jahrhunderts*, ed. Helmut König, Michael Kohlstruck, and Andreas Wöll (Opladen/Wiesbaden: Westdeutscher Verlag, 1998). On the different periodization models, see note 60 below.

17. One could only imagine the loss in research findings if, for example, the South African experience of coming to terms with the past were to be studied within exclusively secular frameworks, and theological inputs in the process itself were to be left out of consideration. On the comparability and utility of such experiences, see the conclusion in this book. On the theologically informed approach to the study of coming to terms with the past, see John Paul Lederach, *Building Peace: Sustainable Reconciliation in Divided Societies* (Washington, DC: US Institute of Peace Press, 1997).

18. Assmann and Frevert, *Geschichtsvergessenheit*, 91.

spiritual resources at the disposal of the victims and their descendants, who used them to help the perpetrators and their later generations arrive at insights that were otherwise inaccessible to them. This book seeks to acknowledge this extraordinary and indispensable assistance in understanding what it means "to turn," and the corresponding willingness and openness to receive that assistance.

An early German volunteer at Aktion Sühnezeichen, an initiative based on the idea of "atonement" (*Sühne*),[19] has documented how she came to know the Jewish meaning of "mercy" from her Hebrew teacher: "Jehuda explained to us that the word 'mercy' does not fully render the meaning of 'chessed.' Mercy is something that comes from God to us while we remain passive receivers. 'Chessed' means much more; it means 'God's solidarity' with us. God stands by us. 'One must not only receive chessed, but *also do it*,' said Jehuda. 'Only then will we know what it means.' "[20] Another time she was "taught" in Israel by a "Chaverim" from America about what "repentance" means: " 'You know what,' Mats said, 'you can't run around in chains forever, just because your fathers are guilty. . . . When a person realizes his guilt, the obvious thing for him to do is to learn and to *repent* (*umkehren*) and to *better himself* (*sich bessern*). . . . The first thing we wish from you Germans is not that you come here and speak about 'atonement' or 'sign of atonement,' but that Germany becomes another Germany because it has learned from the past. Then, what was hurtful to us will also become less hurtful."[21]

Needless to say, such views do not "represent" Jewish thinking in any quantitative sense. Yet they do touch upon, as I shall argue in this book, some of the fundamental tenets of biblical repentance: namely, the role of mercy in repentance, the sin of the fathers, and the possibility of renewal. Without the intellectual infrastructure, the "cultural ground" (Assmann) furnished by these ancient

---

19. See P5.

20. Christel Eckern, *Die Straße nach Jerusalem: Ein Mitglied der 'Aktion Sühnezeichen' berichtet über Leben und Arbeit in Israel* (Essen: Ludgerus-Verlag Hubert Wingen, 1962), 18 (emphasis added).

21. Ibid., 111 (emphasis added).

notions from the Bible, which at times of grave moral crises can be the only remaining recourse to argumentative legitimacy, the key questions of how a nation can come to terms with its past risk become intractable, or merely matters of personal taste. Can the past be "mastered" (*bewältigt werden*)? Can something be "made good again" (*wiedergutgemacht*) through reparation? If the names are logically false, can one still affirm their referents, or must these be rejected as based on "illusions"? With what "promise" or hope can those Germans engaging in VgB substantiate their claim that their words and deeds would contribute to their renewal as a people and to their reconciliation with their victims? Is it possible at all "after Auschwitz"? Without some form of preexisting "frames of meaning,"[22] shared by both the victims and the perpetrators (at least historical-culturally, not necessarily religious-ideologically, as was manifest in Nazi "Christian" theology),[23] how can one answer these questions with a reasonable degree of satisfaction—that is, in a way that is acceptable to those who live within these frames?

III

In the immediate period around the time of military defeat in 1945, some German intellectuals both inside and outside the country were engaged in reflection on what was in store for their nation after Nazism. Ubiquitous in this reflection was the assessment that the existential crisis (the "German question/problem") begotten by the twelve preceding years was of such a catastrophic proportion that only through a fundamental "returning"—whether it be to Germany's religious roots, humanistic tradition, or Western democratic civilization—could postwar Germany have any hope of survival.

---

22. Clifford Geertz, *The Interpretation of Cultures* (New York: Basic Books, 1973), 28.
23. See Susannah Heschel, *The Aryan Jesus: Christian Theologians and the Bible in Nazi Germany* (Princeton, NJ/Oxford: Princeton University Press, 2008).

Alfred Weber, in his *Abschied von der bisherigen Geschichte* (Farewell to Previous History),[24] written before the war ended and published in Hamburg in 1946, called what was then still unfolding a "catastrophic historical collapse," which in effect would seal the end of the history that had been led by European states up until then.[25] "The first great and fundamental sin (*Sünde*), which the West (*Abendland*) has committed against itself," for which it had "to pay a high price," was having erected a state system in which state behavior is placed "outside general morals," "outside any effective idealistic supervision of actions," as in the so-called moral-free state actions.[26] Weber then proceeded to explore the "dogmatizing" tendencies in European history, culminating in the "nihilism" predominant in the epoch, which was allegedly the "deep cause" of the catastrophe. For him—the younger brother of Max Weber—the way forward was "to organize Europe and especially its German center on a free democratic basis that represents human dignity and humanity."[27] The German people must engage in self-education for self-renewal and self-transformation, by returning to the "undogmatic European prototypes (*Vorgestalten*)."[28] "That is what we need. Here lies our future."[29]

Carl-Hermann Mueller-Graaf (a.k.a. Constantin Silens) concurred with Weber that the age in which "Europe was the head and the lord of the world" was coming to end.[30] But in his 1946 book, *Irrweg und Umkehr* (Misguided Path and Repentance), Silens focused on what he called the "German problem" instead of "Europeanizing" it.[31] For him, who professed to belong to "that Christian and conservative Germany," "the great German guilt (*deutsche Schuld*), the guilt of many decades, is the turning away

---

24. Alfred Weber, *Abschied von der bisherigen Geschichte: Überwindung des Nihilismus?* (Hamburg: Claaßen und Goverts Verlag, 1946).
25. Ibid., 12.
26. Ibid., 20.
27. Ibid., 251.
28. Ibid., 251–53.
29. Ibid., 253.
30. Constantin Silens, *Irrweg und Umkehr* (Basel: Birkhäuser, 1946), 245.
31. Ibid., 10.

(*Abwendung*) from the Christianness of the West (*Christlichkeit des Abendlandes*)," turning instead to Darwin, Nietzsche, and Spengler, the "true misleaders."[32] As such, the Germans, who "are guilty of our fate," must do repentance, "not repentance (*Buße*) in the sense of worldly revenge. . . . [but] repentance in the great sense of Christianity, which means realization (*Erkenntnis*) and confession (*Bekenntnis*) of the wrong done," "repentance as regretful (*reuig*) realization of one's own evil."[33] "They must understand that they need a truthful response before God and for their own sake, so that they break a better path to their children's future, better than the one that has led them to today's misery."[34] Without the spiritual outlook derived from the "spirit of Christian regard for the neighbor," the author—an official in trade and economic affairs both during and after the Nazi years[35]—was convinced that "there can be no German future."[36]

Silens, a Lutheran, could easily find a cohort in other German Christians of his time, such as Johannes Hessen, a Catholic theologian. Hessen held a series of public lectures in the winter semester of 1945–46 at the University of Cologne, where he taught philosophy, musing about "reconstruction" (*Wiederaufbau*) of postwar Germany in different spheres, from science to law to religion. He found no more fitting description of the destruction he witnessed in the Germany of 1945 than the first verse from the book of Lamentations, traditionally attributed to the prophet Jeremiah: "Wandering through the ruins of our great cities, one wants to join in the lament of the prophet: 'How forlorn the city lies, once full of folks.'"[37] Yet, Hessen immediately added, "worse than the material is the intellectual devastation (*geistige Verwüstung*) of Germany. . . . National Socialism has proved to be . . . an assassination

---

32. Ibid., 253.

33. Ibid., 248–49.

34. Ibid.

35. See Matthias Pape, "Mueller-Graaf, Carl-Hermann," *Neue Deutsche Biographie* 18 (1997): 497–98.

36. Silens, *Irrweg und Umkehr*, 10.

37. Johannes Hessen, *Der geistige Wiederaufbau Deutschlands: Reden über die Erneuerung des deutschen Geisteslebens* (Stuttgart: August Schröder Verlag, 1946), 10.

of all intellectual culture."[38] Like Silens, he advocated the avowal
of German guilt, of a "common guilt" (*Gemeinschuld*), in order to
work together toward the "intellectual-ethical rebirth of our people": "In the final analysis, we have all become guilty. . . . There is
not only guilt of the individual, there is also guilt of the community
(*Schuld der Gemeinschaft*). Since we belong to the people, whose
leadership has unleashed this war and with it brought unspeakable
suffering and misery to humanity, each of us has after all become
guilty before humanity and before God."[39] He presented Nazism
(especially Alfred Rosenberg's racial theory) as an antithesis to
Christianity and proposed "reconstruction in the religious sphere"
following the prophetic path of individual Christians like Martin
Niemöller and Clemens August Graf von Galen.[40]

Beyond the intellectual-ethical "reconstruction," a distinguished
economist of his time, Wilhelm Röpke, proposed "revolutions"
in the political and socioeconomic spheres. Though also for him,
these revolutions were dependent on the "moral revolution, just
as the German question is always in essence an intellectual-moral
one."[41] The threefold revolution was deemed a necessary undertaking after the "physical, political, and moral suicide (*Selbstmord*)"
of the Germans, "a tragedy without parallel in history, a real
tragedy, in which guilt and fate are enchained to one another."[42]
Now that the Germans had become a pariah Volk, "odium generis
humani," "one of the most problematic, most complicated, and
most hated peoples," "one of the worst wellsprings of infection
(*Ansteckungsherd*),"[43] "it is the hour of 'regret (*Reue*) and rebirth
(*Wiedergeburt*),' of which the German philosopher Max Scheler
had spoken after the First World War."[44] The German people as a

---

38. Ibid.

39. Ibid., 103–4.

40. Ibid., 19, 25, 72.

41. Wilhelm Röpke, *Die deutsche Frage* (Erlenbach-Zurich: Eugen Rentsch, 1945), 222.

42. Ibid., 9.

43. Ibid., 10–13.

44. Ibid., 222. See Max Scheler's essay, "Reue und Wiedergeburt," in *Vom Ewigen im Menschen*, vol. 1, *Religiöse Erneuerung* (Leipzig: Der Neue Geist, 1921), 5–58.

whole, said Röpke, "will not commit suicide, but repent (*umkeh-ren*), if he is shown the way back."[45] The professor of economics, who had been "retired" in 1933 for being a Nazi opponent, pleaded with his Swiss readers to "nurture the delightful first signs of repentance (*Umkehr*) of German intellectuals," so that one might eventually really speak of "Germany's rebirth."[46]

Without going any further into the early primary German responses to the "catastrophe" of the long decade of Nazi Germany, one can already see from the brief survey above the prolific use of the theologically charged terms "sin," "guilt," and "repentance" to perceive, analyze, and to propose solutions to the "German problem."[47] Though one might disagree with their diagnoses—for instance, would an unqualified returning to Christianity be a sufficient "German repentance" when the German churches themselves were by and large compromised?[48] Would a mere returning to the democratic West be a satisfactory answer to the millions of victims of Nazism, many of whom were from or still in the then undemocratic East?[49] On the other hand, European Jewish intellectuals were also engaging in reflection on whether and how "Jewish remnants" should help Germans attain the "moral renewal" they desperately needed, from remaining in postwar Germany to exercise justice (Eugen Kogon) to leaving for Palestine to establish a model civilized state (Hans Klee).[50] Irrespective of the actual validity of these, their act of employing biblical concepts to communicate with one another is a historical fact and, insofar as it is continual, a social phenomenon that is itself a legitimate object

---

45. Röpke, *Deutsche Frage*, 224.

46. Ibid., 225.

47. There is certainly much to explore between biblical notions and German thought, above and beyond the contemporary problem of coming to terms with the past. See, for example, Daniel Purdy, *On the Ruins of Babel: Architectural Metaphor in German Thought*, Signale (Ithaca, NY: Cornell University Press and Cornell University Library, 2011).

48. See more on this problem in **P2**.

49. See **P1** and **P3**.

50. See **P10**.

of phenomenological investigation.[51] The results will show, inter alia, that the broader discourses went actually much further than just (re)turning to Christianity and democracy: whereas an aspect of Nazism was to cut Christianity from its Jewish roots, postwar Christian reflection in Germany was characterized by its returning to this foundation through using scriptures from the "Old Testament" in VgB sermons, and opening itself to Talmudic sources and Jewish voices in general.[52] Postwar political reform also went way beyond building democratic structure and culture to cultivating individual concern for the suffering of the others, based on the biblical idea of the "new heart" of vulnerability.[53]

IV

Without some substantial basis for evaluating the discourse on "(re)turning," it would seem that all proposals have equal validity, which certainly is not the case.[54] Yet, "turning" in the Bible is not an *empty* concept: not all turnings or returnings are repentant turnings.[55] This book begins therefore with an exploration of the idea

---

51. Husserl points us to the phenomena of subjects and intersubjectivity—not as merely psychological-natural objects, but in relation to the *Lebenswelt*, that pregiven, preexisting "ground" on which potentialities and possibilities in theory and praxis stand—as a new field of science toward which philosophy should strive, as phenomenology. My work can be considered as phenomenological investigation insofar as it looks at and seeks to describe that "pregiven, preexisting ground," that source of "selbstverständliche Evidenz" (what I call intellectual infrastructure), on which Germans and Jews could think, talk, act, and judge about how to deal with the aftermath of the Shoah. In this sense, this book presupposes that the biblical concept of repentance is a constituent part of that *Lebenswelt* in which both perpetrators and victims find themselves.

52. This of course does not mean that deep-seated anti-Judaic notions have disappeared overnight. See, for example, the pitfalls of the earlier German Christian confessions in **P14**.

53. See **R6**.

54. See, for example, the maneuvers of shoveling punishment of German guilt onto the few Nazis and positioning Germany as the victim of Hitler in Röpke, *Deutsche Frage*, 240; and Silens, *Irrweg und Umkehr*, 231–32.

55. See **R6**.

of "turning" in the Bible. The purpose is not to produce new theological knowledge, but to outline the main features of this biblical concept that are pertinent to *collective* repentance.[56] The present book proceeds from the principles guiding "turning" between God and the individual sinner, and moves on to those concerning specifically interhuman, collective relationships. Modern German translations of the Bible (Einheitsübersetzung and Lutherbibel, etc.) are used—not for technical but anthropological reasons[57]—together with traditional Jewish exegeses (such as those by Moses Maimonides and Rabbeinu Yonah) and inputs from those contemporary Jewish thinkers (such as Martin Buber, Abraham Joshua Heschel, and Franz Rosenzweig) who have attained referential status in the German-Jewish cultural world. The linchpin of this biblical investigation is the *Bußpsalmen*, or the Psalms of Repentance: a selection of seven Psalms that are traditionally used by Christians for the expression and education of repentance, with the fourth *Bußpsalm*, Psalm 51, recognized by Jewish sources as *the* Psalm of Repentance.[58] The first part of this book presents fourteen "potencies" with regard to biblical repentance—divided into two chapters, one on divine-human and the other on interhuman

---

56. This method is modeled after John Paul Lederach's approach in his *Building Peace*. Lederach observes how Psalm 85:11 was employed by Nicaraguan conciliators in their village meetings mediating between the Sandinista and the Yatama, and draws a theoretical framework out of this text to analyze the tensions among "truth, mercy, peace and justice" in collective reconciliation. It is Lederach who maintains that sociocultural resources (such as shared religious texts) are of paramount importance for sustaining reconciliation (93–97).

57. Consequently, unlike the usual practice of contemporary biblical research, focus is placed on what *is* being translated into German as such, rather than which is the *most accurate* translation according to the source texts in their original languages. Lederach likewise also depended on the actual Spanish translation (Reina Valera) used by the reconciliation workers he was observing, hence the unusual English translation of the verse based on the Spanish words "la verdad, la misericordia, la justicia, y la paz" he had heard. John Paul Lederach, pers. comm., 30 Aug. 2010.

58. See, for example, Rabbeinu Yonah, *The Gates of Repentance*, trans. and comm. Yaakov Feldman (Northvale, NJ/Jerusalem: Jason Aronson, 1999), 38, 49, 70.

repentance—which together form a system of affirmations, or "relational movements" (i.e., **R1–R14**):

R1 The sinner is not sin
R2 The twofold damage of sin
R3 Mercy precedes repentance; repentance responds to mercy
R4 Recognizing punishment as just
R5 Confession as the only acceptable sacrifice
R6 Repentance as inner death and rebirth
R7 "Helping others repent" as the new task of the repentant
R8 Repentant disagreement
R9 Even God repents
R10 Repentance's representative minority
R11 Justice between abused perpetrators and abusive "victims"
R12 The sin of the fathers as cross-generational guilt
R13 Remembrance for life as cross-generational responsibility
R14 Reconciliation as turning to each other through turning to God

These will be employed in the second part of the book to analyze and categorize the historical data. Hence unlike Assmann, I do not begin with VgB "catchwords" and trace backward to their biblical origins, but start with biblical concepts and work forward to identify their equivalents in VgB discourses. In this way I seek to render more visible that intellectual infrastructure on which these discourses take place. In this regard, my approach also differs markedly from Stern's, who has chosen to conduct his investigation of the German-Jewish relationship outside the "realm of special Jewish historiography" and to argue instead for the analytical strength of the "triangular relationship between Americans, Germans and Jews,"[59] I examine how a repentance-informed outlook of history with its

---

59. Frank Stern, *The Whitewashing of the Yellow Badge: Antisemitism and Philosemitism in Postwar Germany*, trans. William Templer (Oxford/New York/Seoul/Tokyo: Pergamon Press, 1992), xv, xx.

God-victim-perpetrator triad (**R2**) may have an impact on the relationship between Jews and Germans in the aftermath of the Shoah.

The historical part of the book (part 2), which is by far the more substantial part, consists of fourteen chapters (i.e., **P1–P14**), all of which are analyses of primary responses (by Germans and non-Germans, but chiefly in German) to the Nazi atrocities, especially the Shoah:

P1 "People, not devils"
P2 "Fascism was the great apostasy"
P3 "The French must love the German spirit now entrusted to them"
P4 "One cannot speak of injustice without raising the question of guilt"
P5 "You won't believe how thankful I am for what you have said"
P6 "Courage to say no and still more courage to say yes"
P7 "Raise our voice, both Jews and Germans"
P8 "The appropriateness of each proposition depends upon who utters it"
P9 "Hitler is in ourselves, too"
P10 "I am Germany"
P11 "Know before whom you will have to give an account"
P12 "We take over the guilt of the fathers"
P13 "Remember the evil, but do not forget the good"
P14 "We are not authorized to forgive"

Each chapter seeks to demonstrate the correspondence between the set of responses documented and the particular feature of biblical repentance in the corresponding section in part 1 of the book. Since it belongs to the nature of biblical repentance that it is a never-ending, ever-renewing process (**R6**), I do not attempt, like some other historians of German VgB do, to offer a narrative with an artificial time frame, to determine the "turning points" in history and to characterize each time period.[60] Rather, in each chapter

---

60. See, for example, Norbert Frei's four phases of "Umgang mit der NS-Vergangenheit" in his *1945 und Wir: Das Dritte Reich im Bewußtsein der Deutschen*

of this discourse and historical analysis, concrete formulations and expressions of particular turning movements are presented, connected, and compared—at times also with countermovements in order to highlight the contrast—with priority given, when it is possible to trace, to pioneering manifestations in the early postwar period. (Hence the names of key pioneer-"turners,"[61] such as Eugen Kogon and Alfred Grosser, to whom recognition is due, will appear and reappear in different historical chapters, simply for the reason that their formulations have "precedented" several aspects of repentance.) Despite this structural disregard of the time-narrative element, there is still a "natural" progression of time as the chapters progress, if only for the obvious reason that some questions and answers only arose when their social conditions came into being, such as those relating to generational guilt and responsibility (**P12–P13**) coming up when the "second generation" came of age in the 1960s.

This structuring of the book therefore allows for two ways of reading it: vertically and horizontally. One may begin with the chapters on biblical repentance to have a grasp of its overall spirit, and then proceed to the chapters on historical repentance to see the correspondence between the two; or alternatively, one may read each of the fourteen biblical-historical sections-chapters by pairs (e.g., **R12** on biblical repentance concerning generational guilt,

---

(Munich: C. H. Beck, 2005), 26–27; and Assmann's three phases of "deutsche Erinnerungsgeschichte," in *Geschichtsvergessenheit*, 143–45. According to these periodization schemes, "Vergangenheitsbewältigung" is only one of the phases (running between the late 1950s to the late 1970s or early 1980s). The use of VgB here in this book deviates obviously from these frames; it is used namely as the name of that phenomenon that was manifest in these different "phases," rather than being limited to one or some of them. Despite the differences in approaches and intentions, I think both Frei and Assmann would concede that it is the name "Vergangenheitsbewältigung," rather than "deutsche Erinnerungsgeschichte" or "Vergangenheitsbewahrung," "Umgang mit der NS-Vergangenheit" or "deutsche Lernprozesse" (or Adorno's "Vergangenheitsaufarbeitung," for that matter), that has, at least judging from the present and despite its referential limitations, become *the* household word for that reality that we are all observing and analyzing.

61. "Turner" is used in this book to refer to those who pronounce messages of turning—whether concerning changes of attitude, mind-set, course of action, way of perception, etc.—that correspond with the spirit of repentance. See more on this in part 2 of this book.

and then **P12** on equivalent ideas as expressed in the history of German VgB). Boldface phrases throughout the book function as pointers to specific sections and chapters to help the reader navigate the book.

This method of using the "expansive" concept of biblical repentance, with its multiplicity of turning movements, rather than a "restrictive" definition of VgB as the historiographic principle, has the advantage of contextualizing historical data that are otherwise considered irrelevant to the history of "coming to terms with the past." (As a result of this, the contributions of Victor Gollancz, Rabbi Robert Raphael Geis, Günther Anders, and some others recorded here are rarely given prominence in most histories of German VgB.) The "downside" of this method is of course the explosion of potential materials. In fact, I am convinced that there is enough historical evidence for each of the fourteen chapters to be expanded into a book-length study. Yet without the context of the whole, the parts risk the loss of meaning aside from a pedantic interest. Hence I have chosen to argue for the contextualizing strength of biblical repentance, aside from its dialogue-enabling potentials, instead of focusing on any one of its fourteen "movements" identified.

Notwithstanding the lack of clear temporal and geographical delimiters, I am looking mainly at German materials that have generated responses from within or without (hence in most cases already "publicized"), between the early postwar years, when taking a particular turning posture bore clear personal risks, and the early postreunification period, after which turning expressions tended to become more of a reaffirmation or reformulation of previous expressions. Exceptions are those materials that have occasioned substantial responses in the German cultural world (e.g., Daniel J. Goldhagen's thesis), and those that have a significant intellectual contribution to German responses (e.g., Rabbi Harold Schulweis's spiritual legacy in Holocaust remembrance). Especially helpful to me as source materials, aside from texts published in book form, are circulated periodicals such as the *Frankfurter Hefte*, *Die Wandlung*, and the *Freiburger Rundbrief*. The digital archives of *Die Zeit*, *Der Spiegel*, and the *Hamburger Abendblatt* have provided me with additional pertinent reference materials.

This book is not about how popular or unpopular "turning" was in Germany. It must be said at the outset that with but extremely rare exceptions, such as Willy Brandt's *Kniefall,* for which there was contemporaneous research done on public opinion regarding the gesture (see **P5**), it is impossible to gauge statistically in retrospection the German and non-German audiences' opinions toward the responses recorded in this study. It is possible to trace, say, the sales figures of a particular book or journal cited,[62] but a higher sales figure does not of course necessarily mean agreement with its message(s) (a problem further compounded by the discrepancy between intended and interpreted meanings)—one cannot even be sure if it indicates readership, for buying is not the same as reading, much less reading with or without sympathy. I think therefore it is only prudent not to make any claim of majority support for the responses—though some of the responses analyzed here, such as the Lichterkette (**P6**), were mass movements instead of individual actions. Perhaps it is safer to assume that these were minority opinions, given the historical contexts in which they were uttered.

Though I in no way lay any claim to the exhaustion of the sources available, much less to the "representativeness" of the examples cited, I do feel confident that with the present "sedimentation" of evidence in each of the fourteen historical chapters, a strong case has already been made for the correspondence (at least "on the surface") between biblical and historical "turning." When I continue to "discover" documented and perhaps even stronger examples of correspondence, the consideration of length and the avoidance of unnecessary repetition prevent me from accumulating further historical sediments.

---

62. The *Frankfurter Hefte,* for example, had done its own quantitative study of circulation and readership in April 1947 (with about 2,600 completed questionnaires). The study showed that most of its readers were in North Rhine–Westphalia (33.9 percent), most in the age group of 35–49 (43.4 percent), most with higher education degrees (63.6 percent), and most interested in topics related to religion (17.4 percent) and politics (14.9 percent). Readership (including shared reading) was estimated at 150,000 (the sample, however, was admittedly "not *entirely* representative" of the population). See the entire report by Valentin Siebrecht, "Selbstbildnis der Leser: Zahlen und Tatsachen aus der Umfrage der *Frankfurter Hefte,*" *Frankfurter Hefte* 2, no. 12 (1947).

From a broader perspective, the human possibilities in expression and in action opened up by shared cultural resources are what this book is about. As a Chinese living in an era of gradually deteriorating Sino-Japanese relations, which are ostensibly burdened by "history problems," I feel a compelling need for the study of German VgB—which Karl Jaspers once defined as *Umkehr*, as distinct from "forgetting" or "shame"[63]—from which *alternative responses* to past atrocities (for both perpetrators *and* victims) can be deduced. Through revealing the relational dynamics of the German "model," that is, the contribution of Jewish ideas as communicated/carried out by Jewish and non-Jewish counterparts, I hope to raise questions about the constitutive aspects of Chinese responses and traditional ideas shared in East Asia in the problem of Japanese VgB. We may discover that the lack of certain critical "turnings" (on one or both sides) may have not so much to do with the will to "repent" and to "reconcile" as with shared traditional understandings of what is (im)possible and (un)desirable in the aftermath of intergroup atrocities in the first place. In other words, the so-called history problems can very well be in fact reflective of the problems of our shared ethical paradigm.

Though the presence of a resource does not automatically mean its employment—one only needs to ask why "mutual-turning" had not happened or succeeded among enemy states in Europe in the interwar years—the neglect or ignorance of it does mean foreclosed possibilities. In this sense, the study of the influence of scripture on history through human agency should sharpen one's perceptibility of potential courses of action that have been either forgotten or obscured.

---

63. "'*Coming to terms with the past*' does not take place through forgetting, not through 'shame' in which a secret apologia still lurks, but only through repentance (*Umkehr*), one that is attested to by—among other things—the *unreserved recognition of the consequences of war*." Karl Jaspers, *Wohin treibt die Bundesrepublik? Tatsachen, Gefahren, Chancen* (Munich: R. Piper, 1966), 238–39 (emphasis in the original).

PART I

The Jewish Device of Repentance: From Individual, Divine-Human to Interhuman, Collective "Turning"

Create in me, O God, a pure heart;
give me a new and steadfast spirit.

PSALM 51:12

I shall give you a new heart
and put a new spirit within you.

EZEKIEL 36:26

"No other tradition has invested as much as Judaism in *tshuvah* [repentance]," proclaimed Rabbi Pesach Schindler to a group of Chinese educators at Yad Vashem learning about how to teach the Holocaust in China.[1] This may sound like a startling claim, considering the existence of similar ideas in other religious traditions.[2] Yet, when one considers the Holy Scriptures, in which the prophets' calls for repentance are a constant fixture, in which stories of repentance (David's, Jacob/Israel's, Naaman's, Nineveh's, etc.) abound, in which expressions of repentance in confessional prayers

---

1. Remarks delivered at the International School for Holocaust Studies, Yad Vashem, 4 Oct. 2010. The author of this book was in the audience.
2. See Amitai Etzioni and David E. Carney, eds., *Repentance: A Comparative Perspective* (Lanham, MD: Rowman & Littlefield, 1997).

and songs suffuse the entire biblical fabric, not to mention the annual ritual of Yom Kippur, or the Day of Atonement, it would hardly be an overstatement to claim that the idea of "turning," which the Hebrew word *tshuvah* literally conveys, is central to the Jewish tradition. Indeed, the potency of this theological emphasis can also be felt in its "offshoot." The litany of "confession literature" in the Christian world has caused Chinese literary scholars to reflect on the almost complete absence of such a genre in the history of Chinese literature.[3] The Reformation began when a German monk went public against the church about what repentance (*Buße tun*) should be and should not be.[4]

The richness of this biblical tradition of repentance is also attested by the need to codify and explicate it for the benefit of Jewish communities. Maimonides's *Doctrine of Repentance* and Rabbeinu Yonah's *Gates of Repentance*, from the twelfth and thirteenth centuries respectively, are among the best-known references. In the historical period around the time of the German plunge into Nazism, the idea of repentance was also prominent in the epoch-defining works of the German-Jewish cultural world, such as Franz Rosenzweig's *Stern der Erlösung* and Martin Buber's *Ich und Du*. In the words of Buber, "The event that is called repentance (*Umkehr*) from the side of the world is called from God's side redemption (*Erlösung*)."[5] For Rosenzweig, inner repentance (*innere Umkehr*) is that event through which fundamental attitudes toward "nothing" and "something" are reversed by revelation (*Offenbarung*).[6] The uniqueness of the biblical paradigm is in fact rooted in its point of departure—it does not begin "speculations" with the "good" and the "perfect," but with the "fallen" and the "broken," not with the "pure" and the "unblemished," but with the "messed-up" and the "downtrodden"—hence the need for "turning."

---

3. See Liu Zaifu and Lin Gang, 罪與文學：關於文學懺悔意識與靈魂維度的考察 [Confession and Chinese Literature] (Hong Kong: Oxford University Press, 2002). This bespeaks of course not the Chinese lack of imagination but of different frames of meaning circumscribing imagination.

4. See the first three "propositions" of Luther's 95 Theses.

5. Martin Buber, *Ich und Du* (Heidelberg: Lambert Schneider, 1979), 141.

6. Franz Rosenzweig, *Der Stern der Erlösung* (Frankfurt a.M.: J. Kauffmann Verlag, 1921), 113–14.

Given this prominence of "repentance" in the Jewish and Christian symbolic universe in general and the German-Jewish one in particular, it is only legitimate to ask how this wealth of conceptualizations might have a bearing on the perceptions of the Shoah and, more precisely for our interest, of its *aftermath*. In other words, how might a repentance-informed perspective change how those affected by the Shoah see catastrophes, human atrocities, the perpetrators, the victims, the bystanders, and the "solutions"? And, if followed through, how might this repentance-informed course of action change the way they relate to each other *after* what is done is done and cannot be undone?

A mere section of a book is obviously not sufficient to provide even an outline of a sketch of the hermeneutical and theological significance of biblical repentance; were it possible, it would not have been really as pivotal as has been touted. What will be attempted here is to merely explore the few potencies that have the clearest relevance, in my view, to our inquiry into how human groups can "turn" after unspeakable atrocities have been done by one on the other. We will attempt to do this by reciting the Bußpsalmen, or the Psalms of Repentance, as keys (especially Psalm 51),[7] to link up with and shed light on some other biblical passages, which promise together to unravel the cluster of knots (i.e., questions regarding justice and revenge, change and making amends, etc.) engendered by human wrongdoing. The aim is not to "unearth" anything theologically new, but to outline a paradigm that is "usable" in the subsequent historical analysis.

According to Christian tradition, the seven Psalms of Repentance are Psalms 6, 32, 38, 51, 102, 130, and 143 (following the Hebrew numbering system). The exact origins of this selection are unknown: though as early as in the third century, there were already references to the repentance psalms (without specifying which were included); only from the sixth century do we have a concrete record (by Cassiodorus) of the use of these seven psalms as we know them today. From then on the collection *Psalmi poenitentiales* was often

---

7. The scriptures cited in this study are not arbitrarily chosen. Most of them stem from the "daily readings" of German Catholics in the period 2009–13. Portions of Psalm 51, for instance, are read regularly during Lent, when repentance is emphasized.

used (collectively and individually) in the liturgy of the church in the Middle Ages, which then was carried forward into Protestantism as "Bußpsalmen" by Luther, who had published an exegesis of these seven psalms even before the Reformation.[8]

It is important to keep in mind, however, that in the Jewish tradition not all of the seven are recognized—either as a group or individually—as particularly relevant to repentance. According to Willy Staerk, only Psalm 51 is explicitly captioned as a "repentance song."[9] It is therefore imprudent to assume that the Bußpsalmen represent Jewish understanding of repentance, even as the contents are, no doubt, from the Hebrew Bible. When the texts are used in this book as the starting point of its theorizing, it is by no means an affirmation of this false assumption; rather, this study proceeds again from the anthropological viewpoint: What do these texts—used and continuing to be used by German Christians and Germans in a Christianized culture—offer the perpetrators as "raw materials" for conceiving repentance, which are nonetheless not irrelevant to the victims? After all, the fact that the "Old Testament" is being used by Christians does not mean it stops being the Bible for the Jews. It is precisely this "bridging" characteristic of the Bußpsalmen—and the Psalms in general—that makes them a veritable spiritual resource in the wounded German-Jewish relationship.[10]

We'll now first deal with the God-human relationship, and then turn to the interhuman, when repentance and reconciliation are concerned. We'll demonstrate that, in the biblical tradition, both concepts are understood in specifically *relational* terms. We'll further explore the boundaries (and problems) of transference, that is, the seeing of the interhuman *in light of* the God-human relationship.

---

8. See Willy Staerk, *Sünde und Gnade nach der Vorstellung des älteren Judentums, besonders der Dichter der sog. Busspsalmen* (Tübingen: J. C. B. Mohr [Paul Siebeck], 1905), 58–68. Also Heinz-Günter Beutler-Lotz, ed., *Die Bußpsalmen: Meditationen, Andachten, Entwürfe* (Göttingen: Vandenhoeck & Ruprecht, 1995), 9–12.

9. Staerk, *Sünde und Gnade*, 58.

10. See the contemporary use of the Psalms of Repentance in the German context in Beutler-Lotz, *Bußpsalmen*; and also Ludwig Schmidt, ed., *Umkehr zu Gott: Themagottesdienste zu Passion, Karfreitag, Bußtag und zu den Bußpsalmen* (Göttingen: Klotz, 1982).

1

"Turning" in the God-Human Relationship (R1–R9)

In this first chapter, we'll explore the conceptualizations of the God-human relationship given the condition that humans have already "messed up"—that is, they find themselves in a situation of inextricable guilt. In particular, we'll ask how God relates to the sinner as presented in the biblical texts and how "repentance" (*Umkehr/Buße tun*) and "redemption/healing" (*Heil/Heilung*) are described and prescribed.

To organize our observations in this chapter, we employ a visual of a triangle to signal the triangular relationship between God and human, and the interhuman.

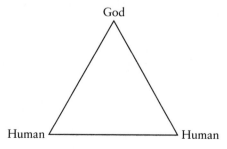

R1: The Sinner Is Not Sin

Psalm 51:4 Wash me thoroughly of my wrongdoing, and purify me of my sin.

Psalm 51:5 For I acknowledge my wrongdoing, and have my sin ever in mind.

Psalm 51:9 Cleanse me with hyssop, so I can become clean; wash me, so I can become white as snow.

Isaiah 1:18 Though your sins be as red as scarlet, they shall become as white as snow. Though they be red like crimson, they shall become like wool.

The first three verses above are taken from the fourth Bußpsalm (i.e., Ps 51), which, according to tradition, was a song of David's after the prophet Nathan had admonished him for his iniquity against Uriah the Hittite and his wife Bathsheba (2 Sm 11–12). A subtle but clear distinction has been made, or rather, reiterated:[1] that I, my wrongdoing (*Missetat*), and my sin (*Sünde*) are distinct entities but entangled as a result of "my doing." That the sinner is not sin, and the criminal is not crime itself, is an essential distinction—though insufficient by itself—that makes "repentance" possible; for if a sinner/criminal is equated with sin/crime, or recognized as the embodiment of sin/evil itself, then "repentance" can have no meaning other than self-mortification, or suicide, and "reconciliation" becomes either an impossibility, or a "moving forward" that "sees no evil, condemns no evil."

The biblical image of the sinner is not one of a "broken mirror" or "outpoured water," that is, one whose "original perfection" is beyond repair.[2] Rather, as portrayed in the Bußpsalmen, the sinner is someone who is sullied by sin/misdeed, whose inherent

---

1. Needless to say, the fundamental affirmation of the value of human beings and their redeemability are among the core tenets of Jewish teachings (e.g., Gn 4:7; Ps 25:7).

2. These are common Chinese metaphors used to describe broken relationships and destructive acts, signifying perhaps pessimism about (complete) reconciliation.

dignity as a being created "in the image of God" (Gn 1:27) is nevertheless not thereby destroyed. As Maimonides put it, "The one who does repentance should not think of himself being very far removed from that high rank of the pious ones because of his wrongdoings and sins; for it is not the case; rather, he is just as beloved and sought after before the face of the creator as if he had never sinned."[3] In a striking passage in the book of Isaiah (19:21–25), this indestructible human dignity is explicitly granted even to the traditional enemies of the Israelites: the Egyptians and the Assyrians; hence the universal applicability of the sin/sinner distinction.[4]

Sin/misdeed can be "washed away"; the sinner can be "pardoned," "excused," and "purified"—but these actions, as emphasized by these verses, can only be completed by God, the injured party, the victim, not by the perpetrator himself, who must "turn to" his victim to seek purification.[5] The promise of God to do just that (Is 1:18) is therefore the only hope left for those entangled in their own sins.

R2: The Twofold Damage of Sin

Psalm 51:6a Against you alone have I sinned; what is evil in your sight I have done.

This peculiar verse comes early in the fourth Bußpsalm. It is a repetition of David's own answer to Nathan in the historical account

---

3. Moses Maimonides, "Die Lehre von der Buße," in *Mischne Tora—Das Buch der Erkenntnis*, ed. Eveline Goodman-Thau and Christoph Schulte, Jüdische Quellen (Berlin: Akademie Verlag, 1994), 479. This German translation dates back to the mid-nineteenth century.

4. But whether this "universal applicability" is universally accepted—that is, *reciprocal*—is another question. See also comparable formulations in Malachi 2:10 and Romans 3:29.

5. Nevertheless, Rabbeinu Yonah also stressed the importance of the participation of the sinner in this cleansing, hence interpreting Psalm 51:4 together with Jeremiah 4:14. Rabbeinu Yonah, *The Gates of Repentance*, trans. and comm. Yaakov Feldman (Northvale, NJ/Jerusalem: Jason Aronson, 1999), 12.

(2 Sm 12:13) and seems to answer directly the prophet's accusatory question: "Why did you despise Yahweh by doing what displeases him?" (v. 9) The verse is peculiar because, in our secular age, the victim in this case can only be Uriah the Hittite. Why is God offended when a wrongdoing has been committed by a human against a fellow human? And why did David, as in this verse from Psalm 51, recognize God *alone* as the one whom he had sinned against? Regardless of the theological explication of this peculiarity,[6] one ramification of this way of seeing *victimhood* (the sinned-against-ness) is that both the perpetrator and the "victim" are called to see *beyond* each other, to "someone/thing else" that is the common focal point, in a situation where the relationship between them has been harmed by the wrongdoing of one (or both) of them, hence summoning the basic triangular structure of relationships.

Yet this triangular way of seeing is in no way a "diversion" from one's own guilt—which happens when the particular disappears in the general or universal. For in a biblical passage explicating this triangular relationship among God, the sinner, and the righteous, in which the human, balance-sheet-style "justice" is judged inferior to God's justice (Ez 18:21–28; see **R4**), it is specifically expressed that the sinner must *see* (v. 28) his wrongdoing/guilt/sin[7] so that he can turn away from it and live.[8] Hence it is not diversion or "dilution" that will result when one adopts the biblical triangular-relational paradigm, but rather an *insight* into one's own involvement—and hence guilt—in wrongdoing, for there is the extra dimension of sin. In this sense, David's seeing his crime against Uriah the Hittite

---

6. See also the same peculiarity in Luke 15:18, 21. One simple answer may lie right within the biblical text concerned: in 2 Samuel 12:9–10, a clear substitution has taken place in which the sword wielded by David on the family of Uriah is turned backward to his own family, and in which Yahweh substitutes Uriah as the injured party. In other words, Yahweh is presented as a god who takes offense when humans offend one another, who does not remain quiet in the face of injustice (Ps 50:21), and who will take vengeance on behalf of the victim.

7. The Lutherbibel (1984) uses *sehen*, which denotes a more general sense of seeing, whereas the Einheitsübersetzung (1980) uses *einsehen*, which implies understanding, realization, and conviction.

8. Cf. the negative formulation in Isaiah 6:10.

as a "sin against God" is not a "sidestepping" of his own guilt, or his responsibility toward the victim(s),[9] but rather the recognition that something graver than what is purely legal or ethical has been breached—a divine order of existence has been damaged by the "evil done."

A further collateral implication is that the healing potential of re-lationship, the bringing back to life of what has been devastated be-yond human remedy, ultimately comes from God (or that "someone/ thing else") alone. Consequently, re-cognizing and re-turning to this "center,"[10] which exists above and beyond the perpetrator and the victim, are hallmarks of those inspired by this spirit of repentance.

On the interhuman level, sin is also perceived as a sickness-/ wound-inducing and chasm-generating relational event.[11] A sinner, or perpetrator, in this sense, is precisely one who has done that which hurts/ails particular relationships,[12] as the perpetrators of specific massacres and genocides have wounded specific, collective relationships, not only of their own generation, but of subsequent generations as well, because of the cross-generational properties

---

9. In fact, as we shall see in **R14**, facing God cannot replace facing the human victim.

10. "Umkehr ist das Wiedererkennen der Mitte, das Sich-wieder-hinwenden." Martin Buber, *Ich und Du* (Heidelberg: Lambert Schneider, 1979), 119. It is re-markable that this formulation of repentance links *tshuvah* (turning) and *meta-noia* (change of mind).

11. A question can be raised here: What about relationships that are "en-hanced" *because of* sin? When soldiers watch each other's back as they abuse their victims, for instance, and when father and son conceal each other's wrongdoings, are their exclusive relationships not "improved"? Upon closer scrutiny, this "im-provement" is in fact *impoverishment*: according to Wayne Cristaudo, instead of enjoying the full richness and abundance of human relationships, these sick de-pendencies close off this possibility by building upon a logic of damage, which ultimately gnaws back inward. See his *Power, Love, and Evil: Contribution to a Philosophy of the Damaged* (New York: Rodopi, 2008).

12. The real and significant differences between "sin" (*Sünde*) and "crime/ wrongdoing" (*Verbrechen/Missetat*), and hence, "sinner" (*Sünder*) and "perpetra-tor" (*Täter*), are not to be understated. Sins are not necessarily crimes, and vice versa. The migration in word choice from "sinner" to "perpetrator" can thus only be justified where the wounding of relationships by the act of the sinner/perpetra-tor is concerned.

of sin (see **R12** in the following chapter). In the Bußpsalmen, we hear specific references to the sickening effects of sin and wrongdoing in interhuman relationships, as when the psalmist/perpetrator expresses loneliness (Ps 102:8). Not only has enmity among his enemies increased (Ps 6:8–9), but his friendships, love relationships, and neighborly relationships are also negatively affected (Ps 38:12). This is attributed to the self-inflicted, sin-induced wounds in himself (Ps 38:5–6).

In the Buber-Rosenzweig translation, "guilt" and "wrongdoing" in the Bußpsalmen are often expressed by a more relationally charged word, *Abtrünnigkeit,*[13] which can be translated as "unfaithfulness" or "infidelity," and is etymologically related to *Trennung,* or "separation."[14] One practical implication of this way of conceptualizing problems of interhuman—including international—relations is that it points to realities that are beyond justice and material reparation, and indicates that there is more to adjudicating between right and wrong, settling scores or national interests. The restoration of relationship—or the healing of relational wounds, "incurable" as they may seem (Jer 15:18)—becomes the binding vision of *both* the repentant perpetrator and the victim, with divine promise of participation (Jer 30:12, 17).

R3: Mercy Precedes Repentance; Repentance Responds to Mercy

Psalm 51:3 Have mercy on me, O God, in your love. In your great compassion blot out my sins.

Psalm 6:3–5 Have mercy on me, O Lord, . . . rescue me for the sake of your love.

Psalm 102:14 Arise, have mercy on Zion; this is the time to show her your mercy.

---

13. See, for example, Psalms 51:4–5, 13; 32:2, 5.
14. See *Duden Deutsches Universalwörterbuch,* ed. Werner Scholze-Stubenrecht (Mannheim/Zurich: Dudenverlag, 2011), s.v. "abtrünnig."

Isaiah 65:1, 24 I let myself be sought by those who did not ask for me.
I let myself be found by those who did not seek me. . . . And before they
call, I answer; while they are still speaking, I hear them.

If the distinction between sin and sinner has made "repentance"
possible conceptually, "mercy" (*Gnade/Barmherzigkeit*) makes it
a *real* possibility. In the biblical tradition, God's mercy is the bed-
rock of all repentive transformation. The message is unambiguous:
it is not the sinner's own "strength" or "merit" that enables him to
achieve repentance as a self-transformative strategy, but that God
has, out of his own will, mercy, and goodness, enabled the sinner
to do so, to partake in the healing process. As Maimonides put it,
interpreting Lamentations 3:38–41, "The healing of this sickness
lies accordingly in our hands, just as we have sinned out of our free
choice, so can we repent (*sich bekehren*) and come back (*zurück-
kommen*) from our evil actions."[15] But repentance is ultimately an
ability that comes from God, who can and did according to tradition in certain circumstances "withhold repentance" from sinners, who then no longer had the option to choose repentance after
freely choosing sin. "God sometimes punishes man by not granting him free will with regard to repentance so that he does not
repent."[16] Thus Rabbeinu Yonah also stressed the necessity to pray
for divine help: "Pray to God, when you do *tshuvah*, to always
help you with it. As it's said, 'Turn me back, and I will return. For
You are God my Lord'" (Jer 31:18).[17]

But if he chooses to exercise this given ability to repent, the sinner will not be rejected. A core biblical message reverberates in the
Bußpsalmen: if a sinner confesses to God, he will be heard (we'll
come back to the central demand of confession later, in **R5**). For
instance, when the sinner calls to his God to show him the way of
repentance—"Show me the way I should walk, for to you I lift up

---

15. Moses Maimonides, *Acht Capitel: Arabisch und Deutsch mit Anmerkungen von M. Wolff* (Leipzig: Commissions-Verlag von Heinrich Hunger, 1863), 61.

16. Ibid., 67–69. The chief example given by Maimonides is the "hardening"
of the Pharaoh's and his servants' hearts (Ex 10:1). See also Maimonides, "Lehre
von der Buße," 471–73.

17. Yonah, *Gates of Repentance*, 61.

my soul" (Ps 143:8)—he has already been assured—"I will teach you, I will show you the way to turn to; I will guide you with my gaze" (Ps 32:8). Indeed, the only direct response from God in the otherwise monological Bußpsalmen is this positive reassurance of guidance. We see the corresponding unswerving trust in the repentant sinner's self-reassurance: "The Lord has heard my cry. The Lord has heard my plea. The Lord will grant all that I pray for" (Ps 6:9–10). He is so sure of this that it doesn't even seem inappropriate to him that he should ask God to "hurry up" (e.g., Ps 143:8; 79:8).

Mercy, however, as encapsulated in the Bußpsalmen, is not "forgive and forget," but a promise to "show the way" and to "keep an eye" on the sinner (rather than to discard and close the file, so to speak). The "gaze" is not one of a distrustful, watchful eye, but one of accompaniment and forewarning, what Maimonides called "the forerunner of repentance"[18]—before the sinner wanders too far on the misguided path again and before the damage is too great. The mistrusting gaze is characterized by the preoccupation to protect the self (against the *perpetual* sinner); the latter has the well-being of the other (i.e., the *former* sinner) as the point of departure; that is why the enduring love of God for the sinner is recalled and resorted to throughout the Bußpsalmen, and is reinforced elsewhere in the Bible: "For whom the Lord loves he reprimands, like a father does the son he's pleased with" (Prv 3:12). Hence admonishment in the form of "pangs of conscience" is also mercy—a warning before catastrophe. We are brought to *feel* this in the Bußpsalmen, for instance, with the descriptions of "burned bones,"[19] "frightened and weakened bones,"[20] and "bones left without flesh."[21] These "sensations" are first associated with the sinner's own sins ("There is nothing wholesome in my bones because of my sins"[22]) but also

---

18. Maimonides, "Lehre von der Buße," 449.
19. Psalm 102:4. See also Ezekiel 24:10.
20. Psalms 32:3 and 6:3.
21. Psalm 102:6.
22. Psalm 38:4.

attributed to their divine origin *and intention* ("Let me hear joy and gladness, let the bones you have crushed rejoice"[23]).

But just as mercy is granted out of free will, repentance, according to the biblical tradition, can also only be exercised freely—it cannot be forced. It can only be a *response*, not a reaction. In the Bußpsalmen, there is a peculiar verse pointing to the undesirability of "forced or *reactive* turning":

> Psalm 32:9 Do not be like the horse or the mule—without understanding and led by bit and bridle.

The juxtaposition of "instructing, showing, and watching over/leading" (Ps 32:8) to being "led by bit and bridle" clearly conveys the message that, when forced, it is not repentance, which does not belong to the "action-reaction" logic of nature. Even pangs of conscience can be overcome and "mastered." But the repentant sinner *responds* to mercy. "Just as man becomes sinner through his own free will, so must he do repentance with full consciousness and out of free will."[24]

The idea that mercy precedes repentance, or presents a proactive call to repentance, is ubiquitous in the biblical tradition. See, for example, the story of Elisha the prophet and Naaman the Aramean general (2 Kgs 5), in which the national enemy who was also a leper asked for healing from Israel, and Elisha granted him just that without asking for anything in return—except turning him to Yahweh (see also the similar "instruction" of the Aramean soldiers with power and mercy; 2 Kgs 6:8–23).[25]

Overflowing with gratefulness from inside out, the repentant one is not mindful of his vulnerability—this inevitably exposes him to the risks of abuse (e.g., by those who contrive to benefit from their claimed "victimhood," and by those mockers and cynics; see

---

23. Psalm 51:10. See also the promise of rebirth from "dry bones" in Ezekiel 37:1–14.

24. Maimonides, "Lehre von der Buße," 469.

25. See also Romans 2:4.

Ps 1:1). As Maimonides advised, "The repentant ones are used to being humble and utterly modest; if the fools reproach them for their former actions and say: 'You have acted in such and such a way, and said so and so,' they do not have to care about that, but listen to these with serenity, as they know this is also beneficial to them, for the shame of their earlier sins and the blush before these increase their merit, and obtain for them an even higher place."[26] Furthermore, Yahweh is the one who will deal with these scorners, impostors, and profiteers. We will come back to this important point when we look at another character in the story of Naaman: Gehazi the servant (see **R11**).

R4: Recognizing Punishment as Just

> Psalm 51:6b You are right when you pass sentence and blameless in your judgment.

> Psalm 130:3 If you, O Lord, should mark our evil, O Lord, who could stand?

> Psalm 143:2 Do not bring your servant to judgment, for no mortal is just in your sight.

> Psalm 6:2 O Lord, in your anger do not reprove me; nor punish me in your fury.

> Daniel 9:18 Incline your ear, my God, and listen . . . for we do not rely on our justice, but your mercy.

Mercy, however, does not preclude just punishment or catastrophe.[27] Biblical scholars concur that acts of repentance, as recorded and represented in the Bible, are not always "successful" as a

---

26. Maimonides, "Lehre von der Buße," 485. On the meaning of the "higher place," see **R7**.

27. As Rabbi Yaakov Feldman explains, referring to Yonah's interpretation of Psalm 51:6, the roots of "just" and "charitable" in Hebrew are the same, hence the double meaning. See Yonah, *Gates of Repentance*, 63–64.

strategy to avert these.[28] A prime example of this, in our context, would be David himself—he sinned and repented, and was also "forgiven" (his sins being "taken away") by Yahweh, so that he would not die, but his first child with Uriah's wife was to die (2 Sm 12:15), and no amount of fasting and weeping could avert that. A "collective" example of this can be found in 2 Kings 22–23, when even after Josiah's religious reforms, neither the anger of Yahweh nor the punishment of Judah was averted (2 Kgs 23:25–27).[29]

It is even questionable whether the "avoidance of punishment" is a legitimate motivation for genuine repentance. In the conclusion of his *Doctrine of Repentance,* Maimonides stressed that love for God (as expressed in the Song of Songs) rather than fear of divine punishment should be the ultimate motivation of all those who turn to God.[30] Likewise, even as Rabbeinu Yonah called repentance an "escape hatch," repentance was for him ultimately not about getting away from punishment, but coming back to God: "And the greater the degree of your *tshuvah,* the closer to God you get."[31] In the Christian tradition, the distinction between "attrition" and "contrition"—that is, merely fearing punishment and genuinely recognizing the wrongfulness of sin—is also a noted example of this concern. In the Bußpsalmen themselves, we hear expressions of recognition, on the part of the sinner, that God's judgment (and punishment) is just, so much so that if God is to be true to his own words, as expressly recognized by the repentant sinner, he can't help but mete out just punishments to all (e.g., Ps 51:6; 130:3; 143:2).

But then how are we to understand the seemingly contradictory entreaty to God to refrain from punishment (as in Ps 6:2)? When the centrality of mercy is recalled, it seems that the sinner's

---

28. See Terence Fretheim, "Repentance in the Former Prophets," in *Repentance in Christian Theology,* ed. Mark Boda and Gordon Smith (Collegeville, MN: Liturgical Press, 2006), 36–37.

29. It would be instructive, though, to compare Josiah's case with Ezra's in Nehemiah 8–10 and see the contrast between the two in terms of the common people's relative passivity and proactiveness.

30. Maimonides, "Lehre von der Buße," 503–9.

31. Yonah, *Gates of Repentance,* 12.

recognition of God's right to justice does not exclude him from beseeching his God to exercise his freedom of mercy instead. In fact, in the biblical tradition, as reflected in the Bußpsalmen, the two often, if not always, go together. The "rod against wrong-doings" and the "strikes against sins" do not preclude love for sinners, or their faithfulness (Ps 89:31–34). What appears to counter this biblical spirit of repentance, though, is the *reversal of values*: when mercy becomes a requirement, and the right to justice is not recognized.

To move from an individual example to a collective one, the most striking instance of the recognition of God's judgment/punishment as just, or of catastrophe as a possible manifestation of such, may very well be the prophetic interpretation of *the* historical trauma of Israel—the Babylonian captivity. In a way that is inconceivable to our modern, nationalistic mind, both Jeremiah and Ezekiel un-ambiguously attributed the foreign invasion and the subsequent exile to the sinfulness of Jerusalem and Judah (Ez 12:13; 17:19–20; Jer 19:15; 20:4). It was Yahweh who delivered Jerusalem to the Babylonians, according to these prophets. Consequently, it was not to the Babylonians that Israel had to *turn* with remembrance of hatred and revenge,[32] but it was Yahweh alone that they must face and *return* to. The evildoers of the invasion and captivity would have to face Yahweh in their time (Jer 30:16; Is 10:12).[33] As in the case of the individual sinner, the community of sinners was prom-ised restoration if they repented.[34]

According to this biblical conception of repentance, then, one may safely conclude, the concern of the repentant sinner is not directed primarily to punishment/catastrophe or the fear of such, but to the *promised* restoration of relationship. Repentance in this

---

32. Rather, one finds "peculiar" places in the Bible where the "good memory" of Babylonians is preserved (e.g., 2 Kgs 25:27–30).

33. See the idea of the "nonmutual cancellation of guilt" in **R11**.

34. Linguistically, the Hebrew terms for "repentance," "turning" and "return-ing," and "restoration," all bear the same root, *sub*, thus pointing to their sym-bolic and essential oneness. See Mark Boda, "Renewal in Heart, Word, and Deed: Repentance in the Torah," in Boda and Smith, *Repentance in Christian Theology*, 11–12.

conception is not a mechanical, causal device—that is, "with this and this input, and the outcome will be that." Nothing concerning the consequences of sin is "guaranteed" in advance—only the restoration of relationship made possible through mercy and repentance. When this is in focus, whether something is "punishment" or "atonement" is a moot point, for that which is conducive to the healing of wounded relationships is welcomed, or even sought after,[35] by the repentant sinner. That is why punishment is no substitute for repentance[36]—for without turning, it is only suffering without meaning.

Yet, as the *Bußgebet,* or prayer of repentance, in Daniel reminds, human justice is not what the repentant sinner ultimately relies on and hence attempts to "satisfy," for God's justice is not human justice (Ez 18:25; see **R6**). The acceptance of punishment as just is hence not without qualifications—the justifiability and limits of human justice (whether it be the victors' or the victims') are always subject to the light of the triangular relationship with God.

R5: Confession as the Only Acceptable Sacrifice

Psalm 51:19 The sacrifices that please God are a broken spirit; a broken and contrite heart you, O God, will not despise.

Psalm 32:5 Then I made known to you my sin and no longer concealed my guilt. I said: "To the Lord I will now confess my trespasses." And you forgave my sin, you removed my guilt.

Psalm 130:6 My soul waits for the Lord, more than the watchmen for the dawn; more than the watchmen for the dawn.

---

35. Freud pointed to the sickening side of what he called *Strafbedürfnis,* or the "need for punishment." Luther, on the other hand, proclaimed that "sincere contrition (*aufrichtige Reue*) desires and loves penalty" (the 40th of his 95 Theses). There is indeed only a thin line between recognizing punishment as just (or the healing effect of atonement) and yearning for punishment as such. See Sigmund Freud, *Unbehagen in der Kultur* (Vienna: Internationaler Psychoanalytischer Verlag, 1930), 99.

36. Maimonides, "Lehre von der Buße," 411. It is granted, though, that repentance, especially where cross-generational guilt (**R12**) is concerned, acts as "armor (*Panzer*) against God's punishment" (469).

> Jeremiah 31:6, 9, 13 There shall be a day when watchmen will call out:
> "Come, let us go to Zion, to Yahweh our God!" . . . They will come
> weeping, but I will accompany them, comforting them, . . . I will turn
> their mourning into joy.

That the repentant sinner should confess his sins to God should
strike one as odd: why the need to tell someone something he already knows? But in the Bible it is not uncommon to see such paradoxical "communications," as in the book of Genesis where God
is presented as asking Adam after he had eaten the forbidden fruit:
"Where are you?" (3:9). Does he not know the whereabouts of his
creatures? Or is he giving Adam a chance to *acknowledge* (both
to get to know and to make known) his "lostness," or his having
wandered away from God? Without such knowledge and acknowledgment, how could the lost one begin to *turn back*?

If we follow this line of interpretive argument, then the act of
confession, as exists between human and God, is first of all an act of
open self-dialogue: it is not to say what the other wants to hear, but
to listen to what oneself needs to hear. When a person confesses,
he identifies his sins—that is, he does not, in effect, identify his self
with Sin. He is of course through his confession inviting demands
for penalties and indemnification, but he is no longer the Sin that
needs to be exterminated. He is simultaneously walking away from
Sin and owning up to the consequences of his sins.

In the Bußpsalmen, confession, acting as a severance between
the sinner and his sins and wrongdoing (Ps 32:5), is clearly conceived as a *relief* for the sinner, for keeping silent about one's sins
and misdeeds saps one's strength (Ps 32:3).[37] Confession is thus a
process of overcoming the impulse to conceal, an act of "letting
light pass through" oneself, so that what was hidden, including the

---

37. Maimonides warned, though, that one should only confess publicly sins
against fellow humans (especially when it comes to deceased victims who could
no longer be asked for forgiveness), not those against God ("Lehre von der Buße,"
421–23, 427–29). This caveat calls for reflection on some demands for "public
apology" that neglect the nature of the wrongdoings and the question of who is
truly entitled to receive the apology.

tendency to hide, is now in "broad daylight"—hence the image of "dawning" (Ps 130:6). But this "dawning," if it is to be valuable as a sacrifice, cannot be coerced (as when someone "confesses" only because the facts are against him) but longed for—more than the "watchmen" for the dawn. This curious character of the "watchman," which is repeated in Psalm 130:6 twice,[38] deserves closer attention.

In the prophetic books, the watchman is frequently used to symbolize the community's *conscience*, "posted there" by God to give warnings to the community (Ez 3:17, 33:7; Is 21:6), but sometimes the watchmen became "blind," "dumb," and "asleep" (Is 56:10), and other times their warnings were not heeded (Jer 6:17)—hence the downfall of the community. Therefore, the reform and restoration of conscience, which will now see and tell what it sees and will be listened to, are hallmarks of the confessing sinner. In Jeremiah 31:6–13, we have an image of a sinner or a community of sinners heeding their restored conscience—the "watchmen," turning and returning to God weeping, who then turned their mourning into joy.

This brings us to another important function of confession: to provide an occasion for "curative mourning." It is not the case that only the repentant sinner weeps for his wrongdoing and his guilt (Ps 6:7; 102:10); God also weeps for the damages and consequences of sin (Jer 14:17, 48:31–32; Is 22:4, 16:9, 15:5). Hence in a later section (**R14**), when we explore interhuman relationships, we'll see how confession is linked to curative mourning—which is itself a difficult "turning" for the victim[39]—in which the turning from mourning to joy becomes apparent.

In the Bußpsalmen, finally, confession is further construed as an act of *sacrifice*: through confessing, the sinner offers his "broken

---

38. See also Psalm 127:1.

39. The victim can, of course, choose *not* to make this turning—turning to the sinner, to his confession—by turning away from him, by refusing to listen, because to listen to a confession, while curative, is to allow access to a wound that still hurts.

spirit and contrite heart," which is the only sacrifice by a sinner acceptable to God (Ps 51:18–19). In return, God promises to renew both the heart and the spirit, so that the sinner can *live* and the broken relationship can be *restored* (Ez 36:28).

R6: Repentance as Inner Death and Rebirth

> Psalm 51:12 Create in me, O God, a pure heart; give me a new and steadfast spirit.

> Ezekiel 36:26–27 I shall give you a new heart and put a new spirit within you. I shall remove your heart of stone and give you a heart of flesh. I shall put my spirit within you and move you to follow my decrees and keep my laws.

> Ezekiel 18:32 I do not want the death of anyone, word of Yahweh, but that you repent and live.

Repeatedly, the biblical conception of repentance revolves around one's heart and spirit, as is also reflected in this central verse of the fourth Bußpsalm. In the Torah, for example, we hear exhortations to the "circumcision of the heart" (Dt 10:16, 30:6), which are repeated in the Prophets (Jer 4:4) and the Epistles. The images of changing or circumcising the heart should point one to the apprehension of coming to—or through—death, for how else could one accomplish something like that? In this conception, however, one kind of death is required, and another not. And for the right kind of death to be achieved, the essential asymmetric mutuality between God and human is stressed.[40]

---

40. It is of no small significance that Rabbeinu Yonah begins his *Gates of Repentance* with an enigmatic line: "[*Tshuvah* is] among the favors God has done *with* us, His creations." This "with" is noted by the translator and commentator of the work, Rabbi Yaakov Feldman, as pointing to the conception that "tschuvah is a means of solidifying and deepening our and God's mutual love." Yonah, *Gates of Repentance*, 4 (emphasis added).

At the very least, the circumcision should call to mind the voluntary "cutting off" of oneself, which is extremely painful, as it is so deep within one's innermost being, as symbolized by the heart. In fact, inner callousness, or the inability to feel pain, is suggested by the "heart of stone," which needs to be replaced by a "heart of flesh," one that can and does feel pain (Ez 36:26–27). But to feel pain for what? Or for whom? The immediate images of "bloodshed" and "cannibalism" in Ezekiel (36:13, 18) suggest insensitivity to the suffering of fellow human beings, and hence to the suffering of God.[41] In other words, the "heart of flesh" can mean a *vulnerable* heart[42] that feels for others, whose suffering is made invisible time and again by hard-heartedness and misguiding spirits, that is, "justifications" such as national interests, racial superiority, class struggle, religious identity, and so on. These utmost "frames of mind," as we now call them, or orientations that have been taken to one's heart—that is, held sacrosanct as part of the "self-identity"—are part and parcel of what needs to be put to death.

But when the repentant sinner is able (and only he is able) to put his innermost self in mind and spirit—which led him to sin in the first place—to death,[43] and to feel again the pain of the victims of his wrongdoings or negligence, chief among them God himself (see **R2**), he is also by this act of inner self-mortification exposing himself to the danger of despair—outright despair ("Nothing is possible for *me* anymore"). This is in fact what happens when people are unable to bear the magnitude of their guilt, as they begin to *see*

---

41. It is Heschel's thesis that prophecy is the communication of the divine *pathos*—including jealousy, disappointment, and frustration—to the people, in order to bring about the needed *sympathy* as a human response. See Abraham Joshua Heschel, *Die Prophetie* (Kraków: Verlag der polnischen Akademie der Wissenschaften, 1936). The extended English version of this work by Heschel appears as *The Prophets*, Perennial Classics (New York: HarperCollins, 2001).

42. Becoming *vulnerable* is a central theme of repentance. See Yonah, *Gates of Repentance*, 6, 12.

43. Even here, however, there is divine assistance (Hos 6:5).

the enormity of their misdeeds—they commit suicide.[44] Hence in the Bußpsalmen and the Torah in general, the creative/redemptive power of God[45] is stressed: to create and to give a pure heart and a new spirit (Ps 51:12); not only is one called to participate in the circumcision of the heart ("[You shall] circumcise your hearts . . ."; Dt 10:16), but God has promised to participate in it too ("Yahweh, your God, will circumcise your heart and the heart of your descendants"; Dt 30:6). It is within this relational reality that repentance, as inner death and rebirth, as can be gleaned from the biblical tradition, is understood and accomplished. It is not, and cannot be, achieved by the sinner alone.

The sinner is not called to repent through death, bodily death, but to repent so that he may have life (Ez 18:32). Nor is he asked to cover his shame by changing his face or his name as a way of hiding.[46] The idea that the right way to achieve repentance is by killing oneself or being killed is nowhere to be found in the biblical tradition. "There is no sin that cannot be atoned for by repentance," Maimonides unequivocally asserts. "Everyone must strive to do repentance . . . so he may die as a repentant [i.e., when the hour of death comes, he has already done repentance, like the "godless sinner" Ezekiel had spoken of in 18:21], and in this way gain entry to life in the world to come."[47] In other traditions, however, the

---

44. See Paul's differentiation between "Godly" and "worldly sorrow" in 2 Corinthians 7:10.

45. Stressing this prerogative of God's, Luther commented on this verse: "A clean hand . . . is easy to do and within human power; but a pure heart . . . is the work of the creator and of divine power." See his "Auslegung der sieben Bußpsalmen," in *Dr. Martin Luthers Sämtliche Schriften*, vol. 4, *Auslegung des Alten Testaments: Auslegung über die Psalmen*, ed. Johann Georg Walch (Groß-Oesingen: Verlag der Lutherischen Buchhandlung Heinrich Harms, 1987).

46. To be sure, name changing can also be a sign of the repentant, but never as an attempt to hide or evade responsibility. It is rather a signal that "he has become another being, no longer the same as the one who had committed the bad deeds." See Maimonides, "Lehre von der Buße," 421.

47. See Maimonides, "Lehre von der Buße," 445, 479. According to Yonah, however, there is a sin of which only "death" absolves the sinner: the profanation of God's name (*Gates of Repentance*, 300). But even here, Rabbeinu Yonah, in disagreement with the masters he was quoting, granted an "escape hatch": using one's whole life for the sanctification of God's name (310). Likewise, when

idea that "only through death can one's honor and the honor of one's family name be saved" is not uncommon. There is the Chinese idea of "using death to apologize" (*yisi xiezui* 以死謝罪), for instance, and that of *seppuku* or *harakiri* in the Japanese tradition. It may seem a moot point to argue about whether death is meted out as punishment or considered a requirement of repentance, when the sinner will die all the same,[48] but it is in fact a fine and important difference when death, especially suicide, is seen as an ideal of repentance or as a consequence of sin. The first precludes the life-saving power of repentance; the latter does not: just as God is justified in demanding death from the sinner, but can and does choose to exercise his freedom of mercy, so too can those created in his image. Indeed, it has been a repeated call of the prophets that God desires mercy, not sacrifice (Hos 6:6), and this is repeated by Jesus (Mt 9:13). There is no injunction against the "year of mercy" (Lv 25:10; Lk 4:19). The story of Jonah illustrates succinctly that even a prophet of Israel cannot withhold repentance, as a life- and

---

Maimonides indicated that such a sin is atoned for "only through death," he was not being self-contradictory. For the biblical passage (Is 22:14) that he cited in its support sheds light on why this is the case: the people have mocked the call to life through repentance, and chose death instead; hence it is only a logical conclusion that death becomes the only outcome when the option for life, that is, repentance, is rejected. The same is true in Amos 9:10, where repentance is not seen as a necessity for life; when the severity of sin's consequences is not recognized by a dumb optimism, death results for sinners. See Maimonides, "Lehre von der Buße," 415–16.

48. See, for example, the passages in the Bible where the death penalty is sanctioned (Ex 21; Lv 24:10–23). One may argue that these penal laws were actually meant to increase leniency—that is, to limit the penal violence to the wrongdoer himself in proportion to the crime he had committed—or that the death penalty is used to highlight the sanctity of life (i.e., "Murder is a serious crime!"). Historically true as these arguments may be, no attempt is made in this book to justify or gloss over these biblical passages that seem to run counter to the "spirit of repentance" I'm trying to outline here. It is readily conceded, rather, that a living tradition is far from "consistent," and that intratraditional tensions are the rule rather than the exception. The questions for the present generation seem to be the following: Where do we stand? Which voice do we *choose* to listen to, and why? Rabbeinu Yonah, for example, asserted that even the biblically "sanctioned" capital punishments can be averted through *tshuvah*, Yom Kippur, and tribulations (*Gates of Repentance*, 308).

relationship-saving device, when it is granted by God himself to human beings, even to pagans. But to avail oneself of this device, besides the courage to circumcise one's heart, patience is required. When the sinner's will to return is "like the morning mist and the early dew," which disappears almost as soon as it appears, the "divine operation" can be of but little help to him (Hos 6:1–4). The repenting sinner, as depicted in the Bußpsalmen, is a soul that waits (Ps 130:5).

The "reborn" sinner—that is, in the sense of one with a renewed heart and spirit—is certainly no saint, nor is this rebirth guarantee of any "proof" against future relapse. This is a recognized fact in the biblical tradition, as when we hear that even circumcised hearts at times need to be "humbled again" (Lv 26:40–42). Martin Buber's well-chosen biblical example (Jer 34:15, 16, 22) of repentance-as-return also illustrates the multifarious kinds of "return"—the return to God, the return to one's former evil ways, and the return of enmity among human beings.[49] Even dogs and fools do "turning"— but only to their own vomit and folly (Prv 26:11). Hence, as Rabbeinu Yonah insisted, before Luther, repentance should be a "lifelong" exercise.[50]

R7: "Helping Others Repent" as the New Task of the Repentant

Psalm 51:15–17 I will teach the wrongdoers your ways and sinners will return to you. . . . Of your justice I shall speak aloud. O Lord, open my lips, and I will proclaim your glory.

Jeremiah 15:19 If you repent, word of Yahweh, . . . you can stand before me again . . . and you will be as my own mouth again.

---

49. See Martin Buber and Franz Rosenzweig, *Scripture and Translation*, trans. Lawrence Rosenwald and Everett Fox (Bloomington: Indiana University Press, 1994), 35.

50. Yonah, *Gates of Repentance*, 109.

Psalm 130:12–13 For you have turned my wailing into dancing, removed my sackcloth and clothed me with joy, so I praise you and will
not remain silent.

The last of Rabbeinu Yonah's "principles of *tshuvah*" is a curious one: "Turning Others Away From Sin as Much as You Can."[51]
Indeed, in contrast to some other traditions where a sinner appears no longer good for anything (even with repentance), and the
"less-than-immaculate" has no right to teach others, in Judaism
and Christianity the repentant sinner is valued precisely for his repentance. In the words of Maimonides, "[The repentant one's] reward is even greater [than that of the pious], for he has already
tasted sin, but nonetheless renounced it and subdued his evil inclination. The sages said: The place the repentant ones occupy is
not allowed even the most pious ones, which is to say, their place
is higher than that of those who have never sinned, because they
have more cravings to rein in than these."[52] What the repentant
one has learned is of such high value that he is even required to
proactively teach others the way to repent, as exemplified by the
verse above from Psalm 51. Aside from David, the ascribed author
of this psalm, Paul also serves as such a paradigmatic figure: having been blinded by his own murderous fanaticism, after returning to sight he preached against others' blindness (see Acts 9:8–9,
13:9–11).

So important is this duty to warn others—which is not reserved
to the repentant—that Maimonides considered it one of the more
significant sins if one omitted to fulfill it. "To this category belongs
also the one who has the power to turn his neighbors aside from
the sin but does not do it; this is relevant to the single individual as
well as to an entire community, if he lets it fall prey to the sin."[53]

---

51. Ibid., 70. He in fact derived this principle from Psalm 51:15 as well as from
Leviticus 19:17: "Criticize your neighbor diligently, and do not bear sin on his
account."

52. Maimonides, "Lehre von der Buße," 481.

53. Ibid., 447.

This renewed spirit to speak out,[54] however, is characterized not by a sense of "pride" of having accomplished repentance, nor by a sense of victimhood ("Why should I be singled out to repent but not *them?*"), but by gratitude and joy about having been "turned around" by God. Psalm 51 again exemplifies this characteristic by emphasizing the link between this "new speech" and the "new spirit": in the space of a few verses (vv. 12–17) the word "spirit" is mentioned three times ("a new and steadfast spirit," "your holy spirit," and "a willing spirit"[55]), and three manners of speaking out have been proposed ("teaching . . . your ways," "speaking aloud of . . . your justice," and "proclaiming . . . your glory"). Divine ways, divine justice, and divine glory are the central themes of the new speech; the (past) sinfulness of the repentant sinner/speaker and the (present) sinfulness of the audience are pointed out *only* in relation to these themes.

The tradition of "confession literature" in the West, starting with Augustine, exemplifies this spirit. And the Hebrew Bible, if read historiographically, is also astonishing in this self-critique: not only of the kings and the "elite," but of the people, the "masses" themselves.[56] It is as if only from that height of a new self, through "the change of heart and spirit," that one can bear to look back and recount that old self, which is no longer alive (i.e., *effective* in the sense of determining one's thinking and action), but neither is it disowned.[57] Duty bound, the repentant sinner has to criticize his neighbor diligently so as not to suffer the consequences of his sin (Lv 19:17). Yet, being the last *tshuvah* principle according to Rabbeinu Yonah, this duty can be understood as the *consummating act*

---

54. The connection between "spirit" and "speech" is of course more apparent and natural if we recall the biblical synonyms of "spirit" and "breath" in Ezekiel 37.

55. Maimonides further interpreted Psalm 51:14 as David's call to God not to "withhold repentance" from him. "Lehre von der Buße," 475.

56. A prime manifestation of this spirit is Ezra's prayer in Nehemiah 9:6–37.

57. Rabbeinu Yonah's interpretation of Psalm 51:5 is that the repentant sinner should always remember his sins and his self having sinned, while not necessarily repeating the same confession (*Gates of Repentance*, 313).

of a long and arduous process of repentant efforts, rather than the beginning of these. Indeed, as we have already seen in the previous sections (especially **R4**), speaking of the guilt of others is highly suspicious as an act of impenitence. It is therefore a hard-won duty, a thankless task, and a narrow path between self-righteousness and paralyzing "humility."

R8: Repentant Disagreement

> Psalm 51:5 For I acknowledge my wrongdoing, and have my sin ever in mind.
>
> Isaiah 43:16, 18–19, 25 Thus says Yahweh . . . "Do not dwell on the past, or remember the things of old. Look, I am doing a new thing: now it springs forth. Do you not see? I it is, I am He who blots out your offenses for my own sake, and remembers your sins no more."
>
> Psalm 51:7 See, I have been guilt-ridden from birth, a sinner from my mother's womb.
>
> Ezekiel 18:4, 20 All lives are my possession, the life of the father and the life of the son are mine. Only the one who sins shall die. . . . The son shall not bear the guilt of his father nor the father the guilt of his son.

In this "mutual-turning" of repentance, turning *to* each other, one remarkable feature is that both sides often *disagree*. As the first example quoted above shows, whereas the repentant sinner insists on always remembering his past sins, God speaks of not dwelling on the misdeeds and sins of the past, but invites the sinner to see the "new" coming into being instead of wallowing in disbelief. Indeed, one can even argue that whereas confessing one's past sins, atoning for them, and remembering one's "capability to sin" are characteristic of the biblical spirit of repentance, "dwelling on the past" as an end in itself is not. For the emphasis of this spirit is always and only on the *present*: there *is* a sickened/wounded relationship that *needs* healing; and there *is* a choice to be made to "return" and be a conduit of healing power, or not.[58] In this light, the "new" (heart/spirit and the relationship between the reborn and his God) is not at all a "compromised old at best," a "broken mirror" that is scarred forever even after repair, but something altogether better than it has ever been. All the "going back to the past," "remembering," and "apologies" lose their meaning the moment one loses sight of the sole reality of relationships and their healing potential at present. These efforts become "futile," for "the past cannot be undone."[59]

Another instance of "repentant disagreement" that we will look at here concerns "generational guilt." Whereas David or the psalmist accepts the link between God's judgment on him and the sins of his former generations, and assumes personal responsibility for them,[60] God speaks of "everyone for his own sins," that sons and fathers should not be made to bear each other's guilt.[61] While we must explore the inherent ambiguities more deeply (e.g., couldn't "generational sin" also be a way to evade responsibility,

---

58. Buber, *Ich und Du*, 63.

59. This is in fact a popular criticism of present-day efforts at reconciliation—at times betraying the underlying defensiveness of the critic, at times bespeaking a sense of despair of those attempting "repair" without any affirmation of possible success.

60. See also Jeremiah 14:20.

61. There seems to be a "divine disagreement" here as well: for wasn't it also the same God who said: "For I, the Lord your God, am a jealous God, punishing the children for the wrongdoing of the fathers to the third and fourth generation, *who hate me*" (Ex 20:5). Once again, the relational context and the respective audience may shed light on the seeming discrepancy. In Exodus, the cited text appears in the pronouncement of the Decalogue—in particular, the prohibition against idol worship; thus the principal relationship in question is between God and his chosen people. The thrust of the text is clearly toward warning the listener (i.e., the present generation) of the dire consequences of sin (especially idol worship), which may lead to a cross-generational rebellion against or hatred toward God, which then necessitates a "turning around" by punishment. In Ezekiel, the cited text appears in the comparison between divine justice and human ways of judging (see Ez 18:2, 25). The thrust of this text is then toward limiting indiscriminate interhuman punishment, which is based on fallible human judgment. In fact, the possibility of repentance by later generations with regard to idol worship is explicitly recognized in this text (Ez 18:15), thus bearing out the interpretation of the Exodus text above.

and if one is "born into sin," how can one be held accountable for something one had no choice about to begin with?), which we will do in a subsequent section dealing entirely with generational guilt (**R12**); suffice it to say here concerning "repentant disagreement" that the unreconciled ones often in fact fundamentally agree with each other, whereas the "mutual-turning" ones (i.e., those inspired by this biblical spirit of repentance) often "disagree."[62] On the assignment of guilt, for instance, these often "contradict" each other in content (if one sees their responses *only* in the dimension of argument with premises and categories, etc.), while the essential emphasis—if one is able to see theirs as relational gestures and responses—is always each other. Establishing logical consistency in terms of rules and ideas is never their primary concern, but the reestablishment of their relationship.[63] It is as if through, and only through, *going further than* what is required/right in the "objective" sense in opposite directions that "mutual-turning" is accomplished, and healing ensues.

R9: Even God Repents

Genesis 6:6 The Lord regretted having created men on earth, and it pained his heart.

Genesis 8:21 And the Lord said to himself: "Never again will I curse the earth because of man, even though his thoughts are evil from youth. Never again will I exterminate all those that live like I have done."

Exodus 32:12–14 Turn away from your burning anger, and let yourself regret the evil that you are thinking of doing to your people. . . . Then the Lord lets himself regret the evil He had threatened his people.

---

62. Perhaps this is why those who avoid "confrontation" at all costs often fail to achieve reconciliation. For in avoiding disagreements, they also miss those that are necessary for healing.

63. Yet this tentatively termed "relationism" must be differentiated from relativism: at the very least, the first is grounded in the asserted reality of relationships (in the triad of God and human beings) and proceeds from a particular understanding of how these relationships are wounded and healed; the latter is not.

Hosea 11:8 How could I give you up, Ephraim? And deliver you, Israel? . . . My heart turns against me, all my compassion[64] is ablaze.

An element of repentance is not spoken of in the Bußpsalmen, and it is only right that this is so. For it entails a "turning" on the part of God that is beyond the turning in terms of mercy (**R3**) and of participation in the renewal of the sinner (**R6**). It refers to the "regret" (*Reue*) of God when faced with the sinfulness of men. Had the repentant sinner voiced this aspect of turning, as if he could now *demand* the repentance of God—that God should look into his own guilt in the sinfulness of his creature—it would have nullified every other expression of repentance on his part. For then the sinner would be in effect blaming God for his sin, like Adam,[65] rather than owning up to it himself.

Yet elsewhere in the Bible, references to the turning of God himself in this distinct aspect are readily found right from the very beginning. The quoted verses above and their related passages portray a God who is not only concerned about justice and mercy, but is also self-blaming and willing to change himself in response to the sinfulness of men. If not, the flood and extermination would have been perceived as "justice served" rather than something "never to be done again"—even *without* any prior guarantee from man that his heart and his world would never be filled with that much evil again (Gn 6:5; likewise in Hos 11:1–9). If not, the threats of punishment would have been counted as "merciful reminders" rather than as something to regret (*reuen*).[66] If not, furthermore, human wickedness should have aroused only divine anger and disappointment, not regret and pain. This regret thus arises from the consciousness of both the guilt of one's *constitutive* part in the sin committed against oneself, and the consequence of being caused by the human evil done to think and/or to do evil as a *reaction*.

---

64. The King James Version (1611/1769) uses "repentings" here, whereas the German versions use "Mitleid" and "Barmherzigkeit."

65. When asked by God whether he had eaten from the forbidden tree, Adam shifted the blame back to God via Eve: "The woman *you* put with me gave me the fruit from the tree" (Gn 3:12).

66. See also similar references in 2 Samuel 24:16 and Jonah 3:10.

In translating Amos 7:3 into English, Abraham Heschel adopted the verb "repent": "The Lord repented concerning this; / It shall not be, said the Lord."[67] God's repentance, of course, as emphasized by Heschel, is not indicative of his "wrongdoing" or wrong judgment, but rather of his mercy as "perpetual possibility" against the iron law of cause and effect. An illustrative biblical example of this chain reaction—and the divine regret that breaks it—can be found in Exodus, where the idolatry of the "molten calf" almost brought about the extermination of the people of Israel (Ex 32). When the people corrupted themselves and "turned away" from the way of God, this effected divine anger and their imminent destruction (Ex 32:7–9). And as in the case of Jeremiah (7:16), Moses was commanded by God not to stand in the way of this outpouring of fury. But Moses disobeyed and rejected the temptation to become "a great nation" (vv. 10–11). He asked God to turn away from his anger, and to let himself regret (*reuen*) the evil or disaster he had in mind for his people (v. 12).[68] He even "threatened" God by daring him to "blot me out of your book" if forgiveness was not to be granted (v. 32).[69] The Lord let himself regret the evil that he had conceived for his people (v. 14).[70]

---

67. Heschel, *The Prophets*, 43. In the German original, Heschel used "gereuen": "Der Herr ließ es sich gereuen" (*Die Prophetie*, 59). This is more in line with common German translations using "reuen." By contrast, the Buber-Rosenzweig translation reads: "IHM wards dessen leid." See Martin Buber and Franz Rosenzweig, *Die Schrift: Bücher der Kündung* (Stuttgart: Deutsche Bibelgesellschaft, 1992).

68. See also Psalm 106:23.

69. This is in sharp contrast to Aaron, who tried to assign the guilt solely to the people while saving himself by claiming passivity (Ex 32:22–24). On the representativeness of prophetic repentance, see **R10**.

70. To be sure, the people of Israel did not escape punishment altogether, a plague (Ex. 32:35) and a self-initiated violent purge (vv. 27–29) did follow. But as we have seen in **R4**, punishment is not the same as the termination of relationship, which, even when "punishment-free," is perceived to be worse than the worst punishment. The Israelites' refusal to go away "freely" without their God points to this understanding (Ex 33:4).

2

Interhuman and Collective Repentance (R10–R14)

In this second chapter, we will turn our attention to the interhuman relationships, especially the victim-perpetrator, *in light of* the God-human relationship, for in the biblical tradition, the latter is often upheld as the hermeneutical context for the former.[1] The God-human relationship is the one "line" that cuts across all other relational lines.[2] We will therefore employ a visual of a modified triad to undergird our discussion.

---

1. See, for example, 2 Chronicles 36:14–23.
2. In Buber's words, "The world of It has its context in space and time. The world of Thou has no context in either. It has its context in the center, in which the extended lines of relationships cross each other: in the eternal Thou." Martin Buber, *Ich und Du* (Heidelberg: Lambert Schneider, 1979), 119.

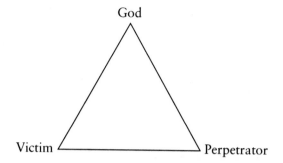

R10: Repentance's Representative Minority

Psalm 51:20 Shower Zion with your favor: rebuild the walls of Jerusalem.

Psalm 130:7–8 O Israel, hope in the Lord, for with him is mercy and redemption. He will deliver Israel from all its sins.

Nehemiah 1:5–6 O Yahweh, God of heaven. . . . May your ears be attentive and your eyes open to listen to the prayer of your servant! I am now in your presence day and night, praying for your servants, the Israelites. I confess to you the sins we the Israelites have committed against you: I myself and the family of my father have sinned.

Genesis 18:32 And he said: "Let not my Lord be angry, for I will speak but one more time. Perhaps ten could be found there." And He said: "I will not ruin it for the sake of ten."

In the interhuman dimension, which seeks in the biblical tradition behavioral and judgmental guidance from the divine-human, sin can be understood as an injury- and separation-causing act, after which relational healing is called for (**R2**). In this process, questions concerning representative repentance, abuses, inherited guilt and responsibility, and the place of remembrance in turning as the narrow path toward reconciliation are among the major issues addressed in the Bußpsalmen and related biblical passages on repentance.

Regarding "representation," religious and political figures are recognized "mediators" between God and nations when expressing repentance and pleading for mercy are concerned in the biblical tradition. Josiah the king and the long line of major and minor prophets were all examples of this mediation. Two particularly relevant questions concerning this will be dealt with here: What are the common characteristics of the mediators, and in what sense are they "representative"? How many repentant sinners are necessary for an entire nation to be judged as having "repented enough"?

Concerning the common characteristics, their voluntary *participation in* relation should be noted first and foremost. They differ from most of those whom we call "social critics" today in that with their social criticism they implicate themselves in instead of extricate themselves from the society in which they live (e.g., Neh 1:4–7; Jer 14:19–21). They are not jurists who distance themselves from the accused as they pass sentence on them, but are shepherds who feel personally guilty for the unfaithfulness of their flock.[3] They also possess an unusually acute sense of God's pain,[4] and are able to "cross over" from grief over personal/communal tragedy to an alertness toward the suffering of the others (examples range from Hosea as a betrayed husband to Amos's social justice to Malachi, the champion of foreigners' rights). Often as guiltless as anyone could possibly claim to be, they draw shame upon themselves (symbolically and literally smashing their "respectable image" by tearing their fine garments and smudging their body with ash) when pleading to God for forgiveness for his community (e.g., Josiah in 2 Kgs 22:11–13). As if echoing Psalm 51:19, they offer their "broken hearts and spirits" as an atoning sacrifice, a sacrificial victim that is perfect and blameless (itself an "injustice," no doubt, but an *inverted* injustice), in an effort to appease the anger of a God infuriated by the injustice and unfaithfulness of the nations concerned.

On the one hand, these mediators become the "representatives" of God vis-à-vis the sinful nation, calling their own communities' attention to the justice and wrath of God if the offer of repentance as mercy is ignored or taken advantage of (e.g., Moses's reminder

---

3. See the inclusive "we" in the collective confessions of Israel in Maimonides, "Die Lehre von der Buße," in *Mischne Tora—Das Buch der Erkenntnis*, ed. Eveline Goodman-Thau and Christoph Schulte, Jüdische Quellen (Berlin: Akademie Verlag, 1994), 425.

4. See Heschel's idea of "divine pathos" in R6.

of Yahweh's "generational punishment" before his enduring mercy in Deuteronomy 5:9–10).[5] The "mediators" are not supposed to give false comforts when there are real causes for trepidation (Is 5:20; Jer 8:11). But on the other hand, they become "representatives" of a nation, not in the modern sense of the word, as statistically or democratically representative, for that they are most certainly not.[6] Rather, they become "representative" by voluntarily sharing the guilt of their nation, by embodying the change of heart that is taking place and by representing the new spirit that the nation can be. In this sense, to risk an exaggeration, a nation's prophets give hope not only to the people, but to their God as well, that change is still possible from *within*. Hence Isaiah the prophet, even as he himself was despondent about his utility, was addressed by God as Israel the people, "in whom I will be glorified" (Is 49:3–4). "Blot me out of your book if you don't forgive them," declared Moses, boldly challenging his God (Ex 32:32) to have more hope in his people, who had sinned against him. At times, the prophet is the only one standing in the way of divine wrath (Ps 106:23), and he is designated as *the* bond between God and his people (Is 42:6).

As for how many such "representatives" are sufficiently representative of a repentant nation, that is, a nation whose relationship with God is not severed for good, two particular biblical passages are worth reading together closely: the passage in the book of Genesis in which Abraham interceded for Sodom and Gomorrah, and that in Jonah in which the Ninevites as a nation responded to Jonah's prophecy. In the first, Abraham "negotiated" with his God about whether Sodom would be destroyed if one finds[7] fifty or even ten righteous people among the population, and the promise is that "for the sake of ten good people," Sodom would not be destroyed (Gn 18:16–32). From the story itself we do not know the population of Sodom at the time, but it is safe to assume that ten was

---

5. As Rabbeinu Yonah notes, the only ones to whom repentance is denied are those who think: "I'll sin first and do repentance later." Rabbeinu Yonah, *The Gates of Repentance*, trans. and comm. Yaakov Feldman (Northvale, NJ/Jerusalem: Jason Aronson, 1999), 72–73.

6. True prophets are often unpopular among the people (e.g., Is 30:10–11).

7. The present tense here is important: a nation cannot be content with having "the righteous" among them in the past; righteousness needs to be kept alive in each generation in the present.

most probably not a "significant representation" of it. From this account alone, then, it seems that God's leniency and patience are being emphasized, as shown by his "absolute minority rule," which his believers, that is, those created in his divine image and loved by him, are called to emulate (Hos 6:6; Mi 6:8; Dt 10:12, 19; Lv 19:2).

The story of Jonah, however, introduces a different viewpoint. The story is that Jonah, the reluctant prophet, after some rebellion against his God's will, finally proclaimed his message to the Ninevites: "Forty days more and Nineveh will be destroyed" (Jon 3:4). Despite the uncharacteristic prophetic message (for there is no explicit mention of God's mercy, nor of the chance for repentance),[8] "the people of the city believed God; they declared a fast, and *all of them*, from the greatest to the least, put on sackcloth to repent" (v. 5; emphasis added).[9] It was only after this first collective and spontaneous act of repentance that the king of Nineveh "got up from his throne, took off his royal robe, put on sackcloth, and sat down in ashes" (v. 6). He then issued a decree asking "*everyone* [to] call aloud to God, turn from his evil ways and violence" (v. 8; emphasis added). Then we have the resolution of God's "repentance" (see **R9**) as turning away from his vengeful thoughts: "When God saw what *they* did and how *they* turned from their evil ways, he regretted the evil that he had threatened to bring upon them and did not carry it out" (v. 10; emphasis added). Thus from this account it seems that collective repentance is "valid" if and only if *everyone* partakes in it—not just the king or the prophet (or in this case, despite the reluctant prophet) or a handful of "righteous" citizens, but every single individual in the community.[10] Indeed, if

---

8. It must be noted, however, that mercy and the chance for repentance are already implied in the postponement of punishment and in the prophecy itself. Otherwise, why would God bother to send a prophet and then wait for forty more days?

9. Slightly different from the English translations, both the Einheitsübersetzung (1980) and the Lutherbibel (1984) emphasize the repentant symbolism of putting on sackcloth (*Bußgewänder/Sack zur Buße*).

10. Again if we recall the case of Josiah (where the king led the way while the people appeared only to be "following orders") and the case of Ezra (where the people responded spontaneously), as mentioned in note 29 in **R4**, further credence is accorded to this interpretation.

the Bußpsalmen are taken as a whole, it is glaringly obvious that they are primarily expressions of *personal* repentance; only scant and secondary references with a collective or representative nature can be found (e.g., Ps 51:20; 130:7). "God has no grandchildren," it is popularly said.[11] So one can also say, "Repentance has no proxy."[12]

How are we to resolve this apparent contradiction between the "absolute minority rule" in Genesis and the "absolute totality rule" in Jonah? And what can we then say about "collective repentance," if there is such a thing at all? For Maimonides, these questions hinge not only on the numbers of the righteous/repentant vis-à-vis the wrongdoers/impenitent but also on the "dimensions" of the acts, and the prerogative to judge rests with God alone. Explicating the case of Sodom and Gomorrah and other related passages, Maimonides said: "The assessment of sins and good deeds is not according to the number, but to the dimensions of these. . . . The weighing can only take place in the wisdom of the omniscient and omnipotent one. He alone knows how the good deeds and the sins are to be compared."[13]

Furthermore, as already noted, logical consistency and statistical accuracy are not the primary concerns of *relational speech*, whose sole consideration is the relational *directions* of God and human, and between human and human—that is, whether they are *turning to* each other, or away from each other. God is willing to "repent," that is, to turn to and to restore the sinners, to turn from destructive wrath to loving patience, exercising his freedom to be merciful to the full (and the sinners are asked to imitate him, when the time comes). But if the sinners abuse this mercy and think a handful of "righteous/repentant" ones will be enough to save all, then they are not doing their own "repentance," that is, turning *to* God and *away* from their evil ways; instead, they're turning away

---

11. See also Ezekiel 18:4.

12. As Maimonides noted, even at times when the high priest could offer atonement sacrifice in the Temple for all of Israel, "only those who had taken this opportunity to do repentance could partake in the pardon," thus emphasizing the primacy of personal repentance in the collective, symbolic act. Maimonides, "Lehre von der Buße," 411–13.

13. Maimonides, "Lehre von der Buße," 429–31.

from him. That is why Maimonides advises individual human beings to think of the whole community/world as half just and half
guilty; thus if a person commits a sin or makes a good deed, the
scale will be tilted toward the ruin or salvation of the world.[14] Thus
those attuned to the spirit of repentance in the biblical tradition are
sensitive to those who are being spoken to *through* the Bible: The
sinners before God? Or the wrongdoers before their fellow human
beings? The "victims"? Or the "perpetrators"? As we have seen
in "repentant disagreement" in **R8**, the issue of audience and the
problem of "contradictions" are integral to the biblical conception
of repentance, and hence also to the issue of representativeness.

R11: Justice between Abused Perpetrators and Abusive "Victims"

> Psalm 38:20–21 My foes are many and mighty; they hate me for no
> reason; they pay me evil for good and treat me as an enemy because
> I seek good.

> Psalm 102:9 All day long I am taunted by my enemies; they make fun of
> me and use my name as a curse.

> Psalm 143:1 O Lord, hear my prayer; in your truthfulness, listen to my
> cry; in your justice, answer me.

> Jeremiah 30:15–16 Why cry out for your plight and your wretched suf-
> fering? I have done these because of your immense guilt and your many
> sins. But all those who devoured you shall be devoured, and all your op-
> pressors shall be taken captive; who plundered you will be plundered,
> and I will make those who preyed upon you a prey.

It is not true that the Bußpsalmen concern only the perpetrator and
his God in a binary mode. Many references point to relationships
with others, friends as well as foes. Some of these relationships
are wounded because of the perpetrator's own wrongdoing, as explored in **R2**, but some others are wounded by the wrongdoing

---

14. Ibid., 433.

of *other* perpetrators: "They hate me for no reason; they pay me evil for good and treat me as an enemy because I seek good" (Ps 38:20–21). Some other fellow human beings take advantage of the perpetrator's perhaps well-deserved suffering as a consequence of his own sins: "All day long I am taunted by my enemies; they make fun of me and use my name as a curse" (Ps 102:9). The Buß-psalmen thus, like other biblical passages (e.g., Jer 30:15–16),[15] recognize the reality that perpetrators may be victimized by other perpetrators,[16] and their pleas to God, not from a self-righteous heart but from a broken one, that is, one that recognizes their own part in contributing to their suffering, will be heard (Ps 102:18).

The most peculiar inclusion in the Bußpsalmen is perhaps the seventh, Psalm 143. For unlike the other six, which first and foremost implore God for "mercy" (*Gnade/Barmherzigkeit*) and "peace" (*Frieden*), Psalm 143 asks God to exercise "truth" (*Wahrheit*) and "justice" (*Gerechtigkeit*) instead.[17] Why would a perpetrator want his God to do that? Would not a judge upholding truth and justice *above all* be disadvantageous to the accused? It is clear that this psalm, taken as a whole, speaks of one besieged by perpetrators. But unlike other "lamentation psalms" (e.g., Ps 44), this is a psalm by one who also identifies himself as a perpetrator: "Do not bring your servant to judgment, for no mortal is just in your sight" (v. 2); "Show me the way I should walk. . . . Teach me to do

---

15. A corollary of this triangular vision of guilt is the important idea that *guilts do not cancel each other out*: the perpetrator's guilt is not canceled out by the victim's or the abuser's guilt, and vice versa. Regardless of the recognition or rejection of the "just punishment" thesis by the perpetrator (see R4), each of the three is reminded by this vision that they will have to face the one judge to account for their own wrongdoing per se. In view of this, it is only logical that the biblical paradigm also rejects the idea of interhuman retaliation or vengeance (see R13)—for no guilt is "evened out" in the process; the total guilt is only increased.

16. It is thus characteristic of sin as relational sickness (R2): it drags love relationships into victim-perpetrator relationships in which nobody "gains" and everybody suffers. Repentance, in this sense, promises to break apart precisely this dragging force: so that not only the perpetrator is redeemed, but also the victim, for the "chain reaction" of sin is broken.

17. There is, of course, wide variation in the translation of these biblical terms. The Buber-Rosenzweig version, for example, uses *Treue* (faithfulness) and *Wahrhaftigkeit* (truthfulness) instead.

your will. . . . Let your Spirit lead me on a safe path" (vv. 8–10). These are familiar expressions of repentance in other Bußpsalmen.

Given the "vulnerability" (**R6**) of the repentant perpetrator, abuse by fellow perpetrators or even the victims (aside from those whose claim to "victimhood" is dubious) is only to be expected. And the biblical tradition is not oblivious to this. Besides the Bußpsalmen, in which we hear the complaints of the repentant and the promise of a "truthful" and "just" God, in Kings there is an instructive story (already mentioned in **R3**) about someone trying to gain from a vulnerable, repentant perpetrator: the story of Naaman and Gehazi, the servant of Elisha the prophet (2 Kgs 5). Struck by both the power to heal and unconditional mercy,[18] Naaman, the commander of a foreign army hostile to Israel, "returned/repented/converted" (v. 15). Meanwhile, disappointed by his master's mercy and justifying his greed, Gehazi contrived an implausible lie to extort "silver and clothing" from Naaman. The *new* man (v. 14), true to the spirit of repentance, that is, vulnerable and willing to risk possible injustice/harm to himself in the course of atonement, gave Gehazi the benefit of the doubt, even giving double what was asked—a spontaneous sign of a repentant with overflowing gratefulness from his circumcised heart (**R6**) for the mercy received. The "man of God," Elisha, knew everything all along, and he gave Gehazi a chance to confess (v. 25). But the servant did not seize the opportunity for repentance, and hence was made to suffer the punishment that was originally Naaman's (i.e., leprosy).

All in all, one may conclude, then, that the repentant perpetrator is encouraged to exercise vulnerability and not to be thwarted by possibilities or even actual incidents of being "abused." "Truth" and "justice" (Ps 143:1) are assured to him (just as they are to other victims); he does not even need to worry about defending himself against animosity amid just accusations, for God himself will be the judge (Ps 38:14–16). Victims or pseudovictims, on the other

---

18. The layers of mercy in this account of course go beyond Elisha's refusal to accept "gifts in return" (v. 16); they extend also to the unnamed young Israelite girl, who, despite her real victimhood of having been kidnapped and reduced to servitude, proactively pointed the way to healing to Naaman (vv. 2–3).

hand, are reminded that they, too, will have to give an account to God as to how they deal with the repentant sinner. Exploiting a neighbor's shame for one's own benefit belongs, according to Maimonides, to those sins that threaten "partaking in the future life."[19]

R12: The Sin of the Fathers as Cross-Generational Guilt

Psalm 51:7 See, I have been guilt-ridden from birth, a sinner from my mother's womb.

Psalm 51:16 Deliver me, O God, from the guilt of blood; you who are my God and savior.

Psalm 102:20–21 From his holy height in heaven, the Lord looks on the earth, he hears the groaning of the prisoners and sets free the children of death.

Deuteronomy 5:9–10 For I, the Lord your God, am a jealous God, visiting the iniquity of the fathers upon the children unto the third and fourth generation of those who hate me, and showing mercy unto the thousands of those who love me and keep my commandments.

Ezekiel 18:2–3 What's that for a proverb you use in the land of Israel: "The fathers have eaten sour grapes and the children's teeth are set on edge"? "As I live," said the Lord God, "none of you shall use this proverb again."

In collective reconciliation, some of the most relevant questions asked across nations and cultures concern generational guilt and generational responsibility: To what extent are the (grand)children of perpetrators guilty of the wrongdoing of their forefathers? Is it justified at all that later generations of the victims should demand "apology" and/or "repentance/atonement" from later generations of the perpetrators, who were not even born when the atrocity took place? What are the responsibilities of the subsequent generations of the victims? And of the perpetrators?

---

19. Maimonides, "Lehre von der Buße," 445. See also Yonah, *Gates of Repentance*, 31.

The Bußpsalmen, as a whole, express an awareness of both the cross-generational "properties" of sin, as exemplified by Psalm 51:7 quoted above, and the ability (and eagerness) of God to break the chain of condemnation (i.e., the "blood-debt" in Ps 51:16 and those condemned to death in Ps 102:21). Indeed, the "guilt of the fathers" is a frequent motif in the Bible (e.g., Ex 34:7; Nm 14:18; Dt 5:9), and sons (and daughters) are encouraged to confess (i.e., to uncover) and to learn from their former generation's wickedness in order to reform themselves and their present society (e.g., 2 Kgs 22:13; Neh 1:6–7). The commandment to "honor father and mother" (Ex 20:12) does not seem to have precedence over the demand to turn away from them when they have sinned: the "sons of Levi" responded to Moses's call to engage in a violent purge against even their closest relatives after these had turned to a false god (Ex 32:26–29).[20] We have already dealt with the "repentant disagreement" concerning generational guilt in the God-human relationship (see **R8**); we will continue here to explore its implications for victim-perpetrator and intraperpetrator relationships.

When a generation "confesses" the sins/wrongdoings of the former generation (e.g., Neh 1:6–7), they recognize both the cross-generational longevity of sin (e.g., in human nature, customs, and institutions) and the cross-generational consequences of sin (e.g., natural and social disasters).[21] By this very act of recognition, they are also exercising the freedom to break away from wrongful practices and frames of mind, and shouldering the responsibility for the aftermath of crimes and wrongdoings. As Jeremiah exclaimed in the face of such responsibilities, "Mine is this affliction; I must bear it" (10:19),[22] so is the attitude of a

---

20. Whether this text can be cited in support of intergenerational violence against apostasy is of course highly controversial. In the relevant text itself, one does not find an explicit demand from Yahweh to Moses for such a drastic measure. Rather, God was shown, before and after, to be willing to "turn away from anger" and to "change his mind" (Ex 32:11–14).

21. Natural degradation because of previous exploitation, and the loss of social trust following totalitarian regimes, are only two of the more obvious examples.

22. Compare the rather unusual translation from the Lutherbibel (1912)—"Es ist meine Plage; ich muß sie leiden"—with more contemporary versions.

repentant generation. But when a man acts as a judge and con-demns entire families/communities/nations for the sins of one or some among them, he in effect denies them such freedom and hence, by extension, negates real personal responsibility (see the biological causality of the proverb condemned by both Jeremiah 31:29 and Ezekiel 18:2). Or when a person blithely thinks that simply by virtue of being born late and having the benefit of his-torical hindsight, he is "free from the guilt/sinfulness" of his for-mer generation(s), he is in fact blind to the cross-generationalities, that is, the *presentness* of sin, and hence fails to make the nec-essary turning. This blindness also often misleads a person to consider himself a "victim" in having to deal with the "unfair" consequences at all.

In the victim-perpetrator relationship, then, reconciliation seems to hinge on the particular configuration of "repentant disagree-ment": whether on the "generational punishment" side, there is generational confession in the "perpetrator-nation" that seeks re-pentance and responsibility, or generational condemnation in the "victim-nation" that seeks perpetual blame and punishment; and whether on the "generational absolution" side, there is repentance aversion in the "perpetrator-nation" that bespeaks reluctance and/ or indifference, or repentance acceptance in the "victim-nation" that assumes the fundamental redeemability of human beings. Again, "mutual-turning" requires nothing less than deliberate "repentant disagreement" of a particular kind—a kind that the biblical tradition appears to advocate. After all, in the book of Jeremiah, it is the prophet who speaks of generational condem-nation when "representing" the "perpetrator-nation" to face God (14:20), while it is Yahweh who responds with generational abso-lution when proclaiming restoration (31:29–30).

R13: Remembrance for Life as Cross-Generational Responsibility

Psalm 143:5 I remember the earlier days; I reflect on what you have done and speak of the work of your hands.

Psalm 38:13, 16 Those who seek my life lay snares for me; those who wish to hurt me speak of my ruin. . . . But I put my trust in you, O Lord; you will answer for me, Lord God.

Psalm 102:19 Let this be written for future generations, and the Lord will be praised by the people he will form.

Psalm 40:11 I do not hide your righteousness in my heart; I speak of your faithfulness and your help. I do not remain silent about your kindness and truth before the great community.

In biblical repentance, if the intraperpetrator relationships (i.e., in this context, the intergenerational relationships within a perpetrator-nation) are "difficult," for coming to terms with "the sin of the fathers" can only be discomfiting, to say the least, the intravictim relationships are no less demanding. The later generations of the victims also have to deal with the set of questions related to the perpetrators and the later generations of the perpetrators, and also those related to the dead, the survivors or *remnants*, and the generations that are yet to come. We have already discussed the generational aspects of the problem above; we'll now turn to the responsibilities of later generations of the victims with regard to justice for the victims, vengeance/revenge and remembrance.

"The Lord Yahweh will wipe away the tears from all cheeks and eyes," declares Isaiah (25:8). Thus the restoration of the victims, especially the dead, for whom the living can apparently do no more than commemoration, is assured. This is of course not to replace human justice, or more precisely, the endeavor for justice as much as humanly attainable,[23] but rather, to *complete* it, especially where it fails or where it is impossible to fulfill. To employ the prophetic vision of human sins as relational wounds (**R2**) once again, it is clear to anyone who has dwelt with any adequate depth on human atrocities against each other that the wounds are beyond human cure (Jer 14:19, 15:18)—even in the case of "perfect" justice with the most complete compensation and punishment as humanly possible. In this sense, if the ultimate duty of the victims'

---

23. After all, to do justice is a fundamental duty of the believer (Mi 6:8).

descendants/compatriots is to achieve *full* justice for them, disappointment seems inevitable. "Our entire justice is like a piece of filthy clothing" (Is 64:5). It is with this understanding of the "not-nearly-enough" quality of human justice—all the more so, the more heinous the iniquity—that the hope for full restoration and retribution is placed, in the biblical tradition, in God and God alone. For even as God also speaks of the incurable wounds, he has promised to heal them as well (30:12, 17).

Unlike in some other traditions, human vengeance is not elevated to a moral duty in either Judaism or Christianity. "Vengeance is mine," declares the Lord, who will give justice to his people in his own way and time (Dt 32:35–36). Seeking revenge is expressly prohibited to the victims (and their later generations) (Lv 19:18). Rather, the later generations' attention, as we have seen in part, is deflected from enemy hatred and self-pity to self-critique: to reflect on their own (and their fathers') possible sinfulness as the "original cause" in their national calamity, whether it be foreign invasion, captivity, or oppression. As exemplified in Ezra's prayer in Nehemiah (9:6–37), three times it is mentioned that it was God who had "handed the [Israelites] over to their enemies" because of their unfaithfulness, thus orienting the victim-perpetrator relationship staunchly within the God-victim-perpetrator triad.

In this three-dimensional vision, it is not just justice and mercy that have acquired different meanings (i.e., as compared to the unilinear victim-perpetrator-only relationship), but also remembrance. Whereas memory can—and often does—become a servant of intercommunal hatred, it is by and large employed in the Bible to serve the God-human relationship. "Thou shalt remember . . ." is a frequent formulation in the Torah. Invariably, the faithfulness of God and the destructiveness of sin are the two major themes of this remembrance, under which the memory of the perpetrators themselves is subsumed, as captured also in the Bußpsalmen verses above. "Remember that when you were a slave in the land of Egypt," reads a "reasoning" in the Decalogue in Deuteronomy (5:15); yet it does not follow that the Egyptians are the ones to be remembered, for "it was the Lord your God who brought you out with a mighty hand and a stretched-out arm." And as if to

counter the prevailing and powerful culture of mutual justification of wrongdoings, the centrality of the God-Israel relationship
is cited as the only "remembrance reason" for Jewish victims of
oppression and slavery and their subsequent generations to refrain
from imitating the Egyptians in their own relationships with *their*
others. "You should love him [the stranger] like yourself, for you
were strangers in the land of Egypt. I am the Lord, your God" (Lv
19:34). The "mighty hand" and "stretched-out arm" that freed
Israel can also turn against him, should he venture to become "like
the nations" in their idolatry and wickedness (Ez 20:32–33).

It is true that the Lord "forgets not," but his nonforgetfulness is
not the same as a human grudge. "Can a woman forget her child, a
mother her own son? Even if she might forget him, I do not forget
you" (Is 49:15). Furthermore, as Maimonides emphasized, remembrance is not to serve the purpose of shaming: "It is also a great
sin to say to the repentant: Remember your former actions, or to
bring him to the memory of these, just to shame him. . . . All this
is forbidden and prohibited in the general commandments of the
Torah."[24] In other words, a loveless reminding that does not serve
the purpose of turning is incompatible with the biblical precept of
remembrance.

We will take a closer look at but one other biblical example
to illustrate the intricacies of this triangular relational structure of
memory, into which the details of the past are placed and from
which their meanings are derived: the "remembrance of Amalek"
(Ex 17:14–16; Dt 25:17–19).[25]

According to tradition, the Amalekites attacked the wandering
Israelites after the latter had found a new source of water. With
the help of Yahweh, the attackers lost, and Moses was instructed
by God himself to "write this in a book as something to be remembered . . . that *I* will wipe out the remembrance of Amalek

---

24. Maimonides, "Lehre von der Buße," 485.

25. I am grateful to Rabbi Pesach Schindler for pointing me to these passages by
linking them to Simon Dubnow's entreaty to the Jewish survivors to "record accu-
rately all the tragic details of the Holocaust." See Schindler, *Hasidic Responses to
the Holocaust in the Light of Hasidic Thought* (Hoboken, NJ: Ktav, 1990), 1, 139.

from under heaven" (Ex 17:14). Moses then took this to mean that "Yahweh is at war with the Amalekites from generation to generation" (v. 16). In Deuteronomy, this incident is recounted with two instructions: "Remember what Amalek did to you when you were on the road, coming out of Egypt. He went out to meet you on the way and when you were weak and tired attacked all who were left behind. He had no fear of God" (25:17–18); "*You* shall wipe out the remembrance of Amalek from under heaven. Do not forget" (v. 19).

The probable confusion on the part of the reader is well justified: What is not to be remembered? And what is not to be forgotten? Or what does it mean to not forget to wipe out remembrance? The key to a possible interpretation pertinent especially to our relational viewpoint is highlighted in italics in the quoted scriptures above: the "I" of Yahweh God and the "you" of the Israelites in the wiping out of "the remembrance of Amalek." One must ask, indeed, if Moses's interpretation was all there was to understand, then what could be left for the Israelites to wipe out? And if everything should be wiped out, then what could be left to remember?

That Yahweh's faithfulness—all the more important in these times of fratricidal treachery[26]—is the main theme and content to be remembered has already been mentioned above. In fact, the monument erected by Moses right after the war was not called "Victory against Amalek" or "The Accursed Amalekites," as one might have expected, but was an altar with the name "Yahweh My Banner" (v. 15).[27] What is also to be remembered seems not the Amalekites themselves or their name, for only the righteous are worthy of remembrance (Prv 10:7), but their *wrongdoings* (the taking advantage of the weak strangers, the tired, and the left behind) and their "godlessness," which the Israelites are called to remember so as not to commit the same themselves (Ex 22:20; Dt

---

26. According to tradition, Amalek was a grandson of Esau—the brother of Jacob/Israel (Gn 36:12).

27. See contrasting examples in ancient Rome in D. S. Levene, " 'You shall blot out the memory of Amalek': Roman Historians on Remembering to Forget," in *Historical and Religious Memory in the Ancient World*, ed. Beate Dignas and R. R. R. Smith (New York: Oxford University Press, 2012), 220.

10:19).[28] Indeed, the immediate verses preceding the instructions concerning remembrance of Amalek in Deuteronomy speak clearly of this danger: holding one set of standards against oneself, and another against the "others," the "enemies" (Dt 25:13–16). The Amalekites themselves had been victims of foreign oppression (Gn 14:7), yet they not only failed to remember the good that Abram/Abraham had done for them (i.e., by subduing their conquerors), but also committed the same or even worse crimes against others, even their benefactors, Abraham's descendants. On the other hand, the victory of the Amalekites & Co. over the Israelites was presented elsewhere in the Bible as the (reluctant) divine response to the repeated mis-turnings of the latter (Jgs 3:12–14).

All in all, the injunctions concerning the "remembrance of Amalek" could be the following: to remember God's faithfulness, to remember sins and wrongdoings, and to make an effort in overcoming the natural remembering of the perpetrators in one's heart—for

---

28. Rabbi René-Samuel Sirat has raised a complementary point when interpreting the text of 1 Samuel 15:18, in which he points out that the Hebrew text did not say "to destroy the Amalekite sinners," but "to destroy sins (of which Amalek is but a symbol)." See Sirat, "Judaism and Repentance" (paper presented at the Religions and Repentance Conference: Growth in Religious Traditions, Facing a New Era, Elijah Interfaith Institute, Jerusalem, 21 Mar. 2000). Indeed, the apparently divinely sanctioned violence against the Amalekites in 1 Samuel 15, in which the prophet Samuel told Saul the king to kill every single Amalekite, including children and infants, has always been problematic in biblical theology. At one extreme, it seems as if the "wiping out of remembrance" meant genocide (1 Sm 15:2–3). However, a counterexample of the vengeful Gibeonites (2 Sm 21) used by Maimonides points to the problem of this interpretation ("Lehre von der Buße," 427). Furthermore, with the Abrahamic plea for Sodom and Gomorrah in Genesis already mentioned (R10), one might ask whether even in the event of a clear and direct divine order of violence, one should not actually be bold enough—like Abraham—to *disagree* with God and try to placate him, instead of simply offering an "obedience" that is indifferent to the injustice inherent in any indiscriminate punishment. It is thus legitimate to ask whether both Saul *and* Samuel had in fact failed the "Abrahamic test" (Gn 22:1), and whether God regretted (1 Sm 15:11) that Saul had failed to kill all, or that he had *just* spared the strong and the useful, instead of having compassion for the weak and those of "no value" (15:9). For relevant exegetical possibilities, see Louis H. Feldman, *'Remember Amalek!'* (Cincinnati: Hebrew Union College Press, 2004), 46–53.

it is the only place "under heaven" where God needs the victim's "help" in wiping out the remembrance of the perpetrators. Yet this inner wiping out takes time and is, like other turnings, not to be accomplished under force (**R3**). Hence it is only with peace and security that this active and selective remembrance and forgetting are to be achieved (Dt 25:19).

R14: Reconciliation as Turning to Each Other through Turning to God

Psalm 51:11 Hide your face from my sins and blot out all my offenses.

Psalm 102:3 Do not hide your face from me when I am in trouble. Incline your ear to me; make haste to answer me when I call.

Psalm 32:5 I said: "I will confess my wrongdoings before the Lord." Then you forgave me the guilt of my sins.

Psalm 143:7 Answer me quickly, O Lord, for my spirit is dying. Do not hide your face from me, so that I will not be like those who go down to the pit.

Psalm 80:20 Turn to us, O Lord, God of hosts; let your face shine so we can be saved.

The Bußpsalmen repeatedly express the repentant perpetrator's/ sinner's wish to seek God's *face*, that is, for "divine turning": from being fixated on the sins and wrongdoings to turning toward the perpetrator himself. It is as if sin (given birth into reality by the sinner) has effected a double turning-away: the sinner's turning away from God, and God's turning away from the sinner. Correspondingly, when repentance as "(re)turning" is spoken of in the Bible, it is meant to be "mutual-turning," in which it is invariably the God-victim who makes the turning *first*—in the various forms of mercy (**R3**), in the enabling of and participation in the sinner's repentance (**R6**), and not the least in repenting himself (**R9**). The various turnings on God's side implored—as opposed to being demanded[29]—by the sinner are expressed in concrete actions: "incline your ear," "answer," "carry away," "hide (not)," "cast out not." In this last section, we will review some aspects of mutual-turning in light of further examples of *interhuman* reconciliation in the Bible, in order to bring out certain elements that are obscured or overlooked in our exploration of repentance in the God-human relationship (**R1–R9**).

Interpersonal Reconciliation between Joseph and His Brothers (Genesis 37–50): The Link between Confession and Curative Mourning

> Genesis 42:21, 24 They said among themselves, "Alas! We are guilty toward our brother! For we saw the fear of his soul when he pleaded with us, but we did not listen; that is why this misery has come upon us. . . ." And Joseph turned and wept.

In the book of Genesis, Joseph, son of Jacob/Israel, who had been betrayed and sold into slavery by his brothers, wept seven times.[30] Two instances of particular importance were occasioned by his brothers' confessions. The first time he wept was after the *internal confession* among his brothers, in which they drew the link between their present predicament (i.e., being imprisoned) and their past sin against their brother Joseph, hence recognizing the punishment as just (see **R4**).[31] The third time, in which he "wept aloud" and finally revealed himself to his brothers, after testing their resolve of repentance,[32] was upon Judah's *public confession* of sin.

---

29. Divine turning is not a matter of "right" that the sinner can demand from God. It is rather always a matter of divine initiative in the dead-end situation in which the sinner rightfully finds himself.

30. Genesis 42:24; 43:30; 45:2, 14–15; 46:29; 50:1 and 17.

31. Genesis 42:21–22.

32. Why would Joseph keep first Simeon and then Benjamin, but let his other brothers go? It is possible that he wanted to see whether his brothers had really learned and turned: Would they let Simeon, their brother of the same mother (Leah), languish in slavery, as they had done to Joseph? Would they do that to Benjamin, regarded not as their brother but only their "father's son"—as Joseph was regarded (Gn 37:32)—of their mother's rival (Rachel)? In other words, were they still constrained by a narrowly defined notion of kinship love? As Maimonides has

Judah said: "God has found out the iniquity of your servants" (Gn 44:16). Rather than pleading their actual innocence of theft, Judah attempted to shoulder all the guilt by substituting Benjamin (44:34). Finally, seeing that his brothers were still burdened by the fear of retribution and a conception of guilt that enslaves, Joseph wept for the seventh time and "comforted" them (50:17, 21).

Hence, although in the Bible one does not read of divine "tears of joy," but only God weeping for our sins (see **R5**), we can see at least from this example of interhuman reconciliation the *curative* potential of confession. That is, even though past wrongdoings cannot be undone, even though a confession may not reveal anything that is not already known—in other words, even though a confession "does nothing"—by confessing a sinner/perpetrator still has much to contribute to healing—not only of the wounded relationship but also of the wounded victim.

International Reconciliation between the Israelites
and the Edomites (Genesis 25–33): The Difference
between Reconciliation and Integration

> Genesis 33:10, 16–17 Jacob answered [Esau]: ". . . I saw your face, as if
> I was seeing the face of God. . . ." Esau returned that day on his way to
> Seir. And Jacob went to Succoth.

Perhaps the most relevant and direct question with regard to the original intention of this biblical investigation is, Where are the examples of "collective reconciliation" in the Bible? With our conceptual preparation up to this point, we shall now finally deal with this question squarely, by looking at the story of Israel (or the Israelites) and Esau (or the Edomites) in Genesis 25:21–33:20. This story is assuring in one sense and "surprising" in another. It is assuring because conflicts between "nations/peoples" (25:23) are framed within the triad of relationships (**R2**), pointing to the *shared origins*

---

said, the test of "complete repentance" (*vollkommene Buße*) is when the sinner is given a chance to commit the same sin again but does not sin even though he can. Maimonides, "Lehre von der Buße," 417. Judah, who had led the group in selling Joseph into slavery (37:26–27), also took the lead in passing both of these tests.

of the conflicting parties (first through Rebekah their mother but ultimately to Yahweh-God, the God of Abraham and the God of Isaac).[33] It is also assuring that the "causes" of these conflicts are not conceived as "black and white," or in terms of a good-versus-evil or us-versus-them kind of historiography; rather, natural disparities (25:23) and parental favoritism (25:28) are cited, alongside the conflicting parties' own respective sinful behavior (**R1**), that is, Jacob's lying and Esau's disregard for the sacred right of the firstborn, for instance. It is also assuring that the Israelites were in effect taught through this particular scripture to see themselves not as "pure and innocent" (**R11**) in their conflicts with the Edomites; rather, Jacob (Israel) had every reason to repent and to proactively seek reconciliation with Esau (Edom), just as Esau did with Jacob. And for Jacob to be "motivated" to do so, the only thing he could and did count on was God's mercy and power (32:10–13), rather than his own "self-power" of "self-transformation" (**R3** and **R6**), of overcoming past mistakes and their consequences. Indeed, even before he met Esau, he was already made a *new man,* "Israel" (32:28). Finally, it is assuring that in international reconciliation, the "forgetting and anger-self-dissipating" approach[34] is judged not reliable (**R13**); the guilt-bearers have to *turn to* their victims, who in turn have to be willing to "face again" their former perpetrators and their shared—yet differentiated—guilt and pain (33:3–4). They both have to face their God and see each other (33:10) if reconciliation is to take place between them.[35] It is only "surprising" that the story does not end with "And they lived happily ever after," as we might have expected. Instead, the two still parted ways (33:16–17).

---

33. See also Obadiah 1:10, 15.

34. Rebekah told Jacob to flee until Esau forgot what Jacob had done to him and his anger "turn[ed] itself away from him" (Gn 27:44–45). It didn't happen.

35. The same occurred in Joseph's reconciliation with his brothers: first, when he turned to them as a "God-fearing man" (Gn 42:18); then, as he took away their guilt by accusing God of delivering him to the Egyptians in order to save the entire family (Israel) from famine (45:5–8). The entire human act of fraternal betrayal was thus enveloped and interpreted in a greater act of divine "culpability" and, ultimately, mercy, which is typical in the biblical paradigm (e.g., Ps 105:25; Ex 11:10).

All of this shows, on the one hand, the challenges for those seeking inspiration for collective reconciliation from the Bible, and on the other, the challenges for the conception of "reconciliation" itself. Does it have to mean "integration," as in intermarriage, similar schooling and worldview, same language and laws, and so on? Does it mean "world peace," in which not only are past relational wounds healed but future wounds are also forestalled, which immediately renders "reconciliation" unattainable as the problem is intractable? Does it mean "going back to the past when things were good,"[36] which brings to the fore both the impossibility of "going back" and the paucity, if not outright absence, of the "original state of good relationship" between communities? Or can it mean a "renewal of relationship," in which wounds are being tended to while a *new* relationship of a *new* liveliness (still under the ever-present threat of new wounds and illnesses) that *has never been* (Is 43:19) is coming into being?

The question of interhuman reconciliation therefore does not have to be burdened with unrealistic expectations on the one side, and is not to be confused with social integration on the other. As Yahweh commanded Jeremiah, "If you return, I will return to you. . . . Let them return to you, but do not return to them" (Jer 15:19).[37] It is repentance to God rather than reconciliation with one another per se that stands at the core of mutual-turning efforts. In the biblical vision, for both the human victims and the perpetrators, drawing closer to God (both themselves and each other) takes precedence over merely drawing closer to one another; should both be turning to God, then no contradiction will arise from their turning to each other. In fact, as we have seen, both—but especially the perpetrator—benefit from the other's efforts in turning to God. But should interhuman mutual-turning give rise to the danger of turning *away* from God, as in "compromises" in issues concerning

---

36. As implied by a common Chinese formulation that is used to express "reconciliation": 和好如初 (literally, "harmonious and good as in the beginning").

37. In this single verse, the verb "repent/return" appears four times—possibly no other verse in the Bible contains more instances of turning. That even God "repents/turns" is not, as we have seen in R9, an alien notion in the Bible. Cf. Zechariah 1:3.

truth and justice,[38] then such "reconciliation" in the human sphere, according to the scripture cited above, is to be rejected in favor of repentance to God.

But can one simply choose to repent *only* to God—that is, without turning to the human victims, who can be much more difficult, if not impossible, to restore than the merciful, ever-ready-to-turn God? From the experience of Jacob, this "sidestepping" of the human victims is to be refuted, for even as the new man, Israel, was already formed *before* facing Esau, his wronged brother, he had to meet him nonetheless, bearing the full risk of rejection—or even abuse (**R11**)—of his genuine repentance. Indeed, such is the high price for human iniquity: a double healing is necessary for the double damage of divine-human and interhuman relationships (**R2**). Had the reconciliation with God alone sufficed, then the Lord would not have to bring famine to the Israelites, his people, in order for them to face the Gibeonites, to atone for Saul's "guilt of blood," through which he annihilated the non-Israelites "in his zeal for Israel and Judah" (2 Sm 21:1–14). It is as if God will not allow himself to be reconciled to the sinners unless they have made at least earnest attempts—so long as these are still humanly possible—to repent also to their human victims.[39] For when the prophet proclaimed, "For the wound of my people I am wounded,"[40] it was indicative of the "divine pathos" (Heschel) when relationships among the children of God remain damaged. Hence according to Maimonides, the Jewish "Day of Atonement/ Reconciliation" (*Versöhnungstag*)[41] is a time for all to repent, as

---

38. See, for example, the problems of premature "healing/reconciliation" and "unjust peace" in Jeremiah 6:13–14.

39. The need to seek reconciliation with the victims of one's own sinful acts before seeking reconciliation with God is also stressed in the Gospels. For if the victims are asked to leave their gifts at the altar to go and face their siblings who had done wrong against them (Mt 5:23–24), shouldn't the perpetrators have all the more reason to summon up the courage to seek the face of their human victims—rather than just seeking absolution from the confessors?

40. Jeremiah 8:21.

41. Yom Kippur is usually translated as "Day of Atonement" in English (see, e.g., Lv 23:27), but the common German translation, "Versöhnungstag," can also mean "Day of Reconciliation." This is probably due to the etymological

individuals and as a community. But "repentance, and the Day of Reconciliation as well, only have the power to forgive sins that man has committed against God. . . . The injustice that a man has done to another . . . will never be pardoned until he compensates his neighbor, to the extent he is guilty toward him, and placates him . . . and begs him for pardon."[42] And should the victims be dead before pardon can be asked for, the guilty ones are to make a public confession before an audience in front of the graves of the dead victims: "I have sinned against the Eternal One, the God of Israel, and against so-and-so; in this and that way I have done injustice against them."[43] To seek the face of the victim—irreplaceable and unrepresentable—is thus liturgically enforced in Judaism. Before the face of God, on the other hand, the victim is also reminded of his own sinner-hood (Eccl 7:20–22). And though it is his prerogative to withhold forgiveness for his victimizer, nevertheless it is not recommended that he do so toward the repentant one.[44]

Toward the end of the book of Genesis, Joseph's brothers feared that the death of their father, Jacob, would remove the inhibition of Joseph's revenge against them. And so they put words in the mouth of the deceased to request forgiveness from Joseph: "Forgive your brothers . . ." (Gn 50:17). But Joseph did not utter that one word they were seeking. Instead he answered: "Am I in the place of God?" (v. 19). It is one thing to consider oneself capable of issuing forgiveness yet withholding it; it is another not to consider oneself to be "in the place" to issue forgiveness, as in the case of Joseph, who, although the undisputed victim of his brothers' wrongdoing, considered himself indebted to God, who had turned the evil intentions of men and his misery into salvation for many (v. 20).

---

link between *Versöhnung* (reconciliation) and *Sühne* (atonement), which at once points to the need for atonement in reconciliation and the conciliatory nature of atonement.

42. Maimonides, "Lehre von der Buße," 423–29.

43. Ibid.

44. Maimonides went so far as to claim that if even after repeated attempts on the part of the repentant to seek forgiveness privately and publicly from his victim, who nonetheless is unwilling to grant it, the guilt will then rest with the unforgiving victim. Maimonides, "Lehre von der Buße," 427.

Instead of forgiveness, Joseph offered his brothers much more: care, comfort, and companionship (v. 21).

Conclusion: A Review of Biblical Repentance

The common translation of the Hebrew word *tshuvah* as "repentance/penitence/penance" in English and "Buße" in German (which derives from "Besserung," or "betterment")[45] has its pros and cons. The most obvious loss of connotation in these translations is the mutuality of turning. For the immediate import of the close linguistic proximity between *tshuvah* and *turning, returning, restoring*—turning away from one's evil ways, turning back to God, turning on the part of the sinner as making amends (Jer 26:13), turning as "re-facing" the sinner (Ez 39:29), and turning as restoring (relationally as well as geographically) on the part of God—is that "repentance" is very much a mutual act, involving both the perpetrator and the victim (in this case, God himself). Although there are crucial differences between what each side needs to turn from and to (re)turn to, hence an *asymmetry*, the overall "structure" of biblical repentance is one of "mutual-turning,"[46] rather than a unilateral turning to be "accomplished" by the sinner alone. In other words, if God did not turn to the sinner in the first instance—to offer him the chance (and guidance/encouragement/admonishment) for repentance—the sinner would have

---

45. See *Kluge Etymologisches Wörterbuch der deutschen Sprache*, ed. Elmar Seebold (Berlin/New York: Walter de Gruyter, 2002), s.v. "Buße." In verb form (*büßen*), it assumes the meanings of "to make better" (*verbessern*) and "to make good again" (*wiedergutmachen*). See *Duden Deutsches Universalwörterbuch*, ed. Werner Scholze-Stubenrecht (Mannheim/Zurich: Dudenverlag, 2011), s.v. "büßen."

46. The problem with mutual-turning, one must never fail to remember, is when it becomes a "requirement" by the perpetrator of the victim, as when the French intellectual Pascal Bruckner demands "absolute reciprocity," in terms of official apologies, from the victims of French colonialism. See Bruckner, *The Tyranny of Guilt: An Essay on Western Masochism*, trans. Steven Rendall (Princeton, NJ/Oxford: Princeton University Press, 2010), 43.

no recourse to turning at all. To borrow Franz Rosenzweig's formulation, repentance is in essence an "evented event" (*ereignetes Ereignis*).[47]

The words "repentance" and "Buße" convey at best only the sinner's side—indispensable nonetheless—of *tshuvah*, that is, of regret, of self-bettering. At worst, they convey only punishment, as, for example, *Bußgeld* (a fine) or *büßen* (to suffer). Although all these elements (including the Greek *metanoia*, roughly, "change of mind"), as has been demonstrated in this part of the book, belong to the conceptualizations of "turning" in the Bible, none alone "defines" what biblical repentance means. The one advantage "repentance" has over "turning" is its religious specificity: not all turnings correspond to biblical repentance, as is shown in the example in Jeremiah 34:15–22 (see **R6**). In cultural contexts where the word "turning" does not enjoy an intuitive link with penitential "turnings" as meant in the Bible, the imperfect translations are necessary compromises. In this sense, although *Umkehr* (turning back) most resembles *tshuvah* in its non-closed-endedness, it suffers from the same nonspecificity as "turning" in English, as in *umgekehrt* (conversely) or *Umkehrung* (reversal).

The problem of biblical repentance does not lie in its imperfect translations into German and English alone, which is a general problem with all cultural borrowings and is not insurmountable with careful clarification. More significant for the purpose of this investigation is the problem of relational transference. To what extent can the God-human relationship be the "model" for the inter-human one? What are the limits of this "trans(re)lation"?

To begin with the obvious, the victim is not, by virtue of the wrongdoing and the resultant victimhood, the perpetrator's "god";

---

47. This term is used in the context of love in revelation. Franz Rosenzweig, *Der Stern der Erlösung* (Frankfurt a.M.: J. Kauffmann Verlag, 1921), 203. See also Bernhard Casper, "Transzendentale Phänomenalität und ereignetes Ereignis: Der Sprung in ein hermeneutisches Denken im Leben und Werk Franz Rosenzweigs," in *Der Stern der Erlösung*, by Franz Rosenzweig (Freiburg im Breisgau: Universitätsbibliothek, 2002).

rather, in the biblical paradigm, they both have the one God to face, who acts as the judge between them (1 Sm 2:25). This seemingly insignificant point is in fact of crucial significance if we consider the problems of interhuman reconciliation, when the perpetrators feel beholden to the victims' demands for "repentance"—even those totally uncharacteristic of the spirit of biblical repentance (see **R11**)—as if the latter were now also the "God-victim."

Secondly, the issue of power is also problematic. Whereas in the God-human relationship, power and mercy on the part of God often come hand in hand (whether as the power to punish or as the power to heal), this does not always correspond to the interhuman. Not all victims are in a position to ponder judgment or clemency, punishment or magnanimity. Quite often, they are still locked in a semidependent, underprivileged relationship with the perpetrators. One cannot exercise mercy, so to speak, if one cannot not exercise it. In this sense, the "restoration of the victims" is of primary importance in interhuman reconciliation, although unnecessary in the God-sinner relationship.

Finally, if God's mercy is the beginning of repentance, temporally and ontologically, as we have demonstrated (**R3**) that the repentant sinner/perpetrator seems to be able to overcome the obstacles to the "circumcision of the heart" (**R6**) only by counting on it, where is the promise of turning in the interhuman? It is not mercy as automatic impunity—this we have seen is not the biblical idea of mercy (**R4**)—but mercy as the promise to restore, that is, to "face again," to hear and speak to again, in short, to reenter into relation with. And if there is no such "guarantee" from the human victims' side, but in its place the possibility—if not already the reality—of permanent condemnation, regardless of whether one repents or not, then where can another motivational force be found?

"Repentance is the most optimistic device," Rabbi Schindler told us at Yad Vashem. We did not know what he meant until he referred to the biblical texts about remembrance ("For you were strangers in the land of Egypt") and then turned to the present-day Israeli-Palestinian conflict. Indeed, without such optimism, difficult questions regarding one's own or one's nation's past and present can be much harder to come to terms with, if at all. Turning to the next chapter, we shall look at how this "device" has been at work—insofar as it is visible—in the history of German *Vergangenheitsbewältigung*.

PART II

Mutual-Turning in German Vergangenheitsbewältigung: *Responses and Correspondence*

The Hebrew word for repentance, *teshuvah*, means *return*.
Yet it also means *answer*. Return to God is an answer to
Him. For God is not silent. . . . The stirring in man to turn to
God is actually a "reminder by God to man." . . . The most
precious gifts come to us unawares and remain unnoted.
God's grace resounds in our lives like a staccato. Only by
retaining the seemingly disconnected notes do we acquire the
ability to grasp the theme.[1]

ABRAHAM JOSHUA HESCHEL

In the two previous chapters on biblical repentance, we have sought
to delineate the salient features of "repentance" in the biblical texts,
deriving conceptions for interhuman, collective "mutual-turning"
chiefly through transference from repentance between God and
human. Moving forward from this textual analysis, we will now seek
to concretize this biblical paradigm with realities created in dealing
with the German guilt situation. We will look at a selection of responses from those affected or burdened by Nazi atrocities—that
is, the victims, the perpetrators, the bystanders, and their respective
later generations—and attempt to establish their correspondence
with the biblical paradigm of repentance.

---

1. Abraham Joshua Heschel, *God in Search of Man: A Philosophy of Judaism*
(New York: Farrar, Straus and Giroux, 1983), 141–42 (emphasis in the original).

The idea is not to trace individual motivation, nor to describe general trends of public or intellectual opinion. Rather, the aim here is to highlight the *formal resemblance* between such words and deeds and the biblical conceptions of repentance. In fact, these responses were often "minority opinions," expressed by individuals who were upheld and castigated at the same time by their respective communities. Yet, as we shall see, this "minority" was not confined to a particular segment of society, namely, the "religious professionals" who are experts in the biblical paradigm and are religiously motivated. The broad distribution of the samples of this "minority" thus proves nothing regarding the broad *acceptance* of their opinions; it indicates rather the broad *presence* of the biblical paradigm.

For want of adequate preestablished categories, one might call this minority the "turners," for they all sought in effect to turn their respective audiences to or away from certain viewpoints, attitudes, and behavioral patterns, which were in unison or conflict with the biblical paradigm of repentance. Needless to say, it is the spoken word, not the speaker, that bears validity, that is, not everything a "turner" says necessarily corresponds with repentance; rather, it is always contingent upon the particular expression identified to be in correspondence with biblical turning that a turner is named as such in this study. It is also never the intention to evaluate particular individuals as whole persons, but to recognize their particular contribution to mutual-turning.

In the following chapters, these "turning" responses will be organized according to the ideational framework established in part 1 of this book (e.g., **P6** contains historical expressions corresponding to the theological positions in **R6**). In each chapter certain phrases appear in boldface for convenient navigation.

3

"People, Not Devils" (P1)

The idea that **"sin" and "sinner" are not to be equated** has found ample expression in the postwar period—in exceptional cases, even *before* the war actually ended. Toward the end of World War II, as the atrocities committed at Buchenwald and Auschwitz came increasingly to light, contempt for "the Germans" grew in Allied countries. Some "turners"—many of Jewish descent—took it upon themselves to challenge a particular understanding of "collective guilt"—that is, that all the Germans should be punished as criminals. One early "turner," Victor Gollancz, a British-Jewish publisher and writer, penned a pamphlet in April 1945, *What Buchenwald Really Means,*[1] precisely challenging this tendency to equate crime/sin (the Buchenwald concentration camp) and the "criminals/sinners" (the Nazis/Germans), by looking more deeply

---

1. Victor Gollancz, *What Buchenwald Really Means* (London: Victor Gollancz, 1945). See also **P10**.

into the nature of the crime/sin itself. "Victor's pamphlet was directed to spelling out in precise detail how Buchenwald proved the opposite: all the Germans had not been guilty; there was ample evidence that hundreds of thousands of heroic gentiles had been persecuted for resisting the Nazis."[2] Seizing on this single fact among facts, Gollancz, the champion hitherto of the cause of European Jewry,[3] denounced any "collective punishment" being visited on the Germans, whether it be expulsion or starvation.[4]

Also in the early postwar years, while Gollancz was standing up for the German case in Britain by using his own publishing company and the press, a young Jew in France was following suit in fighting against the sin-sinner-flattening tendency in public perception. Alfred Grosser, then a twenty-two-year-old aspiring lecturer, returned to Germany in 1947, which he, as a German Jew, and his family had fled because of Nazi persecution. He traveled through all three Western zones to witness the living conditions there. After his return, he published a series of articles in *Combat*, a French newspaper of the Resistance.[5] Among other things, Grosser urged his French audience to reconsider the collective punishment of the Germans, especially in view of the "innocence" of German youth. Because of the unjust sufferings young Germans now faced, he said in one of these articles, "[The German youth] does not hold himself responsible for the murderous madness of the Hitler regime. And he is right. There is no collective guilt, no collective responsibility for children and adolescents."[6]

Plainly agreeable as Grosser's plea might be, at least where guilt rather than responsibility is concerned, one might still object to

---

2. Ruth Dudley Edwards, *Victor Gollancz: A Biography* (London: Victor Gollancz, 1987), 402.

3. See, for example, Gollancz's *Let My People Go* (1943) and *Nowhere to Lay Their Heads* (1945).

4. Matthew Frank, "The New Morality—Victor Gollancz, 'Save Europe Now' and the German Refugee Crisis, 1945–46," *Twentieth Century British History* 17, no. 2 (2006).

5. Martin Strickmann, *L'Allemagne nouvelle contre l'Allemagne éternelle: Die französischen Intellektuellen und die deutsch-französische Verständigung 1944–1950* (Frankfurt a.M.: Peter Lang, 2004), 156–57. The said articles are reprinted in German in Alfred Grosser, *Mit Deutschen streiten: Aufforderungen zur Wachsamkeit* (Munich/Vienna: Carl Hanser, 1987), 11–25.

6. Quoted in Strickmann, *L'Allemagne nouvelle contre l'Allemagne éternelle*, 159.

this "natural" approach to guilt assignment. For if one accepts that children are not guilty, then what about the adults? Is there collective guilt for them? One might ask the similar question with regard to Gollancz's formulation: if Buchenwald proved that not all Germans were guilty because there were those who had resisted and those who had suffered persecution, then were all those who *had not* resisted and/or suffered in the camps guilty, and did they therefore deserve collective condemnation? In other words, is separating "good Germans" from "bad Germans"—whether by age or affiliation—an effective expression of the biblical conception? Is this not only an "improvement" at best, in the sense that those sinners to be condemned for their sin are only the few "bad" ones?

Another Jewish "turner," Hannah Arendt, tackled precisely this problem even earlier, in a publication that appeared in January 1945, "Organized Guilt,"[7] in which she countered that "even the more serious discussions between the advocates of the 'good' Germans and the accusers of the 'bad' . . . [sometimes] adopt unsuspectingly the racial theories of the Nazis and reverse them (*kehren sie um*)."[8] Like Gollancz, Arendt was concerned that the Germans would be collectively, indiscriminately punished for Nazi crimes: "The central thesis of this [political] warfare [of the Nazis] . . . is that there is no difference between Nazis and Germans. . . . The extermination of 70 or 80 million Germans . . . would also only mean that the ideologies of the Nazis had won."[9] That the Nazis or Hitler "had won" would become a recurring theme in the postwar period, as we shall see, calling the victors' and the victims' attention to what it really means to fight Nazism/antisemitism, or to fight sin rather than the sinner.[10]

---

7. First published in English as "German Guilt" in *Jewish Frontier* in Jan. 1945; subsequently published in German as "Organisierte Schuld," *Die Wandlung* 1, no. 4 (1946). In a letter to Karl Jaspers dated 29 Jan. 1946, Arendt referred to the German text as "the original," written in dedication to Jaspers. See Lotte Köhler and Hans Saner, eds., *Hannah Arendt Karl Jaspers Briefwechsel 1926–1969* (Munich/Zurich: R. Piper, 1985), 68.

8. Arendt, "Organisierte Schuld," 337.

9. Ibid., 333, 338–39.

10. See, for example, Eugen Kogon's and Avraham Burg's expressions in **P10** and **P9**, respectively.

But still, can one now simply distinguish the Nazis from the Germans, and condemn the former while leaving the latter in peace? Here is Arendt's answer: because the Nazis had surely seen to it that—by way of false documents and witnesses—no living German could be left with an untarnished anti-Nazi record, therefore "whether someone in Germany is a Nazi or an anti-Nazi can only be determined by one who is capable of looking into the human heart, which, as we all know, no human eye can penetrate."[11] In other words, the human ability to judge sinners—rather than sin—is cast into doubt, and the prophetic message of Jeremiah that only God can fathom hearts and minds (17:9–10) is reaffirmed.[12]

Appearing in tandem with the conceptual separation between sin and sinner in the biblical paradigm is the **reaffirmation of the inherent dignity of human beings**—even the most egregious sinners are included. In the postwar period, the expression of this idea is probably the most significant contribution of Victor Gollancz. His book *Our Threatened Values* first appeared in English in June 1946 and was translated into German the following year.[13] In it he argued that Western civilization's "central value. . .—the value that includes all our other values—is respect for personality," the "real test" of which "is our attitude toward people we 'don't like', toward those whom . . . we 'don't respect', and to all whom we think of as enemies or criminals or sinners."[14]

If the requirement of *respect for personality* in "normal" circumstances is accepted with little difficulty, it is only reasonable to ask why we should still accord such respect to "abnormal" individuals, such as mass murderers, who have arguably forfeited their right to respect through their own disrespect for others. Gollancz based his argument chiefly on the "three interrelated religious doctrines [of the West]: that God created all men in His own image, that God is

---

11. Arendt, "Organisierte Schuld," 336. See also a similar effort at "anonymizing the good Germans" by Max Picard in **P9**.

12. Cf. 1 Samuel 16:7.

13. Victor Gollancz, *Unser bedrohtes Erbe*, trans. Adolf Halfeld (Zurich: Atlantis-Verlag, 1947).

14. Victor Gollancz, *Our Threatened Values* (London: Victor Gollancz, 1946), 9–10.

the Father of all men, and that all men are therefore brothers."[15]
Quoting the prophet Amos (9:7) and the Talmudic legend in which
God admonished the angels for joining the human celebration of
the drowning of the Egyptians—that is, those who were *also* his
children—in the Red Sea, Gollancz exhorted his fellow Jewish
readers to consider the following question and its implications: "Is
not my God also the God of the Nazis?"[16]

Mindful that he was addressing a largely Christian or "Christianized" audience in Britain, Gollancz did not refrain from adopting a Christian discourse to condemn the sin-sinner-flattening
tendency. Quoting John 8:7, he repeatedly challenged his British
readers who would dare "to throw the first stone" at the Germans
or the so-called collaborationists.[17]

A corollary to the affirmation of the sinner's inherent human
dignity is the **rejection of his demonization** by others. Hence it is no
surprise that both Gollancz and Arendt came to the fore to denounce
the tendency to think and speak of Nazi criminals as monsters. In
her "report" on the trial, after enumerating Eichmann's various
"cardinal vices," including vanity, bragging, self-centeredness, ha-
bitual lying, pretentiousness, and a love of clichés (i.e., the *banality*
of evil), Arendt concluded that "despite all the efforts of the prosecution, everybody could see that this man was not a 'monster'."[18]
Gollancz, on the other hand, sought to counter a more subtle form
of the dehumanization of the sinner—by "counting him out," as
if his death were not a human death. Hence in his own report on
the Eichmann case (published before the proceedings ended), he

---

15. Ibid., 12.

16. Ibid.

17. This verse was first used in *Buchenwald*, when Gollancz asked his readers
to "imagine themselves as ordinary Germans." It was used later in *Our Threatened Values*, in specific reference to a woman in France being mocked and shaved
for supposedly having had intercourse with a German or a collaborationist. And,
finally, it appeared in a proposed collective statement from the victors to the Germans, observing that "we have all sinned, and no one of us can cast stones." See
Buchenwald, 9–10; *Our Threatened Values*, 25, 28. See further the meaning of this
self-inclusivity in **P10**.

18. Hannah Arendt, *Eichmann in Jerusalem: A Report on the Banality of Evil*
(London: Faber, 1963), 40–49.

concluded his analysis of the "sin" and "guilt" of Eichmann by pleading for his life: "Do not kill Adolf Eichmann. . . . If six million have been slaughtered, what can it profit to make the number six million and one?"[19]

The drive against demonization was orchestrated not only by those who had not suffered in the Nazi concentration camps themselves, but also by those who had. Hermann Langbein, an Austrian who had survived Dachau and Auschwitz and was recognized as "Righteous Among the Nations" by Yad Vashem in 1967, pointed to the erroneous trends of either demonizing the Nazis or depersonalizing them to the point where they were only small parts in a big machine. He himself preferred to call them, realistically, "people, not devils."[20] He quoted a fellow inmate of Auschwitz approvingly:

> Grete Salus was able to avoid any demonization. . . . She writes: "I am afraid of people. I fear nothing as much as people. How good and how bad can they become? There is no measurement, no foundation, no certainty for that. . . . Here there were petty officials, craftsmen, young girls and women. Under different circumstances all the malice inside them could at most have expressed itself in gossip, cheating, tyranny in the family circle, and the like." Those who kept the machinery of murder going in Auschwitz were not devils; they were humans.[21]

Strong voices against demonizing the Nazi sinner could also be heard in Israel. As documented in Tom Segev's *Seventh Million*, which was translated into German in 1995,[22] some Jewish intellectuals living in Israel—among them Martin Buber, Shmuel Hugo Bergmann, and Yehuda Bacon—were also active participants in the endeavor to turn the Jewish public from the sin-sinner-flattening

---

19. Victor Gollancz, *The Case of Adolf Eichmann* (London: Victor Gollancz, 1961), 60.

20. Hermann Langbein, *People in Auschwitz*, trans. Harry Zohn (Chapel Hill: University of North Carolina Press, 2004), 3, 294–301; originally published in German as *Menschen in Auschwitz* (Vienna: Europaverlag, 1972).

21. Langbein, *People in Auschwitz*, 296–97.

22. Tom Segev, *Die siebte Million: Der Holocaust und Israels Politik der Erinnerung*, trans. Jürgen Peter Krause and Maja Ueberle-Pfaff (Reinbek bei Hamburg: Rowohlt, 1995).

tendency. For Bergmann, killing the sinner (even such a sinner as Eichmann) was objectionable because of the (unjustifiable) preclusion of repentance. In response to his students who were wondering why he was organizing a petition against sentencing Eichmann to death, the aged professor of philosophy at the Hebrew University explained: "Who gave them permission to take life, and in so doing to take from the defendant **the possibility of doing penance for his sins** while he is still in this world? Only he who creates life has the authority to take life."[23] Bergmann was one of the group gathered at Buber's house that drafted the letter to Israeli president Yitzhak Ben-Zvi to ask him to commute the execution of Eichmann. Among the twenty signatories to the letter was Bacon, who was a teenager when he arrived at Auschwitz and became a witness at the Eichmann trial. Their petition was in vain, including in the court of public opinion: "The press rejected the petition with near unanimity. 'A pardon for Eichmann?' *Maariv* asked—and answered, 'No! Six million times no!'"[24]

But if the sinner is not sin and the perpetrator's inherent worth is not destroyed by his crime, there is still the problem of "purifying" and "cleansing," which, according to the biblical paradigm, can only come about when **the perpetrator *turns* to his victim.** For Gollancz, this is precisely the hope that is afforded by sparing Eichmann's life: so that his "divine spark" may shine out from his corruption when he *repents*.[25] In Arendt, the requirement to "turn to the victims" is made even more explicit. In her appreciative critique of Karl Jaspers's *Schuldfrage*, which deals mainly with the assumption and differentiation of guilt and will be analyzed in the next chapter, she asserted that "the assumption of responsibility has to be more than the acceptance of defeat and the collateral consequences. . . . [It] has to come with a positive political declaration of intention (*Willenserklärung*) *addressed to the victims*," such as constitutionally renouncing antisemitism and re-welcoming Jews

---

23. Tom Segev, *The Seventh Million: The Israelis and the Holocaust*, trans. Haim Watzman (New York: Hill and Wang, 1993), 362.

24. Ibid., 365.

25. Gollancz, *Case of Eichmann*, 47.

to live in the future Germany as Jews.[26] Jaspers responded by saying that he agreed "completely" with Arendt on this requirement, but was unoptimistic about getting Germans to agree on that at the time.[27]

This "turning" in the form of a positive, collective statement toward the Jewish people did come, albeit partially and belatedly, in 1990, when the newly reunified Germany opened itself to Jews coming from the former Soviet Union to settle there as their new homeland. And the revised legislation against "incitement to hatred" (*Volksverhetzung*; section 130 of the German Criminal Code), covering antisemitism, expressed in the form of assaults on "human dignity," was also adopted in 1960—as a measure against the "new wave" of antisemitic violence in West Germany in the late 1950s[28]—with amendments dealing with the denial of the Holocaust added in the 1980s and 1990s.[29]

Yet in the making of this piece of legislature, something unexpected happened: the victims refused to have a law specifically addressed to themselves; rather, they proposed a general law coming out of the realization of the **universal damage of sin**. The Social Democrat Adolf Arndt, whose father was Jewish and whose own career was hampered as a "half Jew" during the Third Reich,[30] raised his objection in early 1960 against the proposed legislation of the Christian Democratic Union (CDU) government at that time: "No special law! No special protection!"[31] He argued that

---

26. Letter from Arendt to Jaspers, 17 Aug. 1946, in Köhler and Saner, *Arendt Jaspers Briefwechsel*, 89 (emphasis added).

27. Letter, 19 Oct. 1946, in Köhler and Saner, *Arendt Jaspers Briefwechsel*, 98.

28. Torben Fischer and Matthias N. Lorenz, eds., *Lexikon der 'Vergangenheitsbewältigung' in Deutschland: Debatten- und Diskursgeschichte des Nationalsozialismus nach 1945* (Bielefeld: transcript, 2007), 85.

29. Peter Reichel, *Vergangenheitsbewältigung in Deutschland: Die Auseinandersetzung mit der NS-Diktatur von 1945 bis heute* (Munich: C.H. Beck, 2001), 152–57.

30. See Dieter Gosewinkel, *Adolf Arndt: Die Wiederbegründung des Rechtsstaats aus dem Geist der Sozialdemokratie (1945–1961)* (Bonn: J. H. W. Dietz Nachf., 1991), 21–63.

31. Adolf Arndt, "Kein Sondergesetz! Kein Sonderschutz!," *Sozialdemokratischer Pressedienst*, 3 Feb. 1960.

"the riots of antisemitism are directed in reality against the dignity of each and every human being and against the equality of rights," which one could only "atone for (*sühnen*) through the use of law of the constitutional state."[32] In other words, it is not *only* the Jewish name or the Jewish community that is at stake in antisemitism, but humanity itself; consequently, a victim-targeted measure is not enough to solve this universal—that is, all-threatening—problem. "The intellectual and ethical triumph over the racial mania can only be achieved when the equality of human beings becomes self-evident consciousness."[33] Arndt's was not the lone Jewish voice in this matter, as he could cite the support of the representatives of the Jewish communities in Germany, Heinz Galinski and Henrik G. van Dam. In fact, van Dam himself, then secretary-general of the Central Council of Jews in Germany (ZdJ), took a similar line: "No conservation park for Jews."[34] In response to this unexpected stand, the editor of *Die Zeit*, the newsweekly that published van Dam's article, remarked: "What is odd is that the Central Council of Jews does not approve of [the proposed special law] at all."[35] It is difficult to understand indeed without comprehending the universalizing perspective of "sin" in viewing human wrongdoing. In Arendt's formulation, "The differentiation between German *Übermenschen* and Jewish *Untermenschen* has turned both to *Unmenschen*."[36] Turning in such a situation requires simultaneously a specific "turning to" the victims of wrongdoing, and insight into the universal aspects of the wrongdoing in question.[37]

---

32. Ibid.
33. Ibid.
34. H. G. van Dam, "Kein Naturschutzpark für Juden: Zum Gesetz gegen Volksverhetzung," *Die Zeit*, 19 Feb. 1960.
35. Ibid.
36. Letter, 17 Aug. 1946, in Köhler and Saner, *Arendt Jaspers Briefwechsel*, 90.
37. See "repentant disagreement" in **P8**.

4

"FASCISM WAS THE GREAT APOSTASY" (P2)

On the evening of 17 October 1945 in Markuskirche (St. Mark's Church) in Stuttgart, Pastor Martin Niemöller gave a sermon on a text from the book of Jeremiah:

> Even if our wrongdoings accuse us,
> You Yahweh, please help for the sake of Your Name.
> Many have been our rebellions, and great is our sin against You.[1]

According to an observer's account, the sermon was powerful. In it Niemöller insisted: It does not suffice to give the guilt to the Nazis, the church must also confess its guilt, for Nazi crimes would not have been possible if the people of the church out of a genuine

---

1. Jeremiah 14:7. The sermon was based on a longer segment of the scripture (vv. 7–11).

Christian faith had persisted.[2] The following day, during the council meeting of the Evangelical Church in Germany (EKD) then taking place in Markuskirche, a document of confession was created: the so-called Stuttgarter Schuldbekenntnis (Stuttgart Confession of Guilt). It was formally presented to the visiting delegation of the World Council of Churches on 19 October.

"We know not only that we are in a community of suffering (*Gemeinschaft der Leiden*) with our people, but also in a solidarity of guilt (*Solidarität der Schuld*)," read the confession. "Endless suffering has been brought through us to many peoples and countries."[3] "We accuse ourselves for not bearing witness with more courage, for not praying with more faith, for not believing with more joy, and for not loving with more zeal" in the fight against that spirit that had found its terrible expression in Nazism. "We turn to God in hope . . . that the spirit of peace and of love may come to reign, in whom alone can the tormented humanity find healing."[4] The undersigned of the document include Niemöller and Theophil Wurm, then chairman of the Council of the EKD.

The Stuttgart Confession of Guilt was one of the published responses by the EKD in the early postwar years that either dealt specifically or were in some way related to the issue of Christian guilt. These included the Treysa "message" of 1945,[5] the "word" of 1947 concerning the political path of the German people,[6]

---

2. See Willem A. Visser't Hooft, *Die Welt war meine Gemeinde: Autobiographie*, trans. Heidi von Alten (Munich: Piper, 1972), 231.

3. See the full text of the original in German as well as its prehistory in Armin Boyens, "Das Stuttgarter Schuldbekenntnis vom 19. Oktober 1945: Entstehung und Bedeutung," *Vierteljahrshefte für Zeitgeschichte* 19, no. 4 (1971): 374–97.

4. Ibid., 374–75.

5. English translation: "Message to the Congregations (Treysa Conference, August 1945)," in Matthew Hockenos, *A Church Divided: German Protestants Confront the Nazi Past* (Bloomington: Indiana University Press, 2004), 185–86.

6. "Ein Wort des Bruderrats der Evangelischen Kirche in Deutschland zum politischen Weg unseres Volkes," *Flugblätter der Bekennenden Kirche*, Darmstadt, August 8, 1947.

the "message concerning the Jewish question" of 1948,[7] and the Berlin-Weißensee "declaration" of 1950 regarding Christian guilt toward Israel.[8] One common feature of these statements is the explicit reference to both the sins of Christians against God, and the need to turn back to God.

The Treysa message (1945) features the following: "Today we confess: Long before God spoke in anger, He sought us with the Word of His love and we did not listen. . . . We call to our people: turn again to God!" The "word on political path" (1947) has the following: "We went wrong . . . , we have put our own nation on the throne of God." The message about the "Jewish question" (1948) says this: "Now we have to face the judgments of God which are coming upon us one after the other, so that we may bow beneath the mighty hand of God in sincere repentance, both as a Church and as a nation. . . . Through our suffering and our guilt He made us aware of His Word anew."

This preoccupation—or rather, *preconception*—of "sin against God" rather than crimes against the victims (e.g., the Jewish people) has led some observers to criticize the lack of direct reference to the latter.[9] Notwithstanding this valid criticism, these early statements did specifically refer to the triangular relationship of God-victim-perpetrator (the "mysterious link between Israel and the Church, created by God"),[10] and directed the audience's

---

7. English translation: "Message Concerning the Jewish Question (Council of Brethren of the Evangelical Church, Darmstadt, April 8, 1948)," in Hockenos, *Church Divided*, 195–97.

8. "Erklärung der Evangelischen Synode in Berlin-Weißensee vom April 1950 zur Judenfrage," *Freiburger Rundbrief* 2, no. 8/9 (1949/1950): 18–19. See the pitfalls of these early texts in **P14**.

9. See, for example, Peter Reichel, *Vergangenheitsbewältigung in Deutschland: Die Auseinandersetzung mit der NS-Diktatur von 1945 bis heute* (Munich: C.H. Beck, 2001), 70: "Only in the year of 1950 . . . was a 'word of guilt visà-vis Israel' found in the EKD synod in Berlin Weißensee." But in fact, already in the Bruderrat "Wort" of 1948 mentioned above, explicit reference to the Protestant churches' wrongdoings against the Jewish people can be found: "We recognize with shame and grief what a great wrong we have done to Israel, and how deep our guilt is." Hockenos, *Church Divided*, 211.

10. Hockenos, *Church Divided*, 195–97.

attention to the kind of *turning* ("repentance [*Umkehr*] to God and turning [*Hinkehr*] toward the neighbor"[11]) that is necessary in such a relational setting.

In other words, it is not enough for the repentant sinner/perpetrator to stop at the state of "self-absolution"—a self-forgiving realm of Christianity and the "West"; he must move forward to face both God and neighbor.[12] Hence, "it is not enough now merely to repair the damage caused by National Socialism. Our task goes further."[13] The reorientation of the repentant covers his wrongdoings and their consequences, but is not itself centered on these.

The expression of Christian guilt in light of this triangular relationship was not limited to the Protestants in the German-speaking world. Hans Küng, among others,[14] reformulated a new triad of relationship among the Jews, Christians, and their Christ: "The sufferings of the Jewish people begin with Jesus himself. . . . Jesus was a Jew and all anti-Semitism is treachery toward Jesus himself."[15] Furthermore, by linking National Socialism and the millennia-long "Christian" antisemitism, Küng and others like him sought to turn postwar Christians away from falsely counting themselves as "pure victims" vis-à-vis the Nazis and thereby sidestepping repentance: "Nazi anti-Judaism was the work of godless anti-Christian criminals; but, without the almost two-thousand-year-long pre-history of 'Christian' anti-Judaism which also prevented Christians in Germany from a convinced and energetic resistance on a broad front,

---

11. "Wort zum politischen Weg."

12. Yet there is an ambiguity in this "turning toward the neighbor," for in point 6 of the same "word on political path" (1947), it seems as if turning to Christ is itself *enough* for the absolution of guilt—"By recognizing and confessing this, we know we are as a community of Jesus Christ absolved (*freigesprochen*)"—without an explicit word on turning toward the *victims* for forgiveness. See subsequent attempts at rectification in **P14**.

13. "Message to the Pastors (Brethren Council, August 1945)," in Hockenos, *Church Divided*, 181–83.

14. See also Johann Baptist Metz's "memory of suffering" in **P6**.

15. Hans Küng, "Introduction: From Anti-Semitism to Theological Dialogue," in *Christians and Jews*, ed. Hans Küng and Walter Kasper (New York: Seabury Press, 1975), 11–13.

it would not have been possible!" Hence, he concluded, "Christianity cannot evade a full avowal of its guilt."[16]

If this triangular way of seeing relationships were only confined to the religious realm, to the clerics and theologians, then its effect would only be thus limited. To the contrary, explicit or implicit reference to this relational structure can be found in postwar philosophical and "secular" realms as well. An example of the former is Karl Jaspers's philosophy of guilt. In his conceptualization, all living Germans must present themselves to four "courts" (*Instanzen*) in order to deal with their four layers of guilt arising from the preceding twelve years: criminal, political, moral, and metaphysical. The first two are dealt with when the guilty one faces other human beings: the judges and the victors. Moral guilt is dealt with as he is confronted by his conscience. The last of these, metaphysical guilt, can only be dealt with as he faces his God.

> There is a solidarity among human beings as human beings that makes each co-responsible for all the wrongs and all the injustice in the world. . . . If I fail to do whatever I can to prevent them, I am co-guilty. . . . Jurisdiction rests with God alone.[17]

If in Jaspers's *Schuldfrage*, the emphasis on the self in its own purification has led to doubts as to whether this "self-centered" approach to guilt—or optimism regarding the human ability to achieve "self-illumination"[18] and "self-purification"—has anything to do with the biblical conception of repentance, with God being the center between victims and perpetrators, in his subsequent work, *The Origin and Goal of History*, the links between this "faith in man," in his ability to approach his guilt, and "faith in God" are more forcefully emphasized:

> Faith in man is faith in the possibility of freedom . . . that he, bestowed upon himself by God, shall thank or blame himself for what becomes

16. Ibid.

17. Karl Jaspers, *Die Schuldfrage* (Heidelberg: Lambert Schneider, 1946), 31–32.

18. Cf. Buber's "self-illumination" in P6.

him. . . . Faith in man presupposes faith in the Deity through whom he is. Without faith in God, faith in man degenerates into contempt for man, into loss of respect for man as man, with the final consequence that the alien human life is treated with indifference, as something to be used and destroyed.[19]

For Jaspers, it was the loss of this faith that had made the concentration camps a reality, and it was those who remained "intact as human souls" in the camps who "encourage us to hold fast to the ancient faith of man."[20]

The anchoring of this triangular vision in the biblical paradigm comes with the *insight* of sin. **The seeing of sin,** rather than the sole focus on the crime and the guilt of the perpetrator, is thus also a hallmark of postwar reflection on the Nazi era. In fact, as we have seen in the introduction, the theological vocabulary of sin has allowed German intellectuals (such as Wilhelm Röpke, Alfred Weber, Johannes Hessen, and Constantin Silens) from both inside and outside Germany to speak to the internal and external audiences about what they thought the Germans must turn from. Jaspers's contribution, however, was distinctive, for it avoided the traps of self-victimization (Silens), of "Europeanizing" German guilt (Weber), of separating good, ordinary Germans from the bad, leading Nazis (Röpke), of placing oneself on the better side of Germany (Hessen and Röpke),[21] and of presenting German Christianity as if it were uncompromised (Silens and Hessen). Jaspers's all-living-Germans-are-guilty thesis laid the foundational standpoint for each and every postwar German to do specific repentance

---

19. Karl Jaspers, *The Origin and Goal of History*, trans. Michael Bullock (London: Routledge & K. Paul, 1953), 219–20. See further exposition on the relationship of the two in Jaspers, *Einführung in die Philosophie: Zwölf Radiovorträge* (Munich/Zurich: Piper, 1989).

20. Jaspers, *Origin and Goal of History*, 148. He had also made a similar point previously, characterizing the problem as a "crisis of spirit, of faith." Jaspers, *Die Schuldfrage*, 78–79. Cf. Rabbi Harold Schulweis's refutation of the "bias against man" in **P13.**

21. This is also a problem with Friedrich Meinecke's *Die deutsche Katastrophe: Betrachtungen und Erinnerungen* (Wiesbaden: Eberhard Brockhaus, 1946). See **P8.**

according to the nonmutually-exclusive types of guilt involved.[22] And concerning Christianity, though one could argue that "Christian" Nazis and Nazi sympathizers were in fact anti-Christian (i.e., there is a "true" Christianity to be rescued from these false "Christians" or un-Christian pagans), an unqualified presentation of Christianity as "the way out" could be misleading (to Christian self-victimization, for instance, rather than to repentance even for persecuted Christians, as Niemöller and those behind the Stuttgart Confession had called for). Jaspers's contribution then was notable for basing his message of turning not on an unrealistic image of the church, but on prophetic hope: there is guilt, real guilt in various dimensions, some more visible than others; but there is also hope, real hope, based on "repentance as an individual before God" and not on the "false pathos" of self-pity.[23]

To make German "sins" visible, postwar Germans also received **help from the outside.** In his acceptance speech for the 1951 Peace Prize of the German Book Trade (Friedenspreis des Deutschen Buchhandels), Albert Schweitzer pointed to the pride of "superman" attitude as the sin that had brought humanity to the age of fear and confusions of the time. "In a certain sense we have become supermen through the might we possess, in that we command the powers of nature. . . . But this superman suffers from a deficiency (*Unvollkommenheit*); because its rationality has not become supermanly like its might. . . . He does not possess that level of highest rationality, which would allow him not to set his mind on using the might over the powers of nature to exterminate (*Vernichten*), but to employ it for building up (*Erbauen*)."[24]

Perhaps earliest of all, Abraham Joshua Heschel, who grew up in Poland and studied in Germany before fleeing to the United States, where he would become one of the most-respected Jewish

---

22. What Jaspers had left out, however, was the later generations of Germans born after 1945. Habermas would carry the "guilt question" forward in the 1980s (see **P12**).

23. Jaspers, *Die Schuldfrage*, 99–101.

24. Albert Schweitzer, "Dankesrede," accessed 31 Aug. 2012, http://www.friedenspreis-des-deutschen-buchhandels.de/sixcms/media.php/1290/1951_schweitzer.pdf.

thinkers of the twentieth century, already propagated this sin perspective in assessing the early Nazi years and the unfolding crimes therein, as he spoke to a group of Quaker Christians in Frankfurt in early 1938: "In the beginning of this epoch was blasphemy. The holies of the world: the Law, Peace, and Faith were abused and desecrated. And then the desecration degenerated into the unprecedented disgrace."[25] It is also in Heschel, whose influence extends to postwar Christian theological thinking,[26] that one can find lucid expressions of the **triangular, God-centered relationship**: "Religious observance has more than two dimensions; it is more than an act that happens between man and an idea. The unique feature of religious living is in its being *three-dimensional*. In a religious act man stands before God."[27] "He does not take a direct approach to things. It is not a straight line, spanning subject and object, but rather a *triangle*—through God to the object."[28]

Though bemoaned as lonesome voices at the time, these responses to the Nazi era—sometimes from the perpetrator side, sometimes from the victim side—generated further responses, some of which will be further analyzed in the chapters below. To cite but one example here, in which we'll see how one response that framed Nazism as a sin against God evoked another in kind, Victor Gollancz's *Our Threatened Values*, parts of which were already cited above, was taken up in postwar Germany, abbreviated, and commented on as a "report" before it was translated in full. Whereas Gollancz as a British-Jewish intellectual promoted the sin perspective to his British readers, his German counterparts took it as a tool of orientation to guide German readers. Responding to Gollancz's characterization of Nazism as not just

---

25. Abraham Joshua Heschel, "Versuch einer Deutung," in *Begegnung mit dem Judentum: Ein Gedenkbuch*, ed. Margarethe Lachmund and Albert Steen (Berlin: L. Friedrich, 1962), 13. On the further significance of this speech, see **P9**.

26. See Byron Sherwin, *Abraham Joshua Heschel* (Atlanta: John Knox Press, 1979).

27. Abraham Joshua Heschel, *Man's Quest for God: Studies in Prayer and Symbolism* (New York: Scribner, 1954), 133.

28. Abraham Joshua Heschel, *The Prophets*, Perennial Classics (New York: HarperCollins, 2001), 29 (emphasis added).

an evil regime but a "religion of evil,"[29] a German promoter of his message wrote:

> [The opponents of Western civilization] are the people, who consciously negate God, even only as a philosophical concept, and instead of him worship something else, the state above all. Fascism was, seen in this way, the great *apostasy*, the armed rebellion against God. That human beings were tortured to death in National Socialist Germany and their last dignity was deprived of them had its deepest cause in this hatred against God and against the sparks of Godliness.[30]

The aforementioned sin insights are of course in no way exhaustive or "representative" in the statistical sense; they are meant only to demonstrate the diverse forms through which the biblical concept of sin has found expression in the early postwar period or even during the Nazi years, and also to show how "sin" as a way of seeing approaches the problem of past atrocities very differently from the approach of "crime and guilt" *alone*. We have seen that, generally speaking, in introducing this extra dimension of seeing, the "viewers" are brought to realize the *link*—whether actual in the past or present, or potential in the future—between oneself and the crimes/atrocities in question that was hitherto invisible. Hence, these "turners" who have adopted a sin perspective (even in implicit, "secular" forms) have paved the way for another—and more difficult—step of "mutual-turning," the realization of one's own "co-sinfulness." As Gollancz had perceived in 1945, the expulsion of Germans from different parts of Eastern Europe was a sign that the "Nazi spirit" had already *infected* the victors.[31]

However, one is justified to ask, Would not this *sin* perspective, which tends to abstract and generalize concrete historical events, divert too much attention from the *crimes*, the victims, and the

---

29. Victor Gollancz, *Our Threatened Values* (London: Victor Gollancz, 1946), 15–16.

30. Friedrich Mayer-Reifferscheidt, *Victor Gollancz' Ruf: Rettet Europa!* (Munich: Verlag Kurt Desch, 1947), 13 (emphasis in the original).

31. Matthew Frank, "The New Morality—Victor Gollancz, 'Save Europe Now' and the German Refugee Crisis, 1945–46," *Twentieth Century British History* 17, no. 2 (2006): 237. See more on this in P9.

perpetrators themselves? And would not the "all-guiltifying" effect[32] of the sin perspective unwittingly weaken the critical self-reflection of the Germans, who, no matter how one looks at the Holocaust and the atrocities committed in the Nazi era surrounding it, have arguably the greatest need and responsibility to engage in such a process?

In this sense, it could only be a sign of reassurance to the outside world that German "turners" themselves were not unaware of this problem. Jaspers, for example, warned explicitly against such a pitfall:

> It would be in fact **an evasion and a false excuse** if we Germans wanted to mitigate our guilt through reference to the guilt of humanity. This idea can bring no relief but drag us deeper. The question of original sin shall not become a way of dodging German guilt. The knowledge about original sin is not yet insight into German guilt. The religious confession of original sin shall also not become clothing of a false collective German confession of guilt, that in dishonest ambiguity one substitutes for the other.[33]

---

32. As Hannah Arendt said in 1945, "When all are guilty, *none can judge* in the final analysis"; she then went on to criticize those who had fled Nazi persecution and now adopted an "unbearable element of self-righteousness," just because of "the luck of being Jews." For her, this was but a "vulgar reversal (*Umkehr*) of the Nazi doctrine." Arendt, "Organisierte Schuld," *Die Wandlung* 1, no. 4 (1946): 339. It is interesting to note that whereas her original German text says "none can judge" (*kann im Grunde niemand mehr urteilen*), an English version available at present says "none can be judged." Peter Baehr, ed., *The Portable Hannah Arendt* (New York: Penguin Books, 2000), 150. But in light of the overall thrust of her response, and inasmuch as she sought to turn away from the collective condemnation of the "perpetrators" and from the self-righteousness of the "victims/accusers," I think "none can be judged" would misrepresent her response as a "see no evil, condemn no evil" kind of acquittal for all.

33. Jaspers, *Die Schuldfrage*, 87–88 (emphasis added).

5

"The French Must Love the German Spirit Now Entrusted to Them" (P3)

In late 1965, Polish Catholics must have read with bewilderment and disbelief their bishops' letter to their counterparts in both East and West Germany.[1] First, the bishops included a short spiritual history of Poland in the letter that made it seem as if Poland *needed* Germany, saying: "We truly have much for which to thank Western—and German—culture and civilization." Second, the bishops portrayed Polish suspicion and hatred of the Germans not as a direct and legitimate reaction to what the Germans had done to the Polish people, but as "our generation's problem." Third, in addressing the then-unresolved Oder-Neiße border dispute, the bishops recognized the "suffering of the millions of Germans who had fled or been expelled" above all, thus conceding that the annexation of the "German eastern territories (*Ostgebiete*)" was unjust

---

1. The Polish bishops' letter, dated 18 Nov. 1965, was addressed to bishops in both the Federal Republic of Germany and the German Democratic Republic.

to begin with. And finally, and most bewildering of all, the bishops not only offered forgiveness to the Germans, but also asked for forgiveness. According to a contemporary observer, the "message of reconciliation" was difficult not only for the Communist regime then in power to accept, but also for common Polish Catholics.[2]

Indeed, the biblical message that when it comes to reconciliation the burden of *initiative* (i.e., of enabling mutual-turning) rests with the "victim" is one that contravenes a popular understanding of how reconciliation "works": the perpetrator *first* repents, and then, and only then, the victim may consider whether to grant forgiveness or not. As we have seen in part 1, this is not the case in the biblical tradition, where it is God who, as the victim, first "turns" in multifarious forms of "mercy" to the sinners/perpetrators, who now, and only now, have the opportunity to "re-turn" to God, as a response to his divine initiative. This chapter is dedicated to these forms of turning in the postwar period, and some of the immediate responses they evoked.

In October 1945, a group of church leaders from the Netherlands, the United States, Britain, France, and Switzerland arrived in Stuttgart; their mission: to tell the Germans that "we are here to seek your help, so that you can help us to help you."[3] They perceived that if the relationships between their respective peoples and the Germans, under whose name they had suffered immensely, were to heal, the Christian Church, which had preached and continues to preach reconciliation and renewal through repentance, would have to take this duty seriously. Yet, as one of the initiators and participants noted, "The estrangement between nations cannot be overcome by simply turning a new page or by conceding blithely that the war was a great tragedy for all and therefore

---

2. See Tomasz Kycia and Robert Zurek, " 'Die polnische Gesellschaft war auf einen solchen Schritt nicht vorbereitet': Gespräch mit Tadeusz Mazowiecki," in *'Wir vergeben und bitten um Vergebung': Der Briefwechsel der polnischen und deutschen Bischöfe von 1965 und seine Wirkung*, ed. Basil Kerski, Tomasz Kycia, and Robert Zurek (Osnabrück: Fibre, 2006).

3. Willem A. Visser't Hooft, *Die Welt war meine Gemeinde: Autobiographie*, trans. Heidi von Alten (Munich: Piper, 1972), 230–31.

everyone is guilty of this sin. It's not that simple. A specific word of repentance was necessary."[4]

What was meant by "a specific word of repentance"? A word of *apology* dedicated to the "victim-nation"? No. For the foreign delegation made clear on 18 October 1945, the first day of the "surprise meeting" with their German counterparts, in Stuttgart: "[We] hope that we can talk to one another, as if we were standing before the face of God." The delegation also expressed that they were not there representing their churches to "cancel out each other's trespasses," to issue a blank-check absolution, so to speak, but to acknowledge to the German church that they, too, were "ready to recognize and accept their co-responsibility for what had happened in Germany."[5]

The church leaders who came to proclaim this message of "turning" did not leave Germany empty-handed. On the next day of the meeting, Bishop Theophil Wurm, representing the newly established EKD, read to the foreign delegation a statement from the German church, the Stuttgart Confession of Guilt (see P2), which later enjoyed an enthusiastic reception abroad, but suffered—at the time—scathing criticism at home, even within Christian churches.[6]

This and other similar early gestures of mercy (in the form of turning toward and reaching out) from the Christian ecumenical movement were apparently so impressive—or have made subsequent initiatives look relatively commonplace—that it did not seem inappropriate to the German bishops to respond to the Polish bishops' letter of 1965 by recounting how the French and the British Christian leaders had already undertaken similar initiatives in the early postwar years.[7]

At the heart of these gestures of mercy is the recognition that the relationship between the victims and the perpetrators is important—not important for something else, but important in

---

4. Ibid., 228.

5. Ibid., 232. More on the idea of nonmutual cancellation of guilt in **P11**.

6. Visser't Hooft, *Autobiographie*, 232–34.

7. "Die Antwort der deutschen Bischöfe an die polnischen Bischöfe vom 5. Dezember 1965," in Kerski et al, *Briefwechsel*, 223–28.

itself. In fact, it is so important that the victims are willing to take a risk, the risk of nonresponse or further humiliation,[8] to turn and communicate this perceived importance to their victimizers. As Raymond Aron, a French-Jewish intellectual who also contributed to German-French reconciliation after World War II, put it, all questions concerning war guilt, demilitarization, and change become intractable when the quintessential, orientational idea is lost—the relationship between peoples.[9] He demanded from France such a relationship-centered reorientation when criticizing Charles de Gaulle's "obsession with security" after 1945.[10]

It was out of the same fixation on relationship—concrete relationships between human persons and peoples rather than metaphorical, compartmentalized "relations"—that "turners" like Gollancz would not be satisfied by an act of "mercy" toward the German people that was undertaken out of self-interest. When spearheading the "Save Europe Now" campaign in Britain to stave off the impending famine in Germany in the winter of 1945, Gollancz and his supporters lambasted not only the voices favoring the starvation of the Germans, but also some of the arguments *for* saving the Germans. The British people should not save the Germans only because they feared suffering the resulting epidemic themselves, argued Gollancz, but because it was simply right to help starving *neighbors.*[11] In other words, it could not be self-interest, or even "enlightened" self-interest, but the *concern* for the well-being of

---

8. As a matter of fact, the Polish bishops were disappointed by the initial response from their German counterparts, whose reservation was more indicative of careful political calculations than spontaneous and courageous turning. The contemporaneous Protestant and subsequent lay Catholic expressions have to some extent remedied this insufficiency (see below). Robert Zurek and Basil Kerski, "Der Briefwechsel zwischen den polnischen und deutschen Bischöfen von 1965: Entstehungsgeschichte, historischer Kontext und unmittelbare Wirkung," in Kerski et al, *Briefwechsel*, 32–42.

9. See Martin Strickmann, *L'Allemagne nouvelle contre l'Allemagne éternelle: Die französischen Intellektuellen und die deutsch-französische Verständigung 1944–1950* (Frankfurt a.M.: Peter Lang, 2004), 347.

10. Ibid., 355.

11. Matthew Frank, "The New Morality—Victor Gollancz, 'Save Europe Now' and the German Refugee Crisis, 1945–46," *Twentieth Century British History* 17, no. 2 (2006): 238.

the other, the wrongdoer, that should characterize mercy-turnings. Unconcern was for Joseph Rovan, a French-Jewish survivor of the Dachau concentration camp, the "terrible canker (*Krebsschaden*) that Fascism had left in our hearts."[12] In 1945, just a few months after his own liberation from the camp, he asserted unabashedly that "it is not enough that the material life [in Germany] is maintained . . . , it is necessary that the administrator, just because he is French, feels himself duty-bound to 'his' Germans."[13] "The French . . . must honor, respect, and love the German spirit, which is now entrusted to them."[14]

It is with this fundamental form of mercy, expressed as the victims' concern for the perpetrators, that other forms of mercy—such as **"showing the way"** and guiding with an **"accompanying gaze"**— can begin to take on meanings other than "exercising control" or "lingering mistrust." Some turners, such as Alfred Grosser and Joseph Rovan, took it upon themselves to engage in postwar German "reeducation" (*Umerziehung*). As Grosser told his French audience in 1947, "The German youths are groping their way; if they feel themselves isolated, as if shut out for eternity, the danger is that they will first lose courage completely, and then fall for whichever ideology that promises them a glorious future."[15] Grosser then went on to "open doors and windows" for the German youths to encounter the outside world, not the least by contributing to the radio education project of Jewish historian Henri Brunschwig in the French occupation zone. Rovan, on the other hand, focused on political reorientation, on imparting the "democratic knowledge,"

---

12. Joseph Rovan, "L'Allemagne de nos mérites: Deutschland, wie wir es verdienen," in *Zwei Völker—eine Zukunft: Deutsche und Franzosen an der Schwelle des 21. Jahrhunderts* (Munich/Zurich: Piper, 1986), 90. The essay was first published in French in *Esprit* on 1 Oct. 1945. The original French word Rovan used was *chance*. Quotations from this essay are translated from the German version.

13. Rovan, "L'Allemagne de nos mérites," 96.

14. Ibid., 100. A German reviewer of Rovan's writings took him as living proof of the fact that "people from the other side of the border are concerned and unsettled by the same worries we have here in Germany." See Rüdiger Proske, "Ein Weg zur Verständigung," *Frankfurter Hefte* 2, no. 4 (1947): 324–26.

15. Quoted in Strickmann, *L'Allemagne nouvelle contre l'Allemagne éternelle*, 160.

the "spirit of universalism and human dignity," which "must be taught through and with the example [of France]."[16]

Other turners like Gollancz and those concerned with the justice of the war crime trials employed an even more stringent approach of "showing the way": not by holding oneself as already knowledgeable of the way to which the perpetrators must turn, but by *turning oneself* as an object lesson. The British publisher, for instance, considered those who talked about the "reeducation" of the Germans arrogant, who must first do repentance themselves. "The very word [reeducation] is detestable, so instinct is it [*sic*], as commonly employed, with an odious pharisaism.[17] . . . 'We, being without sin,' is what we are saying, 'will graciously teach you, very gradually we are afraid, to become a decent people—in fact, to become in the end perhaps almost as good as ourselves.' "[18] Noteworthy, however, is not the apparent disagreement between Gollancz and Rovan regarding "reeducation," but their shared commitment to the use of "example," the self as example, in turning-education. As Gollancz conceded, "Re-education, properly understood . . . is more important than almost anything else in European politics today. . . . There is really only one way to re-educate people, and that is by force of example."[19]

These and other similar "self-turnings" as object lessons of "showing the way" no doubt expose oneself to risks of abuse or rejection—especially when the other party clings to the contents

---

16. Rovan, "L'Allemagne de nos mérites," 94.

17. The term *pharisaism* is highly contested in Jewish-Christian discourse, especially because of its historical links with anti-Judaism and antisemitism, that is, since the Pharisees are often portrayed as morally questionable and spiritually misguided in the New Testament (e.g., Mt 23; exception: Acts 5:34–39) antisemites have in various times used the label to stigmatize the entire Jewish people, with the implied assumption that "pharisaism" essentially defines Jewishness. The use of this term by Gollancz (and Arendt and Kogon, etc., as we will see in subsequent chapters) as a vehicle of turning must therefore be evaluated with this etymological background. See Martin Buber, " 'Pharisäertum,' " *Der Jude: Sonderheft; Antisemitismus und jüdisches Volkstum* 1 (1925–27): 123–31.

18. Victor Gollancz, *Our Threatened Values* (London: Victor Gollancz, 1946), 28–29.

19. Ibid.

rather than the spirit of these turnings. Yet, it is precisely in this act of turning, by the "victims," that an essential lesson of repentance is taught: **voluntary vulnerability.** As we have seen its central idea before (**R11**) and will see its concrete manifestations later (**P11**), *willed* vulnerability is a hallmark of biblical repentance, which characterizes both of the mutual-turning parties.

By "showing the way," in both positive and negative forms, the victims "liberate" the perpetrators from being "stuck" in conceptualizations that leave no "escape hatch" (**R6**). By granting a "guiding gaze," also with its positive and negative forms, the victims conform with the biblical conception of repentance as one of "accompanied passage" rather than a "wandering in seclusion." In postwar Germany, this continual "gaze"—whether it be in guarding against reverse-turnings to Nazism, antisemitism, or nationalism—has been furnished by many, not the least by the Zentralrat der Juden in Deutschland (Central Council of Jews in Germany, or ZdJ), established in 1950. While the ZdJ's **"moral watcher"** role has been loathed by some and scathingly criticized by others,[20] a place for it, for an "external inspector," had already from the beginning been prepared in Karl Jaspers's conception of German "purification" (*Reinigung*): "We must be ready to receive reproaches . . . we must seek out rather than avoid attacks on us, because they are for us an inspection (*Kontrolle*) of our own thoughts."[21] And even as in moral guilt and metaphysical guilt a person faces the judgment of his own conscience and his God rather than that of other people, "communication" and "talking

---

20. See **P7**.

21. Karl Jaspers, *Die Schuldfrage* (Heidelberg: Lambert Schneider, 1946), 105. It is important to note the apparent contradiction of Jaspers in this regard. A couple of pages before he had also said: "Purification is not the same for all. Everyone goes his own personal way. It is not to be led forward or shown by somebody else" (103). In light of his broader work, it becomes clear that he was in fact fighting two "mis-turnings" simultaneously: first, Germans *turning to* each other to assign blame and to escape guilt, and second, Germans *turning away* from the outside world from which accusations came. It is important therefore to keep in mind to whom and of whom Jaspers was speaking in each instance. In this sense, the suppression of "internal judgment" in favor of "foreign interference" is itself an important turning that reverses the internal/external order of precedence.

to one another" can help a person attain "moral clarity," especially with "fellow human beings" (*Mitmenschen*) who are "lovingly concerned about my soul."[22] Hence when in today's Germany the necessity of a Jewish "inspector" in safeguarding democracy against racism of all kinds is recognized across the political and religious spectrum,[23] the formational idea remains that mercy in the form of "guiding gaze" is essential for continual repentance, rather than something to be rejected by the "repentance-accomplished."

This "accompanying inspection" does **not only criticize (prodding) but also encourages (comforting)**. It does not speak out only when the other is doing wrong or about to do wrong, but also when the other is doing right, especially when in doubt or challenged. Hence at a time when many—not the least in Germany—criticized the newly established Bonn democracy in 1950, it was Raymond Aron who stood up to challenge the doubters in France, and to affirm the political path that the (West) Germans were taking at the time.[24] At times also when the hope of repentance and reconciliation is mocked for its seeming impossibility or insurmountability, voices of encouragement and affirmation continue to speak out from across the relationship. Commenting on the postwar "acts of repentance" in Europe, especially by the Germans, René-Samuel Sirat, former chief rabbi of France, spoke of Jewish "astonishment and admiration."[25] When the proposed Berlin memorial for the murdered Jews of Europe was hindered by resistance on the one

---

22. Jaspers, *Schuldfrage*, 31–32.

23. See "Eine wichtige Instanz—Politiker und Kirchen gratulieren dem Zentralrat der Juden zum Sechzigsten," *Jüdische Allgemeine Wochenzeitung*, 19 Jul. 2010. This reading of the expressions, of course, does not answer the doubt concerning "political correctness." Yet, to reject all these expressions as unauthentic just because they seem to conform to mainstream consensus requires a presumption of intention, which is arguably no less difficult to prove. Rather, the criticism itself is also revealing: why would such a demonstration of self-mistrust be politically correct in Germany in the first place, when it is hardly so elsewhere in the world? In other words, it is not to be taken for granted that the necessity of external inspection is recognized by the political consensus.

24. Strickmann, *L'Allemagne nouvelle contre l'Allemagne éternelle*, 358.

25. René-Samuel Sirat, "Judaism and Repentance" (paper presented at the Religions and Repentance Conference: Growth in Religious Traditions, Facing a New Era, Elijah Interfaith Institute, Jerusalem, 21 Mar. 2000).

hand and skepticism on the other,[26] James Young, the only Jewish member of the Findungskommission tasked to break through the impasse, stood up in critical moments to reassure his German counterparts of the value of their initiative:

> The memorial comes as close as humanly possible to meeting Germany's insoluble [memorial] problem. . . . With his decision to create a space in the center of Berlin for the commemoration [of the murdered Jews of Europe], the federal chancellor [Kohl] reminds Germany and the entire world of the self-inflicted void in the heart of German culture and of German consciousness. This is a courageous, difficult act of repentance (*Akt der Reue*) on the part of the government.[27]

These responses of *mercy*—that is, the conscious "turning to" from the compulsive "turning away"—in its various forms (encouragement, admonishment, appreciation, etc.) were not expressed in vain. On several occasions in the postwar period, "acts of repentance" could be identified as clear and direct **responses to mercy**. Before analyzing the multifarious forms of these acts in the chapters to follow, we will cite a few examples here to highlight the responsiveness of these acts.

Right after Alfred Grosser's call to bring German and French youths together in 1947, a public response came from Hamburg, with a proposal to send German youths to help rebuild the French village of Oradour-sur-Glane, destroyed by the Nazis in 1944, thus prefiguring the subsequent atonement-volunteerism in postwar Germany. Even as the offer was eventually turned down by the few survivors in the village, Grosser affirmed the attempt by the German youth as a sign of commendable readiness to do atonement.[28]

---

26. For a comprehensive documentation of these debates, see Ute Heimrod, Günter Schlusche, and Horst Seferens, eds., *Der Denkmalstreit—Das Denkmal?* (Berlin: Philo, 1999).

27. See James E. Young, "Die menschenmögliche Lösung der unlösbaren Aufgabe," *Der Tagesspiegel*, 25 Aug. 1998. Later he also praised Germany, for "no other nation has yet attempted to reunite itself on the foundation of remembrance of its crimes." Young, "Was keine andere Nation je versucht hat," *Berliner Zeitung*, 18 Dec. 1998.

28. Strickmann, *L'Allemagne nouvelle contre l'Allemagne éternelle*, 160.

While responding to these "positive" gestures of mercy could be rather straightforward, responding to its "negative" forms could be delicate. For there exists the problem of "seeing the contents but not the spirit," already mentioned above. That is, if the repentance seeker merely repeats the contents of these "negative," self-guiltifying, "showing-the-way" expressions from the victims, then he is not doing his own turning, or even falling into the **traps of self-victimization and other-blaming.** This is the problem of subject-position—that is, the same thing said by a Jewish survivor or an ordinary German can have the opposite relational effect. This problem is not something that can be simply "spirited away" by claims to academic objectivity.[29] To deal squarely with this problem of turning-direction, a German publisher of Gollancz's works had taken the step of issuing what amounts to a "precaution" to the readers: "The following report [of Gollancz's works] is not published to earn applause from the wrong side. . . . What they read here is their shame. . . . Under their reign, writings like Gollancz's would be impossible."[30] Rather, it should serve as a source of hope for the young, the old, and the active opponents of the Nazi regime: "May his voice be a shimmer of hope for them."[31]

The hope that was "received" consisted partly of the sin perspective of Nazi atrocities, as we explored in the previous chapter, which made repentance conceptually possible. But mainly it was the concern expressed in Gollancz's writing, which the report-writer did not fail to pick up from the biblical texts and ideas quoted by Gollancz to call for mercy.[32] In one critical passage of the original work, Gollancz condemned the formulation—which he attributed to Bernard Viscount Montgomery—that **repentance should precede mercy,** and asserted: "[It] seems to me, as a Jew who believes in Christian ethics, a somewhat heretical application of Christ's

---

29. See Dominick LaCapra, *Representing the Holocaust: History, Theory, Trauma* (Ithaca, NY: Cornell University Press, 1994).

30. Rudolf Schneider-Schelde, "Vorwort des Herausgebers," in *Victor Gollancz' Ruf: Rettet Europa!* by Friedrich Mayer-Reifferscheidt (Munich: Verlag Kurt Desch, 1947), 5–6.

31. Ibid.

32. Ibid., 50, 11–13, 25, 26, 41.

teaching: and fifty bishops will not make me, who can read the New Testament as well as they, think otherwise."[33] In reference to this delicate passage, the report-writer tactfully hid the quoted saying of Montgomery's while retaining Gollancz's own words, thus dampening his critique.[34] Although this would make the "reversal" Gollancz was talking about less intelligible, it was perhaps deemed necessary to prevent this message of mercy from being "misapplied" in turn to justify German impenitence. In the same spirit, Dolf Sternberger, editor and publisher of *Die Wandlung*, took great care in presenting another work of Gollancz's, *In Darkest Germany* (1947), to his German readers:

> This incomparable book . . . is ruthless (*erbarmungslos*) regarding the facts and full of mercy (*Erbarmen*) regarding the people. . . . It is critical against those responsible in the zone and those in England. . . . What Gollancz says to his Londoner friends . . . does not concern us, or almost not at all. I mean: in the moral sense. Everyone should mind his own business (*Jeder kehre vor seiner Tür*)![35]

The one initiative of turning that has evoked probably the most memorable response in postwar Germany, culminating in the quintessential symbol of German repentance, Willy Brandt's spontaneous[36] *Kniefall* in Warsaw in 1970 (which will be analyzed in P5), was the Polish bishops' letter of reconciliation in 1965, already cited at the beginning of this chapter. Its groundbreaking impact was evidenced by the fact that, as late as 1968, when (West) Germany was on the verge of a transformation that would have far-reaching societal and also political consequences, a group of German Catholics (mostly lay intellectuals but also clerics and

---

33. Gollancz, *Our Threatened Values*, 115.

34. Mayer-Reifferscheidt, *Gollancz' Ruf*, 49–50. The "heretical application" was summarily rendered as "When Christianness (*Christlichkeit*) is made a condition, then the true spirit of Christianity (*Christentum*) is lost."

35. Dolf Sternberger, "Im dunkelsten Deutschland," *Die Wandlung* 2, no. 3 (1947): 197.

36. This point was emphasized not only by the German media reports at the time, but also by Willy Brandt himself. See Brandt, *Begegnungen und Einsichten: Die Jahre 1960–1975* (Hamburg: Hoffmann und Campe, 1976), 525.

theologians) spontaneously published their own response to the Polish initiative. They were the "Bensberger Kreis," or the "circle of friends of Pax Christi," meeting in Bensberg, near Cologne.

This initiative grew partly out of the disappointment with the German Catholic responses to the Polish bishops' letter thus far. "It is depressing for us . . . that German Catholicism has not summoned up the courage and the power to protest" for the rights of Polish victims, but obstructed reconciliation with their "lethargy" instead.[37] Indeed, although the German bishops' letter in response expressed the "turning around" of values between homeland and people-to-people relationships, saying that "no German bishop wants and demands anything other than the brotherly *relationship* between the two peoples," and that the German claim of "right to homeland" had really no "aggressive intention in it,"[38] it still left too much to be desired. Whereas the Polish bishops had taken great risks in turning their own people from the fixation on their own victimhood to see that of others, their enemies', and consequently, to see not only the need to forgive but also their own need for forgiveness, the German bishops' response was incommensurate in "determination, courage, and readiness for reconciliation,"[39] especially in light of the earlier initiative of their Protestant counterparts, which threatened to tear the EKD apart with its taboo-breaking contents (see **P4**).

Hence the "Bensberger Memorandum" of 1968 by the German lay Catholics was significant in this regard—to bring about a risky, hence meaningful,[40] "turning" that would measure up, as far as possible, to the Polish one. It was also this spontaneous act that was perceived by the Polish press at the time as a genuine

---

37. Bensberger Kreis, *Ein Memorandum deutscher Katholiken zu den polnisch-deutschen Fragen* (Mainz: Matthias-Grünewald-Verlag, 1968), 6, 25.

38. "Antwort der deutschen Bischöfe," 223–28.

39. See Zurek and Kerski, "Briefwechsel," 35.

40. The authors of the text had acutely perceived this point as they sought to convince their fellow German Christians to seize the moment to recognize the Oder-Neiße border: "When [such recognition] has become the order of the day, then it will no longer mean anything as a gesture." Bensberger Kreis, *Memorandum*, 20.

"change" in the Polish-German relationship.[41] While its contents will be further analyzed in subsequent chapters, suffice it here to highlight one important message of the memorandum: the German Catholics' **gratefulness for the Polish initiative**, not only in a general sense, but also specifically for the Polish bishops' "help" in making German turning less difficult, by not relying on untenable "historical arguments" in the claim of the Ostgebiete: "We thank the Polish bishops, that they . . . had based their argument rather on the new facts: the loss of territories in eastern Poland . . . and the life and work of the new settlers."[42] Likewise, the "lethargy of the German public sphere, especially the Catholics," which was deemed "the greatest obstacle to the work of peace," was juxtaposed to the initiatory "message of reconciliation" of the Polish bishops, which was regarded as a necessary "intervention in the historical process."[43]

As we have seen in the previous chapter, repentance as a response to mercy is not without risk, the **risk of being abused**. Rather than first ensuring that his own justice is well secured before making any turning, the repentant sinner, out of his gratefulness for mercy, ventures forth to take that risk. So it was with the Bensberger Memorandum. In one of the steps that went beyond the EKD Ostdenkschrift of 1965, which served as an indispensable basis of it, the Bensberger Kreis not only asked fellow Germans to accept the impossibility of getting back the lost territories, because of the new injustice that the process of regaining would inevitably bring upon the Polish people who had grown up and were now living there (this point was already in the EKD document; see **P4**), but also demanded that the government review its reparation (*Wiedergutmachung*) policy—which at the time excluded those concentration camp survivors who were citizens of states with which the (West) German government did not yet have diplomatic relations—so that the Polish victims could be compensated like the others. "These should in no way be reparation claims from one state against

---

41. See Zurek and Kerski, "Briefwechsel," 46.
42. Bensberger Kreis, *Memorandum*, 19–20.
43. Ibid., 25.

another, but the claims of individual persons on a state. . . . 'Damages should be repaired where injustice had been suffered. . . . no matter [to] which nation [these victims] belong.' "[44]

Skeptics could easily find fodder in this "naive" proposal. Just as the renunciation of the German eastern territories could be framed not as a "reparation" for Nazi crimes but as a "concession" to the new evil—Communism—reparations to individual Polish victims at a time when West Germans enjoyed hardly any confidence of the Communists in the East could equally be disparaged as quixotic at best, just as the abovementioned German youth's proposal to rebuild a Nazi-ravaged village in France was deemed "unrealistic."[45] Yet it must be said that it is not the chance of success but the willingness to become *vulnerable*—precisely when "success" appears most unlikely—that is appreciated by the counterpart in a relationship, that is more "effective," or affective, in evoking responses of turning.

But still, one serious problem exists in this model of collective reconciliation through "mutual forgiveness": to put it bluntly, could the Polish bishops forgive on behalf of *all* the victims of Nazi atrocities? Not only Poles but also Polish Jews and non-Polish victims? Can Christian communities forgive each other when the Christian Church as a whole bears the guilt of bystander if not co-perpetrator vis-à-vis its victims—chief among them the persecuted Jews of the Shoah? We thus have arrived at a typical problem for collective reconciliation, namely, when *internal* mutual-turning poses potential obstacles *externally*, or mutual-turning in one relationship threatens the neglect of another wounded relationship. In this regard, the legitimacy of the forgiveness-issuers should not be taken for granted, as we shall discuss in **P14**.

---

44. Ibid., 22–23. They were quoting Heinrich Lübke's 1965 Bergen-Belsen speech as president of the Federal Republic of Germany (1959–69). This demand would be (partially) fulfilled in 1980, when a 400-million-Mark "Hardship Fund" was set up to address precisely this deficiency, which unfortunately was marred by the Nachmann affair. More on this in **P11**.

45. Strickmann, *L'Allemagne nouvelle contre l'Allemagne éternelle*, 160–61.

6

"One Cannot Speak of Injustice without Raising the Question of Guilt" (P4)

A towering figure in German *Vergangenheitsbewältigung*, where the *self-initiated* prosecution of Nazi-related crimes and the restoration of justice are concerned, is Fritz Bauer (1903–68), state attorney general of Hesse during the turbulent years of the 1960s. Among others, he was pivotal in the Remer trial in Braunschweig (1952),[1] the Eichmann trial in Jerusalem (1961),[2] and, finally, the Auschwitz trials in Frankfurt am Main (1963–65). Furthermore, his legacy in postwar Germany went far beyond the judicial realm. Norbert Frei credited him with having given a boost to the

---

1. Otto Ernst Remer was tried for calling the German resisters of the 20 July coup attempt "traitors." He was convicted but escaped punishment by fleeing Germany.

2. Bauer was the first to receive information on Adolf Eichmann's whereabouts in Argentina, passed this information to Israel, and demanded that Bonn request extradition, to no avail. For his role in the capture of Eichmann, see Irmtrud Wojak, *Fritz Bauer 1903–1968: Eine Biographie* (Munich: C. H. Beck, 2009), 284–302.

developing field of contemporary historical research,[3] and Michael Stolleis concluded simply that "Fritz Bauer has changed the Federal Republic."[4]

Paradigmatic as Bauer is, he is also an enigmatic figure who has been subject to misinterpretation. Because of his German-Jewish ancestry,[5] for example, he was accused of spreading "typical Jewish lies" against the "fatherland-loving Germans,"[6] while he was hailed by others as a "prophet of the Old Testament."[7] It is therefore imperative to understand how, and with what specific forms of expression, Bauer saw it as a German duty to "come to terms with the past" by "holding proceedings over ourselves,"[8] as a means of conducting German "self-purification" or the "self-healing of a sick society."[9]

Indeed, the series of *German* prosecutions against former Nazis and their helpers, which continues to the present day,[10] and in which Bauer played a pioneering role, has served to reassure the victims of Nazi crimes that postwar Germany did not stop at the level of "handshake reconciliation," which was opposed by Bauer,[11] but instead spontaneously moved *inward* to address questions of justice and punishment. But just as in other areas of repentant acts, "coming to terms with the past" in the judicial realm is also subject to the problem of ambiguous interpretation, namely, **the dilemma of condoning and scapegoating.**

---

3. Quoted in Wojak, *Fritz Bauer*, 24–25.

4. Michael Stolleis, "Geleitwort," in Wojak, *Fritz Bauer*, 9.

5. Fritz Bauer was born in Stuttgart of Jewish parents, and was "doubly hated" in Nazi Germany for being a Jew and a Social Democrat (Wojak, *Fritz Bauer*, 14). He survived the concentration camp and exile in Scandinavia, and returned to Germany in 1949.

6. Wojak, *Fritz Bauer*, 19.

7. By Rudolf Wassermann; quoted in Wojak, *Fritz Bauer*, 24.

8. Fritz Bauer, *Die Wurzeln faschistischen und nationalsozialistischen Handelns* (Frankfurt a.M.: Europäische Verlagsanstalt, 1965), 66.

9. Wojak, *Fritz Bauer*, 15. See also Fritz Bauer, "Der Zweck im Strafrecht," in *Vom kommenden Strafrecht* (Karlsruhe: C.F. Müller, 1969), 36.

10. One recent example as of this writing is the trial of Oskar Gröning in Lüneburg.

11. Fritz Bauer, "Im Kampf um des Menschen Rechte," in *Die Humanität der Rechtsordnung: Ausgewählte Schriften*, ed. Joachim Perels and Irmtrud Wojak (Frankfurt/New York: Campus, 1998), 45.

On the one hand, the pursuit of Nazi criminals or former Nazis could be interpreted as a postwar German attempt to scapegoat—for not all Nazis were prosecuted, and hence the "line-drawing" between the "bad ones" to be punished and the "unburdened rest" could be a false distinction, especially when the latter used it as justification to disengage themselves. On the other hand, if postwar Germans did not undertake this pursuit, whether in false or genuine agreement with Arendt's dictum that "when all are guilty, none can judge in the final analysis" (see **P2**), then the charge would be that they condoned the Nazi crimes by "doing nothing" of their own accord about the perpetrators.

Although, as we have seen in the corresponding biblical section (**R4**), satisfying demands and conceptions of human justice is not the primary concern of the repentant perpetrator, these accusations from opposite directions are not entirely groundless. Hence their resolution—satisfactory or otherwise notwithstanding—in Bauer's lifework is instructive. If nothing else, Bauer's two great achievements were bringing Nazi perpetrators to justice, and reforming *German* justice. It is in this double goal that a viable way out of the dilemma can be found.

According to Bauer's writings concerning the **reform of justice**, a chief problem of postwar German justice was that it resembled "justice" during the Third Reich in its foundation on "guilt and punishment" (*Schuld und Sühne*),[12] which is characterized by revenge (*Rache*) and retaliation (*Vergeltung*). Thus he quoted a high judicial official in the Nazi era disparagingly: "Guilt calls for punishment! This demand for punishment is for us Germans so old an idea, as old as our people itself. . . . The demand for punishment

---

12. *Sühne*, of course, is more akin to "atonement" rather than "punishment" in English, which is in most situations matched by *Strafe* in German. But in view of the broader context of Bauer's opposition to the concept, it is deemed necessary to render it as "punishment" in order to highlight the reason why Bauer was against it in the first place. The fact is that in many instances he spoke of *Vergeltungsstrafe* and *Sühnestrafe* interchangeably in his "Der Zweck im Strafrecht"; hence it is clear that Bauer was opposed to *Sühne* applied as *Vergeltung* (e.g., by the Nazis to exact damage on the "criminals") rather than the concept understood religiously as a way of purification, which we shall see below.

lives in us."[13] And Bauer condemned this application of the concept, which is essentially, in my view, the shame-culture application of guilt:[14] "Guilt as blamability (*Vorwerfbarkeit*) was also taught and practiced in the 'Third Reich.' . . . This formulation does not correspond with reality, for it tries to locate the entirety of the conditions and facts of the case in the person of the perpetrator, whereas it exists in truth in the heads and souls of the others."[15]

For Bauer, *Sühne*, when understood properly as atonement, is not the province of the courts:

> Who can speak here of guilt and atonement with good conscience, when they concern not isolated consideration of [individual crimes], but the whole person? Intent and negligence are excellent juridical concepts; it is neither necessary nor responsible to conflate them with a morally or religiously tinted "guilt," like the proponents of retaliation-punishment (*Vergeltungsstrafe*) do. . . .
>
> Atonement (*Sühne*) means that the perpetrator, through voluntarily taking upon himself the suffering of punishment, cleanses his self from sin (*Sünde*) and guilt (*Schuld*), with which he had stained himself by his wrongdoing.[16]

In contrast to the Nazi conception of justice (i.e., "retaliation-punishment"), which was ultimately based on the idea of "evening out" (*Ausgleich*), Bauer argued for the reformed goal of justice, human justice, as "betterment" (*Besserung*) through the reintegration (*Wiedereingliederung*) of the perpetrators and the protection of society.[17] Thus he quoted Augustine's letters: "We do not want revenge for the sufferings of the servants of God through the imposition of the same pain by the law of retaliation. Greater is the necessity for judicial investigation than for punishment. . . . Fight evil with good. . . . Lengthen the respite for repentance (*Frist zur Buße*)."

---

13. Fritz Bauer, "Die Schuld im Strafrecht," in Perels and Wojak, *Humanität*, 274.

14. That is, the identification of the whole person, or the whole nation, with the wrong done. See **R1**.

15. Bauer, "Schuld im Strafrecht," 259, 256.

16. Fritz Bauer, *Das Verbrechen und die Gesellschaft* (Munich/Basel: Ernst Reinhardt, 1957), 176.

17. Bauer, "Zweck im Strafrecht," 35.

He ended with his own conclusion: "This is the Western ethic that is passed on to us and in the spirit of which the Basic Law of our democratic and social constitutional state was created."[18]

The link between betterment and repentance is of course not Bauer's invention. For in the German language, one of the two commonly used terms for repentance, *Buße* (*tun*), the other being *Umkehr*, is etymologically linked with betterment (*Besserung*).[19] What is new, perhaps, is Bauer's conceptualization of social or societal betterment/repentance through the reintegration of perpetrators. Interpreting the Sermon on the Mount,[20] he said:

> The Sermon on the Mount does not forbid the judgment on the question, who the perpetrator is, not the determination of damages to be repaid (that is the *Wiedergutmachung*[21] of the perpetrator), not the socialization or resocialization of the perpetrator (that is the *Wiedergutmachung* of the society in the sense of repaying evil with good); it does not also forbid the protection of society.[22]

In other words, there are two levels of repentance/betterment (individual and collective), and they entail, among other things, different forms of *Wiedergutmachung*. Whereas the perpetrator/sinner himself has an important responsibility to repay the victims, where repaying is possible, the society as a whole, from which the crimes emerged, is responsible for reintegrating the perpetrator/sinner. If the society casts him away or leaves him alone to repay his debts, it is not doing its *Wiedergutmachung*, for then it is not recognizing its own share in the perpetrator's crime. "If human behaviour is the

---

18. Bauer, "Schuld im Strafrecht," 275–76.

19. See chapter 2.

20. Matthew 5–7.

21. *Wiedergutmachung* is usually translated as "reparation" in English, and is in fact mostly used in the postwar period to refer to the material reparations to the victims of Nazi crimes. It can be translated literally as "making good again." Constantin Goschler, however, observes that the concept actually covers an "exceptionally broad range of subject matters," and is ultimately an "untranslatable peculiarity of the German language." See Goschler, *Wiedergutmachung: Westdeutschland und die Verfolgten des Nationalsozialismus 1945–1954* (Munich: R. Oldenbourg, 1992), 12.

22. Bauer, "Schuld im Strafrecht," 275.

product of nature and nurture . . . then we as his neighbors—the ones who nurture him [the perpetrator]—can make an impact if we act neighborly."[23]

While Bauer's application of Paul's dictum of "fighting evil with good" (Rom 12:21) in resocialization may be unconvincing in itself as an argument, his peculiar conception of individual and collective repentance—at least where *Wiedergutmachung* is concerned—does pose a plausible way out of the "condoning/scapegoating" dilemma. It is not condoning crimes, for the Nazi perpetrators will be identified and tried in court, and will have to repay the damages. It is not scapegoating either, for the punishment of the perpetrators is not the goal, nor is it employed to pay for the guilt of Germany, but the entire society will engage itself in the resocialization of the perpetrators, and reeducate itself—this time not forced by the Allied victors but voluntarily—through the court proceedings.[24]

"What the word of the Bible forbids," declared Bauer, "is 'loveless judging' (*das 'liebelose Richten'*), is retaliation as the affliction of evil for the sake of evening out evil. The state and its judges do not have the function of the Last Judgment; that would be arrogance and asking too much of us humble human beings."[25] For him, our "justice" is but "inadequate work of human hands," not "wisdom and justice with finality."[26]

Thus the kind of relational attitude to which Bauer wished to "turn" postwar German society is clear: prosecution without self-justification and ostracization,[27] motivated by a love that seeks to heal not only the victims but also the perpetrators and those

---

23. Ibid., 277. In the context, it is clear that Bauer's determinism seems hostile to the idea of human free will only because it is perceived as being (mis)used in history to support "guilt and punishment."

24. On Bauer's goal of "second reeducation" through German-initiated court proceedings, see Matthias Meusch, *Von der Diktatur zur Demokratie: Fritz Bauer und die Aufarbeitung der NS-Verbrechen in Hessen (1956–1968)* (Wiesbaden: Historische Kommission für Nassau, 2001), 137–38.

25. Bauer, "Schuld im Strafrecht," 275.

26. Ibid., 259.

27. The same year that Bauer published his *Das Verbrechen und die Gesellschaft* (1957), he also founded an association for the resocialization of prison inmates, which was named after him posthumously as Gefangenenbildungswerk

judging them. This is the key to understanding his otherwise enigmatic words as he began his plea in the Remer trial: "The goal of this trial is not to sow discord, but to build bridges and to reconcile, certainly not through a dubious compromise, but through the clarification by a democratic, independent court of the question, 'Were the men of the 20 July plot traitors guilty of high treason?' "[28] His goal was not so much about punishing the perpetrators, but rather to bring the society to *insight*.[29]

At the end of the Auschwitz trial in Frankfurt in 1965, although the much-hoped-for confession or "breaking of silence" by the accused did not materialize,[30] the judgment itself at least came close to Bauer's vision in terms of humility and circumspection. Applying Karl Jaspers's guilt concepts,[31] the verdict issued by presiding judge Hans Hofmeyer displayed not the kind of high-minded judgment that Bauer condemned, but instead refrained from adjudicating anything more than criminal guilt, conceding that it was not in the court's purview to discuss and prove political, moral, and metaphysical guilt.[32] The massive publicity given to the trials also meant that after "the Auschwitz trials had laid bare in front of the German population the dreadful details of the process of mass murder of European Jewry—no one can deny these anymore."[33] Hence Bauer's striving for "betterment," at least where the societal part of it is concerned, was not at all futile, although he himself was disappointed by the results.[34]

Toward the final phase of the first Auschwitz trial, on 12 May 1965, the BRD and the State of Israel formally established

---

Dr. Fritz Bauer (renamed in 2000 Berufsbildungswerk Dr. Fritz Bauer). See Wojak, *Fritz Bauer*, 17.

28. Fritz Bauer, "Eine Grenze hat Tyrannenmacht," in Perels and Wojak, *Humanität*, 169.

29. Wojak, *Fritz Bauer*, 8. See also **R2**.

30. Wojak, *Fritz Bauer*, 342–43.

31. See **P2**.

32. Quoted in Peter Reichel, *Vergangenheitsbewältigung in Deutschland: Die Auseinandersetzung mit der NS-Diktatur von 1945 bis heute* (Munich: C. H. Beck, 2001), 175.

33. Wojak, *Fritz Bauer*, 360.

34. Ibid.

diplomatic relations. About two months after the verdict was issued, the EKD issued what came to be remembered as the *Ostdenkschrift*, or the position- and discussion-paper on the "situation of the expellees and the relationship between the German people and their eastern neighbor."[35] In the *Ostdenkschrift*, the EKD continued with its tradition that began right after the war: to promulgate the way of *seeing* postwar German suffering as **just punishment for German guilt.**

Beginning with the "message to the pastors" of 1945, the link between the "harsh reality" in postwar Germany and the crimes of Nazi Germany was clearly emphasized: "We confess our guilt and bow under the burden of its consequences. . . . It is God *who in everything is punishing us* with his merciful justice."[36] "God's angry judgment has broken out over us all. God's hand is heavy upon us. . . . Cowardice in the face of suffering has brought upon us this immeasurable grief."[37]

From these embryonic, general forms of acknowledgment of "just punishment," which mimicked the prophetic interpretation of national calamity in the Bible (see **R4**), subsequent expressions pointed only further in the same direction, differing only in the specificity of the suffering in question. Thus one reads in the *Ostdenkschrift*, published twenty years later:

The violent loss of homeland is placed in relation with God's intervention in history. . . . One must speak of the connection between God's judgment and human sin. . . . One cannot speak of the injustice of the expulsion [of Germans from the Ostgebiete] without raising the question of guilt. In the name of the German people, the Second World War was started and suffered in many foreign countries. Its total destructive violence ultimately turned back (*sich gekehrt hat*) to its initiator. The expulsion of the German population and the fate of the eastern territories is one part of the disaster that the German people has brought upon

---

35. Kirchenkanzlei der Evangelischen Kirche in Deutschland, *Die Lage der Vertriebenen und das Verhältnis des deutschen Volkes zu seinen östlichen Nachbarn: Eine evangelische Denkschrift* (Hannover: Verlag des Amtsblattes der EKD, 1965).

36. Matthew Hockenos, *A Church Divided: German Protestants Confront the Nazi Past* (Bloomington: Indiana University Press, 2004), 181–83.

37. Ibid., 185–86.

itself and other peoples. . . . None of the guilt of the others can explain or exculpate German guilt.[38]

The practical input of this way of seeing suffering is that one no longer counts oneself as victim—victim of unjust suffering. Where there is an overarching "framework" of responsibility not only for one's own unjust actions, but also for the resulting unjust *reactions*, then the "turning" toward self-victimization (by choosing to focus on a set of facts/interpretations to identify oneself as the victim) is blocked. The drafters of the 1948 "message concerning the Jewish question" had clearly seen this danger: "Today when retribution is being meted out to us for what we did to the Jews, there is increasing danger that we may take refuge from God's judgment in a new way [*sic*] of anti-Semitism, thus conjuring up all the old devils once again."[39]

Yet, just as the dilemma of condoning/scapegoating exists in juridical prosecution, the **dilemma of indifference/self-victimization** exists in dealing with social suffering. Are not these proponents of the "just punishment perspective" only doing that because they themselves are not the victims and are therefore indifferent to the suffering of these? And when the champions of the rights of the expellees, rape victims, and retaliatory war victims emphasize the victimhood of these Germans, thereby highlighting German victimhood, are they not moving toward identifying Germany as victim rather than perpetrator?[40]

In this sense, the resolution of this dilemma—through what one might call **"substituted atonement"**—in the EKD *Ostdenkschrift* is instructive. The text began first of all with the recognition of the

---

38. *Ostdenkschrift*, 15, 40.

39. Hockenos, *Church Divided*, 195–97. See, however, the failure of this 1948 statement in **P14**.

40. It is indeed a thin line between identifying *with* the individual victims of particular crimes and identifying oneself *as* a "victim-national." See Werner Konitzer, "Opferorientierung und Opferidentifizierung: Überlegungen zu einer begrifflichen Unterscheidung," in *Das Unbehagen an der Erinnerung: Wandlungsprozesse im Gedenken an den Holocaust*, ed. Ulrike Jureit, Christian Schneider, and Margrit Fröhlich (Frankfurt a. M.: Brandes & Apsel, 2012), 119–27.

expellees' victimhood, but transformed this victimhood from an outwardly to an inwardly directed one, that is, not the victimhood caused by *outside* aggression, but the victimhood from *inside*—that is, German—indifference. The nonexpellee German society was judged "guilty" for being complacent about economic "integration" of the expellees but neglected their other human needs;[41] the German churches were blamed for not taking up this *human* integration challenge seriously enough. And when the idea of "just punishment" was inculcated, the authors of the text decreed that the expellees must not be left alone to face it: "Only a yes to God's judgment can make way for the new purposes [of our life], but this yes must be said *together* with the entire people in the solidarity of a unique, immense guilt- and liability-community (*Schuld- und Haftungsgemeinschaft*). . . . In no way should the expellees be made *especially* responsible for their fate."[42] In other words, the unspoken assumption was that the victims of expulsion also had responsibility for their own suffering—for they also shared the guilt of German aggression, but the resulting punishment weighed disproportionally heavy on them. That was why they were *internal* victims, victims of the unequal distribution of a just punishment,[43] which could only be addressed, as proposed in the *Ostdenkschrift*, when the nonexpellee German population assumed this guilt and debt toward the expellees.

But was this substituted atonement acceptable to the victims of expulsion themselves? Some contemporary responses demonstrated its rejection.[44] On the other hand, the recognition of "just punishment" would undoubtedly be more effective, in the sense of

---

41. *Ostdenkschrift*, 14.

42. Ibid., 17, 15 (emphasis added).

43. It must be emphasized, though, that the EKD in no way condoned ethnic expulsion as just (*Ostdenkschrift*, 40). For the possibility of perceiving an act of injustice as just punishment by God, see **R4**.

44. The official response to the *Ostdenkschrift* published by the Bund der Vertriebenen (Federation of Expellees, or BdV) in 1966, for example, did not consider this part of the EKD message, even though it was a direct response to the expellees' Charter of 1950, which had demanded a more proportional distribution of atonement (see **P11**). Instead, the rebuttal focused solely on the issue of rights and international law. See Ausschuß für gesamtdeutsche Fragen, *Die völkerrechtlichen*

overcoming obstinacy to such turning, when uttered by the individual victims of expulsion themselves.

In the late 1950s and especially the early 1960s, Marion Gräfin Dönhoff, a journalist and later editor in chief and publisher of *Die Zeit*, repeatedly called for more engagement with neighbors in the East, particularly Poland. She criticized fellow Germans for being complacent with regard to their reconciliation with former enemies in the West, while being indifferent to the East.[45] She brought home to her readers the present-day consequences of Nazi occupation in Poland—that is, the sufferings of the Polish people still living. When the "Tübinger Memorandum,"[46] which supported the recognition of the Oder-Neiße border, was published in 1962, Dönhoff penned a commentary, which appeared on the front page of *Die Zeit*, urging readers to lend an attentive ear to the memorandum's arguments, and praising the memorandum authors as "lobbyists of reason."[47] In subsequent years, her support for the "just punishment" thesis would become more explicit: "Poland is the first victim of the Second World War, initiated by Hitler. For that reason the Polish people shall now be formally guaranteed [by the Germans] . . . that they have the right to live within secured borders, which shall not be put into question by German territorial claims. . . . This means for all Germans, who once had land on the other side of the Oder as their *Heimat*, a painful incision."[48]

If the same had been uttered by any other German journalist, suspicion of "magnanimity out of indifference" would be justified. Yet Dönhoff herself had every right to claim victimhood—as a fugitive fleeing East Prussia and as a resister in Nazi Germany; in other words, she was punished for a crime that she had actually fought

---

Irrtümer der evangelischen Ost-Denkschrift (Bonn: Bund der Vertriebenen— Vereinigte Landsmannschaften und Landesverbände).

45. Marion Gräfin Dönhoff, *Polen und Deutsche: Die schwierige Versöhnung; Betrachtungen aus drei Jahrzehnten* (Munich: Goldmann, 1991), 21.

46. Carl-Friedrich von Weizsäcker et al., "Das Memorandum der Acht," *Die Zeit*, 2 Mar. 1962.

47. Dönhoff, "Lobbyisten der Vernunft," *Die Zeit*, 2 Mar. 1962.

48. Dönhoff, *Polen und Deutsche*, 12–13.

against. Yet, she and others like her refused to identify themselves as victims, victims of "unjust punishment," but instead sought to turn fellow fugitives and expellees from self-victimization to embracing Polish victimhood. Dönhoff represented someone who was inside the core of the wounded German-Polish relationship, who could not be rejected on the ground that "she's not the victim, of course she can 'forgive'." Hence when she passed away in 2002, the Federation of Expellees eulogized her as someone who "had fought with the expellees and their unions over the shaping of the Ostpolitik," who was "confrontational and fond of debates," but above all, a "homeland-loving East Prussian."[49]

Other promoters of the "just punishment" thesis have less claim to this "oneness" with the victims. Rather, these **"pseudoturners"** of various degrees of "outside-ness" have probed the limits of the legitimacy and illegitimacy of "turning." In recent years, the remembering of German suffering during and after the war has been greeted with "anti-victimizing" responses: when speaking of the rape that German women had suffered toward the end of the war, it has been countered that these women were not "uncompromised" to begin with, for they had been "enthusiastic supporters" of the Hitler regime, and "had also sent their children to the Hitler Youth or League of German Girls."[50] When the suffering of German citizens in the Allied air bombing was in focus, it was countered that the Wehrmacht had also been compromised in its conduct of war. These and other similar pairs of responses often neglect the issue of subject position: when the same views are upheld by the actual victims of these wrongdoings themselves, then it represents their efforts to do their "turning"; but when these are held by the various "outsiders"—experiential, national, and generational, who are not even attempting substitutive atonement, then it becomes the

---

49. Bund der Vertriebenen, "Zum Tode von Marion Gräfin Dönhoff," accessed 15 Jul. 2013, http://www.bund-der-vertriebenen.de/presse/index.php3?id=13& druck=1.

50. Mary Nolan, "Air Wars, Memory Wars: Germans as Victims during the Second World War," *Central European History* 38, no. 1 (2005): 32.

latter's refusal of their own "turning," as they remain spectators who, by resorting to the "just desert" thesis, refuse to see the suffering of the other and their own connection to it. We will return to this problem of the "abuse of the repentant perpetrator" in a subsequent chapter (**P11**).

7

"You Won't Believe How Thankful I Am for What You Have Said" (P5)

In June 1966, Willy Brandt, who had not yet become foreign minister or chancellor of the Federal Republic of Germany (BRD), expressed his vision for reconciliation with its eastern neighbors: "A peace settlement, if it comes one day, will *demand sacrifices.* These sacrifices would be understood . . . as the price for the war that was initiated and lost by Hitler."[1] And he also knew that the territories east of the Oder-Neiße border, which were already lost in fact, could not therefore be an adequate sacrifice.

Brandt found the "sacrifice" that would be acceptable four and a half years later, when he came to Warsaw as chancellor to sign the treaty that would formally recognize the Oder-Neiße border. As an accompanying journalist wrote in a later article that appeared in *Der Spiegel,* "This unreligious man, who was not co-responsible

---

1. Willy Brandt, *Begegnungen und Einsichten: Die Jahre 1960–1975* (Hamburg: Hoffmann und Campe, 1976), 242 (emphasis added).

for the [Nazi] crimes, who was not even there . . . , now kneels down at the former Warsaw Ghetto—he kneels not for his own sake. . . . He confesses to a guilt that he himself does not have to bear, and asks for forgiveness, which he himself does not require. He kneels there for Germany."[2]

This eyewitness account of Brandt's *Kniefall* in Warsaw on 7 December 1970, though without explicit reference to biblical texts, is unmistakably rich in religious symbolism, especially surrounding the idea of the **"guilt- or atonement-sacrifice"** (*Schuld-/Sühnopfer*). For in the book of Isaiah (chap. 53), one reads an almost identical description, with these details: the sin-offering (v. 10),[3] who has done no injustice (v. 9), bears "our" crime/guilt/sin (vv. 5, 6, 8, 11, 12), willingly[4] and silently (v. 7).

The "vicarious sacrifice" himself, though, did not think of guilt and innocence in these terms. Writing some years later, Brandt explained that he had only done "what humans do, when words fail," that he "also remembered that, despite Auschwitz, fanaticism and suppression of human rights have *not yet ended.*"[5] In other words, not only the "pastness" of German guilt arising from Nazi crimes, which Brandt shared as a German, but also the "present-ness" of attitudes, tendencies, and frames of mind as roots of the crimes, was called into attention by the silent confession. It was not a confession to end all confessions, nor was it *only* a confession of past crimes that cannot be changed,[6] but a confession of present, ongoing failures, a self-opening—to critique, accusation, and scrutiny and even risks of abuse—that has now become the new attitude, rather than a one-time-only event.[7]

---

2. Hermann Schreiber, "Ein Stück Heimkehr," *Der Spiegel*, no. 51 (1970).

3. The Einheitsübersetzung (1980) uses *Sühnopfer*, while the Lutherbibel (1984) version uses *Schuldopfer*. Common English translations tend to use "offering for sin."

4. Only the Lutherbibel uses the word *willig*.

5. Brandt, *Begegnungen und Einsichten*, 525 (emphasis added).

6. Ibid., 526.

7. According to a contemporary survey by *Der Spiegel*, though, a slight plurality of Germans (48 percent vs. 41 percent) found Brandt's gesture in Warsaw "exaggerated" (*übertrieben*) rather than "appropriate" (*angemessen*). "Kniefall angemessen oder übertrieben?," *Der Spiegel*, no. 51 (1970).

One immediate response to Brandt's spontaneous confession, which exposed not only the Federal Republic but also himself personally to unforeseeable risks and dangers,[8] was *mourning*. Brandt recalled that his friends in the delegation had "tears in their eyes," and that then Polish prime minister Józef Cyrankiewicz had told him how his wife had "wept bitterly" talking over the phone about Brandt's *Kniefall* with a friend.[9] Inge Meysel, a German-Jewish actress who had suffered persecution in the Nazi period, said some years later that she had "wailed" (*geheult*) after seeing the image of the kneeling Brandt.[10] In the succinct words of the same *Der Spiegel* reporter, "This December is bleak and bitter. . . . But now one is almost thankful for this wind, which is icy-cold, that [one can say] one's eyes become wet because of it."[11]

Yet this weeping is not the type that hurts—such as crying for justice, or rather, the kind of weeping that is an expression of the present, unattended wound that is still inside. The weeping in Warsaw in the December 1970 belongs to another category, to what one may call **"curative mourning"** (see **R14**). Writing for *Die Zeit*, Hansjakob Stehle, himself a veteran contributor to Polish-German understanding, spoke of the "liberation of healing" that unfolded on 7 December, which exorcised the "spectres of the past." A close associate of Wladyslaw Gomulka, then leader of the Polish Workers' Party, told Stehle that he had never before seen his chief "so liberated" in the presence of Western visitors. And another "otherwise cool Polish observer" was moved by Brandt's gesture to whisper to Stehle his newfound admiration for the Federal Republic.[12]

Though praised by Stehle as having "contributed more than all the speeches" with his speechless gesture, Brandt was quick

---

8. Brandt, *Begegnungen und Einsichten*, 539; Schreiber, "Ein Stück Heimkehr."

9. Brandt, *Begegnungen und Einsichten*, 525.

10. Cited in Christoph Schneider, *Der Warschauer Kniefall: Ritual, Ereignis und Erzählung* (Konstanz: UVK Verlagsgesellschaft, 2006), 67.

11. Schreiber, "Ein Stück Heimkehr."

12. Hansjakob Stehle, "Schlußpunkt unter die Vergangenheit," *Die Zeit*, 11 Dec. 1970.

to direct the "gratefulness for the sacrifice made" to where he thought it belonged: the sacrifice of the expellees. He recognized their "great suffering," and thanked them for not having, on the whole, mobilized themselves to form a hostile revolt against the Warsaw treaty of 1970.[13] Indeed, it is undeniable that Brandt's act of turning, which was a representative act of "German turning" (see the problem of representation in **P11**), entailed an act of injustice vis-à-vis the expellees, in the sense that the former forsook his responsibility of fighting for the latter's justice. In this situation, it appears inevitable that collective turning involves **a choice of guilt**: the prioritization of others' justice (i.e., that of outside victims, victims of one's own wrongdoings) over one's own (i.e., that of internal victims). It is true, however, that German turners such as the EKD *Ostdenkschrift* supporters have resorted to "substitutive atonement" vis-à-vis their internal victims (see **P4**), but ultimately the issue of internal guilt was not thereby definitively resolved.

It is important therefore to recognize that even here an act of mutual-turning was in order. Once again, Marion Gräfin Dönhoff rose to the task. For even before Brandt went to Warsaw, as a victim herself she had already begun the process of **de-victimization**, itself a painful turning for the victims of expulsion, in support of the recognition of the Oder-Neiße border. Speaking to her fellow refugees and expellees in a front-page article on *Die Zeit* in November 1970, she defended the treaty by arguing that it was Hitler—not the "representatives of Bonn"—whose "brutality and reckless insanity had wiped out 700 years of German history" and thereby lost the eastern territories.[14] She urged the expellee organizations to "stop their polemics," for the return of those territories would invariably lead to violence and "the expulsion of millions of human beings again—which is exactly what no one wants."[15] Recalling also the three-time participation of Prussia in the division of Poland, Dönhoff in effect reiterated the "just punishment" thesis

---

13. Brandt, *Begegnungen und Einsichten*, 541.
14. Marion Gräfin Dönhoff, "Ein Kreuz auf Preußens Grab," *Die Zeit*, 20 Nov. 1970.
15. Ibid.

(see **P4**), and pushed it forward not by basing it only on the "war by Hitler" argument (i.e., German guilt), but by bringing the guilt closer to home (i.e., Prussian guilt). With this guilt-consciousness, she sought to offer her fellow Germans a "new beginning" fore-stalled by the one-sided "accounting" of guilt: "No one is without sin. But the attempt to bring each other to account is not only senseless; it would lead to a situation in which the curse of an evil act gives birth to further evil. That's why a new beginning? Yes, or else the escalation would find no end."[16]

Brandt's "bold confession of guilt"[17] in Warsaw would indeed be unthinkable without these previous contributions by earlier turners like Dönhoff. Brandt himself repeatedly conceded that "understanding and reconciliation cannot be furnished by statesmen, but must grow and mature in the human hearts themselves on both sides,"[18] and this was cultivated by exactly the kind of work Dönhoff and Stehle did. Brandt gave credit to the German churches for "psychologically preparing" the German population for the Warsaw treaty,[19] and particularly the EKD *Ostdenkschrift* of 1965 (see **P4**), for initiating this psychological "decramping" (*Entkrampfung*). "The conversation of the churches and their communities was ahead of the dialogue by politicians."[20]

Indeed, a closer analysis of Brandt's expressions on this theme shows that many of these were in fact the **fruits of previous turnings**. His point that postwar Germans were not "collectively guilty" but "collectively responsible"[21] was but an adaptation from early German-speaking Jewish turners who had sought to broaden the scope of responsibility to include themselves (see **P9**). His assertion that the recognition of the Oder-Neiße border should in no way be construed as the legitimization of expulsion,

---

16. Ibid.

17. Torben Fischer and Matthias N. Lorenz, eds., *Lexikon der 'Vergangenheitsbewältigung' in Deutschland: Debatten- und Diskursgeschichte des Nationalsozialismus nach 1945* (Bielefeld: transcript, 2007), 189.

18. Brandt, *Begegnungen und Einsichten*, 534, 541.

19. Ibid., 540.

20. Ibid., 240–41.

21. Willy Brandt, *Mein Weg nach Berlin* (Munich: Kindler, 1960), 22.

but rather, as a *Schlußstrich* to the chain reaction of injustice, even at the expense of a just claim, had already been forcefully argued by the *Ostdenkscrift*, which also lent him the important insight of turning to the integration of expellees in West Germany in the debate on the border problem.[22] His already cited recognition that collective reconciliation is not within the purview of interstate politics, but is in the realm of interpeople, interpersonal relationships, was already highlighted by the Bensberger *Memorandum* of 1968.[23] Finally, the idea that reconciliation requires sacrifice was of course not "new"; what was new was the realization of the idea at the particular time with the particular meaning in the Warsaw of December 1970. For if one could chase the line of sacrifices that had led to this point, then one would arrive at the point in 1965 when the Polish bishops made the first "willing sacrifice for reconciliation" between the Germans and the Polish people. As the drafter of the Polish letter, Boleslaw Kominek implored his German counterpart, Julius Döpfner, in the interval between the publication of the Polish letter and the response from the German bishops: "Please pray that the letter will not also scandalize us too much. . . . But there is a price to pay for bridge building; *it demands sacrifices.*"[24]

In regard to the reception of Brandt's *Kniefall*, though as mentioned above more Germans were initially negative about it than supported it, the facts are that the treaty was ratified by a majority in the Bundestag in May 1972 (with the opposition abstaining), that Brandt's Social Democratic Party (SPD) was reelected the same year, winning the highest percentage (45.8 percent) of votes ever in party history, that Brandt was awarded the Nobel Peace

---

22. Brandt, *Begegnungen und Einsichten*, 527.

23. Bensberger Kreis, *Ein Memorandum deutscher Katholiken zu den polnisch-deutschen Fragen* (Mainz: Matthias-Grünewald-Verlag, 1968), 21.

24. Quoted in Robert Zurek and Basil Kerski, "Der Briefwechsel zwischen den polnischen und deutschen Bischöfen von 1965: Entstehungsgeschichte, historischer Kontext und unmittelbare Wirkung," in '*Wir vergeben und bitten um Vergebung*': *Der Briefwechsel der polnischen und deutschen Bischöfe von 1965 und seine Wirkung*, ed. Basil Kerski, Tomasz Kycia, and Robert Zurek (Osnabrück: Fibre, 2006), 34–35 (emphasis added).

Prize in 1971 and named "Person of the Year" by *Time* magazine in 1970,[25] and that, finally, some three decades after the *Kniefall*, a commemorative plaque in his honor was erected in Warsaw, and the image and footage of the confession are still prominently remembered in museums from Bonn to Berlin.[26] Though one can never say with exactitude how many victims of Nazi atrocities have accepted this confession, it is probably not an exaggeration to conclude that the "face of the confessant" (Schreiber) was met with the face of an appreciative community.

Hence this act of confession and the responding act of its appreciation together formed a **voluntary loss of honor** and its restoration from the other. The voluntary "loss of face" on the part of the wrongdoer, or the representative of wrongdoers, in the symbolic act of *lowering* oneself, and in so doing attracting negative attention to oneself, demonstrated or sought to demonstrate the "broken spirit and contrite heart" that are demanded in the biblical understanding of confession. Considering the historical circumstances at the time, a West German chancellor could easily—and very reasonably—have adorned himself with quite a different spirit when concluding the Warsaw treaty of 1970. For the recognition of the disputed border (and hence the loss of the Ostgebiete) could have already been touted as *the* sacrifice for reconciliation, a concession made to save one's face. In other words, it could have been a spirit that says: Take this compensation, and leave me alone and my nation's honor intact. But to the contrary, Brandt had already declared in Moscow, before coming to Warsaw, in a way that is baffling in terms of negotiation tactics or self-interest paradigms: "[This treaty] is no giveaway; what was lost was already long gambled away, not by us, who in the Federal Republic of Germany

---

25. In the cover image, Brandt was further portrayed as the "crucified iron chancellor," thus hinting at his status as "vicarious sacrifice" for Germany.

26. In the Haus der Geschichte in Bonn, for instance, Brandt's *Kniefall* is prominently displayed, together with his Nobel Peace Prize, the *Time* "Person of the Year" cover, and the *Der Spiegel* survey. Not far from this exhibit, the letters of the Polish and German bishops, together with the EKD *Ostdenkschrift* and the Bensberger *Memorandum* are also on display (author's observation made on 17 Jul. 2011).

have borne and continue to bear political responsibility, but by a criminal regime."[27] This was consistent with what he had already expressed in the 1966 speech quoted above: "Many people behave as if we still possessed the territories east of the Oder-Neiße. . . . But I want to say to you. . . : One is not doing any good, when one promises more than he can give."[28]

Indeed, a confession is ultimately an act that "does nothing" in material terms. The sacrifice made is neither tangible nor quantifiable. It can either be read and understood in symbolic terms, or rejected as an act of self-interest by a political actor. Hence it is inevitable that skepticism should arise as to "what comes next" after this confession: Does it replace or come with atonement—in both material and human terms? As Tadeusz Szymanski, a Polish concentration camp survivor, remarked, "The treaty . . . was an essential step forward. . . . But [it] must be fulfilled *with life.*"[29] He then went on to commend the German volunteers of Action Reconciliation Service for Peace (ASF),[30] who since 1965 had come to Auschwitz and other concentration camp locations in Poland to pay homage and to provide conservation services.[31] "Every group [of volunteers] that comes to Poland can be of great help in this regard," said Szymanski, who also spoke of a personal experience in which a weeping and forgiveness-seeking German student had "helped me understand the young German generation better," despite the survivor's professed prejudices and doubt resulting from the concentration camp ordeal.[32]

Indeed, long before Brandt's *Kniefall* in Warsaw, German volunteers had already been **"seeking forgiveness with their hands"**[33]

---

27. Brandt, *Begegnungen und Einsichten*, 525–26.

28. Ibid., 242.

29. Quoted in Karl-Klaus Rabe, *Umkehr in die Zukunft: Die Arbeit der Aktion Sühnezeichen/Friedensdienste* (Bornheim-Merten: Lamuv Verlag, 1983), 122 (emphasis added).

30. The German volunteer organization Action Reconciliation Service for Peace was founded by a group of Protestant leaders in 1958. See later chapters for more on the activities of ASF.

31. Rabe, *Umkehr in die Zukunft*, 65, 72.

32. Ibid., 121–22.

33. This is a formulation derived from the founding document of the ASF by Lothar Kreyssig, "Wir bitten um Frieden." Rabe, *Umkehr in die Zukunft*, 14–15.

in Poland. By the time Brandt arrived in December 1970, these volunteers had already completed (re)building projects and/or been providing social services not only in Poland, but also in Israel, the Soviet Union, the United States, and other Western European countries.[34] And even as the problem of reparation (*Wiedergutmachung*) to the millions of qualified victims in Poland would still have to be dealt with in the subsequent years, especially the difficulty of ensuring that the material compensation would actually arrive in the hands of individual victims, rather than disappearing in the state budget for other purposes,[35] previous compensation agreements between (West) Germany and other "victim-nations" had at least on this point demonstrated the will of the (West) German people,[36] on the whole, to do "atonement" in this regard.[37] Hence, the question has never been whether confession can or does replace atonement, but rather, whether the same would be acceptable if one is without the other, and vice versa.

At Easter in 1960, when ASF volunteers arrived in Servia, Greece, which was conquered by the German army in 1941, they were so shocked by the hospitality they received from the local population that some of them asked themselves: "Is reconciliation here necessary at all?"[38] They were told by the locals that "the Turks were often even more brutal than the Germans and the Italians; in

---

34. See ASF's own timeline: *Aktion Sühnezeichen Friedensdienste 1958–2008: Eine Chronik in Stichworten; 50 Jahre im Überblick* (Berlin: ASF, 2008).

35. See Constantin Goschler, *Schuld und Schulden: Die Politik der Wiedergutmachung für NS-Verfolgte seit 1945* (Göttingen: Wallstein, 2005), 316–22.

36. The readiness or unreadiness of East Germans to atone for Nazi crimes does not, of course, lend itself to sweeping judgment. To cite one example, while it is true that the East German government had refused to participate in ASF projects because it "felt no responsibility for national socialism, but it had rather stood firmly in the tradition of anti-fascists," it is also a fact that the majority of willing volunteers at the beginning of ASF were from East Germany. See Rabe, *Umkehr in die Zukunft*, 20–21. In view of this internal tension, one could perhaps appreciate even more the various projects within East Germany that the ASF was able to pull off after all.

37. See, however, the ASF's reservation about *institutionalized* (as a substitute for *personal*) Wiedergutmachung. Rabe, *Umkehr in die Zukunft*, 15, 78–79.

38. Rabe, *Umkehr in die Zukunft*, 30–31.

the civil war [of 1946–49] we were exceedingly harsh and brutal against one another. Besides, war is war: in which human beings are under other laws."[39] Though this response was in all likelihood uncommon in any given population, it was nevertheless a *typical* response of victims seeking to **take the guilt away** from the perpetrators. One "method" is *turning* to the shared nature of sin/guilt, including oneself, to "neutralize" the distinctiveness of the perpetrator. But as Willem Visser't Hooft said, "A confession is only valuable when it is spontaneous";[40] this taking away of guilt through comparison can only be a voluntary act by the victims themselves, not by others, who have no valid claim to victimhood, and least of all by the perpetrators themselves, who must, if the biblical paradigm of reconciliation through repentance is to be realized, be the first and the last to emphasize the distinctiveness of their guilt and not let it "pale in comparison" with others' guilt.

This will to hold onto the single fact of one's own guilt in one's own confession, which has been (re-)generated multiple times in the postwar period, was demonstrated by a young German volunteer of the first group to Israel in 1961. When asked during a televised interview about their motivations in joining the ASF project, some said, "Serving world peace," but one of them said, "It's what had shocked me most [in the last war], the persecution of the Jews," and then went on to recount what she had heard from her parents and from books.[41] As with Brandt's confession, this act of self-opening furnished the victims with a much-needed occasion for curative mourning.

> The same evening, a Jewish woman called up . . . to see if she could visit the group [of ASF volunteers]. The next day she was with us . . . and told us of

---

39. Ibid.

40. Willem A. Visser't Hooft, *Die Welt war meine Gemeinde: Autobiographie*, trans. Heidi von Alten (Munich: Piper, 1972), 230.

41. Christel Eckern, *Die Straße nach Jerusalem: Ein Mitglied der 'Aktion Sühnezeichen' berichtet über Leben und Arbeit in Israel* (Essen: Ludgerus-Verlag Hubert Wingen, 1962), 22.

her hatred of the Germans, and of how the short TV interview the evening before had so moved her, as if suddenly light had pierced through darkness. . . . Then she came up to me and said: "You won't believe how thankful I am for what you said last night." And she held my hand tight . . . , struggling with tears, she said: "We have the *same Father*, you know." . . . The woman had lost twelve siblings in the concentration camps.[42]

As the first German chancellor to visit Israel, in 1973, some twelve years after the first ASF project in Kibbutz Urim,[43] Brandt was offered a chance to read at Yad Vashem a biblical passage in German in which the God-victim's "removal of guilt" is promised (Ps 103:8–16).[44] A contemporary observer noted the "unusual" reception that Brandt was accorded as a German in Israel, and Golda Meir, then prime minister of Israel, praised him as someone who had "made it easier for Israel to turn a new page in Israeli-German relations."[45] But just as in the case of the reception of previous "gestures of turning," already mentioned in the previous chapters, it was from the German side that voices of reservation were heard.[46]

---

42. Ibid.

43. Rabe, *Umkehr in die Zukunft*, 36–37.

44. Brandt, *Begegnungen und Einsichten*, 593.

45. Quoted in Dietrich Strothmann, "Stirbt die Sünde mit den Menschen?," *Die Zeit*, 15 Jun. 1973.

46. Astounded as he was by Brandt's reception in Israel, Strothmann was nonetheless reserved about the "vague hope" of that "promise of God's mercy" from Psalm 103. He ended the article with his own solemn conviction: "The six million deaths remain."

8

"COURAGE TO SAY NO AND STILL MORE COURAGE TO SAY YES" (P6)

In the Buchenwald concentration camp—which for Victor Gollancz was proof that *not all* Germans were guilty (see **P1**)—was a prisoner named Eugen Kogon, who had spent almost six years there for being both an opponent of National Socialism and a Jew.[1] One of his first acts after liberation in 1945 was to participate in an Allied effort to study "how a German concentration camp was established, what role it played in the National Socialist state, and what the fate of those sent there by the Gestapo and the SS was."[2] The resulting report was the basis for his own expanded work,

---

1. Kogon was born in Munich in 1903 to Jewish parents. See Heiner Ludwig, "Politische Spiritualität statt katholischem Fundamentalismus: Zum 20. Todestag von Eugen Kogon," *Neue Gesellschaft Frankfurter Hefte*, no. 12 (2007); Karl Prümm, *Walter Dirks und Eugen Kogon als katholische Publizisten der Weimarer Republik* (Heidelberg: Carl Winter Universitätsverlag, 1984).

2. Eugen Kogon, *Der SS-Staat: Das System der deutschen Konzentrationslager* (Berlin: Druckhaus Tempelhof, 1947), 13.

Der SS-Staat: Das System der deutschen Konzentrationslager (The SS-State: The System of German Concentration Camps), which was first published in 1946 and remained in print even after his death in 1987. It ranks among the first detailed studies of the concentration camps and the Nazi state. The aim of this work, as Kogon put it, was to contribute to the "necessary purification process" (*Läuterungs-/Säuberungsprozess*) of the German people,[3] the burden of which rested not on the Germans alone; rather, "it was the duty of the Allies' farsighted realpolitik to awaken the powers of reflection in Germanness (*Deutschtum*)."[4] "The goal . . . must be the removal of evil in the soul so that the return of atrocity is made impossible and that spiritual space is made available for a renewed Germany within Europe."[5] In fact, in the spirit of Gollancz and others, Kogon blamed both the victors and even the concentration camp survivors for not doing a better job in this respect. "The plundering, revenge-taking 'plague'. . . . Most German inmates liberated from the concentration camps did what in effect extinguished the last existing remnants of sympathy. . . . The majority did nothing but complain, curse, and demand."[6] Such strong words, no doubt containing partial truths and exaggeration at the same time, could only be uttered with the effect of "turning toward" rather than "turning away" by someone like Kogon himself.

Kogon also criticized the way his contemporaries deployed the collective guilt thesis against the Germans, which, according to him, "confused the heart of the people, and in many indeed the heart was hardened."[7] Despite this general reservation, Kogon nevertheless saw a self-critical glance at the German "national essence" as integral to the purification process. This is evident in his frequent attempts to align the SS spirit and (famed) German cultural traits: for example, the "German inclination to idealistic imagination, which then justifies every barbarity,"[8] such as turning

---

3. Ibid., 12, 367.
4. Ibid., 363.
5. Ibid., 364.
6. Ibid., 366.
7. Ibid., 360.
8. Ibid., 35.

off one's conscience and imagining that the concentration camps were just tools to turn "political pests" and those unwilling to work into productive laborers.[9] German Protestantism was also to blame, for its tendency to separate one's conscience from the power politics of the earthly state, resulting in the absolutization of political authority.[10] In Kogon's view it was the task of postwar Germans to "investigate these historical and collective-spiritual roots of guilt," and to reach the bottom, where "the gold of high German quality" is hidden, in order to "fulfill the true German duty in Europe and in the world."[11]

Remarkable, however, is the fact that Kogon did not utter these pronouncements as a Jewish survivor,[12] making a definitive judgment on German culture, or dictating what Germans should do in order to earn his or the victims' forgiveness, but as a member of postwar German society engaging in self-critique and reorientation. We see this in the passages where he uses "we"[13] to include himself in his (self-)accusations against the Germans:

> The concentration camps are only one of the gruesome facts, which the German conscience must focus on. . . . Should *we* not try . . . to delineate the problem, to lay bare its core, and to pass our own judgment . . . ? Perhaps *we* will grasp the deep meaning of this judgment for Germany and the educational intention of history.[14]

What differentiates Kogon's efforts of "turning" from the others already mentioned is his detailed analysis of the German concentration camp, based on his own experience in Buchenwald, thus providing Germans in the postwar period the necessary materials

---

9. Ibid., 37.

10. Ibid., 370.

11. Ibid., 363.

12. As he was a Catholic with Jewish lineage born in Germany, Kogon's identity is of course anything but self-explanatory. That he could have chosen to identify himself as a persecuted Jew but did not—that is, to be among the plaintiffs instead of the accused—is not to be taken for granted either.

13. This voluntary self-identification as one of the sinners/perpetrators is itself another characteristic of biblical repentance (**R10**).

14. Kogon, *SS-Staat*, 361 (emphasis added).

for the "purification process." What Kogon called a "sociological work" was actually also a psychological and spiritual analysis of the perpetrators, the victims, and the bystanders. If *Der SS-Staat* were the only contribution to German "turning" that Kogon had furnished, he would have counted as one of the great "turners" in postwar German history. In fact, his contributions went much further. In 1946, together with his close associates, among them Walter Dirks and Clemens Münster, Kogon founded the monthly periodical the *Frankfurter Hefte*. In today's media parlance, it would be classified as a periodical about culture and politics, offering articles ranging from literary critique to foreign affairs analysis. But in the founders' original vision, there was an unmistakable "metaphysical" dimension to the work they were trying to achieve with this publication effort. In the words of Kogon in the very first issue of the *Frankfurter Hefte*, in April 1946,

> Something metaphysical has happened to the German people in the twelve rough years of the Third Reich, which the intellect alone can hardly grasp.[15]

> We—the publishers, the coworkers, and the thoughtful readers—believe that we can lend a service to the renewal of Germany. . . . We want to give [the reader] the courage to say no and still more the courage to say yes. We will repeat this, because this is important: *the courage to say no and still more the courage to say yes;* we want to nourish the power of *the heart and the spirit*, which comes with this courage, with insight.[16]

The **death and rebirth** in repentance is thus expressed as a no and a yes.[17] If *Der SS-Staat* consists primarily of what postwar Germans

---

15. Eugen Kogon, "Gericht und Gewissen," *Frankfurter Hefte* 1, no. 1 (1946): 25–26. This is actually the last chapter of *Der SS-Staat*, which Kogon had recommended his readers to read twice.

16. "An unsere Leser!," *Frankfurter Hefte* 1, no. 1 (1946): 1–2 (emphasis added).

17. If we go back a little further in German-Jewish theological-philosophical thought, we can find a comparable formulation in Rosenzweig: "turning" consists primarily of turning from a "No to something" and "Yes to nothing," to a "Yes to not-nothing" and a "No to nothing." See Franz Rosenzweig, *Stern der Erlösung* (Frankfurt a.M.: J. Kauffmann Verlag, 1921), 113–14.

need to say no to, that is, a painful and incisive cut in the national heart where the perceived national essence is concerned, then the *Frankfurter Hefte* appears to be a long-term effort to help postwar Germans distinguish the no from the yes in all areas of life that cut across the individual and the collective,[18] in effect giving content to what Kogon called a "renewed Germany" to fill the spiritual void left by the vacated evil.[19] As one of the few German Jews remaining in postwar Germany,[20] Kogon spent the rest of his rescued life initiating and participating in the renewal of heart and spirit through his publication efforts and political activism.

But why should any German listen to the victors and the victims, if they themselves, as Kogon and the others said, had so much to answer for? In resolving the "victor's justice" controversy, Kogon once again turned to biblical resources to make his case for repentance:

> The judge is not identical to the *executioners of the judgment*. . . . Nebuchadnezzar was named by the prophet [Jeremiah][21] as the "servant of God," sent by him to lead the people of Israel out of the misguided path through punishment. He who goes into the innermost chamber of his own conscience in order to question himself on right and wrong is not interested in the moral suitability of those who have externally brought him to the place of reflection. . . . To him, the others are the "servants of God," whether they themselves are just or not.[22]

In other words, the triangular vision of God and human beings (see R2) of the biblical paradigm was invoked in order to bring postwar Germans to the repentant acceptance of the "punishment" meted

---

18. The *Frankfurter Hefte* was in circulation until 1984, when it was merged with *Neue Gesellschaft*, which is now called *Neue Gesellschaft Frankfurter Hefte* (www.frankfurter-hefte.de).

19. Kogon, *SS-Staat*, 364.

20. According to Kogon, there were fewer than 20,000 German Jews remaining in the Federal Republic in 1949. See Eugen Kogon, "Juden und Nichtjuden in Deutschland," *Frankfurter Hefte* 4, no. 9 (1949): 726–29.

21. The Babylonian king Nebuchadnezzar, who captured Jerusalem in 597 BC and exiled the Jews to Babylon, was referred to as the servant of God three times in the book of Jeremiah (25:9; 27:6; 43:10). Cf. Isaiah 10:5.

22. Kogon, *SS-Staat*, 361 (emphasis in the original).

out *through* the victors as just (see **R4**). Himself a Catholic, Kogon connected this prophetic vision to Christian symbolism to further his case:

> [The self-questioning German] does not think like the tax collector: "Lord, I'm thankful that I'm not like the Pharisee there." For if the latter is not justified as he leaves the temple, then even less justified is the former with such an attitude.[23]

> It is necessary that the world not behave pharisaically, and that Germany not be unrepentant (*verstockt*).[24]

For Kogon repentance is a powerful ancient remedy that is threatened not only by the inability to repent on the part of the perpetrators and bystanders, but also by the inability to believe in the "atoning purification" (*sühnende Reinigung*) of repentance on the part of the "realists" and "skeptics," for whom the "repentant conviction" (*bußhafte Gesinnung*) of a nation is but an outdated mode of thinking and a hindrance to the pursuit of national interests.[25]

Returning to the prophetic vision—that is, repentance is both offered as a remedy and demanded as a response—was therefore an essential element in Kogon's endeavor to give Germany a new heart and a new spirit. Indeed, many German Christian thinkers have used the platform of the *Frankfurter Hefte* to advocate the "turning" of the Christian churches, whether it be in their complicity with the Nazi regime, their failure to mount an active resistance, or their long-standing antisemitism.[26] As if to shore up this collective German effort, other Jewish thinkers, like Martin Buber, also

---

23. Ibid., 362. The parable of the Pharisee and the tax collector, found in the Gospel of Luke (18:9–14), contrasts the arrogance of the "innocent" with the humility of the sinner. By reversing the roles, Kogon challenged German Christians to fight this "hidden arrogance" that can take root in the sinner, not only the guiltless. See, however, the problematic use of the term *pharisaism* in chapter 5, note 17.

24. Kogon, *SS-Staat*, 10.

25. Ibid., 362.

26. A few examples in the early years: Walter Dirks, "Die geistige Aufgabe des deutschen Katholizismus," *Frankfurter Hefte* 1, no. 2 (1946): 38–52; Ida Friederike Görres, "Brief über die Kirche," *Frankfurter Hefte* 1, no. 8 (1946): 715–33; Heinrich Scholz, "Zur deutschen Kollektiv-Verantwortlichkeit," *Frankfurter Hefte* 2,

helped propagate the prophetic vision through Kogon's periodical. In the March issue of 1948, for instance, a German reader could read Buber's text comparing the critique and demand of the Jewish prophets (represented by Isaiah) against Israel's people and their government, and the philosophical understanding of the Greeks (Plato) concerning state power and the role of philosophers. In it the German reader could find a message that was relevant for both Israel (as originally intended by Buber)[27] and occupied Germany at the time: returning to and recognizing the true head of state—the "metapolitical possibility" that human beings (whether philosophers or kings or prophets) are the owners neither of the spirit nor of power, but are only lent these to fulfill particular tasks in history. As such, the political question was never about aligning with this or that world power of the day, but realizing justice in one's own community.[28]

Indeed, Buber's voice was much sought after in postwar German society. Invariably, the themes touched upon prophecy and repentance. In Dolf Sternberger's *Die Wandlung,* for example, Buber talked about "the false prophet,"[29] who "does not know that there is guilt, guilt that makes one fail the task of the hour. . . ; who also does not know that there is **repentance, through which one receives a possibility that did not exist.**"[30] But perhaps the most illuminating text of all, in which Buber explained in detail the inner movements of a repentant sinner, where death and rebirth occur, is his *Guilt and Guilt Feelings,* published in German as *Schuld und Schuldgefühle* in 1958.[31]

---

no. 4 (1947): 357–73; and Werner Koch, "Die evangelische Kirche und die zweite Reformation," *Frankfurter Hefte* 2, no. 6 (1947): 557–67.

27. The editorial note introduced this text as part of Buber's inaugural lecture at the Hebrew University of Jerusalem.

28. Martin Buber, "Die Forderung des Geistes und die geschichtliche Wirklichkeit," *Frankfurter Hefte* 3, no. 3 (1948): 209–16.

29. The biblical example he used was Hananiah (Jer 28).

30. Martin Buber, "Falsche Propheten," *Die Wandlung* 2, no. 4 (1947): 279.

31. Though first published in English in 1957 (as a journal article) and reprinted numerous times as a chapter in various books, the German version (as a book) displays a much more precise and sophisticated terminology. Martin Buber, *Schuld und Schuldgefühle* (Heidelberg: Lambert Schneider, 1958).

In this short text, Buber introduced three spheres in which "atoning for guilt" (*Schuldsühnung*) is both possible for and demanded of the one suffering from "existential guilt" (which is not mere guilt feeling), as a result of his wrongdoing. These three spheres are the law of the society, conscience, and faith. In each of the three spheres, three "events" are required for atonement to be fulfilled. In the sphere of law, admission (*Geständnis*) is followed by the sufferance of punishment (*Strafverbüßung*) and compensation (*Schadloshaltung*). In faith, the third and the "highest" sphere, confession of sins (*Sündenbekenntnis*) is followed by regret (*Reue*) and the offering of repentance (*Bußopfer*). In the sphere of conscience, which is the primary focus in this text, first there is self-illumination (*Selbsterhellung*), and then insistence (*Beharrung*) and atoning (*Sühnung*). The interrelatedness of these last three acts is described as follows:

> First, to illuminate the darkness that still surrounds the guilt despite all previous action of the conscience . . . , second, to insist on the identity of the past and the present person in the newly earned humble knowledge, no matter how high in the reality of his present life he might have ascended from that stage of guilt; and third, to restore (*wiederherstellen*) the order of being—which was wounded by him in the past—through an active, self-giving relationship to the world, in his place and according to his ability, and in the given historical and biographical situations. For the wounds of the order of being can be healed in infinitely many places other than where they were inflicted.[32]

Obviously, this conceptualization involves two "identities" of the guilt-bearer:[33] one is the "old self," who had committed the wrongdoing and hence loaded himself with the guilt to begin with, and the other is the "new self," who has come to look upon that old self and realized his *own* wrongdoing and, through repentance, has "ascended above that station of guilt." This way of conceptualizing repentance is, as we have seen, typical of the turners: compare it with Kogon's no and yes, for example. Interestingly though, in Buber's formulation, the *unabandoning attitude* of the new self is

---

32. Buber, *Schuld und Schuldgefühle*, 40–41.

33. Not the ego (Ich) and the super-ego (Über-Ich), however, which Buber explicitly rejected. Buber, *Schuld und Schuldgefühle*, 44.

stressed—it is not a new identity that says: "The old self is already dead; I don't have anything to do with *him* anymore"; but rather: "The old self is indeed dead, but I am still *the one* who had done such wrongdoing." This is a crucial difference to keep in mind when we explore in a later chapter (**P11**) the similarly unabandoning attitude of the "representatives" of national repentance.

In this understanding of repentance (in the sphere of conscience), the promised new life is expressed in both the idea of a new, atoning relationship to the world, and the idea of past wrongdoings as wounds, which, to be sure, cannot be undone, but are nonetheless not beyond healing (i.e., restoration). This conception thus conforms again to another characteristic of biblical repentance that portrays sin/wrongdoing as *relational illness* (**R2**).[34] This way of weaving the two ideas together has the effect of affirming that the project of restoration is neither dispensable nor doomed to fail. The possibility, indeed, the only possibility, of a new and productive life lies in owning up to the old and destructive life of the past—in cooperation with God and the victim.[35]

It was with this understanding of guilt atoning in the sphere of conscience that Buber warned his readers of the danger of dealing merely with the feeling of guilt instead of with the guilt itself (e.g., by turning to a psychotherapist who is unaware of or refuses to recognize the existence of guilt). He used an example to demonstrate the danger of such a trap:[36] when a person is "cured" of her guilt feeling, but her existential guilt remains intact, she forgoes the chance for atonement and reconciliation, which promise the full unfolding of the potentials of her being in her restored relationships. With this conception of "guilt feeling" we can better appreciate Buber's objection to the execution of Eichmann in Israel

---

34. Buber, *Schuld und Schuldgefühle*, 31.

35. Buber stressed that since both human conscience and human faith can err, they must entrust themselves to mercy/grace. Ibid., 68. Furthermore, "for the Jews," he said, God "forgives" a human being "in a meaningful cooperation with the one to whom [the latter] has become guilty," thus emphasizing the role of the human—side by side with the divine—victim in the guilt atonement of the perpetrator. Buber, *Schuld und Schuldgefühle*, 43–44.

36. The example of "Melanie" in Buber, *Schuld und Schuldgefühle*, 23–25.

in 1962, which, aside from his concern for the one convicted to death,[37] Buber feared might serve as a false guilt-atonement by alleviating the guilt feeling of many young Germans. Hannah Arendt roundly criticized Buber for this: "It is strange that Buber, a man not only of eminence but of very great intelligence, should not see how spurious these much publicized guilt feelings necessarily are. It is quite gratifying to feel guilty if you haven't done anything wrong: how noble . . . they are trying to escape from the pressure of very present and actual problems into a cheap sentimentality."[38] It is clear that in Buber's understanding the "guilt feeling" of contemporary Germans was potentially "healthy" because if they chose to undertake the acts outlined in his *Guilt and Guilt Feelings*, it would lead them to where the existential guilt was, and hence genuine healing of the wounded relationships could begin; in Arendt's understanding, this "guilt feeling" was pure "sentimentality" at best, obstructing young Germans from feeling "indignant" about present-day politics and political institutions (which were staffed with high-ranking individuals who had actual guilt but did not necessarily feel guilty), where a political "turning" was lacking. In light of the foregoing, it is actually rather strange that Arendt, a prominent turner in postwar German history, as we have seen (P1), had failed to see that feeling guilty, when seen in and treated according to the biblical paradigm, does not paralyze or deaden the guilt bearer as she feared, but is the beginning of the death-to-rebirth repentance process that would eventually expand into the kind of social and political regeneration that she was hoping for.

---

37. Buber had, in his earlier work, uttered these words for "evildoers": "He [who utters Thou] has renounced moral condemnation for good. For him, the evildoer is only someone entrusted to him with a deeper responsibility, someone who is more in need of love." Buber, *Ich und Du* (Heidelberg: Lambert Schneider, 1979), 128–29. He repeated this with regard to Eichmann: "It is erroneous to think that the devil unmasked in this trial is new. This sort of devil was always there in the history of humankind. It was always *our duty to turn these human beings* from their way. But it was since time immemorial difficult, for devils do not want to recognize devils." "Stunde der Schwäche," *Der Spiegel*, no. 53 (1961) (emphasis added).

38. Hannah Arendt, *Eichmann in Jerusalem: A Report on the Banality of Evil* (London: Faber, 1963), 229–30.

It was not only Arendt, however, who found something amiss with this "inner" repentance, which is perceived to be lacking in an "outer" political expression. In the 1970s a German theologian also found the "I-Thou" paradigm to be too interpersonal, too "private," to "capture the political senses in which we cooperate with one another in society."[39] He then went on to revamp Christian (Catholic) political theology centering on the remembrance of **the suffering of the others.**

Born in 1928, Johann Baptist Metz survived World War II as a soldier because of an errand as a messenger. Witnessing massive destruction and the deaths of both his companions and "the enemies," Metz suffered a psychological crisis:

> A fissure had opened in my powerful Bavarian-Catholic socialization, with its impregnable confidence. What would happen if one took this sort of thing *not to the psychologist but into the church,* and if one would not allow oneself to be talked out of such unreconciled memories even by theology, but rather wanted to have faith with them and with them speak about God . . . ?[40]

Hence Metz, as if heeding Buber's warning and like Martin Niemöller before him, chose not to "overcome the past" by quieting or suppressing horrible memories and guilt feelings, but rather by embarking on a lifelong engagement in what can be called the "turning" of German Catholic theology. If the guilt of the church, as Niemöller put it in the Stuttgart Confession of Guilt, was failing to have engaged in the affairs of the world enough according to the demands of its faith (see **P2**), the "new political theology," which Metz was part of, was then "to trace the strange lack of political awareness in theology and Christianity back to its (historical-social) roots and to criticize it, since Christianity and theology cannot hold themselves to be politically innocent and uninvolved without deluding themselves or deceiving others. This new political theology

---

39. See J. Matthew Ashley, introduction to *Faith in History and Society: Toward a Practical Fundamental Theology,* by Johann Baptist Metz (New York: Crossroad Publishing, 2007), 10.

40. Quoted in "Johann Baptist Metz," in *The Blackwell Companion to Political Theology,* ed. Peter Schott and William T. Cavanaugh (Malden, MA: Blackwell Publishing, 2003), 243 (emphasis added).

is determined to reveal all the talk about 'pure Christianity' for what it is: a cover under which to evade the practical demands made by a radical Christianity."[41]

The centerpiece of Metz's theology is the memory of suffering, *memoria passionis*, which he called both dangerous and liberating: "It is *a dangerous and liberating memory*, which badgers the present and calls it into question, since it does not remember just any open future, but precisely this future, and because it compels believers to be in a continual state of transformation in order to take this future into account."[42] The future that Metz was talking about was a future in which all become subjects—rather than oppressed objects—in God's presence.[43]

But if Metz's memory of suffering referred only to the suffering of Jesus, then one would be right to doubt whether there was anything new at all about this "new" political theology; for was it not the accusation of "deicide" one of the roots of traditional Christian antisemitism? Yet, the "turning" of Metz's theology occurred precisely here: for the practical remembering of the suffering of Christ lies, according to Metz, in the Christian remembrance of *others' suffering*. Christians are to "heed the prophetic call of the stranger's suffering" and to exercise "the freedom to suffer another's suffering," while the church is to be the "public memory" of this suffering and this freedom against all totalitarian systems.[44] As Niemöller had singled out the guilt of the church in the immediate postwar years, Metz, some thirty years after Niemöller, continued to proclaim the *specific* repentance of the church: the church can regain its authority "only if it continues to be connected with love's concern, a love that searches out its own path through history, following the trail laid down by others' suffering. Only when the Church has an ear for the dark prophecy of this suffering of others . . . will it truly hear the word of Christ."[45]

---

41. Metz, *Faith in History and Society*, xi.
42. Ibid., 89 (emphasis in the original).
43. Ibid., 81.
44. Ibid., 88–90.
45. Ibid., 94. Cf. Werner Bergengruen, "Die letzte Epiphanie," in *Dies Irae* (Munich: Verlag Kurt Desch, 1947).

Indeed, Metz advocated a kind of spirituality for postwar German Catholics that is characterized by an expansive ethic, one that is concerned not only about "action" and "omission," but also about what one "allow[s] to happen to others."[46] Accordingly, neither the "golden" nor the "silver" rule is enough for Christians—either as individuals or as a group—to respond adequately to the political demands of a "radical Christianity." It is as if the "heart of stone"— whether out of indifference or hostility based on difference—were replaced with a "heart of flesh," where compassion for the suffering of Jesus is bound with that for the stranger's.

In a way, this concerted effort to turn German-Christian thinking by Metz, Niemöller, Hans Küng, and others was but a realization of what Rabbi Leo Baeck had called for already in 1946. The preeminent German-Jewish rabbi wrote in *Aufbau*, one of the most significant German print media by the exiles in New York, a piece on the "Jewish situation," in which he expounded on the biblical conception of human right: "Human right is . . . above all the right of *other* human beings."[47] Basing his argument on the biblical idea of humans being created by God in his own image, Baeck asserted that "there is no wrong that was merely done by one on another. Wrong committed against the others is wrong against me, injustice against one is injustice against all."[48]

Yet, as thorough and in-depth as these "turnings" may be in the realm of faith, one is right to doubt how widespread or effective these ideas were in the wider society, or if they were confined only to theological rumination. Were there incidents in the postwar history of Germany in which we can see these ideas *in action*—not necessarily only within the religious realm? Were there indicators by which, although one still cannot be certain of the majority/minority question,[49] one can at least speak of *significant minorities* who are not to be neglected?

---

46. Metz, *Faith in History and Society*, 93.

47. Leo Baeck, "Gedenken zur jüdischen Situation," *Aufbau*, 30 Aug. 1946 (emphasis added).

48. Ibid. See also similar formulations in **P2**.

49. See **P10**.

In the early 1990s, the euphoria of the newly reunited Germany was overshadowed by yet another round of xenophobic violence. Between 1991 and 1992, over 4,000 violent acts by right-wing extremists were recorded—three times the sum total of the previous seven years.[50] Seventeen victims were killed in 1992 alone. The attacks were mainly against foreigners, asylum seekers, Jewish synagogues, and so on. Homes were set on fire, "outsiders" were mobbed, battered, if not murdered. In one particularly notorious case in August 1992, what some called the "pogrom of Rostock-Lichtenhagen," hundreds of asylum seekers and foreign workers were rounded up and attacked by mobs for days while onlookers applauded, before adequate action was taken by the local police to end the televised fiasco.[51] Hence for the first time since 1945 the German population as a whole was put to the test: Would it excuse itself by saying, "We didn't do it (for those were crimes committed by a few 'right-wing extremists')"? Or worse, "It's not *us* who were hurt"? Or would it demonstrate the sense of responsibility that Metz had advocated, which takes seriously the "stranger's suffering" and accepts that there is guilt also in "allowing (atrocities) to happen"—that is, the guilt of bystanders?

The "Chain of Light" (Lichterkette) movement, as a collective response to the xenophobic violence, was described by an unsympathetic observer as an "immense success":

> It became the greatest "antifascist"-motivated demonstration in the history of the Federal Republic of Germany. . . . Crowds formed themselves into long lines with candles in the mostly dark, winter evening hours to express their rejection of hostility against foreigners. The movement reached its climax in the winter of 1992/1993. . . . On the first Sunday in December 1992, over 400,000 people took to the streets in Munich. . . . End of January 1993 [on the sixtieth anniversary of the Nazis coming to power], in many German cities more than half a million people took to the streets. . . . In Düsseldorf around 120,000, in Berlin 100,000 participants were recorded. Besides these, there were bigger demonstrations in Cologne, Regensburg, Nuremberg, Munich,

---

50. "Die heimlichen Rädelsführer," *Der Spiegel*, no. 27 (1993).

51. Julia Jüttner, "Rostock-Lichtenhagen: Als der Mob die Herrschaft übernahm," *Spiegel Online*, 22 Aug. 2007.

Bremen, and Hamburg. . . . The success of the "Chain of Light" campaigns was immense.[52]

Indeed, the massive support for these demonstrations was a shock even to their original initiators. A contemporary report in *Die Zeit* reckoned that, between November 1992 and January 1993, over three million people in the Federal Republic had demonstrated against antiforeign hostility, antisemitism, and assaults by right-wing radicals. In Munich and Hamburg alone, the turnout for the demonstrations represented close to one-third of their entire populations. "No political parties or unions could have mobilized such masses."[53]

Originally a civil initiative in Munich with the slogan "A City Says No," the movement became a model for similarly oriented campaigns in that period. Demonstrators' placards read: "No to Racism. No to Elimination of Asylum Seekers."[54] "All human beings are foreigners. Almost everywhere."[55] "First THEM—Then YOU."[56] "Human dignity is inviolable."[57] "Living with one another—against antistranger hatred and violence." "Silence is guilt."[58] The link between this wave of civil responses and the Holocaust was also omnipresent: "For tolerance, against exclusion and antisemitism." "This time everyone is aware of it."[59] The reference to the excuse of former generations vis-à-vis the Nazi crimes was obvious.

Even reports critical of subsequent "imitations" conceded that "the first Chain of Light movements have transmitted the signal that the majority of Germans do not secretly applaud when stones

---

52. Description taken from Claus-M. Wolfschlag, "Das 'antifaschistische Milieu': Vom 'schwarzen Block' zur 'Lichterkette'—Die politische Repression gegen 'Rechtsextremismus' in der Bundesrepublik Deutschland" (PhD diss., Rheinischen Friedrich-Wilhelms-Universität zu Bonn, 2001), 192–95.

53. Norbert Kostede, "Erleuchtung für die Politik," *Die Zeit*, 29 Jan. 1993.

54. Giovanni di Lorenzo, "Die intellektuelle Feuerwehr," *Der Spiegel*, no. 6 (1993).

55. From the video footage of the Chain of Light on 6 Dec. 1992 in Munich, accessed 22 Dec. 2011, www.lichterkette.de.

56. "Rock links, Rock rechts," *Die Zeit*, 18 Dec. 1992.

57. From Article 1 of the German Basic Law.

58. Cited in Wolfschlag, "Das 'antifaschistische Milieu'," 193–95.

59. Ibid., 196.

are thrown and foreigners burn."[60] "[Supporters of antiforeigner violence] are quick to shut up. . . [for] they only obtain disgust and contempt from the overwhelming majority of the citizens."[61] While statistically questionable, these "majorities" did encompass a broad spectrum of society: "High school students and pensioners, the unemployed and entrepreneurs, landlords and movie stars . . . Rock stars played music, authors conducted readings [in the apartments of asylum seekers] and offered their royalties for them to use."[62]

For the unsympathetic observer already cited, "compassion for the victims" of right-wing violence was the "psychological motive" of these participants in the Chain of Light movements, who also wanted to "unburden themselves of guilt feelings in the face of the cruelties that happened in the National Socialist past."[63] Yet, for him and the like-minded, this path from guilt feeling to compassion, or from guilt-bearing to self-giving engagement with the world (Buber), was a problem rather than a welcomed "turning," for it was allegedly part of the "antinationalism" that was "against the interests of one's own [German] nation, leading to the paralysis of the will to self-determination and to an immense weakening in foreign politics."[64]

But the participants themselves certainly did not see their action as damaging to the nation, much less as "being instrumentalized" by antifascist groups for political power.[65] And the symbol they created did not prove futile. As Giovanni di Lorenzo, one of the four initiators of the Chain of Light in Munich, explained, "Against the shouting of neo-Nazis we have resorted to silent (protest), and against the Molotov cocktail, the candle."[66] Although the Chain of Light "was but a symbol . . . , not a means to fight

---

60. "Overkill der guten Absichten," *Der Spiegel*, no. 5 (1993).
61. Hans Schueler, "Zu spät, zu viel," *Die Zeit*, 18 Dec. 1992.
62. Ibid. Also in Wolfschlag, "Das 'antifaschistische Milieu,'" 193.
63. Wolfschlag, "Das 'antifaschistische Milieu,'" 196, 442.
64. Ibid., 457.
65. Participation by political parties and organizations was in fact rejected by the initiators of the Chain of Light in Munich. See di Lorenzo, "Die intellektuelle Feuerwehr."
66. Kostede, "Erleuchtung für die Politik." Cf. Gollancz's and Fritz Bauer's previous admonition "not to fight Nazis with Nazi spirit/justice" in **P1** and **P4**.

right-wing radicalism and antiforeigner hatred," hence not to be "overestimated," "it is also true that the Chain of Light . . . has restored the courage of exactly those foreigners and Jews to live in Germany."[67] This was not some wishful thinking on the part of some German demonstrator, but the affirmation of those affected by German xenophobia: di Lorenzo is German Italian, while another co-initiator, Gil Bachrach, a German Israeli.[68] Furthermore, public sympathy for antiforeigner discourses and measures did decline dramatically—at least for a period of time—after the Chain of Light movements.[69]

As Kogon had already seen in 1945, a clear no to the perceived "national essence" would—and still will—be regarded by some as "national suicide," which would be vehemently, if not also violently, opposed. That's why courage is required. And certainly not all would share Karl Jaspers's counterintuitive assertion that the acceptance of guilt is the beginning of political freedom: "For only from the awareness of guilt comes into being the awareness of solidarity and co-responsibility. . . . In short: without the purification of the soul there is no political freedom."[70] The negation therein is real and hence all the more terrifying. For self-illumination (Buber) to persist, assistance is required from "the outside." And courage to utter yes is needed—affirming both the possibility of "change in heart and spirit" and the necessity of collaboration in precisely this turning. From the *Frankfurter Hefte* to the *Münchner Lichterkette*, the element of "co-initiation" was present. And this presence was not without risk and resistance: both di Lorenzo and Bachrach had to overcome objections from their own family circles: "Let the Germans do it themselves!"[71] Had they heeded that—by all means reasonable—family advice, one can only imagine the loss in symbol and substance for the German turning recorded in this chapter.

---

67. Di Lorenzo, "Die intellektuelle Feuerwehr," 212.

68. Kostede, "Erleuchtung für die Politik." Di Lorenzo has been editor in chief of *Die Zeit* since 2004.

69. Kostede, "Erleuchtung für die Politik."

70. Karl Jaspers, *Die Schuldfrage* (Heidelberg: Lambert Schneider, 1946), 104.

71. Kostede, "Erleuchtung für die Politik."

9

"RAISE OUR VOICE, BOTH JEWS AND GERMANS" (P7)

The spread of the Chain of Light movement was not confined to Germany. To the dismay of right-wing extremists and their sympathizers, this German response to antiforeigner hatred was adopted in Austria, among other places.[1] Shortly after the Lichterketten in Munich and Hamburg, a "Sea of Light" (Lichtermeer) demonstration was organized in Vienna to fight xenophobia, which was becoming more alarming in Austria.[2] The organizers made use of symbols and examples from the German Chain of Light movements to call for public support, which led to a turnout of more

---

1. Claus-M. Wolfschlag, "Das 'antifaschistische Milieu': Vom 'schwarzen Block' zur 'Lichterkette'—Die politische Repression gegen 'Rechtsextremismus' in der Bundesrepublik Deutschland" (PhD diss., Rheinischen Friedrich-Wilhelms-Universität zu Bonn, 2001), 195.

2. The immediate occasion was a proposed referendum by the Freedom Party of Austria (FPÖ) to limit immigration and the rights of immigrants.

than 200,000 participants with candles or torches filling the Heldenplatz in Vienna on 23 January 1993.[3]

Nor was it the case that the German examples of turning served only as passive inspirational models. As a matter of fact, **a proactive approach** to "helping others repent" could already be seen in the 1960s, and then grew from individual to institutional initiatives, from one limited effort to a diversity of forms in the next decades, which continues in the present. At the same time, infrequent but clear encouragement for Germans to take up this hard-won duty from the side of the victims could also be heard from time to time.

In 1966, when Aktion Sühnezeichen was still in its infancy (see P5), Lothar Kreyssig, its founder, invited his Austrian counterparts to participate in "joint-atonement": "In Poland, where fear and fright still prevail over any of our notions, the meaning of begging for forgiveness would not be perceived clearly enough . . . , *it would therefore be more meaningful and effective if we went there together with the Austrians.*"[4] Volunteers from Austria were ready to take part; however, participation in such AFS projects was met with opposition and hostility from the broader public as well as within Austrian Christian communities.[5]

Similarly in 1967, when an initial willingness on the part of Austrian volunteers to join an ASF operation in Czechoslovakia was hampered by the spirit of self-victimization, ASF leaders again emphasized that Austrian turning was necessary. Responding to his Austrian counterparts' reasoning that they would rather not go to Czechoslovakia because of recent border incidents in which "Austrian sovereignty was . . . grossly disrespected,"[6] and because

---

3. See "Kräfte der Finsternis," *Der Spiegel*, no. 5 (1993).

4. Quoted in Anton Legerer, *Tatort: Versöhnung: Aktion Sühnezeichen in der BRD und in der DDR und Gedenkdienst in Österreich* (Leipzig: Evangelische Verlagsanstalt, 2011), 418 (emphasis in the original).

5. Legerer, *Tatort*, 418.

6. Though unspecified in the quoted part of the letter, the border incidents in question could be the shootings on 27 Aug. 1967: Czechoslovak soldiers were alleged to have shot at individuals who had already crossed the Czech-Austrian border into Austrian territory. See "Der Schießbefehl an der Ost-West-Grenze," *Der Standard*, 24 Apr. 2002.

of their "strong conviction that the ministry of reconciliation has to proceed from [the attitude] . . . that the same rights will be recognized in one another," which "must . . . be demanded from both sides,"[7] Franz von Hammerstein, the soon-to-be secretary-general of the western branch of ASF, spelled out in no uncertain terms the necessary turning—precisely in this attitude—to his Austrian neighbors:

> Your reasoning also does not convince us, for with this attitude we could hardly have gone to a single Communist country. . . . There have also been similar incidents along the German-Czech border. But in Sühnezeichen it was always our Christian conviction that we continue to do further work humbly, even when we are cursed or humiliated. We want exactly to encounter hate with our humble, human service.[8]

This more-than-frank admonishment from the side of the widely recognized and—at least in this case—the self-confessed guilt bearer of the Nazi atrocities could very well be interpreted as impropriety on the part of the perpetrator, who supposedly had "no right to teach others." Indeed, there were signs of its poor reception: neither did the planned "joint atonement" take place, nor is there a record of further correspondence after this.[9]

It was not until one young Austrian, who had participated in an ASF service in Auschwitz in the early 1980s, considered himself "German,"[10] and had lobbied for years for the Austrian government to make a public confession of Austrian guilt in National Socialism, that an ASF-like organization was finally founded in 1992—the Austrian Holocaust Memorial Service, locally referred to as the Gedenkdienst (Memorial Service). Its founder, Andreas Maislinger, though in no way in unanimous agreement with his German counterparts,[11] found in ASF the vision for the Austrian response that he was looking for. When he first wrote to the Austrian

---

7. Quoted in Legerer, *Tatort*, 419. Cf "reversal of values" in R4.

8. Quoted in Legerer, *Tatort*, 420.

9. Quoted in Legerer, *Tatort*, 420.

10. Quoted in Legerer, *Tatort*, 415, 421–22.

11. See, for example, his criticism of ASF's relations with the Communists in Poland. Quoted in Legerer, *Tatort*, 422.

federal president Rudolf Kirchschläger in 1978, after submitting his application to ASF, he lamented the Austrians' relative inactivity in terms of reconciliation attempts and pressed for more initiatives for "understanding" and "atonement."[12] For Maislinger, Austrian victimhood was simply a myth, for during World War II "Austrians were actually there leading the way, when the 'inferiors' were being rooted out in the concentration- and extermination-camps of the Nazis."[13] Through Maislinger's single-minded persistence, and helped in part by concentration camp survivors like Hermann Langbein, Gedenkdienst was at last a reality. "Modelled after Aktion Sühnezeichen in content,"[14] it was recognized by the Austrian federal government as legitimate civil service and an alternative to compulsory military service.[15]

On the intergovernmental level, the German effort to "help others repent" is perhaps most conspicuously represented by its continual promotion of anti-Holocaust denial legislation across the European Union—to the chagrin of some former Allied countries like the United Kingdom, who feared that freedom of expression was at stake.[16] Though the result fell short of their intentions, the German EU presidency of 2007 did successfully get other EU members to agree to the "Council Framework Decision on Combating Racism and Xenophobia," which renders "publicly condoning,

---

12. Quoted in Legerer, *Tatort*, 423. Kirchschläger retorted that "a young Austrian has nothing to atone for in Auschwitz" (425).

13. Quoted in Legerer, *Tatort*, 425.

14. Quoted in Legerer, *Tatort*, 429. "Hermann Langbein an Andreas Maislinger, Wien, 20. Dezember 1980," accessed 23 Jul. 2013, http://gd.auslandsdienst.at/deutsch/archives/letters/1980/2012.php4.

15. Yet, as Legerer has rightly pointed out, the difference between ASF and Gedenkdienst is still substantial. Whereas the former was the inspiration for the latter, the "theological superstructure" of ASF was not adopted—at least expressly—by its Austrian offshoot, which maintains a largely secular outlook (*Tatort*, 457). The central ASF concept of "atonement," which Maislinger had clearly sought to transpose to the Austrian context, was also watered down to "social or humanitarian" effort in the wording of the Austrian legislation (432). That is, the presumption of guilt, which makes ASF unique among peace-promoting NGOs, including other Christian ones (see **P14**), is replaced with the innocence of benignity.

16. See Yossi Lempkowicz, "Germany Pushes for EU-Wide Law on Holocaust Denial," *European Jewish Press*, 19 Jan. 2007.

denying or grossly trivialising . . . crimes of genocide, crimes against humanity and war crimes as defined in the Statute of the International Criminal Court. . . [and] crimes defined by the Tribunal of Nuremberg" "punishable in all EU Member States."[17] In effect, though still subject to national variations in its implementation, the denial of the Holocaust is now a punishable crime not only in German-speaking countries, where the law is strictly interpreted,[18] but across the European Union.

Sometimes, the opportunity for help in turning can come in surprising ways. Already in the early 1950s, German and French historians and history teachers had resumed their work on "turning" in their very own craft of history writing and teaching: the **turning away from mutual prejudices**, what the early pioneers in the interregnum years called "the de-poisoning of school textbooks" (*die Entgiftung der Lehrbücher*).[19] In the 1970s, German and Polish historians followed suit. These and other "joint textbook commissions" stemming from the Georg-Eckert-Institut (GEI) in Braunschweig, Germany, have now become models for nations still suffering from mutual hostilities and prejudices, including Japan and Korea, and Israel and Palestine. Just as in the case of ASF, a proactive approach—often in the form of platforms and workshops for collaboration on history writing and historical reflection[20]—is also manifest in this area of helping others in their turning.

---

17. "Council Framework Decision 2008/913/JHA of 28 November 2008 on Combating Certain Forms and Expressions of Racism and Xenophobia by Means of Criminal Law," *Official Journal of the European Union* 51, no. L328 (6 Dec. 2008): 55–58.

18. See Michael J. Bazyler, "Holocaust Denial Laws and Other Legislation Criminalizing Promotion of Nazism," accessed 31 Oct. 2012, http://www.yadvashem.org/yv/en/holocaust/insights/pdf/bazyler.pdf.

19. See Rainer Riemenschneider, "Transnationale Konfliktbearbeitung: Das Beispiel der deutsch-französischen und der deutsch-polnischen Schulbuchgespräche im Vergleich, 1935–1998," in *Das Willy-Brandt-Bild in Deutschland und Polen*, ed. Carsten Tessmer (Berlin: Bundeskanzler-Willy-Brandt-Stiftung, 2000), 122.

20. See, for example, Klaus Mäding, "Historische Bildung und Versöhnung," *Eckert—Das Bulletin* (Winter 2008): 12–15; Eckhardt Fuchs, "Zusammenarbeit mit Ostasien," *Eckert—Das Bulletin* (Summer 2011): 45–47; Sven Hansen, "Geschichte der Anderen: Chinas Blick auf deutsche Vergangenheitsbewältigung," accessed 15 Oct. 2014, http://www.boell.de/en/node/275908; Peace Research

In all these endeavors, it is remarkable that the German contribution is not just to be a "nice" host who listens (and helps finance such efforts), but also to be a challenging, if not—to paraphrase Metz—a *dangerous* presence (P6). At a 2008 conference in Braunschweig organized for East Asian participants, the Japanese guests stated that many in Japan were of the opinion that "Germany has gone too far in its 'coming to terms with the past,' " whereas guests from China were dumbfounded as to why *their own* historiography and history pedagogy should come under scrutiny if not attack by the German participants.[21] The "moral example" that strikes not only the opponent but the club wielder himself is dangerous indeed.

Hence, as is to be expected, such outspokenness is often the object of attack itself, not the least within intra-German dialogues. In his acceptance speech for the Peace Prize of the German Book Trade in 1998, German writer Martin Walser lamented the use of Auschwitz as a "moral club": "It does not befit Auschwitz to become a threat-routine, an all-season tool for intimidation or moral club (*Moralkeule*) or just an exercise of duty."[22] Though hidden in language that was somewhat elusive, a central thread in Walser's speech could still be identified: **the critique of the critics.** Three times the speechmaker repeated himself: "Whatever one says to another, he should at least say exactly the same to himself." With this he assailed the critics of Germany and of the Germans: "When a thinker[23] criticizes the 'full extent of the moral-political trivialization (*Verharmlosung*)'[24] of the government, of the state apparatus and of

---

Institute in the Middle East, *Learning Each Other's Historical Narrative: Palestinians and Israelis*, preliminary draft of the English translation (Beit Jallah: PRIME, 2003).

21. Mäding, "Historische Bildung und Versöhnung," 14.

22. Martin Walser, "Erfahrungen beim Verfassen einer Sonntagsrede," in *Die Walser-Bubis-Debatte: Eine Dokumentation*, ed. Frank Schirrmacher (Frankfurt a.M.: Suhrkamp, 1999), 13.

23. Though unnamed in the speech, the thinker in question was in fact Jürgen Habermas. See Habermas, "Die zweite Lebenslüge der Bundesrepublik: Wir sind wieder 'normal' geworden," *Die Zeit*, 11 Dec. 1992.

24. In the context of the speech, this trivialization was applied previously to Auschwitz—Walser recounted in the selfsame speech that he himself had been accused of this—and to right-wing terror.

the leadership of the parties, then the impression is inevitable that his conscience is purer than that of the morally-politically trivialized." Just before this he said: "Could it be that the [critic-]intellectual ... had for a second succumbed to the illusion that—since they have worked again in the gruesome ministry of remembrance (*Erinnerungsdienst*)—they were a little bit expiated, that for a moment they were even closer to the victims than to the perpetrators?" Thus in highly veiled language, the age-old rejection of the repentant sinners' outspokenness was repeated: the critic should refrain from criticizing others because of his less-than-immaculate self (see R7). As a self-professed "soul who thirsts for freedom,"[25] Walser chose to "look away" (*Wegschauen*) and "think away" (*Wegdenken*): "Instead of being thankful for the incessant presentation of our shame, I begin to look away."[26] "When the condemned thinks that the judgment is unjust, he is free. That is the freedom of conscience that I have in mind."[27]

Walser's speech sparked a series of heated debates that accompanied those concerning the Berlin memorial for the murdered Jews of Europe, which Walser referred to as "a soccer-field-size nightmare in the center of the capital."[28] Chief among the debate participants was Ignatz Bubis, then president of ZdJ, who retorted that although he fully agreed with Walser that the concept "Auschwitz" should in no way become a routine of threats or intimidation tool or just a compulsory exercise, he did consider it right that Auschwitz should be used for moral purposes. "When Walser sees a 'moral club' in it, he is perhaps right, for one can, should, and must learn morals from 'Auschwitz,' though he need not look upon it as a club."[29] Bubis further asserted that it should not be the duty of the Jewish community alone to take up this moral role, but the wider German society. "It is the society that is demanded here, and

---

25. Walser, "Sonntagsrede," 8.
26. Ibid., 12.
27. Ibid., 14.
28. Ibid., 13.
29. Ignatz Bubis, "Rede des Präsidenten des Zentralrates der Juden in Deutschland," in Schirrmacher, *Die Walser-Bubis-Debatte*, 112.

it cannot be that the fight against racism and antisemitism as well as hostility against strangers is left to the Jews, whereas a part of the society feels rather annoyed by it."[30]

Reading Walser and Bubis together, one can already discern the subtle but significant changes in the use of "moral club": whereas the original nomenclator used it derogatorily, seemingly with the intention to inhibit its use, because it was allegedly employed by some to "injure" others, himself included, his critic upheld it—the moral part of it—and encouraged Jews *and Germans* alike to use it to speak out.

This **encouragement to speak out** was uttered not only by Bubis, but also by representatives from other Jewish communities. Avraham Burg, former speaker of the Knesset, whose father had fled Nazi Germany, proposed in his controversial book *Defeating Hitler* that Germans and Jews should become partners in the moral fight against violations of human dignity: "I propose a walk together, for both Jews and Germans, for the children of victims and perpetrators. I propose that we go there together, wherever human beings are sacrificed at the altar of cruelty, and to *raise our voice* and say: 'Never again, no one, not only Jews. Never again the murder and extermination of human beings.' That is the universal lesson from the tragic relationship between Jews and Germany that we want to derive from 'our Holocaust.' "[31]

And this Jewish encouragement for Germans to speak out includes also perhaps the most inconceivable direction: German critique of Israeli policy. Alfred Grosser, who was already an active "turner" in the early postwar years (see **P1** and **P3**), explicitly demanded that postwar Germans should resist the silencing effect of the "Auschwitz club" and diligently criticize Israel:

A young German, who has nothing to do with the German past—except the responsibility to make sure that something like that should never happen again—such a German must intervene wherever fundamental

---

30. Ibid., 108.
31. Avraham Burg, "Vorwort zur deutschen Ausgabe," in *Hitler besiegen: Warum Israel sich endlich vom Holocaust lösen muss* (Frankfurt/New York: Campus, 2009), 19–20. More on this work in **P9**.

rights are infringed. . . . In this point I stand behind Martin Walser's critique of the Auschwitz club.[32]

The idea that the duty of the repentant to speak out exists *precisely because*—rather than *in spite*—of his guilt in the past has perhaps found clearest expression in Lev Kopelev. A Russian-Jewish writer, Kopelev joined the Red Army during World War II and saw the atrocities committed by Soviet soldiers against Germans in East Prussia.[33] In his book *Aufbewahren für alle Zeit* (To Be Preserved Forever), first published in Russian in 1975 and then in German a year later, he bore witness to these wrongdoings and his own guilt and fate in these. He called it an "attempt at a confession (*Beichte*)."[34] In an opinion piece in *Die Zeit*, which had serialized parts of the book, Kopelev explained to his German readers why he was doing what he was doing:

> I began to write down the memories, because I recognized my guilt. But I know that regret does not repair (*wiedergutmacht*) my guilt, nor does it free me from the responsibility for all that the Party had done, to which I belonged. . . . My guilt remains inextricably bound with me. . . . Only if I resolutely and unreservedly judge myself can I further live. . . . And only determined and unreserved self-condemnation gives one the right, even the duty, to speak against those who try to deny, to trivialize (*verharmlosen*), or to justify the same kind of evil acts.[35]

Kopelev's daring acts of speaking out found immediate resonance in Germany. Heinrich Böll wrote the afterword for Kopelev's book, and cited Kopelev's confession as proof of a long-begun

---

32. Alfred Grosser, "Israels Politik fördert Antisemitismus," *Stern*, 12 Oct. 2007.

33. For trying to stop his colleagues from raping and looting in Prussia, Kopelev was convicted of "bourgeois humanism." See Robert G. Kaiser's introductory note to Kopelev's *Ease My Sorrows: A Memoir*, trans. Antonina W. Bouis (New York: Random House, 1983), xi–x; and Marion Gräfin Dönhoff, "Mitleid mit den Deutschen: Neun Jahre Gefängnis," *Die Zeit*, 6 Feb. 1976.

34. Lev Kopelev, *Aufbewahren für alle Zeit*, trans. Heddy Pross-Weerth and Heinz-Dieter Mendel (Hamburg: Hoffmann und Campe, 1976), epigraph. More on this work in **R11**.

35. "Bekenntnisse eines Sowjetbürgers," *Die Zeit*, 11 Feb. 1977.

and ongoing process of "rethinking" (*Umdenkprozeß*), and of the "inner transformation" (*innere Umwandlung*) in the Soviet Union.[36] Yet, just like those who had quoted Victor Gollancz before him (see **P3**), Böll cautioned German readers not to commit the error of self-victimization when faced with the turning of the other, to "exploit" it while neglecting the "*entire* context" of German guilt and Soviet guilt.[37] In this sense, one might agree with Böll when he called Kopelev "dangerous,"[38] because a genuine turning act is always simultaneously challenging and tempting.

Marion Gräfin Dönhoff, another German writer and a great "turner" in her own right (see **P4**), saw in Kopelev—who was admittedly with the Russian troops when they marched into Dönhoff's native homeland of East Prussia, from which she had to flee in 1945—an exemplary "change" (*Verwandlung*) "from a scrupulous faithful Communist to at first an angry, then disappointed, but finally a fearless man of *great wisdom*,"[39] that is, someone who has much to teach others. Dönhoff's praise for this "turned turner" was unreserved: "I marvel at Lev over and over again. I'm amazed most of all by the freedom that he possesses. Perhaps one might better say the freedom that he begets, that he has summoned out of nothing."[40]

Hence in Kopelev, as appreciated and "promoted" by Dönhoff and others, one finds an example of calling others to repent that is not simultaneously "looking away" from one's national or personal shame, as manifested by Walser. Rather, *looking into* one's own guilt, as argued and shown by Kopelev, is the prerequisite to helping others turn. Confession, according to this paradigm, precedes and *demands* such a duty. The freedom to call for repentance comes from one's own repentance.

Yet, one might want to object, Isn't this in principle what Walser was saying all along, "Whatever one says to another, he should at

---

36. Heinrich Böll, "Nachwort," in Kopelev, *Aufbewahren für alle Zeit*, 596–97.
37. Ibid., 599 (emphasis in the original).
38. Ibid., 602–3.
39. Dönhoff, "Mitleid mit den Deutschen" (emphasis added).
40. Ibid.

least say exactly the same to himself"? Had not Karl Jaspers also said something similar in his *Schuldfrage*, namely, that fellow Germans should stop assigning guilt to others (including other Germans) instead of themselves? And weren't Kopelev and Dönhoff mutually contradictory—one speaking of his "inextricable guilt," and the other of his "marvelous freedom"?

These are indeed complex expressions that do not lend themselves to oversimplified explication. We must therefore turn to the next chapter in which we'll see how, in the postwar period, certain logical "disagreements" actually turned victims and perpetrators/ bystanders toward each other (and thus were "repentant disagreements"), whereas some "agreements" did the opposite.

10

"The Appropriateness of Each Proposition Depends upon Who Utters It" (P8)

After the war ended in the summer of 1945, although different periods were dominated by different sets of questions related to the legacies of the Nazi past, one set seems particularly resilient: questions concerning guilt. One might have expected that, after the Stuttgart Confession of Guilt, Karl Jaspers's *Schuldfrage,* the Nuremberg trials, and so on, the issue of guilt would have been settled once and for all. But this was not so. Not only was guilt a fiercely contested question in the immediate postwar years, but it resurfaced periodically—especially when postwar generations came of age in the 1960s and then in the 1980s respectively—with a seemingly undiminished intensity that dismayed those who opposed the question altogether.[1] Hence it is especially revealing to

---

1. See Walser's complaint of this in his "Erfahrungen beim Verfassen einer Sonntagsrede," in *Die Walser-Bubis-Debatte: Eine Dokumentation*, ed. Frank Schirrmacher (Frankfurt a.M.: Suhrkamp, 1999), 12.

trace the "repentant disagreements" (and their opposites) along the line of postwar debates concerning guilt.

In early 1945, even before the war ended, Swiss theologian Karl Barth did in Switzerland what Victor Gollancz was doing in the United Kingdom (P1) almost simultaneously—he problematized the idea of collective German guilt on the one hand, and "guiltified" the "innocent" audience on the other. Speaking on the topic "the Germans and us" in front of his fellow Swiss citizens, Barth must have tried his listeners' patience by listing the "Swiss sins" in Nazi wrongdoings, from the maintainence of "not only correct but friendly relations" with the Hitler regime to supporting the German war industry to the "newfound" antisemitism of Swiss citizens and peasants. "We have spoken a lot about the Germans, but only very little about ourselves. A complement *on this side* is urgently needed."[2]

Thus when Barth later spoke in Stuttgart in November 1945—the first time after the war before a German audience—about hoping that the Stuttgart Confession of Guilt would also be pronounced "by the other sides" (of German society, that is, aside from the Protestant church),[3] he had already done just that himself *outside:* for and to the Swiss. And when he told the Germans that it was in their best interest now to remain undistracted by **the guilt of others** while focusing on dealing with their own guilt,[4] he himself had given them reasons and "proof" to do what was required. Thus when "the war was the sole guilt of the Germans" was the consensus of Jaspers, Niemöller & Co., Barth, Gollancz et al. were finding guilt in their own national contexts. But apparently for some in Germany, this was not enough. They felt that unless the guilt of the others was also dealt with *together with*—if not prior to—German guilt, a new injustice would have been committed.

---

2. Karl Barth, *Zur Genesung des deutschen Wesens: Ein Freundeswort von draußen* (Stuttgart: Verlag von Franz Mittelbach, 1945), 44–48 (emphasis added).
3. Karl Barth, "Ein Wort an die Deutschen," in *Der Götze wackelt* (Berlin: Käthe Vogt Verlag, 1961), 94.
4. Ibid., 93.

An articulate example of this sentiment would be Helmut Thielicke, a theologian based in Tübingen. On Good Friday (the Friday before Easter) 1947, Thielicke gave a sermon in Stuttgart in which he called the practice of Allied occupation a "scandal" (*Ärgernis*) in the biblical sense, that is, something that causes others to fall.[5] Citing the example of the internment camp in Darmstadt, he criticized the "automatic imprisonment" of both the guilty and the innocent as "undignified for human beings and soul killing."[6] "In the name of denazification, what happens among us is not just injustice: it is the murder of soul and faith (*Seelenmord und Glaubensmord*)."[7] According to Thielicke, the twofold "scandal" that caused a good many Germans to lose faith lay precisely in the "injustice of the occupation powers" and "our silence in the face of it."[8] Sounding almost like Martin Walser, he lamented, "I can no longer listen to the church's guilt confession in public, as long as it is not also publicly, so harshly and mercilessly said vis-à-vis the others."[9]

Thielicke, and the like-minded,[10] saw a "continuity" between the silence of the church in the Third Reich and its silence now under the Occupation; supposedly, the breaking of this continuity *now* would be a repentant act on the part of the church. A letter writer in support of Thielicke's sermon, which he quoted approvingly, formulated this idea more directly thus:

> That the internal front in the Third Reich was not clearly distinguished, and so the good, faithful Germans were left to the followers of satanic powers, it was something that the church's silence then was to blame. But the church's confession of this guilt today will lose it credibility and hence its repentance-effecting power (*Buße wirkende Kraft*), if the

---

5. Thielicke quoted Matthew 18:7 on "scandals."

6. Helmut Thielicke and Hermann Diem, *Die Schuld der Anderen: Ein Briefwechsel* (Göttingen: Vandenhoeck & Ruprecht, 1948), 10.

7. Ibid., 11.

8. Ibid., 10.

9. Ibid., 12.

10. See, for example, the documentation in Matthew Hockenos's chapter "The Guilt of the Others," in his *Church Divided: German Protestants Confront the Nazi Past* (Bloomington: Indiana University Press, 2004).

church continues with its accursed silence today and again contributes nothing to the clear distinction today [*sic*] between the kingdom of God and the reign of Satan.[11]

It was in reaction to this kind of criticism and attack on the credibility of the church that Thielicke exclaimed in his sermon: "Someone should stand up . . . so that it will not be said again that the church remained silent. . . . As caretaker of the soul (*Seelsorger*) and teacher of the church . . . I have the duty to say this out loud to the whole public—precisely so that *the others* can also hear it, for perhaps they have no one who would bring this up to their conscience."[12]

Thielicke obviously knew that "no one" was an exaggeration, for later in his sermon he also praised Gollancz's plea for the Germans (**P1**), whose Jewish mercy should shame the (Allied) Christians.[13] He also quoted an "English reporter" who had dutifully recorded what he had heard from a student in Germany: "For God's sake, don't turn us into Nazis."[14] But instead of assessing and presenting these as initiatives of turning in the outside world and warning his audience accordingly, Thielicke **"agreed" with the turners' self-condemnation**, thus seeing in them the exceptions that prove the rule, that is, the case he was trying to make. "How merciless is this world," he concluded. "Truly, this all is a merciless world. . . . So we stand as messengers . . . in our world of scandals and traps."[15]

According to Thielicke himself, this sermon received largely positive feedback from its audience.[16] But there were others who felt that there was something terribly amiss in this way of sermonizing over the guilt of others. Hermann Diem, a contemporary German theologian, saw that what Thielicke was doing was tantamount to giving poison to his fellow Germans, when they needed medicine

---

11. Quoted in Thielicke and Diem, *Schuld der Anderen*, 34.
12. Thielicke and Diem, *Schuld der Anderen*, 12–13 (emphasis added).
13. Ibid., 14.
14. Ibid., 12.
15. Ibid., 14–15.
16. Ibid., 26.

instead. He wrote in a sharply critical letter to Thielicke: "That was no sermon. . . . The listeners left empty-handed. They have received *stone instead of bread*."[17] A single objection emphasized in Diem's critique was against the tendency to turn the biblical call to confess one's own guilt into an "objective" law, under which even perpetrators can "rightfully" lay claims against the victim:

> I've also succumbed to the temptation . . . to lay down the confession of guilt as a law (*Gesetz*), even as I, as a theologian, should have known that it doesn't work like that. . . . It is entirely out of the question that the "guilt of the others" should mean a scandal for us, or even that we may or must defer the confession of our own guilt because of that. That would mean in effect to defer the comfort of the Good News (*Trost des Evangeliums*) for us and our people.[18]

The only "law" that Diem deemed appropriate for his fellow Germans in their present situation of guilt was to be found in the Torah, which also served as an explanation as to why the sole **focus on one's own guilt** was so crucial. Quoting the book of Exodus (20:5–6), in which cross-generational divine punishment (and also mercy) was proclaimed, Diem said: "[This verse] is more shocking to me than all the news about the present condition in Germany, for then I know why such shocking things happen today in the aftermath of the war. But then I also know that I may do nothing other than preaching this law in the Good News (*dieses Gesetz im Evangelium*) to my listeners, so they can also believe that it is the merciful God before whom they should confess their guilt, in order to be free from it."[19]

Diem castigated Thielicke for committing the grave error of turning the attention of his listeners to the guilt of others instead of their own: "You have contributed in the strongest way to that unrepentant (*unbußfertig*) self-justification of our people. . . [for] such talk leaves the listener no way out other than that which

---

17. Ibid., 19 (emphasis added). See the biblical reference in Matthew 7:9–10.

18. Thielicke and Diem, *Schuld der Anderen*, 20–21. It is noteworthy that Diem saw the "comforting" role of a "carer of the soul" differently from Thielicke.

19. Thielicke and Diem, *Schuld der Anderen*, 30.

leads to national self-assertion."[20] And if, Diem went further, what Thielicke was after was also **the turning of the others,** he should have addressed them directly instead of going through a domestic audience.[21] Thielicke would concede in his defense that "repentance-readiness" (*Bußfertigkeit*) was also his goal; but in order to achieve this, he countered, he needed to shore up his credibility as a preacher by speaking *also* of the guilt of the others.[22] And he questioned whether **audienceship should be prioritized over objectivity.**[23] Again, he cited the "agreement" of foreigners who had heard his sermon as proof of his point.[24]

Concerning the "instrumentalization" of the guilt of others, Diem's rejection was absolute. He insisted on the priority of one's own guilt—even when, as he put it, one could only "believe" in it:[25] "One cannot deal with the guilt of the others simply in order to clear the way for the realization of one's own guilt, because one must first realize and confess in faith one's own guilt, and only then can one be done with the guilt of the others."[26]

In his own sermon on the Day of Repentance (*Landesbußtag*)[27] Diem illustrated how, by using verses from Jeremiah and Isaiah, a preacher could speak of the guilt of the others without losing the central focus on the guilt of the directly addressed community:

---

20. Ibid., 21.

21. Ibid., 19.

22. Ibid., 24.

23. Ibid., 23.

24. Ibid., 26. Thielicke referenced an "American theologian . . . Bodensiek, who subscribes to my sermon."

25. Thielicke and Diem, *Schuld der Anderen*, 20. There is a subtle but significant difference between the "belief in guilt" (*daß man diese Schuld nur glauben kann*), to which Diem referred in his letter to Thielicke, and the belief in the divine origin and purpose of punishment because of one's own guilt, which he actually pointed to in his own sermon (54–55). In any case, I'm of the opinion that it would be a mistake to take Diem to mean a guilt that is beyond intellectual/perceptual grasp. What "one cannot be persuaded and convinced of," as he put it, seems rather the three-dimensional relationship among God and human beings (see R2), which "one can only believe in."

26. Thielicke and Diem, *Schuld der Anderen*, 31.

27. The *Buß- und Bettag* is a Protestant tradition in Germany that can be traced back to the sixteenth century and continues to this day (www.busstag.de).

We must not merely talk about our misery in order to complain and accuse, but in whatever we say, it must resonate like an unmistakable undertone that we have heard and remembered the word of the prophet: "I will not completely destroy you, but I will punish you with moderation, *that you will not consider yourself innocent.*" How completely different would the discussions have been . . . if they came out of this faith, that God has sent us all that, in order to make us conscious of our guilt.[28]

Thus in **"repentant disagreement" with outside turners** such as Gollancz and Grosser, who unequivocally presented the injustice in occupied Germany as Allied guilt rather than "divine," that is, justified punishment for the Germans, Diem and the like-minded[29] invoked a perceptual framework that included this as part and parcel of the legitimate consequences of German guilt. Hence the vehement objection of Diem to his colleague's "reversal espousal."

To be fair, Thielicke was no simple sower of German victimhood, for he could—and did—argue in his defense that he had also matter-of-factly stated at the beginning of his Stuttgart sermon that "what we are suffering is our guilt."[30] He seemed only to be reacting to an accusation against the church that he could not take—namely, the church must speak against injustice *now* or risk its credibility.[31] And above all, he had also suffered Nazi oppression in his time because of his links to the Confessing Church, a status that, if Barth's rule is to be followed, would afford him the authority to speak out against Allied injustice in occupied Germany.[32] As

---

28. Thielicke and Diem, *Schuld der Anderen*, 53 (emphasis added). The quote is from Jeremiah 30:11. The translation used by Diem would seem today unusual, for most versions available at present do not read "that you will not consider yourself innocent (*daß du dich nicht für unschuldig hältst*)," but "I will not let you go unpunished (*doch ungestraft kann ich dich nicht lassen*)." Diem was apparently quoting from the 1912 version of the Lutherbibel, from which the 2017 version quoted above differs. Regardless of which translation is "closer" to the Hebrew original, the fact is that the 1912 translation lends itself readily to justifying his "guilt-consciousness" interpretation, whereas the newer ones do not.

29. See those propagating the recognition of punishment as just in P4.

30. Thielicke and Diem, *Schuld der Anderen*, 7.

31. Ibid., 9.

32. Karl Barth, "Ein Wort an die Deutschen," in *Der Götze wackelt* (Berlin: Käthe Vogt Verlag, 1961), 93. This is again in "repentant disagreement" with

Thielicke explained to Diem, "I'm willing to take the risk in order to bring the credibility of my 'subjectivity' to bear on these uncertain questions—exactly as I [did] in the Third Reich."[33] Yet, all in all, Thielicke's message to his German audience was evidently on the side of "We Germans deserve it, *but* the guilt of the others is there" rather than "The guilt of the others is there, *but* we Germans deserve it." This *but* is a decisive difference, a difference that determines the relational thrust of the message.

Remarkable also was Thielicke's **"repentance tone deafness,"** that is, his inability to discern the turning efforts of the others as such, but taking this self-criticism as "objective proof" of his own accusations against them. This tone deafness was what Diem roundly criticized when he found the German "inconsistency" in rejecting criticism of Germany or the Germans by foreigners as "interference in German affairs," while at the same time gladly embracing foreign criticism of themselves (such as criticizing the Nuremberg trials or denazification) as "*even* the foreigners say so."[34] One could imagine what happens when the same takes place in reverse: that is, outsiders taking German self-criticism as "proof" of their definitive condemnation of them.

About fifty years or some two generations after the Thielicke-Diem debate, the question of German guilt did not just "fade away," but was revived, in 1996, in a controversial book by a young Jewish-American scholar, Daniel Jonah Goldhagen, which dealt specifically with the perpetrators of the Holocaust, *Hitler's Willing Executioners*.[35] The attention aroused in Germany was unusual for an academic work: by the time its German translation appeared, the

---

German turners like Jaspers, who would not allow even surviving Nazi opponents like himself—who shared the "metaphysical guilt" (see **P2**)—to take up this weighty task of "turning the others," until a time "when an atmosphere of trust is there, [and] then one can remind the other of the possibility of guilt (*Schuldmöglichkeit*)." Karl Jaspers, *Die Schuldfrage* (Heidelberg: Lambert Schneider, 1946), 105.

33. Thielicke and Diem, *Schuld der Anderen*, 25.

34. Ibid., 28.

35. Daniel Jonah Goldhagen, *Hitler's Willing Executioners: Ordinary Germans and the Holocaust* (New York: Alfred Knopf, 1996).

number of German essays relating to the book's thesis and reviews of the book itself was so great that a "documentation" of these could already be published as a book by itself.[36] And the debates that the author and his thesis ignited lasted in the German press until 2003.[37]

In the author's own words, which appeared in the preface specifically designated for the German edition, "In no way is a claim on the eternal 'national character of the Germans' made here. . . . I expressly reject such concepts and notions . . . ; I want to make clear why and how the Holocaust happened, why it could become possible at all. . . . The goal of this book is about historical clarification, not moral judgment . . . , I categorically reject the notion of collective guilt."[38] Yet, in addition to these rather (by now) uncontroversial statements, the thesis was packed with explosive convictions: "The Holocaust had its origin in Germany; it is therefore first and foremost a German phenomenon. . . . He who wants to make the Holocaust understood must grasp it as a development in German history. . . . The Holocaust could only occur in Germany, . . . I bring forth in this book evidence that shows the complicity (*Mittäterschaft*) was far more widespread than hitherto assumed. . . . The number of Germans who have committed criminal acts is enormously high."[39]

Indeed, the seemingly inconsistent statements, aims, and outcomes of the thesis, especially when it comes to collective guilt, were conducive to multiple (mis)interpretations; hence a large part of the debate had to do with contesting claims as to what the author, Goldhagen, was *actually* saying and/or trying to say

---

36. Julius H. Schoeps, ed., *Ein Volk von Mördern? Die Dokumentation zur Goldhagen-Kontroverse um die Rolle der Deutschen im Holocaust* (Hamburg: Hoffmann und Campe, 1996).

37. Torben Fischer and Matthias N. Lorenz, eds., *Lexikon der 'Vergangenheitsbewältigung' in Deutschland: Debatten- und Diskursgeschichte des Nationalsozialismus nach 1945* (Bielefeld: transcript, 2007), 296. See also Avraham Barkai, "German Historians versus Goldhagen," *Yad Vashem Studies* 26 (1998): 295–328.

38. Daniel Jonah Goldhagen, "Vorwort zur deutschen Ausgabe," in *Hitlers willige Vollstrecker: Ganz gewöhnliche Deutsche und der Holocaust*, trans. Klaus Kochmann (Berlin: Siedler Verlag, 1996), 6–11.

39. Ibid., 7–12.

with his thesis. One unmistakable critical voice against the Gold-hagen thesis, though, came from a prominent Jew in Germany at the time, Ignatz Bubis (see **P7**). In a colloquium in Bonn in the September 1996, which was solely dedicated to Goldhagen's the-sis and jointly organized by the Friedrich-Ebert-Stiftung and the Deutsch-Israelische Gesellschaft, Bubis flatly rejected Goldhagen's work as "a bad book" containing "many contradictions."[40] He agreed with Goldhagen when he said that the concept of guilt should only be applied when a person in fact had committed a crime. "But right after that Goldhagen said exactly the opposite: 'And every individual is part of the collective.' I think this is very inconsistent."[41] Bubis also found Goldhagen's interchangeable use of "Germans" and "perpetrators" unacceptable. "He mingles the Germans and the perpetrators time and again. In many places he speaks correctly about the perpetrators, but then immediately equates them with the Germans. . . . Goldhagen calls the Germans a people of perpetrators on the one hand, and he rejects the thesis of collective guilt on the other. I don't know what to make of it."[42] For Bubis, the only good thing coming out of Goldhagen's book was the debates.[43]

By calling "ordinary Germans" "willing executioners," Gold-hagen's thesis was in fact a "turning back" of what Arendt, Gollancz, and Grosser had promulgated: that not all Germans were Nazis or criminally guilty. Nazi propaganda would have succeeded if the outside world thought that Nazis and Germans were the same, ar-gued Arendt in 1945 (**P1**). True, Goldhagen did not equate the two; all he did was simply take the "Nazi" out of the historical account, and in its place inserted the "German." In doing this, he was in **"agreement" with German turners** like Niemöller and Jaspers, who had argued that giving the guilt to the Nazis was not enough, and

---

40. Dieter Dowe, ed., *Die Deutschen—ein Volk von Tätern? Zur historisch-politischen Debatte um das Buch von Daniel Jonah Goldhagen 'Hitlers willige Vollstrecker: Ganz gewöhnliche Deutsche und der Holocaust'* (Bonn: Friedrich-Ebert-Stiftung, 1996), 52, 64, 78.
41. Ibid., 52.
42. Ibid.
43. Ibid., 64.

that all living Germans were guilty (in different senses), individually *and* collectively (P2).[44] Furthermore, as in the case of Thielicke, the turning efforts of the others have become "proof" of Goldhagen's accusation against them. In supporting his argument that "because the perpetrators of the Holocaust were Germany's representative citizens, this book is about Germany during the Nazi period and before, its people and its culture," Goldhagen cited the confession of a former Hitler Youth, which contains stark accusations against the "millions of Germans" sharing antisemitism and the "majority of Germans" behind Hitler.[45]

Goldhagen's thesis also overturned, perhaps inadvertently, another "movement" Jewish turners before him had endeavored to bring about, namely, to bridge the perceived gap between their audience (i.e., Jews and non-Germans) and the "German" perpetrators/bystanders, for example, by de-demonizing the latter (e.g., Langbein and Arendt; see **P1**). Time and again, Goldhagen emphasized the "abnormality" of the Germans in Nazi Germany:

> The notion that Germany during the Nazi period was an "ordinary," "normal" society . . . is in its essence false. Germany during the Nazi period was a society which was in important ways *fundamentally different from ours* today, operating according to a different ontology and cosmology, inhabited by people whose general understanding of important realms of social existence was not "ordinary" by *our* standards.[46]

> [They] were living, essentially, in a world structured by important cultural cognitive assumptions as *fantastically different from our own* as those that have governed distant times and places.[47]

This comforting distance between "them" and "us" (assuming "us" as non-Germans) was flatly rejected by Yehuda Bauer. On 27 January 1998, the German memorial day for the victims of the

---

44. In Jaspers's conception, whereas "criminal," "moral," and "metaphysical" guilts are personal, "political guilt" is expressly collective: "There is . . . collective guilt (*Kollektivschuld*) as the political liability (*politische Haftung*) of the nationals of a state (*Staatsangehörigen*)." Jaspers, *Schuldfrage*, 56.
45. Goldhagen, *Hitler's Willing Executioners*, 456, 597.
46. Ibid., 460 (emphasis added).
47. Ibid., 597 (emphasis added).

Shoah, the preeminent Israeli historian from Yad Vashem gave a speech in the Bundestag. Although he did not name the Goldhagen thesis, the reference was nonetheless readily discernible:

> And what is terrible about the Shoah is precisely not that the Nazis were inhuman; what is terrible is that they were human—like you and me. It is only a cheap excuse when we say that the Nazis were different from us, that we can sleep in peace, because the Nazis were devils and we are not, because we are not Nazis. Equally cheap an excuse is the view that the Germans were somehow genetically programmed to carry out this mass murder. Many believe that what happened then could only happen in Germany and that it cannot be repeated because most people are not Germans. This attitude is nothing other than reversed racism.[48]

While Goldhagen's book was criticized by prominent Jews like Bauer and Bubis,[49] it was upheld on the German side by Habermas and others. In 1997, one year after his book first appeared in English, Goldhagen was awarded the "Democracy Prize" in Germany by the *Blätter für deutsche und internationale Politik,* a periodical that was started in 1956 with the support of, among others, Martin Niemöller and Robert Scholl, the father of Hans and Sophie Scholl.[50] In his laudatory address for Goldhagen, Habermas **"disagreed"** with the Jewish critics of Goldhagen's thesis, who had called it "self-contradictory" and "a bad book." While taking note of the fine difference between Christopher Browning's "ordinary men"[51] and Goldhagen's "ordinary Germans," Habermas

---

48. Yehuda Bauer, *Die dunkle Seite der Geschichte: Die Shoah in historischer Sicht; Interpretationen und Re-Interpretationen,* trans. Christian Wiese (Frankfurt a.M.: Jüdischer Verlag, 2001), 317–18. The wording of this speech is slightly different from that available on the Bundestag's website. My translation follows the printed version.

49. To be sure, there were also numerous German critics of the book, including Marion Gräfin Dönhoff. See Dönhoff, "Warum D. J. Goldhagens Buch in die Irre führt," *Die Zeit,* 6 Sept. 1996.

50. See Blätter-Redaktion, "50 Jahre Blätter," *Blätter für deutsche und internationale Politik,* no. 11 (2006): 1284–86.

51. Christopher Browning, *Ordinary Men: Reserve Police Battalion 101 and the Final Solution in Poland* (New York: HarperCollins, 1992). See how Browning himself considers the difference between his "ordinary men" and Goldhagen's "ordinary Germans" in Schoeps, *Volk von Mördern?* 118.

nevertheless saw in the latter not a "stigmatizing reproach" of the Germans, but a "counterfactual reflection (*kontrafaktische Über-legung*) that has the good sense in a historical context to point out the undisputed high dissemination of antisemitic dispositions in the German populace in that era."[52]

Goldhagen's antiuniversalizing focus on the German cultural context was also to praise, for subsequent German generations, argued Habermas, needed exactly this "public use of history" for their self-critical, ethical-political self-understanding:

> In historical retrospection, which parts we attribute to the persons and which to the circumstances, and where we draw the line between being free or forced, guilty or not guilty—these depend [on more than just facts, but] also on a "pre-understanding" (*Vorverständnis*). . . . The hermeneutical readiness to recognize the true extent of responsibil-ity . . . varies with our understanding of freedom. . . . How we see guilt and innocence divided in historical retrospection mirrors also the norms that we mutually, as citizens of this republic, are ready to respect. Here I see Goldhagen's true merit. . . . [His] clarification refers to spe-cific traditions and mentalities, to ways of thinking and perceiving of a certain cultural context. It refers not to something unchangeable . . . but to factors that can be changed through a change of consciousness (*Bewußtseinswandel*).[53]

In a subtle reference, Habermas seemed even ready to compare Goldhagen with Jaspers, who was allegedly mocked by Carl Schmitt in 1948 as "a repentance preacher (*Bußprediger*) who de-serves no interest."[54] Yet, as we have seen in the case of Thielicke, the problem of audienceship—not to mention the content—makes this interpretation of Goldhagen's role and message nearly unten-able, except when embraced and translated by someone from the "inside" to an intra-German message, as was the case with Haber-mas's *Laudatio*.

---

52. Jürgen Habermas, "Warum ein 'Demokratiepreis' für Daniel J. Goldhagen? Eine Laudatio," *Die Zeit*, 14 Mar. 1997.

53. Ibid. "Change of consciousness" is in fact the direct translation of *meta-noia*, or "repentance" in Greek as used in the New Testament. See the introduction.

54. Habermas, "Warum ein 'Demokratiepreis.'"

In a way, the Goldhagen controversy was a continuation of the Historikerstreit, or "the dispute of historians," in the 1980s, in which the main question of historical comparison was discussed, and in which Habermas argued also for the "cross-generational liability" thesis (see **P12**). In his study of this dispute, historian Charles Maier commented on the necessity of "repentant disagreement," or the phenomenon of "asymmetrical obligations of memory":

> If it behooves Germans to stress the anti-Jewish specificity of the Holocaust, it is sometimes important for Jews *to do the opposite.* . . . The obligations of memory thus remain *asymmetrical.* For Jews: to remember that although they seek legitimation of a public sorrow, their suffering was not exclusive. For Germans: to specify that the Holocaust was the Final Solution of the Jewish problem as its architects understood it. The appropriateness of each proposition depends upon *who* utters it.[55]

In an age where the academic consensus is that the mere mentioning of the author's/speaker's biographical background in relation to his book/speech is tantamount to committing the fallacy of ad hominem, Maier's insistence on the **significance of relational position** is remarkable. Yet in the foregoing exposition we have seen precisely the existence of this "repentance disagreement" between German and non-German authors/speakers—in its various contexts with its various opposites—in postwar Germany. In abstract terms, the central questions in this disagreement are those concerning the relation between objective truths (whether historical or moral) and the parties in a wounded relationship. It seems that in the realm of mutual-turning dynamics, a "pre-understanding" (Habermas) is required: that certain objective truths are "medicine"—to borrow the "stone instead of bread" metaphor used by Diem—when spoken outside, but are "poisonous" when expressed inside, and vice versa.

---

55. Charles Maier, *The Unmasterable Past: History, Holocaust, and German National Identity* (Cambridge, MA: Harvard University Press, 1988), 166 (emphasis added).

In this light we can better assess the pitfalls of Friedrich Meinecke's *Deutsche Katastrophe* (German Catastrophe) as a German historian's—or perhaps *the* German historian's—response
to the German downfall.[56] It is not that it lacked a critique of
Nazi Germany and the Germans, or insights into the longer-term,
more culturally rooted "causes" of the catastrophe. The problem
is that instead of concentrating his readers' attention on areas
in which German turning could take place, Meinecke positioned
himself, thereby prepositioning his German readers, as an objective historian (with the credentials of a Nazi opponent) observing
great currents of history and standing *outside* the triad of historical truth, the victims, and the perpetrators. Hence the impulse to
be "fair" in answering the "historical question" and judging the
two human groups: even the victims had their faults,[57] and even
the perpetrators had their merits.[58] This is not the position of the
accused, much less the self-accused sinner, but of the self-elevated,
self-exempted judge. This is altogether different in spirit from the
"historiography of repentant disagreement" required of and by the
turners.

For a successful repentant disagreement to form, one needs to
pay attention to the specific sets of speaker-audience configurations.
This involves risks of abuse for either side of the speaking parties
as they embrace the more difficult parts of the truth, as neither
has control over the response of the other, which they nonetheless
depend on. In the following chapter, we will turn to a particularly

---

56. Friedrich Meinecke, *Die deutsche Katastrophe: Betrachtungen und Erinnerungen* (Wiesbaden: Eberhard Brockhaus, 1946).

57. "The antisemitic movement from the beginning of the 80s brought the first
signs of lightning. The Jews . . . had given rise to various scandals (*mancherlei An-
stoß erregen*) since their full emancipation. They have contributed much to the
gradual devaluation and invalidation of the liberal world of ideas." Meinecke,
Deutsche Katastrophe, 29. Though immediately he also spoke about Jewish intellectual and economic contributions to Germany.

58. "We searched for what could be 'positive' in Hitler's work, and found also
something that corresponded to the great objective ideas and requirements of our
time [i.e., his fusion of the two currents of nationalism and socialism]." Meinecke,
Deutsche Katastrophe, 112. Though again the historian also concluded that Hitler
had left the Germans nothing but rubble.

risky move by the victims—the turning toward their own guilt—
which exposes them to both abuse from the outside and attack
from the inside. Yet it is also this move that completes repentance
as mutual-turning—after turning as mercy in its various forms (**R3**)
and turning as participation in the sinner's renewal (**R6**).

11

"Hitler Is in Ourselves, Too" (P9)

After escaping from Nazi-dominated Europe, Abraham Joshua Heschel, a young rabbi, settled in the United States in the early 1940s at Hebrew Union College (HUC), in Cincinnati, Ohio. He brought with him a message that had first been addressed to a largely German-Christian audience in Frankfurt (see **P2**), but was now "translated" for his new, Jewish-American readers. "The Meaning of This War" he now called it. But what could possibly be *shared* by Germans and Jews when the extermination of European Jewry was under way at that very moment? One can only imagine how dumbfounded HUC *Bulletin* readers were when they saw the opening lines of Heschel's article in 1943:

> There have never been so much guilt. . . . At no time has the earth been so soaked with blood. Fellow-men turned out to be evil ghosts, monstrous and weird. Ashamed and dismayed to live in such a world, we ask: Who is responsible? . . . Few are privileged to discern God's judgment in History. But all may be guided by the words of the Baal Shem:

if a man has beheld evil, he may know that it was shown to him in order that he learn his own guilt and repent; for what is shown to him is also *within him*.[1]

With this prologue Heschel directed his readers' attention to "our failures," which were co-responsible for the outbreak of the atrocities, which ranged from doing nothing when the seeds of hatred and cynicism were being sown to betraying the Torah and the "ideals."[2] "Israel forfeited his message. . . . We have helped extinguish the light our fathers had kindled. . . . Where is Israel?[3]

In short, Heschel was calling fellow Jews to repent. Not a single time—neither in the spoken nor in the printed words—was "Germany" or "German" mentioned. The "spotlight of illumination" (see P6) was solely cast on the self, Israel. In fact, if one compares the German speech and the English text, one observes the noticeably more pointed language in the critique of the Jews, even though it remains consistent with the original message that "it is the believers (*die Gläubigen*), not those nonbelievers, who are being judged [by God]."[4]

For Heschel **self-blaming** was an essential attitude if the return of God was to come about. "Let Fascism not serve as an alibi for our conscience. . . . The conscience of the world was destroyed by those who were wont to blame others rather than themselves."[5] Recalling the biblical passage (Ex 3:6) in which God was about to deliver the Israelites from the Egyptians and showed himself to Moses, Heschel counseled against self-righteousness precisely in this hour: "Like Moses, we hide our face; for we are afraid to look upon Elohim, upon His power of judgment."[6]

---

1. Abraham Joshua Heschel, "The Meaning of This War," *Hebrew Union College Bulletin* (Mar. 1943): 1. I would like to thank Edward Kaplan for generously providing me with all the available versions of this article.

2. In the 1954 version of this article, Heschel changed "ideals" to "prophets." See Heschel, *Man's Quest for God: Studies in Prayer and Symbolism* (New York: Scribner, 1954), 150.

3. Heschel, "Meaning of This War" (1943), 2, 18.

4. Abraham Joshua Heschel, "Versuch einer Deutung," in *Begegnung mit dem Judentum: Ein Gedenkbuch*, ed. Margarethe Lachmund and Albert Steen (Berlin: L. Friedrich, 1962), 13.

5. Heschel, "Meaning of This War" (1943), 2.

6. Ibid.

"But what is the *evil in us* that could plausibly be related to the ongoing slaughter of European Jews?" a Jewish reader of the 1943 text might reasonably ask. Although *tshuvah* is always necessary, it would still be wrong to profane it by using it indiscriminately or exaggeratedly. On this central point, Heschel's message was unambiguous:

> Iron weapons will not protect humanity. . . . The war will outlast the victory of arms if we fail to conquer the infamy of the soul: *the indifference to crime, when committed against others.* For evil is indivisible. It is the same in thought and in speech, in private and in social life. Our victory is in sight, we hope. But when will we start to conquer *the evil within us?*[7]

The charge of indifference, which did not exist in the 1938 speech, indeed seemed to be the focal point of Heschel's 1943 message, which he reinforced in the expanded 1944 version by adding the outcry of the Jews being slaughtered in Poland against the outside world: "We, Jews, despise all those who live in safety and do nothing to save us."[8] This might also explain the modification of the Baal Shem's quote from "repent for what he has come to see" in 1938 to "repent; for what is shown to him is also within him" in 1943 onward.[9] In an interview in 1963, Heschel would also speak of his frustration in these early years in the United States because of the indifference he encountered.[10]

If indifference, among other things, was for Heschel the evil for which non-Germans—including Jews not suffering directly from the Holocaust—needed to repent, another contemporary European

---

7. Ibid., 18 (emphasis added).

8. Heschel, "The Meaning of This War," *Liberal Judaism* 11, no. 10 (1944): 20.

9. The quote in 1938, as reproduced in 1962, read: "Wenn der Mensch Böses zu sehen bekommt, so mag er wissen, daß man es ihm zeigt, damit er seine Schuld erfährt und für das, was er zu sehen bekommt, Buße tut." "Versuch einer Deutung," 12. Judging from the sentence structure of this text, it seems unlikely to be a mere typographical error in the reproduced 1962 text, but an intentional addition in the 1943 version, which was repeated in the 1944 and 1954 versions.

10. See a translation of this interview in Morris M. Faierstein, "Abraham Joshua Heschel and the Holocaust," *Modern Judaism* 19 (1999): 255–75.

Jew saw an even more radical and widespread culpability for the
Nazi phenomenon. In 1946, Max Picard, a Swiss philosopher from
a Jewish family, published a book in German titled *Hitler in uns
selbst* (Hitler in Ourselves).[11] Unlike Heschel and many other turners, Picard did not try to "spare" the Germans. In fact, many of
the sweeping, judgmental, and seemingly self-contradictory statements about the Germans that one might expect to find in Goldhagen's thesis (P8) also appeared in this work by Picard: "The
German today has forgotten all about the defeats that he had only
suffered yesterday"; "The discontinuity in Germany was before
Hitler only a characteristic among many other characteristics; but
then . . . it became essence."[12] Political flip-flop "is characteristic
of the Germans."[13] Picard also discredited the "resisters": *"Most
of the Germans who were against Hitler did that only because
they are against everything that stands before them that is present
at the moment."*[14] He also voiced what many of his contemporaries thought, to which even Goldhagen would explicitly object:
the Germans were incorrigible; "Without inner continuity," he
said, "there is no regret (*Reue*), hence no betterment (*Besserung*).
*What is sinful (das Sündhafte), like everything that happened in
the past, is broken off from the present, in which the German now
lives.* Therefore all attempts to use books and teaching to change
a German who lives in discontinuity are useless."[15] In this sense,
then, was Picard's *Hitler in uns selbst* a philosophical forerunner
of Goldhagen's *Ordinary Germans,* or even surpassed it in its collective condemnation of the accursed nation?

But for one difference this might have been the case. Whereas
Goldhagen endeavored to distance the "ordinary Germans" from
the generation of his present-day readers, which could only include himself, Picard did the *exact opposite.* Indeed, the unifying
structure of Picard's *Hitler* was "in ourselves, *too.*" Every section

11. Max Picard, *Hitler in uns selbst* (Erlenbach-Zürich: Eugen Rentsch, 1946).
12. Ibid., 33, 49.
13. Ibid., 103.
14. Ibid., 104 (emphasis in the original).
15. Ibid., 36 (emphasis in the original).

that analyzes the evil in and through Hitler/National Socialism/ Germany invariably comes to the conclusion that there was shared sinfulness, a real homogeneity between "them" and "us."

> It was already long before the Nazis that a man was considered solely for his 'effectiveness.'[16]

> It was already long before Hitler that the word and the object did not correspond to each other.[17]

> Racial antisemitism was not alone in its inability to see a man as a complete form (*Gestalt*) and being (*Wesen*); it was already long before Hitler that one became used to seeing and assessing oneself and the others under a reduced scheme.[18]

> It is not only the German who has lost the right relationship with time, but also the man of Europe and of America.[19]

> A clear phenomenon found its expression in National Socialism, which was widespread in the German people, and not only in the German people, but in almost every country on earth.[20]

In other words, Picard led his readers to see the contemptible situation of the Germans, the Nazis, and Hitler himself, and then showed them how they were not better than them, for—to paraphrase Heschel quoting the Baal Shem—what was shown to them was also in them.[21] In the section on European literature, Picard

---

16. Ibid., 62.

17. Ibid., 87.

18. Ibid., 135.

19. Ibid., 222.

20. Ibid., 248. See Heschel's agreement in this: "Our world seems not unlike a pit of snakes. We did not sink into the pit in 1939, or even in 1933. We had descended into it generations ago." Heschel, "Meaning of This War" (1944), 19.

21. One might observe, of course, that this "strategy" is the other side of Thielicke's coin (see P8). Yet, aside from the important asymmetry between the victims' and the perpetrators' respective burdens of turning (Maier), there is also the fine difference between a situation where guilt is apparent but its recognition is avoided, which then requires the dismantling of escapist stratagems, and a situation where guilt is mostly hidden, which may call for more intuitive means of demonstration before the counterintuitive turn.

explicitly drew on this point: "It is a sign that discontinuity is everywhere, that we belong to one another in guilt (*daß wir alle zueinander gehören in der Schuld*)."[22] Here he raised the example of "today's literature" as exemplified by Sartre's *L'enfance d'un chef* (1939), in which both obscenity and shamelessness were "surpassed" in the "ephemerality" (*Augenblickhaftigkeit*) so characteristic of the age of discontinuity. "Here is Hitler superhitlered (*überhitlert*). For with Hitler there was still the alternation of one ephemera with another. With Sartre there is only that *one* ephemera, nothing else. . . . If Nietzsche's 'blond beast' was an early sign of the full-blown Hitler-beast, what then is that human like whose early sign is found in Sartre's tales?"[23] So here is where Picard's reflection and Heschel's converged:

> The Hitler regime and its catastrophe have a clarity, a superclarity (*Überdeutlichkeit*): we should *see* what happens when human being is without connection with things, with human beings, with himself, with God. That is directly held out to us and demonstrated to us for instruction (*Belehrung*) . . . the happening is so clear for the sake of *us*.[24]

> Much of the evil that was done in Germany actually happened for the others vicariously (*stellvertretend*).[25]

> The Germans have no right to say that they had taken the evil upon themselves vicariously. . . . But the *other* peoples must say this to themselves, that a monument was erected here for the evil that was also in them.[26]

It was from this common point of departure that Heschel and Picard moved toward other common self-reflective conclusions. In the assessment of modern science, for example, whereas Picard broadly condemned the mechanistic worldview for contributing to the out-of-boundness of Nazi crimes,[27] Heschel, as usual, concentrated

---

22. Picard, *Hitler in uns selbst*, 166.
23. Ibid., 166–68.
24. Ibid., 246 (emphasis in the original).
25. Ibid., 248.
26. Ibid., 250 (emphasis in the original).
27. Ibid., 87–88.

on the Jewish participation in the promotion of this worldview. As
a newcomer to America, he took issue with Albert Einstein, whose
abridged article "Religion of God or Religion of the Good" had
appeared in *Aufbau* in September 1940.[28] Heschel accused Einstein
of propagating a "naturalist" philosophy that the Nazis would up-
hold approvingly, as it invariably leads to the "abolition of human
dignity."[29] Once again, the sin-perspective (see **P2**) made this unlikely, or hidden, link visible: "The hubris, the tragic sin of our
time, is the conviction that there are only laws of nature and tech-
nology, that one can be sufficient in everything alone and organize
worldviews, human breeding, and faith movements."[30]

"Shaky logic" is how one might characterize Heschel's linking of what Einstein—"America's most prestigious Jew" of his
time—was saying and what the Nazis were doing.[31] But as we
have seen in "repentant disagreement" (**R8**), the turners' pronouncements are no mere sets of arguments conforming to the
rules of logic, but first and foremost relational directives that seek
to direct their respective audience to the acts of turning necessary
in each particular situation of guilt. As Heschel himself explained
in his *Prophets*, "The prophets were unfair to the people of Israel.
Their sweeping allegations, overstatements, and generalizations
defied standards of accuracy. Some of the exaggerations reach the
unbelievable."[32]

Likewise, Picard's Pan-European critique (at times also including
the Americans), suggesting their implication in the "Nazi phenomenon," could very well be played down as "unfair" to the subjects
of this criticism, whether they were the Germans or Europe as a
whole.[33] On the other hand, like Hannah Arendt in "Organisierte

---

28. Albert Einstein, "Gottesreligion oder Religion des Guten?," *Aufbau*, 13
Sept. 1940.

29. Abraham Joshua Heschel, "Antwort an Einstein," *Aufbau*, 20 Sept. 1940.

30. Ibid. Cf. Picard, *Hitler in uns selbst*, 176.

31. See Edward K. Kaplan, "Coming to America: Abraham Joshua Heschel,
1940–1941," *Modern Judaism* 27, no. 2 (2007): 140–41.

32. Heschel, *The Prophets*, Perennial Classics (New York: HarperCollins,
2001), 15.

33. Picard, *Hitler in uns selbst*, 110.

Schuld" (see **P1**), Picard anonymized the good people, the "exceptions," who, according to him in a rather "self-contradictory" way, were most numerous in Germany: "In no country are there so many of these individuals as in Germany. . . . [They are] more integral (*vollkommener*) than those with integrity (*die Vollkommenen*) in other countries."[34] Was Picard unfair to the victims of German/Nazi aggression? Or was he unfair to the Germans in accusing them of having mounted no opposition at all to "the monument of evil"?[35] By our "standards of accuracy," he was probably both. But in centering his message on the possibility and necessity of repentance, that is, the enabled reconnection with God, and by directing this message toward his own (as European and Jew), he certainly belonged to the early turners in postwar Europe:

> Before one such man can be taught, he must first return and be *present* (*wieder* da *sein*). And he can only do that if he is connected with the one who is himself Presentness (*Daseinshaftigkeit*), with God.[36]

> [The intervention by God] is a sign that men and earth do not belong only to themselves, but to the One who loves them, who gives a chance to all again and again—probably also to the Germans.[37]

---

34. Ibid., 241.
35. Ibid., 250.
36. Ibid., 255. A similar anchoring presence of God was also emphasized by Jaspers, as when he concluded with an exegesis of Jeremiah's conversation with his servant Baruch (Jer 45): "What does it mean? It means, God is, that is enough. When everything disappears, God is, that is the only fixed point." Karl Jaspers, *Die Schuldfrage* (Heidelberg: Lambert Schneider, 1946), 105. Elsewhere he further elaborated that this "reality" is "the only reality" for someone who has tried their best but "failed" and "lost everything." Jaspers, *Einführung in die Philosophie: Zwölf Radiovorträge* (Munich/Zurich: Piper, 1989), 32. Without mentioning it, then, Jaspers and Picard are in fact reiterating the same affirmation that is also contained in the fifth Bußpsalm (Ps 102:27–28).
37. Picard, *Hitler in uns selbst*, 278. It seems at an early point that Picard was negating the possibility of repentance, when he said that "the structure of the [Nazi] world" had made turning (*Umkehr*) and change (*Wandlung*) impossible (ibid., 67). Yet in light of his entire work and his concluding affirmations quoted above, it is clear that he was not negating repentance per se, but a *shallow* turning (e.g., by "books and teaching") that overlooks the structural, societal, and even civilizational reach of disconnectedness.

This way of self-reflection in the face of wrongdoing against one-self was not a monopoly of one or two "exceptional" Jewish indi-viduals. A brief review of the postwar decades reveals many others who took a similar path,[38] that is, as victims or victimhood-bearers of German Nazism, seeing in the Holocaust their own guilt or a mirror for their guilt in their respective present situations. Already in the 1950s, Jewish historians such as Jon and David Kimche and Hans Günther Adler had written on aspects of Jewish culpability in Nazi atrocities against fellow Jews.[39] These had in turn provided Arendt in the 1960s the arguments she needed to bring Israel to court in the trial of Eichmann (see **P1**).[40] But perhaps the clearest echo of the early turners was provided by André Glucksmann, who, in 1989, published "Hitler bin ich" (I Am Hitler) in a compendium coinciding with the centenary of the birth of the dictator. Like He-schel and Picard, Glucksmann, whose antifascist Jewish family had suffered in Vichy France, wasted no time making the point that Hitler was an occasion for self-reflection, not others-blaming: "To ask oneself how Hitler was possible means to ask Europe how it has made him possible. That means, ourselves. . . . I am the possi-bility of Hitler, I am Hitler."[41]

---

38. The vast differences in terms of intellectual upbringing and political opinion of these individual voices, however, cannot be overlooked. See below.

39. Jon Kimche and David Kimche, *The Secret Roads: The 'Illegal' Migra-tion of a People, 1938–1948* (London: Martin Secker and Warburg, 1954); H. G. Adler, *Theresienstadt 1941–1945: Das Antlitz einer Zwangsgemeinschaft* (Tübin-gen: J. C. B. Mohr [Paul Siebeck], 1955).

40. Arendt cited the Kimches, for example, to argue that "these Jews from Pal-estine spoke a language not totally different from that of Eichmann," and that Jewish racketeers had unjustly profited from the plight of European Jews escaping Nazism. Hannah Arendt, *Eichmann in Jerusalem: A Report on the Banality of Evil* (London: Faber, 1963), 55–56. But in view of the entire work of the Kimches, it is arguable whether the authors were critically assessing the Zionists per se, or merely making claims against different groups in and outside Zionism (i.e., the Revision-ists, the religious Jews, etc.), so that some groups' "pact with the devil" was un-derstandable, and others' passivity vis-à-vis atrocity was not (Kimche and Kimche, *Secret Roads*, 26, 214). In any case, the objective facts unearthed and some per-spectives developed in these studies do lend themselves readily to serving as mate-rials for intra-Jewish self-reflection.

41. André Glucksmann, "Hitler bin ich," *Spiegel-Spezial*, no. 2 (1989): 73.

But unlike Picard, who considered the reconnection to God through Christianity as *the* turning needed for "the disconnected" in Europe, Glucksmann saw Christianity and humanism (at least the naive versions of these) as constitutive of the problem of Hitler: "This blindness vis-à-vis the evil outside us and in us, this incessant demonstration through our good feelings that devils do not exist, is this not exactly what made Hitler possible, because he was unforeseen by and unimaginable for the beautiful souls?"[42]

The turning that Glucksmann advocated was instead rooted in classical philosophy. Quoting the Socratic dictum "Know thyself," he blamed contemporary historians for lacking "the most elemental philosophical reflex of going into oneself (*Insichgehen*)"[43]—hence their inability to see "the same intellectual horizon" shared by the Nazis and the Bolsheviks. Yet this **going into oneself** does not mean a simple identification with Hitler, or his exculpation:

> That Hitler is my reflection (*Abbild*) does not mean that I concede that he had a sheep's soul under his wolf's skin. . . . To dig into the homogeneity between Hitler and me gives rise less to the better representation of him than he actually was, but more to the suspicion of myself, that *I bear evil in me*, which I don't prefer to know.[44]

For Glucksmann, philosophizing about Hitler does not mean to work out a philosophical system from Hitler as if he were a philosopher—which Picard had also warned against;[45] rather, it means "challenging the philosophers and common citizens to discover the Hitlerian side in themselves."[46] As democrat, Communist revolutionary, and Jew, Glucksmann then went on to demonstrate how each in turn could discover a Hitler in himself.

If it is remarkable for someone like Glucksmann—who has only childhood memories of Nazi Europe (he was born in 1937)—to relate in such a way to the Nazi atrocities as if he had to repent

---

42. Ibid.
43. Ibid., 74.
44. Ibid., 73 (emphasis added).
45. Picard, *Hitler in uns selbst*, 195.
46. Glucksmann, "Hitler bin ich," 73–74.

personally, then it is nothing short of extraordinary that even Jews born after the war should seek ways to relate to the Holocaust in the same spirit. In 2007, an Israeli from a German-Jewish family wanted to publish, in Hebrew, a book called "Hitler Won," for he "felt that the wounds and scars were so deep that the modern Jewish nation had no chance to heal. Our Shoah-inflicted trauma seemed like an incurable disease." The book came out, with a more hopeful title: "As it is Jewish custom to give the sick person a new name to facilitate his healing, I changed the book's title in Hebrew to *Defeating Hitler*."[47]

The author, Avraham Burg, was no fringe personality in modern Israel. Aside from being a former speaker of the Knesset and a former chairman of the Jewish Agency and World Zionist Organization, he was also, in the words of a bitter critic, "the scion of one of Israel's most renowned religious Zionist families, a son of the late revered Dr. Yosef Burg, who headed the National Religious Party for many years."[48] With such a curriculum vitae, it is no wonder that Burg's book was loathed by many for delivering weapons of delegitimization to the foes of the State of Israel.[49]

But what exactly can "defeating Hitler" mean for present-day Jews and Israelis? As one reads through Burg's book, two interrelated yet distinct issues become clear as Burg's deepest concerns: a certain way of remembering the Shoah that is ailing Israel's relationships with the peoples of the world,[50] and the **injustice committed by Israelis against the Palestinians.** Hence like Glucksmann and Picard, Burg saw this necessary fight against Hitler *within* rather than without.

Deploying caustic language, Burg lamented the phenomenon of the "Holocaustic soul,"[51] or a traumatized collective mentality

---

47. Avraham Burg, *The Holocaust Is Over; We Must Rise from Its Ashes*, trans. Israel Amrani (New York: Palgrave Macmillan, 2008), 6.

48. Isi Leibler, "Avraham Burg: The Ultimate Post-Zionist," *Jerusalem Post*, 24 Dec. 2008.

49. Ibid.

50. Burg, *The Holocaust Is Over*, 21–22.

51. Burg used "Holocaustic" several times in a critical manner in his book (*The Holocaust Is Over*, 17, 78).

that seeks self-justification in the traumas: "We cling to the tragedy and the tragedy becomes our justification for everything."[52] "All is compared to the Shoah, dwarfed by the Shoah, and therefore all is allowed—be it fences, sieges, crowns, curfews, food and water deprivation, or unexplained killings."[53] And although he explicitly rejected the comparison of modern Israel with Nazi Germany,[54] the time dimension was gradually loosened when names of peoples were used in a timeless manner:

Israeli Arabs are like the German Jews of the Second Reich.[55]

Arabs [are made to be] the heirs of the Jews.[56]

Are the writings on the wall "Arabs Out" and "Transfer Now" different in any way from *Juden raus* [Jews out]? . . . When a radio newsreader says, "An Arab has found death," what does it mean? That he lost death and IDF [Israel Defense Forces] soldiers helped him find it? What does it mean, "Soldiers fired in the air and two boys were killed"? That Palestinian children fly in the air like Marc Chagall creatures, and are hit by our innocent bullets? The dozens of cases of unidentified, unaccounted-for killings, to whom do they belong?[57]

Burg did not only see an image of the self, the Jew, in the other, the Arab, hence transferring the "victim-title" to the latter. He also attributed their victimization to the traumatic experience of having been victimized itself. Thus the message of **turning from the reaction of hate within** was Burg's special contribution. He used the psychoanalytical idea of *transference* to account for this, that is, the displacement of "our anger and revenge from one people to another, from an old foe to a new adversary."[58]

---

52. Burg, *The Holocaust Is Over*, 9.

53. Ibid., 78. A "crown," Burg explained, is Israeli military lingo, meaning "a stifling siege that leads to hunger, thirst, and desperation." Ibid., 61.

54. Burg, *The Holocaust Is Over*, 62.

55. Ibid., 55.

56. Ibid., 59.

57. Ibid., 64. See, for example, Chagall's *White Crucifixion* (1938).

58. Burg, *The Holocaust Is Over*, 79 (emphasis added).

It is chiefly in this *reaction* that Burg saw the "Hitler inside" who needs "defeating."[59] For example, following Arendt, he castigated the Israeli Law of Return, the origins of which were allegedly a reaction against the race laws of Nuremberg: "Until the link between Israeli citizenship and the Nuremberg Laws is severed, Hitler will in effect continue to decide who is Jewish."[60] He also criticized American Jews for their "obsession of exaggerated securitism" created by the "guilt complex over the Shoah,"[61] or the posthumous "influence" by Hitler.[62]

In the foreword to the German translation of his book, which appeared in 2009, Burg brought this theme of comparative spiritual warfare, from Germany to Israel, to the forefront, which was only briefly mentioned in the 2008 English translation:

> It was a spirit (*Geist*) that fed on a national trauma, on humiliation, which was inflicted on Germany by the victors of the First World War. . . . In this way, Germany became Europe's most deeply wounded and humiliated nation. . . . At the same time, a current of equality, freedom, creativity, brotherliness, and original thinking was under way. There was a contest . . . and at the end shame won the upper hand and national trauma defeated the current of hope. . . . In present-day Israel, such a contest between a gory national trauma and a new spirit of Jewish hope and Israeli spirituality is taking place. *The outcome of this competition is not yet decided.*[63]

Critics of Burg have called him a "self-hating Jew," or worse, an "opportunist."[64] Yet for two reasons, the charges of self-hatred and

---

59. See also his critique of intra-Jewish discrimination. Burg, *The Holocaust Is Over*, 29–31.

60. Burg, *The Holocaust Is Over*, 236. Arendt, to whom Burg dedicated his book, also objected to the alleged similarity between the rabbinical laws governing intermarriage and the Nuremberg laws. See Arendt, *Eichmann in Jerusalem*, 5.

61. Burg, *The Holocaust Is Over*, 40.

62. Ibid., 42–43.

63. Avraham Burg, "Vorwort zur deutschen Ausgabe," trans. Ulrike Bischoff, in *Hitler besiegen: Warum Israel sich endlich vom Holocaust lösen muss* (Frankfurt/New York: Campus, 2009), 18 (emphasis added).

64. Leibler, "Avraham Burg"; Inon Scharf, "Avraham Burg in München: Hitler besiegen," accessed 15 Mar. 2012, http://www.hagalil.com/archiv/2009/11/04/burg-4/.

opportunism seem unfounded. First and most important, a litmus test to distinguish a call to repentance from a definitive condemnation is the possibility of turning. Self-hatred (and other-hatred, too, in this limited sense) is precisely characterized by the nonrecognition of this possibility.[65] In this regard, Burg's *Defeating Hitler* is suffused with suggestions of turning; the quotation above is but one of many examples. Elsewhere, arguing from a religious standpoint, he called on his fellow Israelis to reflect on **Abraham's call to God to be a just judge** and their own present situation.[66] He then went on to use the biblical story of Jacob and Esau to present concrete choices to his Israeli readers,[67] imploring them to *return* to being more authentically Jewish rather than becoming more like the Gentiles. "We can defeat Hitler,"[68] Burg reaffirmed in conclusion.

Second, a hallmark of "representative repentance" is self-inclusivity, that is, a social/collective critique that is simultaneously self-blaming (see **R10**). Though again the ubiquitous "we" should suffice to bear this out, in several places in his book, Burg's admission of personal guilt was made even more explicit. For instance, in a section where he recounted an encounter with three Lebanese in which he felt "naked like Adam" as he realized his own guilt in their suffering, he wrote:

> How could it be that I never thought of my responsibility for their suffering? I am responsible, and I have an arsenal of excuses and arguments. . . . Except that when I am alone, as I was with [the Lebanese] in Jordan, I cannot and must not escape the bitter truth. *I must admit*

---

65. I asked Sander Gilman how one might incorporate the biblical idea of repentance in the study of the phenomenon of self-hating; he replied that whereas repentance always leaves room for the emergence of a new identity (see Buber on this point in **P6**), self-hatred does not. Cf. Sander Gilman, *Jewish Self-Hatred: Anti-Semitism and the Hidden Language of the Jews*, Softshell Books (Baltimore/London: Johns Hopkins University Press, 1992); and Robert S. Wistrich, "Jews against Zion," in *A Lethal Obsession: Anti-Semitism from Antiquity to the Global Jihad* (New York: Random House, 2010).

66. Burg, *The Holocaust Is Over*, 88.

67. Genesis 25–33. On the significance of this story in collective reconciliation, see **R14**.

68. Burg, *The Holocaust Is Over*, 232.

it. . . . We have to admit that, post-Shoah, we valued our lives because we wanted to live after so much death. We were not sufficiently sensitive to the lives of others and to the price that they paid for our salvation. *Please forgive us*, and together we will put an end to the unhealthy refugee mindset that torments us all.[69]

Burg also took personal responsibility for the killings of innocent Palestinians, which *"belong to us, to you and me."*[70] This self-inclusivity is all the more authentic when one takes into account that Burg was not somebody who had no personal attachments to the region, hence imposing moral burdens he could not jointly bear: aside from being an Israeli Jew himself, his mother's family had fallen victim to the Hebron massacre of 1929, a point that was not lost on his critics.[71] And when he complained of the problem of transference, he blamed himself for having contributed to prematurely forgiving the Germans, which had allegedly led to this problem.[72] Hence all in all, Burg's critique of Israel was very much a self-critique, not just finger-pointing or utilizing the "Holocaust club" to hit political opponents.

Because of this bond with his people, Burg was simultaneously "written off" and upheld by fellow Jews, so that even among those critics who found his book "exaggerating," some still recommended it as material for soul searching.[73] From the German-speaking world, Burg remarked that some Germans were amazed by the fact that such a debate in such a conflict situation could take place at all, and thus were impressed by the degree of openness in Israeli society.[74]

---

69. Ibid., 83–84 (emphasis added).

70. Ibid., 64.

71. See Leibler, "Avraham Burg."

72. Burg, *The Holocaust Is Over*, 78–79. It is clear, though, that Burg resented not the forgiving of the Germans per se—or else it would have run counter to his lavish praise in the book for German repentance efforts—but rather its unintended consequence of transference of emotional negativities to the Arabs.

73. Cf. Scharf, "Burg in München"; Leibler, "Avraham Burg."

74. "Gespräch mit Avraham Burg am 26. Oktober 2009," accessed 23 Jul. 2013, http://www.3sat.de/mediathek/mediathek.php?obj=15101&mode=play.

While it is still too early to gauge the full impact of Burg's confession in Germany, there are reasons to hope that such an act of self-turning on the part of the victims (or victimhood-bearers) will generate further repentant responses. After all, Heschel's speech in Frankfurt was able to inspire his German listeners to spread the message—despite the personal risks entailed.[75] It is further to be expected that, given the idea that even God could and did repent in the biblical narrative, the use of the Holocaust or Hitler as a mirror for one's own reflection or that of one's own society will continue to be a recurring theme in intra-Jewish and intra-Israeli dialogues. Although the individual turners' proposals for reform—especially in the political dimension—can be diametrically different at times,[76] their common point of departure in self-turning is unmistakable.

---

75. See Edward K. Kaplan, *Holiness in Words: Abraham Joshua Heschel's Poetics of Piety* (New York: State University of New York Press, 1996), 166.

76. The State of Israel and the geopolitical problems besetting it is one example: whereas Heschel saw its creation in general as a "concrete repudiation of Hitler's blasphemy" (Kaplan), Burg saw its own "re-creation" in a critical light, almost blasphemous because of its purported failure to fulfill the divine calling to become a "light unto the nations" in critical moments such as during the Eichmann trial. Glucksmann, on the other hand, was of the opinion that Israel's problems were not entirely in the hands of Israelis alone, and that the West should take a more active role in dealing with the authoritarian regimes in the region. Cf. Kaplan, *Holiness in Words*, 130; Burg, *The Holocaust Is Over*, 119, 139, 144; "Sehnsucht nach Entscheidungen: Interview mit André Glucksmann," *Der Standard*, 17 Apr. 2007.

12

"I Am Germany" (P10)

How many "bad Germans" are enough to prove that Germany is beyond the cure of repentance? For Victor Gollancz, who had fought a lone publicity battle against European apathy toward Jewish suffering during World War II, this was a nonquestion. "What Buchenwald really means" is precisely that not all Germans are guilty, he argued in April 1945, for many German opponents of Nazism had suffered persecution there as well (see P1): "Can you read the various stages of the argument I have tried to set out, and still believe that *all* Germans are 'guilty'? Surely it is not possible."[1] But even then, can one still conclude that since the German resisters were at best an *insignificant* minority, Germany was still guilty *in general*? To counter this line of thinking as well, Gollancz employed theological arguments to reject any

---

1. Victor Gollancz, *What Buchenwald Really Means* (London: Victor Gollancz, 1945), 14–16 (emphasis in the original).

pseudo-automatic minority/majority generalization. He argued that it is "utterly impossible for the Judaeo-Christian tradition ever to compromise with fascism," in the sense that the latter is susceptible to "depersonalisation" and abstractions like "State, Folk or Collective which men have created out of nothing," whereas the former adheres to "the ultimate reality [that] is the human soul, individual, unique, responsible to God and man."[2] He cited **Abraham's plea for the cities of Sodom and Gomorrah** as "the first great protest against the old blasphemy [of depersonalization]," and ended his pamphlet with a "salute . . . to these German heroes of Dachau and Buchenwald. . . [against] whom Hitler employed all his malice, but could not prevail. . . . for all will know some of these outcast Germans suffered more and suffered longer" than the Allied soldiers.[3]

Gollancz's "overestimation" of the few against the many was not at all a common standard among his contemporaries. For example, in June 1945 he received an antisemitic hate-mail from a "home-loving Briton" who accused him of being an "Anglophobe" and "un-British."[4] Yet at the same time, Gollancz could count support among Holocaust survivors who also subscribed to this **disproportional representation of the righteous.** A letter writer recounted his own memories of the "good Germans" during his persecution, and then concluded: "Nobody will ever persuade me that *all these men and women* (and *every* refugee knows *dozens* of those cases) are hopelessly wicked and deserve to be punished."[5] The extension from the few known and concrete individuals to the vague, uncertain many through association—and "exaggeration," most likely—is obvious, which strives toward the conclusion that the "few" rather than the "many" should carry more weight in the judgment of Germany as a whole, which should not be ruined like Sodom and Gomorrah, for the sake of the few righteous ones.

---

2. Ibid.

3. Ibid.

4. Ruth Dudley Edwards, *Victor Gollancz: A Biography* (London: Victor Gollancz, 1987), 403–4.

5. Ibid. (emphasis added).

Gollancz was not the only "Abrahamic advocate" for Germany around this period, but he was often the most obvious example of turners drawing directly from biblical sources of repentance when dealing with the German question. Another contemporary who displayed these Abrahamic tendencies—though not necessarily expressly so—was Joseph Rovan (P3). In a way that was similar to Abraham chiding God for "not being himself," that is, the just judge of the world, if he were to punish the righteous and the wicked indiscriminately, Rovan, coming straight from the Dachau concentration camp in 1945, reminded his French readers of the self-esteem and self-expectation that *the French* should have in their dealings with the Germans—righteous and wicked alike—who were now under their might in the French occupation zone. "The universalist vocation, *the real vocation of the French spirit*, seems to be sleeping. . . . Every Frenchman who is today responsible for a portion of Germany acts, judges, condemns, and governs *in the name of France*. How is his spirit being prepared for this office, for this responsibility?"[6]

Rovan, who was born in Munich as Joseph Rosenthal to a Jewish family, would later explain that his concern for Germany stemmed from the meaning that Gollancz had given to Buchenwald: "Precisely because we have suffered [in Dachau] . . . many of us shared the conviction that we owed *that* to our German comrades" who were already there.[7] In other words, for surviving victims like Rovan and the letter writer just quoted, the "minority of the righteous" has taken precedence over the majority of ordinary Germans—as bystanders and perpetrators—in the moral representation of Germany as a whole. It is "out of proportion," one might say. But it is also a representation that is chosen, not enslaved to given facts and established formulas.

---

6. Joseph Rovan, "L'Allemagne de nos mérites: Deutschland, wie wir es verdienen," In *Zwei Völker—eine Zukunft: Deutsche und Franzosen an der Schwelle des 21. Jahrhunderts* (Munich/Zurich: Piper, 1986), 90 (emphasis added).

7. Quoted in Martin Strickmann, *L'Allemagne nouvelle contre l'Allemagne éternelle: Die französischen Intellektuellen und die deutsch-französische Verständigung 1944–1950* (Frankfurt a.M.: Peter Lang, 2004), 98 (emphasis added).

The representative minority was not only used to convince the victims or victors of the redeemability or not-yet-forsakenness of the enemies, but was also deployed to **give hope to the "perpetrator nation."** In the concluding chapter of *SS-Staat,* Eugen Kogon (**P6**), survivor of the Buchenwald concentration camp, gave a sober assessment of German "individual guilt." Beginning with the cleric "who did not seek out opportunities to help," the judge "who did not prevent the condemned from becoming a concentration camp victim," to the physician, the journalist, the professor, the manager, and the worker, Kogon declared them all guilty of not having done his "true duty . . . for justice and freedom."[8] In the same breath that Kogon made this sweeping judgment, that every living German bore his own personal guilt, he also pointed to the hope that was made available to this majority by a minority who were no longer there—the German resisters who had attempted a coup on 20 July 1944. "Among the 5,000 men and women of all classes who were at that time arrested, there were the true martyrs for the German future.[9] They were the great example of ethical power and personal courage. This great meaning of their action is *not lessened* (*herabgemindert*) by the genuine German lack of that great political good sense. . . . Their example is not lost for the Germans."[10] Once again, the idea that the value of the minority is not to be relegated to a secondary status or even disregarded completely as "insignificant," just because it is the minority was brought forward

---

8. Eugen Kogon, *Der SS-Staat: Das System der deutschen Konzentrationslager* (Berlin: Druckhaus Tempelhof, 1947), 374–75 (emphasis in the original).

9. It is important to note that Kogon did not simply equate the "5,000 men and women" with "martyrs," only *some* among them. In both Judaism and Christianity, the idea of martyrdom is traditionally associated with the tenacious holding on to faith despite death, rather than with armed struggle per se, hence the long-standing tension with the purely nationalistic viewpoint. See the martyrdom of Rabbi Akiva (Ber. 61b) and of Rabbi Haninah (Avodah Zarah 18a), and that of Stephen (Acts 7). Reinhold Mayer, ed., *Der Talmud* (Munich: Orbis, 1999), 431, 437. See also the debates surrounding martyrdom and heroism in Israel in Roni Stauber, *The Holocaust in Israeli Public Debate in the 1950s: Ideology and Memory* (London: Vallentine Mitchell, 2007), 123.

10. Kogon, *SS-Staat,* 375 (emphasis added).

in a collective moral situation where outright condemnation or despair appeared to be the only logical outcome.

These turners who advanced the Abrahamic message of representative minority were also characterized by their **self-identification as a guilt-bearer among the guilty.** As has already been noted (**P6**), Kogon did not assume the position of a "pure victim" meting out a definitive judgment on the Germans, but always included himself in the community of Germans in his call for turning (which was certainly not mere rhetoric, considering the substantiation of this identification with his lifelong engagement in transforming postwar Germany as a German citizen). Rovan identified himself as "a Frenchman who was once a German."[11] Although these political and cultural paths of identification were not an option for Gollancz, he nevertheless appropriated the theological possibility of self-inclusion as a sinner among sinners and admonished his British audience to turn away from the prevailing (and condescending) self/other dichotomy:

> What we should be saying. . . [is] we have all sinned, and no one of us can cast stones. We in Britain have had a fortunate history, which has enabled us to win a large measure of freedom and democracy. Your history, on the other hand, has been unfortunate: when you have tried to advance to freedom and democracy circumstances have thwarted you, and the thwarting has weakened you in independence and civic courage—which is not to deny that there has been a *magnificent minority* that has stood firm against fearful odds.[12]

These were the occasions on which the turners acted as **the "perpetrator-nation's" advocates** in front of a "judging authority," at times reminding the latter that there is still a higher instance, at other times pleading with it for clemency. While Gollancz and Rovan were typical in their critique of the victors of Britain and France respectively, Kogon's approach was markedly different, as he faced a very different audience—the Jewish community remaining in Germany as well as Jewish communities around the world.

---

11. Joseph Rovan, *Erinnerungen eines Franzosen, der einmal ein Deutscher war*, trans. Bernd Wilczek (Munich: Carl Hanser, 2000).

12. Victor Gollancz, *Our Threatened Values* (London: Victor Gollancz, 1946), 28 (emphasis added).

In July 1949, Kogon spoke in Heidelberg at the first meeting of German Jewry since 1932 to discuss the future relations between Jewish and non-Jewish populations in Germany. According to the speaker himself, representatives of world Jewish organizations were among the audience, who actively took part in the discussions. In his speech, Kogon first reiterated the destruction that the Nazis had brought, and remembered the millions of Jewish victims—among them "four-fifths of Germany's Jewry"—who were murdered. He then presented a balance sheet of German guilt. As a persecuted resister himself, he first downplayed the significance of the resistance: "Only extremely few members of the German people have rendered active resistance. A larger number of Germans have, under great personal danger, helped and protected individuals of the persecuted. Many who saw the beginning or parts of the massacre were indignant inside. Not a few have approved of it, without fully realizing the extent of the events. The majority were more or less indifferent. Almost all kept silent, whatever the reasons."[13] Nazi destruction, German guilt, and postwar developments, including help from Jewish organizations abroad for Jews to migrate from Germany, had led to the grave situation that "no more than 20,000 [Jews chose to] remain behind, mostly old and weak Jewish people; the youths are almost gone."[14] Up to this point it was still unclear whether Kogon was primarily speaking as a Jewish Holocaust survivor (i.e., one among the audience) or as a German public intellectual (i.e., one among those being spoken about). But then he made a stunning remark:

Allow me to state this with terrible grief, that this decision [of leaving instead of staying], which is so understandable to you, means *the final triumph of Hitler*. What he wanted to do is now successfully accomplished. He who still is a National Socialist in this country may now rub his guilt-tainted hands.[15]

---

13. Eugen Kogon, "Juden und Nichtjuden in Deutschland," *Frankfurter Hefte* 4, no. 9 (1949): 727.

14. Ibid.

15. Ibid. See similar use of "victory of Hitler" by Arendt (**P1**) and Burg (**P9**). See alternatives in Hans Klee, *Wir Juden und die deutsche Schuld* (Lausanne: Granchamp, 1945), 13–16; Steven Katz, Shlomo Biderman, and Gershon Greenberg,

Kogon continued with an expressly German resolution that the care for "your remnants (*Ihre Zurückgebliebenen*)" in Germany should never be neglected by any living German. The self-identification of Kogon became unmistakable from this point on, as he pleaded with his Jewish audience to exercise the "extraordinary sense of right and wrong, which the Jewish character exemplifies," in tackling the ongoing problem of indiscriminate restitution of Jewish properties giving rise to new prejudices among the less initiated. "You will perhaps find a way . . . ," he suggested, "to eliminate these causes of disorder, by being superior to your opponents in moral terms, in helping the better principle of individual justice to achieve victory even in the smallest of things."[16]

Kogon's speech found approval in Jerusalem, when Martin Buber wrote to the *Frankfurter Hefte* on 21 September 1949, saying how "directly touched" he had been by Kogon's speech, more than any other letter or publication he had seen on the same subject matter, and called the speech a "human voice, vox realiter et essentialiter humana."[17] He further praised Kogon's efforts as publisher of the *Frankfurter Hefte*, which "makes it easier for me to think back to the city which has meant much for my life."[18] For more than a decade before the Nazis came to power, Buber had been active in Frankfurt, where he would return in 1953 to receive the Peace Prize of the German Book Trade, as Albert Schweitzer did before him (**P2**).

In his acceptance speech, Buber asserted that, as a survivor, to listen and to respond to such a "human voice," "vox humana," is a duty, for "genuine conversation among the peoples," rather than the "lonely monologue," is what is required in the struggle against the "demonic power of the sub-human, the anti-human."[19]

---

eds., *Wrestling with God: Jewish Theological Responses during and after the Holocaust* (New York: Oxford University Press, 2007), 103.

16. Kogon, "Juden und Nichtjuden in Deutschland," 728 (emphasis added).

17. Martin Buber, "Brief aus Palästina," *Frankfurter Hefte* 5, no. 1 (1950): 29.

18. Ibid.

19. Martin Buber, "Das echte Gespräch und die Möglichkeit des Friedens: Eine Dankesrede," accessed 18 Jul. 2013, http://www.friedenspreis-des-deutschen-buchhandels.de/.

He explained that the "gratitude" that was being expressed by the surviving Jew was intended as a "solidary confession to the common—also common between Germans and Jews—fight against the anti-human, and also the answer to the fighters' vow heard."[20]

In Buber's re-presentation of German society during the Nazi period, one can gain a glimpse of **the inner workings of the representative-minority paradigm,** which demonstrates how a certain minority is "magnified" so that it is more "magnificent" than even the majority itself. First he presented the "considerable number of German individuals (*deutsche Menschen*)," the "thousands" of them, who had participated in the murder of millions of his people. He could neither identify with, have hate feelings for, nor "forgive" this group of Germans. "Who am I to overestimate myself here to 'forgive'!"[21] Next Buber presented the "German people" (*deutsches Volk*), many of whom were aware of the atrocities at Auschwitz and Treblinka, but did not protest. "But my heart refuses—because it is aware of the weaknesses of human beings—to condemn my neighbor, just because he couldn't summon himself to become a martyr." Lastly, those who had "refused to carry out or pass on orders," and suffered death because of protest or despair, were presented. "I see these people *up close before me (ganz nah vor mir)*," said Buber, "and now awe and love for these German individuals reigns in my heart."[22] This "optical" presentation of German society with one's own viewpoint anchored in the "up-closeness" of the righteous minority necessarily conjures up images of sizes and weights quite different from those derived from, say, an "objective," distanced presentation of it, which projects the majority (i.e., Germans as accomplices and criminals) as the "bigger" part to look at and to draw definitive conclusions from. Buber's re-presentation thus furnished ultimately a possibility of seeing and weighing that would characterize a stream of postwar remembrance efforts centering on the "righteous among the nations" (**P13**).

---

20. Ibid.
21. Ibid. See similar positions in **P14**.
22. Buber, "Das echte Gespräch" (emphasis added).

Obviously, as is the case with many other turning acts on the side of the victims or victors, this "out-of-proportion" way of seeing the righteous as "representative" of the whole is *both* an enabling act of further mutual-turning gestures and a powerful temptation for the perpetrators or bystanders. Will postwar Germans not take it as a point of national pride that, as Rovan put it, German resisters were braver than all the rest? Or as might be inferred from Buber's re-presentation, only a handful of Nazis were contemptible, while the majority of Germans were "only" all too human in their weaknesses, and the German name deserves respect and honor because of the righteous Germans? There is therefore a need for "repentant disagreement" (P8). To actually "get" a turning message from one side, one often needs to "disagree" with it from the other. Hence it was left to German turners in their turn to respond to this representative-minority paradigm in specific configurations of audiences and contexts.

One of the German turners who took up this task was Martin Niemöller (P2). Through preaching and other public speeches, the former persecuted Nazi-opponent brought home to his German audience a particular way of interpreting and relating to the history of German minority resistance. On the occasion of the twentieth anniversary of the Attentat of 20 July, for instance, Niemöller spoke in Frankfurt about conscience and representation. "The victims of 20 July were representatives (*Stellvertreter*) for many," he declared. But immediately he added, "I'm not saying this to somehow reduce our guilt or the guilt of our people, whose members we were and are."[23] The "many" that he meant were the "Communists and Jews and Bible researchers,"[24] who had suffered "just as keenly as the dead of 20 July for their conviction and for their faithful demonstration of their co-human solidarity," an "elite of a special kind" whom his audience should not forget. For Niemöller,

23. Martin Niemöller, *Reden, Predigten, Denkanstöße 1964–1976* (Cologne: Pahl-Rugenstein Verlag, 1977), 28–31.

24. "Bible researchers," or *Bibelforscher*, was a designation used by the Nazis to label inmates in the concentration camps who were mainly members of Christian groups such as Jehovah's Witnesses and the Quakers.

the meaning of 20 July for Germans "today" was precisely in *emulating* the "representativeness" of this minority:

> They have not paid for a guilt/debt (*Schuld*) for which they alone were indebted (*verschulden*) and had by themselves amassed; they paid for the others, in order to help us. And what a blessing it could be . . . if we set our minds on what we ourselves could take up as our responsibility and load it upon our conscience *on behalf of* (*stellvertretend*) the others.[25]

In calling upon the church to take up more guilt than was due it, Niemöller was in fact asking his audience to accomplish two turning acts: first, to *persevere* in recognizing the guilt of Christianity; second, to counter the tendency of "unloading" one's own guilt onto the "guilty representatives," with its exact opposite—the self-offering of vicarious sacrifice.[26] To convince his listeners of the first duty, he consistently affirmed the existence of Christian guilt since the Stuttgart Confession of Guilt (**P2**). According to him, Christianity had—despite its representative minority of resisters—on the whole failed in its prophetic duty to stand up against the Nazis: "The sovereign claim of God . . . was not made in reality and with clarity perceivable by prophetic witness. *Attempts were made here and there, but all in all it must be said*: Christianity did not come out from its defensive position and was too weak and too timid . . . to proclaim in the authority of its prophetic mission: 'So says the Lord!' "[27] For Niemöller, even *his* Confessing Church, a minority of resisters against the absolute state power, was not without guilt for the lack of heroism; that was why "it was precisely the Confessing Church that in the October of 1945 insisted on the Stuttgart Confession of Guilt, in which we spoke out openly [against ourselves]."[28] On top of all this, he accused his minority of committing one fatal error—they thought they needed to "protect" the church, which actually wasn't in need of that, but their neighbors were:

---

25. Niemöller, *Reden, Predigten, Denkanstöße*, 30.
26. See **P6** and **P4**.
27. Niemöller, *Reden, Predigten, Denkanstöße*, 57 (emphasis added).
28. Ibid., 212.

We the Confessing Church . . . had to realize, though unfortunately too late, that we had let ourselves and our conducts be determined more by the enemies of the church than by the people who needed our help. At the end of the war, we had to state that—to my shame . . . the church does not need our protection, because the Lord, her Lord, sees to it that she remains; but the "neighbor," the person on our side, he needs us, we are there to do the service that he needs. But we had . . . cared more about the continual existence (*Weiterleben*) of the church than about the life, the true human life and survival (*Überleben*) of our fellow human beings. Looking back, I suppose I have to say that for me, as for so many other Christians, here is where the real guilt-consciousness originated.[29]

If, to follow Niemöller's appraisal of German Christianity during the Third Reich, even the Confessing Church had so much guilt to reckon with, how much more did the rest? This re-presentation was thus necessary to counter the latent danger of the representative-minority paradigm, namely, to "take shelter" under the righteous minority to avoid turning. In other sermons, Niemöller would expressly argue that **personal repentance is the beginning and essence of collective repentance.** Making use of the Protestant institution of the Day of Repentance (*Buß- und Bettag*), he elaborated on the relationship between personal and collective repentance: "We do not have to wait for the world to change, but we have to let ourselves be led by God's 'goodness, patience, and generosity' to repentance, so that God can use us as his salt to change the world. It is not about the repentance of our people, not the repentance of the peoples, not the repentance of the world, but it is about *my* repentance (*Buße*) and *your* repentance, *my* turning (*Umkehr*) and *your* turning."[30]

With these words Niemöller called on his Christian audience to repent, but not only for themselves as individuals, as in doing what is "enough" for oneself, but also to accomplish the second task, which is to repent *for* the world—that is, to be the change itself within a world that needs changing. These words coming from the

---

29. Ibid.

30. Ibid., 153 (emphasis added). See biblical references in Romans 2:4 and Matthew 5:13. For the idea of "assisted turning," see **R3**.

community of perpetrators and bystanders could sound hollow or even presumptuous, if not also self-congratulatory. But if we recall one of the central tenets of biblical repentance as "helping others repent" (**R7**), and the encouragement in this regard that Germans have been receiving from the victims (**P7**), then Niemöller's call, himself with every justification to claim victimhood under Nazism, could be appreciated as one of the turning voices in this relational context.[31]

This assertion again would also seem blatantly self-contradictory if we looked at the turner as a logician: if repentance has no proxy, then what sense does it make to speak about doing repentance for others "representatively" (*stellvertretend*)? But as has already been demonstrated (**P8**), a turner is not someone who is concerned about establishing universal principles that are valid for all, but someone concerned primarily about the relational direction of his particular audience in their particular situation: hence it is "valid" to urge postwar German Christians to atone *also* for the others, who are not willing to shoulder their own guilt, it is "invalid" for them to think *in reverse*, that is, to be the beneficiary rather than the benefactor, as one is allowed to do under the universal-principle mindset. Niemöller would probably have countered that, having *already* benefited from the vicarious sacrifice of the men and women of 20 July coup (and ultimately of Christ himself), postwar German Christians should have but one response of grateful self-giving.[32] It is no doubt a veritable double standard, but a **reverse double standard.**

Further from religious sermons and public speeches, the theme of representative minority could also be found in the arts and the most intimate private sphere. In one of his letters to Hannah Arendt in 1946, Karl Jaspers challenged his former student to see the "Hegelian thinking" in collectives that was purportedly undermining her otherwise "fantastic" reflections on Fascism and

---

31. See also Kogon's call to personal repentance ("your and my revolution") and reinterpretation of the failed coup on 20 July 1944 in his "Die deutsche Revolution," *Frankfurter Hefte* 1, no. 4 (1946): 17–26.

32. Niemöller, *Reden, Predigten, Denkanstöße*, 275.

antisemitism. In passing, he confided to her a personal example of breaking through this way of thinking:

> In the Nazi period I occasionally said to my wife, "I am Germany" (*Ich bin Deutschland*), in order to preserve our ground for the both of us. Such a statement has meaning only in the situation. The word becomes unbearably *demanding* (*anspruchsvoll*) when taken out of context or even passed on to the others. . . . Now that Germany is eliminated (*vernichtet*) . . . I feel for the first time uninhibited (*unbefangen*) as a German.[33]

The situation that Jaspers was referring to was of course a very intimate one—one that was between him and his Jewish wife, Gertrud Mayer, alone. Because of their marriage and Jaspers's refusal to annul it, the Heidelberg philosopher was not allowed to teach or publish at the height of Nazi terror, and had to live in constant fear of their being sent to the concentration camps.[34] The "inappropriateness" of claiming to be the nation itself, which was by then corrupt to the core, could only make sense under these relational circumstances. Yet in his *Schuldfrage,* which was going to print by the time he was writing Arendt, Jaspers would turn this personal example of representative minority into an argument for **doing collective repentance individually** as a "demand":

> We know ourselves not only as individuals, but as Germans. Each is—if he really is—the German people. Who does not know the moment in his life when he says to himself in oppositional despair of his people: I am Germany, or in jubilant unison with them: I, too, am Germany! The German has no other form than these individuals. Therefore the *demand* (*Anspruch*) of transformation, of rebirth, of purging the ruinous is a duty for the people in the form of a duty for each individual. Since I cannot help feeling collectively in the depth of my soul, being German for me, for everyone, is not an asset (*Bestand*) but a duty.[35]

---

33. Letter from Jaspers to Arendt, 27 Jun. 1946, in *Hannah Arendt Karl Jaspers Briefwechsel 1926–1969*, ed. Lotte Köhler and Hans Saner (Munich/Zurich: R. Piper, 1985), 82 (emphasis added).

34. See Suzanne Kirkbright, *Karl Jaspers, A Biography: Navigations in Truth* (New Haven, CT/London: Yale University Press, 2004), 183.

35. Karl Jaspers, *Die Schuldfrage* (Heidelberg: Lambert Schneider, 1946), 71 (emphasis added).

With a logic that borders on the mind-boggling, Jaspers breached the collective/individual dichotomy and asserted that repentance for a nation is a personal "demand" for each and every member of that nation, and that claiming to be the nation is no privilege or even arrogance, but the humble acceptance of a collective burden on one's own shoulders. It is a claim that is indeed "full of demands" (*anspruchsvoll*), though only at the opposite end of the give-and-take relationship. The philosopher himself conceded that reason alone might not be enough to lead one to this insight: "The given fact of being a German, which essentially means life in one's mother tongue, is of such a lasting effect that I feel—in a way that is no longer rationally comprehensible, or is even rationally refutable—co-responsible for what Germans do and have done."[36]

What a thinker was at pains to bring out in prose, a writer managed to use alternative means to express. If the idea of a representative minority is too difficult to justify rationally, or even outright offensive to the democratic ethos, then it is perhaps only understandable that fiction is employed to get it across. An example of this would be Rolf Hochhuth's *Stellvertreter*,[37] a play first published and staged in 1963. Ostensibly, the "representative" or deputy in the title meant only the head of the Catholic Church, Pope Pius XII, *the* representative of Christ on earth (*der Stellvertreter Christi*), who had died only a few years before the play was published, and whose (in)action during the Third Reich has long been a subject of debate.[38] In the historical drama, however, the various paradigms of representation, of representative seeking and being, were brought into contest through the mouths of different characters, some of whom, like Kurt Gerstein, were real historical figures, and others "pure inventions," according to the author. In one scene, for instance, the otherwise polite and thankful "Jacobson," a Jew

---

36. Ibid., 71–72.

37. Rolf Hochhuth, *Der Stellvertreter* (Reinbek bei Hamburg: Rowohlt, 1963).

38. See John Cornwell, *Hitler's Pope: The Secret History of Pius XII* (New York: Viking, 1999); Pinchas E. Lapide, *Rom und die Juden*, trans. Jutta Knust and Theodor Knust (Freiburg/Basel/Vienna: Herder, 1967); and David G. Dalin, *The Myth of Hitler's Pope: How Pope Pius XII Rescued Jews from the Nazis* (Washington, DC: Regnery, 2005).

under the protection of Gerstein in Berlin, belted out in a fit of fury, after learning that his parents had been "displaced," possibly to Auschwitz, that "*every* German is my enemy. . . . I will *never* forget the Germans, *all* Germans, that my parents—good Germans—were murdered here."[39] This **reverse representative-minority paradigm** is exactly what Gerstein was trying to ward off, as he had said just a few dialogues earlier in the same scene: "The traitors, they alone are the ones saving the honor of Germany now. For Hitler is not Germany, he is only its destroyer—the judgment of history will absolve *us* [the traitors]."[40]

The most striking model of representation, however, was put into the mouth of a fictional character, "Fr. Riccardo Fontana," an Italian Jesuit priest who had visited Germany and was troubled by his own conscience. In the second scene of the third act, which was set in the office of the superior-general of the Salvatorians, a religious order in Italy, who were engaged in saving persecuted individuals, including Communists and Jews, "Riccardo" argued vehemently with the abbot concerning the (mis)conduct of Pope Pius XII and what they could do, as mere priests, to rectify it. Counting on God's promise to Abraham that Sodom would not be destroyed for the sake of the ten righteous, the highly agitated, almost delusional Jesuit turned the representative-minority paradigm around into a principle of action:

> The silence of the pope, which is favorable to the murderers, saddles the church with a guilt (*Schuld*), which we have to atone (*sühnen*) for. And since the pope, who is but a human being after all, can represent even God on earth, so will I . . . so will a poor priest be able to, when push comes to shove, represent the pope—*there*, where he ought to be standing today.[41]

Hence in the words of "Riccardo," who acted as the plaintiff's voice against the pope's silence in the play, we have a reformulated representative-minority paradigm, one that does not exculpate its

---

39. Hochhuth, *Der Stellvertreter*, 73 (emphasis in the original).
40. Ibid., 65 (emphasis in the original).
41. Ibid., 124 (emphasis in the original).

bearer, but obligates him: **from letting the righteous minority represent oneself or one's "group" to becoming the righteous minority that represents.** Hochhuth himself certainly understood well the problem and limits of this kind of representation, which touches not only the past but also the present, as he, a young German Protestant then, hesitated in the beginning to write about and to criticize in no sparing language a Catholic pope: "As a Protestant I'm certainly a poor advocate for the Catholic Church. It is in any case an aesthetic imperfection (*Schönheitsfehler*) that I'm not a Catholic. Pius XII can in fact only be rightly judged from the viewpoint of the Catholic Church."[42] Yet it did not prevent him from assuming this Christian duty, when no Catholic was in sight to take that up in such a way that would so engage the Catholic German public. Though he was roundly criticized by some of his contemporaries for "shaming" a deceased pope, he was thanked by other Catholics for once again reminding them of their guilt.[43] Indeed, if "Riccardo's" claim of representing the pope is anywhere near the truth, then Hochhuth's play is as much anti-representative (with Pope Pius XII as the antagonist) as it is pro-representative (with "Riccardo" the protagonist, who ended up voluntarily wearing the *Judenstern* and died at Auschwitz). The *real* representatives of the Catholic Church upheld by Hochhuth were after all Fr. Maximilian Kolbe and Fr. Bernhard Lichtenberg—the real-life Riccardos—to whom Hochhuth dedicated his drama.

There has been, no doubt, also an inner-Catholic discussion in Germany regarding this subject, which can be traced back to the immediate postwar years. Both Walter Dirks and Eugen Kogon, for example, counseled fellow Catholics to engage in personal repentance instead of merely expecting reformation "from above" in the church hierarchy.[44] This initial emphasis, however, created

---

42. Quoted in "Mein Pius ist keine Karikatur," *Der Spiegel*, no. 17 (1963).

43. See a documentation of the controversy in Fritz Raddatz, ed., *Summa iniuria oder Durfte der Papst schweigen? Hochhuths 'Stellvertreter' in der öffentlichen Kritik* (Reinbek bei Hamburg: Rowohlt, 1963).

44. Eugen Kogon, "Das Porträt: Eugenio Pacelli—Papst Pius XII," *Frankfurter Hefte* 2, no. 2 (1947): 192–94; Walter Dirks, "Die geistige Aufgabe des deutschen Katholizismus," *Frankfurter Hefte* 1, no. 2 (1946): 38–52.

perhaps inadvertently, or even inevitably, a gap in postwar German Catholic reflection, namely, the critical assessment of papal failures during the Nazi period, which was filled, successfully or not, by Hochhuth's *Stellvertreter*. For if everyone should *only* mind his own guilt and own turning, then speaking of the guilt of a pope, a veritable "other" vis-à-vis the self, could only be seen as a suspicious diversion from tackling one's own guilt. If a German Catholic should delve deeper into the guilt of Pius XII, who was not even German, he was further to be exposed to the criticism of attempting to downplay "German" guilt.[45] In short, the hope for a "pitfall-proof" path of repentance seems to be in vain; every step forward has to be made in a moral minefield—whether real or only misperceived.

This shows once again that when deep motivations remain hidden from human view, the presence or absence of the corresponding repentant disagreements (R8)—whether within the German-Jewish, the Catholic-Protestant, or the lay-cleric relationships—can make or break a mutual-turning effort. For acts of turning are always risky for both the victims and the perpetrators: such acts run the risk of nonresponse, the risk of further damage, and the risk of abuse.

---

45. See in this respect the importance of contemporary Jewish appreciation of Hochhuth's intervention in Raddatz, *Durfte der Papst schweigen?* 151.

13

"Know before Whom You Will Have to Give an Account" (Pii)

In May 1988 the Jewish community in Germany was shaken to its core by a scandal that no one seemed to have had the least inkling of: it was discovered that Werner Nachmann, the former president of the Zentralrat who had passed away in January that year, had embezzled millions from German reparation payments, or the so-called Wiedergutmachung funds, dedicated to persecuted Jewish survivors.[1] Heinz Galinski, Nachmann's forerunner *and*

---

1. The particular fund in question was the so-called Hardship Fund (Härtefond), which was set up in 1980 to indemnify the Jewish survivors (estimated to be 80,000 in number) from the states of the Eastern Bloc, who could not otherwise claim reparations. While the actual fund, which amounted to 400 million DM, was not affected, proceeds from accumulated interests (e.g., through delayed transfers) became prey to Nachmann. The amount he pocketed was estimated at 33 million DM, the exact whereabouts of which remains unclear. On the concept of the Hardship Fund in historical context, see Constantin Goschler, *Schuld und*

successor, called the development "the gravest crisis since 1945."[2] Indeed, only a few months before, Galinski had spoken about the need for more "transparency" in Jewish life in order to fight prejudice.[3] Now his words were put to the severest of tests. It was feared that the scandal would spark a new wave of antisemitism and that even well-justified reparation measures would be indiscriminately affected in the future.

None of this came to be, however. The German press, with neither coordination nor external pressure, exercised remarkable moderation in treating this explosive and otherwise ruinous development. The major weekly from Hamburg, *Die Zeit*, ran at first only minimal coverage of the scandal, warning German readers—as if taking a page straight from the Diem-Thielicke book (P8)—that such an example of "human weakness" should not divert Germans from their own guilt: "The Jewish community must do all it can to clean up the table. . . . We, the others, however, have to watch out for self-righteous pharisaism. Nachmann has probably brought guilt upon himself. That does not lessen the guilt of the Germans."[4]

Antisemitism did flare up here and there on the margins, including the unsubstantiated accusation that Galinski might have embezzled more than Nachmann had.[5] But, by and large, as international observers noted, "the German press was extraordinarily restrained" in its handling of the Nachmann affair, which should have elicited a huge response in the media.[6] The sharpest critiques of the wrongdoer and the postwar German-Jewish establishment

---

Schulden: Die Politik der Wiedergutmachung für NS-Verfolgte seit 1945 (Göttingen: Wallstein, 2005), 357–59.

2. Quoted in Joachim Riedl, "Herrenloses Geld," *Die Zeit*, 27 May 1988.

3. Heinz Galinski, "Die Ehrung bedeutet vor allem Verpflichtung: Rede vor dem Berliner Abgeordnetenhaus am 26. November 1987," in *Aufbau nach dem Untergang: Deutsch-jüdische Geschichte nach 1945*, ed. Andreas Nachama and Julius H. Schoeps (Berlin: Argon, 1992), 82.

4. Th. S., "Gewissensgeld," *Die Zeit*, 20 May 1988. See also Hermann Rudolph, "Der Fall Nachmann und die Deutschen," *Süddeutsche Zeitung*, 19 May 1988.

5. "Im Bett des Führers," *Der Spiegel*, no. 23 (1988).

6. Y. Michal Bodemann, "Nachmann Scandal," *American Jewish Year Book*, 1990, 362–65. See also Serge Schmemann, "Germans Are Wary of Jewish Scandal," *New York Times*, 26 May 1988.

came, in fact, from Jewish and Israeli authors, with the voices of Henryk M. Broder and Maxim Biller among the most critical to be heard in this period concerning Jewish and Israeli issues related to the Nachmann scandal.[7]

In a wide-ranging article built on this theme that was published in *Die Zeit* in 1989, Broder called attention to a problem that he called **"the victims of the victims."** "Without Hitler," began his article, "Berlin would still be the capital of the German Reich . . . and Werner Nachmann would never have [had] the chance to embezzle millions from the reparation funds."[8] The son of Jewish Holocaust survivors himself, Broder first rebelled against the survivor generation for making unbearable demands on their children. Already before Martin Walser, Broder complained about the "Holocaust club" (**P7**): "It pissed me off that I could not lead a life like my non-Jewish friends, whose parents were entirely normal in their unbearability and not so burdened like mine, who dragged out the concentration camp club (*KZ-Keule*) even on the most trivial occasions."[9] Broder lamented the "continuation of the victim role," which was, according to him, implicit in the uncritical use of the "second generation" label for the children of Holocaust survivors.

Like Broder, Biller used the Nachmann affair to call on his fellow "second generation" Jews to engender a new, critical attitude toward their own "victimhood" and the other's "perpetratorship." He went even further—or too far—coining the term "Nachmann-Jews" (Nachmann-Juden), which he used to attack postwar German Jews, whom he accused of being self-centered and minding their own business while living in cozy but suffocating ghettos: "Not without reason are they called Nachmann-Jews. They speculate—crafty and circumspect and opportunistic—with the bad conscience of the Germans, exploiting it intellectually and

---

7. See, for example, "Amnon, die Katze," *Der Spiegel*, no. 24 (1988); and Henryk M. Broder, "Rehabilitiert Werner Nachmann," in Nachama and Schoeps, *Aufbau nach dem Untergang*, 299–303.

8. "Die Opfer der Opfer," *Die Zeit*, 14 Jul. 1989.

9. Ibid.

materially. Unscrupulously they milk the Holocaust cow."[10] The author derided his fellow Jews for wielding the "Auschwitz hammer" even against their own rebellious children who wanted a life away from the "ghetto-and-money insipidity."[11]

While one can rightfully object to Biller's and Broder's unsavory language and sweeping generalizations, an important contribution of these young and iconoclastic Jewish writers was their insistence that the **absolution of guilt can neither be bought nor sold.** For long before the Nachmann affair erupted, Broder, together with Michel R. Lang, had already called attention to this problematic German-Jewish "exchange" or "symbiosis." They condemned the practice of Jewish representatives in Germany, whom they attacked as "alibi-Jews" (Broder) or "functions-Jews" (Lang). "They consider themselves as simultaneously an entourage of the Israeli Foreign Ministry and a mouthpiece of German interests. . . . It is symptomatic of the intellectual and political disintegration of the Jewry in the Federal Republic that [Werner Nachmann] and his colleagues can go on speaking in the name of the Jews."[12] These Jewish speakers, according to Broder, were so "busy maintaining contacts with their German patrons" that they neglected the duty of speaking out against them when there was a real cause to do so.[13] Likewise, Biller disparaged their "appeasement policy," which allegedly found an enthusiastic reception among the German Christian parties.[14] "The Germans," said Broder provocatively, "*have* gotten the Jews that they need and deserve."[15]

Of course, whether the Jewish presence and engagement in postwar Germany was a genuine exercise of mutual-turning or, as

---

10. Maxim Biller, "Die Nachmann-Juden," in *Tempojahre* (Munich: Deutscher Taschenbuch, 1991), 173.

11. Ibid.

12. Michel R. Lang, "Fremd in einem fremden Land," in *Fremd im eigenen Land: Juden in der Bundesrepublik*, ed. Henryk M. Broder and Michel R. Lang (Frankfurt a.M.: Fischer Taschenbuch Verlag, 1979), 266–67.

13. Henryk M. Broder, "Warum ich lieber kein Jude wäre; und wenn schon unbedingt—dann lieber nicht in Deutschland," in Broder and Lang, *Fremd im eigenen Land*, 98.

14. Ibid.

15. Ibid., 96 (emphasis in the original).

Broder, Biller, Lang & Co. had charged, some sort of magnanimity for sale, was seldom clearly differentiated. The Nachmann affair was the rare instance in which the two were plainly distinguished. We *now* know there is a difference, but that is only with the benefit of hindsight. What is more apparent is that there have been self-critical Jewish voices against real or suspected abuses, and such voices have helped Germans deal with the challenge of their own turning efforts: rather than doubting or even reversing their own turning ("Why pay reparations to scoundrels?"), they could go further with the reassurance that the necessary turning from abuse on the side of the victims has *already* been taken care of (though not necessarily accomplished).[16] One can only imagine a different outcome of the Nachmann affair, had German Jews been less forthcoming or more self-defensive than self-critical, so that a scaling back in repentant vulnerability (**R3**) would have become inevitable on the side of the perpetrators.

If absolution cannot be purchased with money, then neither can guilt be released by another guilt. The idea that injustice is not "evened out" by another injustice, or that **the perpetrator's guilt is not canceled out by the victim's guilt**, also found expression in the discourse about another abuse of the "perpetrators"—the crimes of the Red Army against defeated Germans, especially German women.[17] In Lev Kopelev's "confession," published in 1977 (see **P7**), the former Red Army soldier tried to relate the crimes of the "Hitler State" and the revenge that even "innocent Germans" in the East were not spared. His point, however, was not that since both had done wrong to each other, each should therefore shake each other's hand, and "forget and forgive." To the contrary, for "the reasons and causes can only explain the blind rage and cruelty of this pogrom, not justify it. *Much less can it wipe out or*

---

16. This can be seen in the German press coverage of the Nachmann affair cited above, which generally focused on the factual details of the case and on how Germans should and should not react to it, while leaving the more critical comments to Jewish voices themselves as a sign of reassurance.

17. On the crimes of rape by Soviet soldiers, see Norman M. Naimark, *The Russians in Germany* (Cambridge, MA: Belknap Press of Harvard University Press, 1995).

even lessen the guilt of those who had taken part in the far more cruel acts of retaliation."[18] By that Kopelev meant the Germans and Nazis who were responsible for the massacres and destruction in Lidice and Oradour-sur-Glane (P3). It was with this "relatively late realization" that the Russian-Jewish writer came to the conclusion that neither Hitler's guilt could justify Stalin's, nor could Stalin's guilt justify his own. He spoke of "my co-perpetratorship" (*Mittäterschaft*), having been a convinced follower of Stalin, and of "my guilt [that] remains inextricably bound with me."[19] In short, the mutual cancellation of national guilt thesis was for Kopelev as antithetical to the spirit of confession as the rejection of one's own guilt because of the guilt of the others.

In his book *Aufbewahren für alle Zeit* (To Be Preserved Forever), which was hailed by Marion Dönhoff as "the first work appearing in the West presenting the view of a Russian going through the Russian victory in East Prussia,"[20] Kopelev reflected on **the abuse of the Germans by the Russians,** and asked how it was possible at all that "so many of our soldiers turn out to be base bandits."[21] In the spirit of "representative repentance" (P11), Kopelev sought an explanation for this "possibility" in his own guilt, although he had actually tried to stop the atrocities and been convicted of "bourgeois humanism" as a result (P7):

> Have we not educated them that way, we, the political workers (*Politarbeiter*), the journalists, the writers . . . industrious, ambitious, but also gifted agitators, teachers, educators, earnest preachers of "holy vengeance"? We taught them to hate, convinced them that the German is evil just because he is German; we glorified death in poetry, in prose, and in paintings. . . . There was a time when I almost felt ashamed of not having a "personal ledger" of murdered Germans. . . . All these must be contemplated. Where did it come from, and where does it lead?[22]

---

18. Lev Kopelev, "Bekenntnisse eines Sowjetbürgers," *Die Zeit*, 11 Feb. 1977 (emphasis added).

19. Ibid.

20. Marion Gräfin Dönhoff, "Mitleid mit den Deutschen: Neun Jahre Gefängnis," *Die Zeit*, 6 Feb. 1976.

21. Lev Kopelev, *Aufbewahren für alle Zeit*, trans. Heddy Pross-Weerth and Heinz-Dieter Mendel (Hamburg: Hoffmann und Campe, 1976), 16–17.

22. Ibid.

Fast-forward one generation, and another Jewish turner would follow in Kopelev's footsteps in contemplating the "coming and going" of victim and perpetrator roles in a context entirely different from that of the Soviet confessor's, contexts that were linked only by the Nazi past and the idea of victim-turning-perpetrator. The occasion was the 2006 Lebanon War. Rolf Verleger, a professor of psychology at the University of Lübeck and son of Holocaust survivors, went public to question the allegedly unquestioning allegiance of ZdJ to Israeli policies. While German-Jewish critics of Israel and Israeli politics were not lacking, Verleger's charge was particularly embarrassing for the ZdJ because he was at the time a member of its directorate.[23] In his original, internal letter dated 23 July 2006 to the top leadership of the Central Council, which would be published on 8 August, the then chairman of the Jewish community in Lübeck expressed that he "cannot and will not remain silent" about the Central Council's open support for the "military measures of the Israeli government against Lebanon."[24] He affirmed the need for solidarity with Israel, but interpreted it as a duty to criticize the "misguided path" the nation was purportedly following. Like the late Yosef Burg, Verleger saw the postwar convalescence of the German-Jewish relationship as hope and a road map for contemporary conflicts between Israel and its neighbors.[25] Further, in the same letter, the religiously active Jewish intellectual admonished his colleagues in the Central Council for forgetting the perennial conflict between Jewish religion and nationalism, between "our prophets and the kings of Judah and Israel," resulting in the one-sided support for the political establishment.[26]

In a book following his "unsuccessful" attempt to turn fellow Jews *and* Germans away from what he perceived to be the misguided path of Israeli politics, Verleger drew support from the

---

23. Verleger would eventually lose his official positions.

24. Documented in Rolf Verleger, *Israels Irrweg* (Cologne: PapyRossa-Verlag, 2008), 74–78.

25. Verleger, *Israels Irrweg*, 77. Cf. Avraham Burg, *The Holocaust Is Over; We Must Rise from Its Ashes*, trans. Israel Amrani (New York: Palgrave Macmillan, 2008), 81.

26. Verleger, *Israels Irrweg*, 77–78.

biblical idea of **triangulation**: that victim and perpetrator do not stand only in a bilateral relationship, but each must also give an account of his deeds and treatment of the other before his God:

> "Know whence you have come. And where you go. And before whom you have to give an account in the future." This motto was given by a teacher by the name of Akabia ben Mahalalel.[27]

Verleger sought to offer his personal answer to the question of being Jewish and pro-Israel to "other Germans" confused by their own attitudes toward Israeli policies and toward the Jewish people.[28] Yet his words also carried weight because of his family history and family connections in contemporary Israel. Therefore, when he criticized Israeli policies, he was not doing so as an unconcerned or even indifferent observer with nothing to lose. In response to disapproval of his critiques of Israel, he would often bring his family history to bear on his claim. In late 2006, for instance, Verleger started a publicity campaign in Germany for ending Israeli injustice against the Palestinians, which drew some support from Jewish and Israeli circles there.[29] A German-Protestant theologian engaged in Christian-Jewish dialogue, however, was "angered" by the presentation of Middle East conflicts with Israel shouldering all the guilt.[30] Verleger responded to this critic by recounting how the injustice his own great-grandfather had suffered in Nazi Germany (i.e., from the "Aryanization" of Jewish property) was *successfully* dealt with when (East) German authorities owned up to their guilt. In the same way, Verleger claimed, "one could make peace in Palestine: recognition of the dignity of the Palestinians, admission of the immense injustice of expulsion, indemnification of the loss of property."[31]

---

27. Ibid., 4.
28. Ibid.
29. See Verleger, "Schalom 5767," in *Israels Irrweg*, 94–102.
30. Hartmut Metzger, "Wie kann es Frieden geben für Israel und Palästina? Das Friedensrezept der 'Berliner Erklärung' stimmt schon im Ansatz nicht," *Rundbrief des Denkendorfer Kreises für christlich-jüdische Begegnung*, 5 Feb. 2007.
31. Verleger, *Israels Irrweg*, 158.

In his most direct attack on the **nationalistic transference of vic-timhood** to date, Verleger took issue with another Jewish "function-ary," Ronald S. Lauder, president of the Jewish World Congress. Lauder had written an op-ed in the *Süddeutsche Zeitung*, in which he tried to connect the duty toward Holocaust victims to the respon-sibility toward a threatened Israel, and criticized the "self-fashioned good people in Europe," who had rejected the Zionist state and used "much more stringent standards" than usual in evaluating Israeli policies.[32] Verleger penned a passionate rebuttal, entitled "Haben Opfer das Recht, Unrecht zu tun?" (Do Victims Have the Right to Do Wrong?), questioning the very foundation of this self-victimizing nationalism. First, he reiterated the triangular vision of accountabil-ity as the "ethics of Jewish religion," which he contrasted with the "alternative ethics" allegedly propagated by Lauder in his essay, in which purported national victimhood takes center stage.[33] He then turned to his own family history to refute the transference of victim-hood and the justification of wrongdoing through it:

I would like to ask Mr. Lauder: The fact that none of my grandparents had survived the Third Reich—did it give the Jewish militia and the Is-raeli army the right to expel in 1947/48 hundreds of thousands of Arabs from Israel?

The Aryanization of my great-grandfather's land in Berlin—did it give the State of Israel the right to confiscate in the 1950s the land and property of the Arab expellees?

The murder of my uncles and aunts by the SS—does it give the State of Israel the right to exercise dictatorship as a regime of occupation for the past forty years?

The shooting of my grandmother Hanna for going to the hairdresser in Berlin without wearing the yellow star—does it give the State of Israel the right at present to starve the population of Gaza?

Generally speaking: Does the fact that we European Jews became victims of an immense injustice give the right to the Jewish state *before God and before man* to do injustice to the others now?[34]

32. Ronald S. Lauder, "Sonntagsreden und Montagstaten," *Süddeutsche Zei-tung*, 25 Jan. 2008.

33. Rolf Verleger, "Haben Opfer das Recht, Unrecht zu tun? Zur 'Außenan-sicht' vom 25.1.2008 ('Sonntagsreden und Montagstaten')," *Süddeutsche Zeitung*, 9 Feb. 2008.

34. Verleger, *Israels Irrweg*, 160 (emphasis added).

To be fair, Lauder did not identify himself and fellow living Jews (except survivors) as victims in his essay. Rather, he always spoke of "our debts" toward the victims of the Shoah, thus distancing himself and his audience from them. But the critical distance between the real victims and the State of Israel demanded by Verleger was indeed missing.

Verleger's central contention—that injustice suffered does not justify injustice done by the "victims"—was also the outcry of another group of victims who felt that their plight had long been neglected in postwar Germany. The German refugees and expellees from the former eastern territories (**P4**) were the veritable embodiment of the identity-boundary-overlapping "perpetrator-victim." Culturally and politically, their name was bound to a "perpetrator-nation" whose "political guilt"—to follow Jaspers (**P2**)—was beyond doubt. But personally, each of these expellees (especially German women and children) had experienced wrongdoing at the hands of the "victims" or victors that were—to follow Verleger—nowhere near justified or proportionate. Their **struggle for justice and truth as the "abused perpetrator"** would thus illustrate yet another aspect of the complex phenomenon of shifting victim/perpetrator roles.

In August 1950 the elected representatives of the German expellees produced a charter that exemplified certain elements of the seventh Bußpsalm, or the psalm of the abused sinner.[35] "Conscious of their responsibility before God and man," began the charter, following the preamble of the new German constitution (1949), "the elected representatives of the millions of expellees (*Heimatvertriebener*) have decided to make this solemn declaration that lays down the *duties and rights* that the German expellees consider as their *basic law* and indispensable prerequisite for the creation of a free and unified Europe."[36] The first article of the charter dealt with the renunciation

---

35. Psalm 143.

36. "Charta der deutschen Heimatvertriebenen," in *Die völkerrechtlichen Irrtümer der evangelischen Ost-Denkschrift*, by Ausschuß für gesamtdeutsche Fragen (Bonn: Bund der Vertriebenen—Vereinigte Landsmannschaften und Landesverbände, 1966), 29 (emphasis added).

of "revenge and retaliation." It hinted at the wrongfulness of all by referring to the "endless suffering that was visited upon humanity especially in the last decade." While committing themselves to peace and reconstruction, the expellees also demanded what they perceived to be divine justice: "We have lost our homeland. . . . God has placed man in his homeland. To separate him by force from his homeland is to kill him in spirit. We . . . demand that the right of homeland (*Recht auf die Heimat*) be recognized and realized as one of the fundamental rights granted by God."[37]

While the "right of homeland" and its purportedly divine origins were greatly contested by fellow Germans,[38] no one could deny the suffering that these expellees had experienced, which was not even mentioned in the charter. The massive sexual abuse by Red Army soldiers described by Kopelev was only part of the ordeal; the summary killings, torture, and humiliation of ethnic German populations by Polish and Czech "neighbors" were so shocking that even the Russians were alarmed.[39] On top of these was the unbearable—if any of these actions were bearable—hypocrisy that the "new perpetrators" sometimes displayed. As the expulsion took place in Brno (Brünn) in May 1945, a Czech remarked to the persecuted Germans, "That's how you have done it to the Jews," only to receive a retort from a German neighbor who asked which of them had taken pleasure from it.[40] By the end of the expulsion

---

37. Ibid., 30.

38. The EKD *Ostdenkschrift* of 1965, for example, concluded, after attacking the "pseudo-religious character" sometimes given to "homeland" (*Heimat*), that "God is not bound to the gift of homeland that he has once granted. . . . A relationship with the homeland based on faith in God should make Christians ready to renounce it (*Verzicht*) just as they have to be obedient in the use of its resources." The Bensberger Memorandum of 1968 reinforced this by proposing that through proactively making such a decision, "we are demonstrating not our powerlessness, but our sovereignty." See *Ostdenkschrift*, 33–34; and Bensberger Kreis, *Memorandum*, 20.

39. See the description of these paradoxical roles of the Russians in Germany in Norman M. Naimark, *Fires of Hatred* (Cambridge, MA: Harvard University Press, 2001); and Benjamin Lieberman, *Terrible Fate: Ethnic Cleansing in the Making of Modern Europe* (Chicago: Ivan R. Dee, 2006).

40. Lieberman, *Terrible Fate*, 237. In this sense, it is perhaps not even appropriate to speak of the "victim turning into perpetrator," but rather, the "new

process, which lasted roughly from 1944 to 1950, an estimated 12 million ethnic Germans had been displaced.[41]

Though the outside world was not unaware of or unconcerned about these abuses,[42] the wounds that these expellees carried with them from the East could last decades, or even a lifetime. A young German girl named Hannelore Renner living in Döbeln, who was born just after the Nazis had risen to power, was fleeing to Leipzig with her mother in May 1945 when she was waylaid by some Russian soldiers, who raped and injured her. She was only twelve. She kept her pain to herself, shunned contact in school, and worked hard for her own and her family's existence. Decades later, her husband, Helmut Kohl, chancellor of the Federal Republic of Germany (1982–98), signed the "Treaty of Good Neighborliness" with the Soviet Union, which sought to "settle with the past for good," and in which the German side promised to "respect and protect . . . the monuments on German soil that are dedicated to the Soviet victims of war and of tyranny."[43] As first lady, Hannelore Kohl had to perform a variety of semiofficial duties; these included commemorating the fallen Red Army soldiers together with the wife of Mikhail Gorbachev in Stukenbrock in 1989. According to her biographer, this "program" was a huge burden for the chancellor's wife:

> She kept her composure and let none notice what went on in her inner being. . . . A change in the ladies' program would be possible but very difficult, and would only have led to irritation. No one could have any idea what kind of memories would come up for the wife of

perpetrator." Naimark also found the Polish behavior against the Germans more understandable than that of the Czechs, who "did not suffer terribly at the hands of the Germans, certainly not in comparison to the Poles." See Naimark, *Fires of Hatred*, 14, 122.

41. See the contested nature of the estimates in Eva Hahn and Hans Henning Hahn, *Die Vertreibung im deutschen Erinnern: Legenden, Mythos, Geschichte.* (Paderborn: Ferdinand Schöningh, 2010), 657–78.

42. Ibid., 361–62.

43. Preamble and Art. 18 of the German-Soviet Treaty of 1990: "Vertrag über gute Nachbarschaft, Partnerschaft und Zusammenarbeit zwischen der Bundesrepublik Deutschland und der Union der Sozialistischen Sowjetrepubliken vom 9. November 1990," *Bulletin des Presse- und Informationsamtes der Bundesregierung*, no. 133 (1990): 1379–82.

the chancellor. . . . The visit to the cemetery revived old trauma, the memory of powerlessness and of being at the mercy of others. . . . The strength that Hannelore had to call up in order to keep going and to finish the rest of the program was enormous. . . . She allowed herself—as always—to betray nothing, she had to hide, to repress, and to exercise the utmost discipline.[44]

The first lady chose to keep everything to herself and her few confidants. It was only after her death that German citizens learned about her ordeal.[45] The tragedy of Hannelore Kohl's life was only one of the better-known cases in which the problem of guilt and atonement assumed intellectually insurmountable dimensions. Hence it was not insignificant that part of the German expellees' charter of 1950 was expressly directed at the problem of **disproportionate allocation of atonement** in (West) Germany. "We demand . . . the same rights as citizens, not only before the law, but also in the reality of daily life. . . [as well as] the just and reasonable *distribution of the burden* of the last war to the entire German people."[46] While the *internal* guilt that the nonexpellee Germans bore in comparison to that borne by the German expellees was a major theme of the EKD's *Ostdenkschrift* of 1965 (**P4**), concern for the expellees' plight in the "reality of daily life" found expression in the early 1950s in a German-Jewish author's short stories. Anna Seghers, an active member of the exiled German resistance during the Nazi years who was best known for her wartime novel, *The Seventh Cross* (1942), published a series of "peace stories" (*Friedensgeschichten*) in 1952–53 in Berlin, which portrayed ordinary individuals in postwar Germany. One of Seghers's characters was Anna Nieth, the "repatriate" (*Umsiedlerin*), a German

---

44. Heribert Schwan, *Die Frau an seiner Seite: Leben und Leiden der Hannelore Kohl* (Munich: Wilhelm Heyne Verlag, 2011), 218–19. See also a contemporary report of the visit, "Der Kremlchef muß am Rhein regieren," *Der Spiegel*, no. 24 (1989).

45. According to Schwan, Hannelore Kohl had never publicly spoken about her own trauma of rape. It was only after years of confidence earned as a trusted friend and trustworthy journalist that the biographer was able to confirm this rumored tragedy with her. Schwan, *Die Frau an seiner Seite*, 7–10, 56.

46. "Charta der deutschen Heimatvertriebenen," 30 (emphasis added).

widow with two children who had to leave her province because of the entry of the Poles. She ended up in a small village called Lossen (possibly the village of that name in Göhren, Thuringia, then part of East Germany), where "after three years she felt as bad as on the first day."[47] Her involuntary caretaker was as uncaring as he was embittered (he had lost his son in the war); the house dog was the only one that was good to her children.[48] The villagers appeared no better. Though living standards had improved for most, Nieth "withered" in a joyless life in her new "home"—a storeroom with her kids, separated like the other repatriates from the locals, especially the rich farmers and the mayor. It was only at the invitation of a district administrator of the working class that Nieth, who was otherwise resigned to her fate, was able to voice her complaints before all the villagers, and thus changed her fate. "When I arrived here, I was crammed into a dump hole with my kids, and I have lived as if in a stall for pigs, and I still live as if in a stall for pigs. I have nothing more to say."[49]

Seghers's *Umsiedlerin* marked the beginning of a literary tradition in East Germany dealing with the problems of integration faced by the German expellees.[50] Although the more gruesome wrongdoings that the expellees had experienced at the hands of the Red Army soldiers were not mentioned (for obvious reasons in the case of someone like Seghers, who was writing and publishing in the DDR), the fact that a German Jew who had herself suffered in escaping the Nazis chose to write on this of all themes made her story particularly poignant. Indeed, as a contemporary literary critic put it, "When it is an embarrassment for Eastern interpreters that Anna Seghers always makes the persecuted and the victims her main characters . . . it is in fact the strength of this author: she writes best when she is indignant."[51] That a victim can become indignant about the injustice suffered by the perpetrator is, of course,

47. Anna Seghers, "Die Umsiedlerin," in *Anna Seghers Gesammelte Werke in Einzelausgaben* (Berlin: Aufbau-Verlag, 1977), 10:272.

48. Ibid., 273. Cf. Luke 16:21.

49. Seghers, "Die Umsiedlerin," 277.

50. Hahn and Hahn, *Vertreibung im deutschen Erinnern*, 578.

51. Rolf Michaelis, "Die Kraft der Schwachen," *Die Zeit*, 10 Jun. 1983.

not at all self-explanatory—even through the prism of the usual left-right political schema.

While fiction can at times lead its readers to see the real problems around them, arouse concern where it is lacking, and frame perspectives of turning where they are hidden, as Seghers's does, it can at other times undermine the weight of reality and turn concerned readers away. And, indeed, a Nachmann-like scandal broke out in the German-reading world of the mid-1990s that threatened to undo the goodwill of Germans and German-speaking nationals toward the survivors of the Shoah. In August 1995, the German publishing house Jüdischer Verlag (a division of Suhrkamp) rolled out a book by an unknown Swiss author, "Binjamin Wilkomirski," that would become a publicity sensation in the three years that followed. The title of the book was *Bruchstücke (Fragments)*, and its author presented it as a first-person narrative of a Jewish child who had survived the Nazi concentration camps. "I wrote these fragments of memory to explore both myself and my earliest childhood," said the author in the afterword.[52] The book would go on to receive distinguished awards (including the National Jewish Book Award in New York), and the author himself would earn a great deal of sympathy from a global readership.[53] All went exceptionally well for the debut of an amateur author except for one thing—the book was anything but a memoir, and the author anyone but a Holocaust survivor.

Although even before the book's publication the authenticity of Wilkomirski's identity had been questioned *internally* within the publishing house,[54] it took the courage and persistent investigation

---

52. Binjamin Wilkomirski, *Fragments: Memories of a Wartime Childhood*, trans. C. B. Janeway (New York: Schocken, 1996), 155. The book was originally published in German as *Bruchstücke: Aus einer Kindheit 1939–1948* (Frankfurt a.M.: Jüdischer Verlag, 1995).

53. See Stefan Maechler, *The Wilkomirski Affair: A Study in Biographical Truth*, trans. J. E. Woods (New York: Schocken, 2001). See especially the chapter "A Global Literary Event."

54. The Swiss journalist Hanno Helbling was the first to bring the suspicion to the attention of the publisher at Suhrkamp. See his letter dated 9 Feb. 1995 to Siegfried Unseld, documented in Maechler, *Wilkomirski Affair*, 94–95.

of a real survivor's son to bring the exposé to the German-reading public. In August 1998, Daniel Ganzfried, a Swiss-Jewish author, made the bold accusation in *Die Weltwoche*, a Zurich-based weekly, that "Binjamin Wilkomirski's 'Fragments,' which is currently the most successful Swiss book, is a fiction," a "borrowed Holocaust biography."[55] Based on documents and photos in the Zurich archive, which contradicted Wilkomirski's assertion that he had "arrived" in Switzerland only in 1948, Ganzfried declared that "Binjamin Wilkomirski is a pseudonym, its bearer was never in a concentration camp as an inmate," and his book was but a work of "fictitious biography."[56] For the whistle-blower, the worst damage of such a lie was not pecuniary,[57] but moral—the Swiss students who had heard the author discuss his life and had believed in him as someone who had come back from hell alive would now believe in nothing anymore. Or worse, they would be inclined to believe Holocaust deniers.[58]

Yet it was clear from even this first attack that Ganzfried was not so much after the "feigned victim" as after those who had made such a fiasco possible. For him, the act of faking an identity deserved no more reflection than the fact of its social veneration, "as if [the book] were some original handwritten copy of the Old Testament."[59] One problem, according to him, lay in the **blind sympathy with the "victim."** "Thoughtlessly sympathetic, we find the hero in the victim, with whom we can fraternize ourselves on the side of morals: Binjamin Wilkomirski. Whoever makes that possible for us does not need any further achievement than showing himself before the entrance of Auschwitz: 'I'm one of those who got out of it!'"[60] Another, greater problem was the opportunism of the "culture business" (*Kulturbetrieb*), which had allegedly con-

---

55. Daniel Ganzfried, "Die geliehene Holocaust-Biographie," *Die Weltwoche*, 27 Aug. 1998.

56. Ibid.

57. Contrary to expectation, *Fragments* did not generate as much sales as mere publicity. See Maechler, *Wilkomirski Affair*, 119, 333.

58. Ganzfried, "Geliehene Holocaust-Biographie."

59. Ibid.

60. Ibid.

tributed to rendering Auschwitz a "source of self-deception" (*Fundus der Lebenslüge*), a kind of "sausage-making" (*Verwurstung*).[61]

Indeed, Ganzfried should count as one of the earliest of the "second generation" of Shoah survivors to point to the problem of procuring benefits from the victimhood of others. In September 1995, that is, at almost the same time that "Wilkomirski" appeared (and five years ahead of Norman Finkelstein),[62] Ganzfried published a novel, *Der Absender,* in which the theme of profiteering from Holocaust remembrance was already apparent. "Perhaps," he wrote, in describing the work of his main character, Georg, as a volunteer at a planned Holocaust museum in New York, "the only outcome of his hectic search in the past was in fact that it lent him justification for a couple of weeks of his present time [to remain in New York]."[63] The author could hardly have anticipated better the role that he would play in the Wilkomirski affair.

Ganzfried's *social* critique aside, however, it must be stated that the success of the Wilkomirski memoir was insufficient to gauge whether a sympathetic German (or German-speaking) audience was in fact guilty of moral profiteering through "fraternizing with the victim," as Ganzfried claimed, or was only fulfilling an essential facet of repentance through "turning to the victim" (**R1**). For there are other, less inconvenient means of "achieving" victimhood without turning to the "other," the victim. It is even doubtful whether a "thoughtful or critical sympathy," which Ganzfried demanded, is compatible, in terms of attitude, with the willed vulnerability

---

61. Ibid.

62. In 2000 Norman G. Finkelstein, son of Shoah survivors, published his controversial book, *The Holocaust Industry,* which was translated into German and published by Piper in 2001. It aroused intense debates in Germany, so much so that within the same year, no less than three compendia of responses were published. The essential difference between Ganzfried and Finkelstein, of course, is that whereas the former exposed a concrete case of fraud with concrete evidence, the latter erected a hypothetical enemy, the "Holocaust industry" through theoretical—some critics would even say, "conspiratory"—reasoning, in which the entire system of reparation is under attack. See relevant debates in Petra Steinberger, ed., *Die Finkelstein-Debatte* (Munich: Piper, 2001). See Ganzfried's own critique of Finkelstein's book in the Steinberger volume.

63. Daniel Ganzfried, *Der Absender* (Zurich: Rotpunktverlag, 1995), 18.

(R3) demanded of the repentant perpetrator. On the other hand, within the "culture business" of which Ganzfried was most critical, the publisher of *Fragments* and Wilkomirski's literary agent did seem—at least judging from the report of the historian they commissioned—to have taken reasonably cautious verification steps before Ganzfried's exposé or even before the publication of the book itself.[64]

Yet precisely because there would be no returning and restoring to begin with if every German audience should demand or be required to demand that the victim *first* prove his victimhood beyond doubt before granting him audience, or that a fraud-proof reparation system be in place *before* such payments will be made, turners like Ganzfried and Verleger, who perform the thankless task of **"victims watching over victims"** (real or fake), are indeed providing an indispensable service to the work of turning—for the perpetrators are not in a position to do it, and without it the continual and ever-renewing process of turning will be choked by abuse. Although abuse or the possibility of abuse is by no means eliminated, with the insider-watcher the repentant perpetrator can at least count on the delivery of "truth and justice" somehow, and that their goodwill is not met with or only with bad faith. While Eugen Kogon counseled his fellow Germans in 1946 to watch out for the self-righteousness of the tax collector vis-à-vis the unjust servant (**P4**), it was the persistent self-watchfulness of these turners that went a long way to keeping that conviction alive.

---

64. See the chapter "The Origins of *Fragments*" in Maechler, *Wilkomirski Affair*. They also retracted the book before the case was definitively settled with the DNA test proving that the biological father of Doessekker/Wilkomirski was indeed a Swiss national living in Switzerland. See "Suhrkamp zieht Bruchstücke zurück," *Berner Zeitung*, 13 Oct. 1999; and Julian Schütt, "Wilkomirski: Alles vergisst," *Die Weltwoche*, 4 Apr. 2002.

14

"We Take Over the Guilt of the Fathers" (P12)

"The guilt haunts me, you know," said "Rudolf," son of Nazi parents who had fled to Argentina. "And those guilty are to be punished. If not here and now, then in another time and in another place. It will also catch up with me. I can't get away from it. . . . The guilt is now with me. My parents, they are already burning in hell. They are long dead, already done with it, this life. And they left me behind. *Born guilty, left guilty.* . . . Why did they come to the absurd idea of having a child after what had happened? . . . Sometimes I wish that it were over. It is so meaningless just to wait. Hopefully, they'll come and get me soon."[1]

These words of resignation from a "postwar German" (Rudolf was born in 1950) were recorded by Peter Sichrovsky, who was himself son of Jewish refugees who had returned to Austria after

---

1. Peter Sichrovsky, " 'Ich war's nicht, verdammt noch mal' II," *Der Spiegel*, no. 7 (1987) (emphasis added).

1945 and settled down there. Sichrovsky wanted to find out how children of Nazi criminals dealt with their parents' past in postwar Austria and Germany. His collection of these monologues and dialogues, published in 1987, was a disturbing account of the destructiveness—whether in despair, dispute, or defense—that Nazi parents had bequeathed to their children.[2] Rudolf was not the only one who regretted his birth; another "born-guilty" child, "Anna," also had doubts about any chance of renewal for herself. "Can wolves become sheep within one generation?" she asked. "It is just the same families, the same parents, grandparents, teachers, priests."[3] Anna's parents had lied to her about their Nazi past; she had to "discover" in school that her father had in fact been a guard leader in a concentration camp. Rudolf's father had, at least once when drunk, "confessed" to and wept for the "horrible time when they had to shoot the children one by one with the pistol, because the idiotic soldiers had aimed too high with their machine guns at the standing adults."[4] Just like Rudolf, Anna expected that she would have to make some sort of mystical repayments for what her parents had done: "They'll be coming, I tell you."[5]

The morbidity of these guilt-ridden children (and grandchildren) is unsettling; it is surpassed only by the intransigeance of those who either staunchly defended their parents ("The history teacher is lying"; "He is our father after all") or rejected any connection whatsoever ("It's not me, damn it!").[6] While modern jurisprudence does not recognize the generational transference of criminal guilt, there is a social expectation that later generations of the perpetrators (and bystanders) should make an effort to reflect on and

2. Peter Sichrovsky, ed., *Schuldig geboren: Kinder aus Nazifamilien* (Cologne: Kiepenheuer & Witsch, 1987). Parts of this book were also serialized in three installments in *Der Spiegel* in early 1987.

3. Peter Sichrovsky, "'Ich war's nicht, verdammt noch mal' III," *Der Spiegel*, no. 8 (1987).

4. Sichrovsky, "Ich war's nicht II."

5. Ibid.

6. See, for example "Stefanie" and "Brigitte," in Peter Sichrovsky, "'Ich war's nicht, verdammt noch mal' I," *Der Spiegel*, no. 6 (1987); and Sichrovsky, "Ich war's nicht III."

to address (rather than get punished for) the wrongdoings of earlier generations when it comes to *national* crimes. The plethora of demands for national apologies and compensations attests to this.[7] In between these two consensuses lie the extreme attitudes of nonchalance on one side and fatalism on the other, as manifested by the responses of the children of Nazi families. The question for educators then is this: How can one help the young ones see the cross-generational properties of the "crimes of the fathers"—for example, their social consequences and cultural prerequisites—without plunging them into despair about an unearned and seemingly unatonable guilt?

Some German and Jewish intellectuals in fact endeavored to counter this dual problem of **false generational guilt and false freedom of the new generation** by clarifying where real guilt and hence real opportunities for turning lie. One of these pioneering turners was Günther Anders. Born to German-Jewish parents and educated in pre-Nazi Germany, the philosopher had to flee as the Nazis ascended to power, only returning and settling down in Vienna some years after the war ended.[8] In 1964, that is, two years after the execution of Eichmann in Israel, Anders published a most unusual book, or rather, a letter, in Munich. It was an "open letter to Klaus Eichmann," the eldest son of the convicted Nazi criminal, with an enigmatic title: *Wir Eichmannsöhne* (We the Sons of Eichmann).[9] Anders began his letter—and reiterated this point throughout—with a reaffirmation of innocence of birth. "Ancestry (*Herkunft*) is not guilt," he told Klaus E. "No one is his origins' (*Ursprung*) smith; you, too, are not."[10] The notion of group punishment, so favored and mercilessly executed by the Nazis, was to be categorically rejected. "Like any other, you mustn't fall victim

---

7. See Alexis Dudden, *Troubled Apologies among Japan, Korea, and the United States* (New York: Columbia University Press, 2008).

8. For an intellectual biography of Anders, see Raimund Bahr, *Günther Anders: Leben und Denken im Wort* (Berlin: epubli GmbH, 2012).

9. Günther Anders, *Wir Eichmannsöhne: Offener Brief an Klaus Eichmann* (Munich: C. H. Beck, 1964).

10. Ibid., 5.

to the principle of 'tribal liability' (*Sippenhaft*)."[11] If so, what sense does it make to speak of "Eichmann's sons" then? In the same way that "Hitler" was not a mere historical personality for Picard (**P9**), "an Eichmann" was also not a mere biological offspring of Adolf E. for Anders. "Never shall [the concept "an Eichmann"] mark the one who descends *from* an Eichmann, but always and only the one who feels, acts, and argues *like* an Eichmann does."[12] As such, the philosopher spoke of not only Eichmann but *Eichmen* (*Eichmänner*): the slavish Eichmen, the shameless Eichmen, the hard-headed Eichmen, the greedy Eichmen, and the cowardly Eichmen, who ran and manned the institutional and factory-like operations (tolerated by the passive Eichmen) to exterminate millions of human beings.[13] And after arguing at length that the phenomenon of Eichmen was by no means over after 1945, Anders sought to provoke the addressee of his letter to consider the hitherto inconceivable:

> Do you notice something, Klaus Eichmann? Do you notice that the so-called Eichmann problem is not yesterday's problem? That it does not belong to the past? That there is no reason at all for us—here I see really only very few exceptions—to feel superior to yesterday? That all of us, exactly like you, are confronted by what is too huge for us? . . . That *all of us* are *likewise Eichmann's sons*? At least sons of the *Eichmannian world* (*Eichmannwelt*)?[14]

Anders even went so far as to identify Klaus E. as a "relative" (*Verwandter*) of the six million Jewish victims of the Shoah, as among the "six million and one."[15] For these, he argued, shared the same "mother"; they were the children of the "one and the same epoch" that had produced their "underserved misery," for which the letter writer expressed his "deep respect."[16]

---

11. Ibid. See the misapplied "agreement" to this notion by a child ("Herbert D.") of a Nazi father below in this chapter.

12. Anders, *Wir Eichmannsöhne*, 5 (emphasis in the original).

13. Ibid., 17–18.

14. Ibid., 56 (emphasis in the original).

15. Ibid., 44–45. See also Victor Gollancz's use of the "six million and one" symbol in pleading for clemency for Adolf Eichmann in **P1**.

16. Anders, *Wir Eichmannsöhne*, 8.

What Anders demanded from Klaus E., then, was **not an apology or atonement** *for* what his father had done, **but "courage"** (*Mut*)—like the courage that is required of the sick "to agree to the operation"—to "move away (*abrücken*) from his origins."[17] This would mean getting rid of the "poison" and cutting oneself off from the "roots" that had made and would continue to make the "Monstrous" possible.[18] "Move away from your father," so that the sons and daughters of Klaus E. would not have to move away from him, their own father, pleaded Anders once again toward the end of the letter.[19] Using the example of the "Hiroshima pilot" Claude Eatherly[20] and employing Christian scripture, the philosopher hoped to turn the addressee of his letter, his *fellow* "Eichmann's son," from the path that he was allegedly taking (based on some news reports of his father-defensive and antisemitic remarks around the time the book was published).[21] The success of such a turning step from the son of Eichmann would mean that

> there is one less Eichmann—that this day would not be just another ordinary day for us. For "one Eichmann less" would not mean to us: one less human being, but: one more human being; and not that a human being is now liquidated, but that a human being is now turned back (*zurückgekehrt*). Or, in the words of a greater one, "that this brother, who was dead, is again alive, and who was lost, is now found" (Luke 15:32).[22]

Like those turners before him, Anders identified what he considered to be the most salient intellectual "roots" that had made Nazi monstrosity possible, which he then used as analytical tools to diagnose the present. What sets him apart is the fact that he spoke

---

17. Ibid., 15.
18. Ibid., 19–21.
19. Ibid., 73.
20. Ibid., 19. Claude Eatherly was a pilot in the US Army, who had personally participated in the operation of dropping the atomic bomb on Hiroshima. He and Anders published their exchanged letters in 1961: *Off limits für das Gewissen: Der Briefwechsel Claude Eatherly Günther Anders* (Reinbek bei Hamburg: Rowohlt).
21. Anders, *Wir Eichmannsöhne*, 65–66.
22. Ibid., 70.

directly to the children of Nazi families—in this case, one very specific "child" (Klaus E. was already twenty-eight the year that Anders published his first letter to him). His demand to break the filial bond as a turning act was also the most direct. In his second letter to Klaus E., published in 1988 and occasioned by the Historikerstreit, this demand was formulated in even more lucid language than in the first letter. "*The truth has to triumph over taboos, over everything. Therefore also over the unassailability of the parents.*"[23] The biblical commandment to honor one's parents is not applicable "*when they are or were despicable.*" Loss-melancholic remembrance is not the same as honor-defensive remembrance.[24]

Though his attempt was "in vain"—for there was no direct response from Klaus E.[25]—his penetrating observation of the psychological needs of those "born guilty" proved remarkably accurate. The "two deaths of the father" that he spoke about in the first letter and employed to denote the problem of coming to know who one's father really was as against whom one remembered him to be was later found in the expressions of the affected children themselves. One of Sichrovsky's interviewees, "Susanne," for example, felt torn apart by her loving but lying father and her beloved son who sought the truth about his grandfather's activities during the war. And when the former, Susanne's elderly father, denied everything, "for me, my father died on that very day."[26] Anders had envisaged that, for Klaus Eichmann, there must have been exactly such a moment like Susanne's when he discovered who his father really was.[27]

We do not know for sure whether Klaus E. had in fact had such a moment, or if he had experienced it like Susanne did, but a psychological problem arising from such a "double loss" (*zweifacher Verlust*) as identified by Anders in the early 1960s would in reality

---

23. Anders, "Zweiter Brief an Klaus Eichmann: Gegen die Gleichgültigkeit," in Anders, *Wir Eichmannsöhne*, 78 (emphasis in the original).

24. Ibid.

25. Anders said he had only come to know of the reaction of the addressee of his letter "indirectly." See Anders, *Wir Eichmannsöhne*, 78–79.

26. Sichrovsky, "Ich war's nicht I."

27. Anders, *Eichmannsöhne*, 9.

occupy German VgB for at least the next two decades—the **burden of mourning**. "I have tried again and again," said Anders to Klaus E., "to put myself in your shoes. . . . The answer . . . was always no. I did not succeed in mourning (*Trauer*), pain, and piety."[28] And his advice to the addressee of his letter was this: "Give up trying to mourn (*betrauern*) your father. Take down that picture on the wall. Stop repeating the old ways. . . . Through this giving up, you could mourn again—not your father's death, though, but the death of *your* mourning (*Tod* Ihrer Trauer). . . . If you could also find the way to this second mourning, then you would no longer be standing alone. But you would be one of us."[29]

Three years after the publication of *Wir Eichmannsöhne*, a German couple would help German youths find that way and propound the problem of mourning, of collective mourning, as the central issue of postwar German reflection on the Nazi past. They called it the "inability to mourn" (*Unfähigkeit zu trauern*). Alexander and Margarete Mitscherlich published their book, of the same name, which was in fact a collection of essays, in 1967, just around the time of the tide-changing 1968 "student movements." The main essay, which bears the title of the book, is difficult for nonspecialist readers, which makes the popularity of the book all the more astounding.[30] At its core, the essay sought to address the problem of a nation that had collectively "externalized" its conscience to the **Führer, the "super-father"** (*Über-Vater*),[31] who proved to be a most misleading (*verführerisch*) conscience. The inability to mourn, which according to the Mitscherlichs manifested itself in the lack of sympathy for the victims of Nazi Germany on the one hand, and the lack of engagement and intellectual creativity in social issues on the other, was the symptom of this underlying problem—of having

---

28. Ibid., 11.

29. Ibid., 15–16 (emphasis in the original).

30. See Tobias Freimüller, "Der versäumte Abschied von der 'Volksgemeinschaft': Psychoanalyse und Vergangenheitsbewältigung," in *50 Klassiker der Zeitgeschichte*, ed. Jürgen Danyel, Jan-Holger Kirsch, and Martin Sabrow (Göttingen: Vandenhoeck & Ruprecht, 2007).

31. Alexander Mitscherlich and Margarete Mitscherlich, *Die Unfähigkeit zu trauern: Grundlagen kollektiven Verhaltens* (Munich: R. Piper & Co., 1967), 62.

internalized the wrong ego-ideal (*Ich-Ideal*), which the Germans
were purportedly unwilling to relinquish:

> The inability to mourn for the suffered loss of the Führer is the result
> of an intensive defense (*Abwehr*) against guilt, shame, and fear. . . .
> Not only does the death of Adolf Hitler as a real person serve as occa-
> sion for mourning, but above all else the dissolution of his representa-
> tion as collective ego-ideal. . . . The defense against mourning for the
> countless victims of Hitlerian aggression follows in second place—an
> aggression that we shared so willingly, so unresistingly in identifica-
> tion with him.[32]

The remedy, as proposed by the Mitscherlichs, lay in *correctly*
mourning the Führer, or what the Mitscherlichs called "mourning
work" (*Trauerarbeit*)—to overcome Hitler in ourselves: "Productive mourning work . . . would mean in our case that we also as-
similate Hitler in ourselves (*Hitler in uns selbst assimilieren*), that
is, to be able to overcome him progressively. The lack of mourning work allows him to continue to exist (*weiterbestehen*) as a
capsuled psychological introjection."[33] Without "painful remembrance work" (*Erinnerungsarbeit*), the "old ideals that have led to
the fatal turning of German history will continue to have effect."[34]
This mourning work would mean an "inner dispute" that should
lead the "incapable" Germans to severance from their loved and
lost object (the Führer and his ideals), and hence the experience of
"tearing and wounding," in order to get back to reality.[35] The reward of such psychological labor would be the regained ability to
mourn and the "discovery of our ability to sympathize with people
(*Fähigkeit des Mitleidens für Menschen*)."[36]

People familiar with psychoanalysis will easily recognize the
work of the Mitscherlichs as a Freudian analysis of postwar German society. In fact, the authors drew explicitly and extensively

---

32. Ibid., 34–35.
33. Ibid., 60.
34. Ibid., 83.
35. Ibid., 78.
36. Ibid., 83. See also other expressions of self-willed wounding and the regaining of *vulnerability* in **P6**.

from Freud's texts on mourning.[37] The divergence between the authors and their intellectual father, however, was just as striking: whereas for the latter, the problem of guilt lay precisely in the unreasonable demands of the super-ego,[38] for the Mitscherlichs, the problem of guilt was—at least for the German readers they were speaking to—that its *reality* was not sufficiently recognized. Time and again the authors spoke of the **"real guilt"** (*reale Schuld*) of Germans as a self-explanatory object.[39]

Though the Mitscherlichs did not elaborate further, what they meant when speaking about the "real guilt" of the Germans was clear in context: the guilt of "action" (*Handlung*) and the guilt of "toleration" (*Duldung*) of the "million instances of murder."[40] Hence although it did not draw explicitly from Martin Buber's *Schuld und Schuldgefühle* (Guilt and Guilt Feelings) (**P6**), *Die Unfähigkeit zu trauern* (The Inability to Mourn) was in fact a direct affirmation of "existential guilt" (Buber) or "real guilt" (Mitscherlich), which cannot be "overcome" (*bewältigt*) simply by alleviating the neurotic symptoms or reducing the tension between the ego and the "over-demanding" super-ego. After all, as the Mitscherlichs reminded their readers, a legacy of the Nazis was precisely the "reversal of the conscience" (*Umkehrung des Gewissens*), so that murderous acts could be committed with the "misleading release from an uncomfortable conscience."[41]

It was therefore no small irony that Alexander Mitscherlich, the founder and then director of the Sigmund Freud Institute in Frankfurt, credited Freud with the discovery of "guilt feeling as the most important problem in the development of civilization,"[42] while speaking

---

37. For example, "Erinnern, Wiederholen, Durcharbeiten" and "Trauer und Melancholie," in Sigmund Freud, *Gesammelte Werke*, vol. 10, *Werke aus den Jahren 1913–1917* (Frankfurt a.M.: S. Fischer, 1991).

38. See Sigmund Freud, *Unbehagen in der Kultur* (Vienna: Internationaler Psychoanalytischer Verlag, 1930).

39. Mitscherlich and Mitscherlich, *Unfähigkeit zu trauern*, 27 (emphasis added).

40. Ibid., 24.

41. Ibid., 72–73.

42. Ibid., 338–39.

decidedly *for* the acceptance of guilt in the postwar German context. The Mitscherlichs praised the **"atoning Germans"** (*Sühnedeutsche*),[43] who did not succumb to the illusion that guilt is to be "historically done away with through denial."[44] The postwar German generations should reject the "error," propagated by some politicians, that "the postwar period is over," the Mitscherlichs advised, for it is "not we alone [who] determine when it is enough to draw consequences" from that erroneous past.[45] Quoting the 1963 EKD statement on the ongoing Auschwitz trials, the Mitscherlichs reiterated the importance of guilt admission—even after more than twenty years since the war's end—as a basis for mourning work and a precondition for reconciliation and psychological health: "As long as we do not finally acknowledge the guilt of 'mass murder executed with indescribable brutality,' not only must our spiritual life (*Geistesleben*) stagnate, but no emotionally solemn reconciliation (*Aussöhnung*) is possible with our former enemies."[46] Therefore, to follow this line of thinking, if the burden of guilt admission and of mourning was not shouldered by the directly guilty generation(s), it would only be "bequeathed"—not metaphysically but sociopsychologically—to the subsequent generations, who would have to deal with the consequences, one way or another.

The **generational rift** in postwar Germany with respect to this problem increased noticeably in the 1960s, even before the 1968 "revolution." In the EKD declaration quoted by the Mitscherlichs, for example, one could already sense the "discontent" of the first postwar generation coming of age, occasioned by the Auschwitz trials between 1963 and 1965. "We *the older ones* are now being questioned once more . . . whether we are willing to face this past, instead of suppressing its remembrance and denying every co-responsibility for it."[47] The EKD advised that schools and church

---

43. The term *Sühnedeutsche* was attributed to Franz Josef Strauß, who had allegedly used it in a derogatory sense. See Mitscherlich and Mitscherlich, *Unfähigkeit zu trauern*, 65.

44. Mitscherlich and Mitscherlich, *Unfähigkeit zu trauern*, 41.

45. Ibid. See comparable expressions of self-insufficiency in repentance in P3.

46. Mitscherlich and Mitscherlich, *Unfähigkeit zu trauern*, 58–59, 65.

47. "Wort des Rates der Evangelischen Kirche Deutschlands zu den NS-Verbrecherprozessen anläßlich der Synode der EKD vom 13. März 1963," *Freiburger*

instruction should see to it that "parents do not dodge the questions of their children."[48] Such inquiry should not be brushed off as "dirtying one's own nest" (*Beschmutzung des eignenen Nestes*), when "it is in truth about cleaning up a very dirty nest."[49]

A young German girl knew only too well what it meant to be accused of "sullying one's own nest" in postwar Germany. She was a favorite of her little hometown when she began asking very innocuous questions for a student contest: how did the "good anti-Nazis" struggle against the "evil Nazis" in her own Bavarian *Heimat*?[50] "**Dirty-nest maker**" soon became her second name. When Anja Rosmus-Wenninger, born in 1960 in Passau, published her findings in 1983 after almost three years of "remembrance work"—that is, literally asking members of the older generations to remember what had happened during the "forgotten" years of Nazi rule— Martin Hirsch, then a member of the German Federal Constitutional Court, contributed a foreword in defense of the young researcher: "Those who resist this tendency [of suppressing the past] were quickly [called] 'dirty-nest maker' (*Nestbeschmutzer*)— as if the one who tries to clean up a nest were responsible for the filth in it."[51] Hirsch, as a member of the older generations, praised the young author for delivering a (thankless) generational service of "putting us, 'the old ones,' to shame."[52]

Indeed, many among the older generations were shamed by Rosmus-Wenninger's work, *Widerstand und Verfolgung: Am Beispiel Passaus 1933–1939* (Resistance and Persecution: The Example of Passau, 1933–1939), for it showed not only how much public support Hitler and the Nazis had enjoyed in Passau (in sharp contrast to the delivered myths of resistance), but how much they still did

---

Rundbrief 15, no. 57/60 (1963/1964), 37–38 (emphasis in the original); quoted in Mitscherlich and Mitscherlich, *Unfähigkeit zu trauern*, 58.

48. Mitscherlich and Mitscherlich, *Unfähigkeit zu trauern*, 58.

49. Ibid.

50. Dietrich Strothmann, "Eine Passauer Passion," *Die Zeit*, 14 Dec. 1984.

51. Martin Hirsch, "Vorwort," in *Widerstand und Verfolgung: Am Beispiel Passaus 1933–1939*, by Anja Rosmus-Wenninger (Passau: Andreas-Haller Verlag, 1983), 9.

52. Ibid., 10.

in the present. Many responded to the researcher's questions with this general judgment regarding the Nazis: "The National Socialist regime may be bad, but the Russians are worse!"[53] The society in general was not a community of "opponents of National Socialism," but rather of bystanders: "Teachers, from whom one could have expected resistance commensurate with their education, were, at least partly, rather open to National Socialism. . . . The local personalities adapted quickly."[54] Rosmus-Wenninger found that in her hometown, "not a few Nazis and bystanders (*Mitläufer*) belonged to the middle-class families," and that the Nazi Party served as the "guiding father figure" (*richtungweisende Vaterfigur*) especially for the lower classes and the workers.[55]

The group of people who needed to feel most ashamed was probably the clerics. In her chapter "Die Kirche Passaus im Dritten Reich" (The Church of Passau in the Third Reich), the whistleblower raised many inconvenient truths about the so-called resistance of the Catholic Church during the Nazi era. In particular, the activities of Emil Janik, a priest who had supervised the church publication, *Passauer Bistumsblatt*, since the 1930s, and was celebrated subsequently as a "towering figure of the resistance,"[56] came under harsh scrutiny. After the war Janik himself had identified several incidents involving his work at the *Bistumsblatt* in which he had been personally persecuted by the Nazi authorities because of noncompliance, while attempting to explain at the same time that the government-friendly articles that had appeared on his watch were only a tactical necessity.[57] In Rosmus-Wenninger's evaluation, however, Janik was nowhere near a forced adapter, much less a resister, but seemed more like an inspired follower of the Führer. Rosmus-Wenninger uncovered articles, some of which were penned by Janik himself, that were, according to her, difficult to justify even under past circumstances. One of these, published

---

53. Rosmus-Wenninger, *Widerstand und Verfolgung*, 160.
54. Ibid., 155.
55. Ibid., 160–61.
56. "Rechter Arm zittert," *Der Spiegel*, no. 18 (1984).
57. Quoted in Rosmus-Wenninger, *Widerstand und Verfolgung*, 102.

in 1939, for example, verged on promoting holy war: "I am confident," wrote a Protestant pastor of the religious services in the infamous Condor Legion,[58] "that in these services held before the enemy, the spoken word of the Bible has born fruit in many hearts, just as it was always a source of strength for our fathers and forefathers in war."[59] Likewise, another article appearing in early 1941 sought to justify the German-instigated war by quoting the book of Genesis in support of the Lebensraum claim.[60]

Janik himself did not shy away from seeking "Christian" justification for German nationalism. Writing in 1939–40 under his own name, he opined that the "unbearable injustice" of Versailles was "repaired" (*wieder gut gemacht*) through the "homecoming of the German city Danzig."[61] The "Western powers" were portrayed as harboring the goal of "the extermination (*Vernichtung*) of the entire German people" and were guilty of "driving a wedge" between the Volk and the Führer: "We pray to God with the words of the Führer, that he may 'let us and all others find the right way.' "[62] With an astounding interpretation of Jesus's weeping over Jerusalem (Lk 19:41), the love of nation was elevated by Janik to be a Christian value: "The Christian German (*Der christliche Deutsche*) knows loyalty. The love of fatherland is a genuine Christian virtue. The Savior himself has shown it in a really touching way. . . . The Catholic Church is no opponent of love of fatherland, but consecrates (*heiligen*) and glorifies (*verklären*) it, elevating it to a moral-religious duty (*sittlich-religiöse Pflicht*)."[63]

Had all these rather enthusiastic responses to Nazi Germany been necessitated by the struggle to survive? Rosmus-Wenninger's work forcefully raised this doubt. And was Janik a "good anti-Nazi"? What was still more troubling, according to the amateur Passauer historian, was that even as late as 1977 the priest was still

---

58. The Condor Legion was Germany's intervention in the Spanish Civil War (1936–39).

59. Rosmus-Wenninger, *Widerstand und Verfolgung*, 103.

60. Ibid., 103–4.

61. Ibid., 106–7.

62. Ibid.

63. Ibid., 105–6.

defensive of the Nazi leadership by asserting in the *Bistums-blatt* that "not everything that the power holders of the Third Reich undertook was absolutely wrong."[64] Although Rosmus-Wenninger expressly stated that the "conclusive assessment of [Janik's] activity is not the intention of [her] book,"[65] this portrayal of the priest, who passed away while she was still working on her book, was enough to catch the attention of the family of the deceased. Rosmus-Wenninger was sued for defamation by Erwin Janik, the brother of the priest, for publicly calling Emil Janik the "brown Emil."[66]

But just like Hochhuth's *Stellvertreter* (P11), Rosmus-Wenninger's *Widerstand und Verfolgung* was no single-minded denunciation of the Catholic "Fathers." In both critiques, the examples of failure were presented side by side the **"good Fathers,"** who had done what the others were supposed to be doing but didn't. In Rosmus-Wenninger's case, her "Fr. Riccardo" was Fr. Dionys Habersbrunner, who "minced no words" in preaching the prophetic concerns for truth and social justice, and suffered for it.[67] The fact that Rosmus-Wenninger had chosen to present the Nazi persecution of the church and the example of Habersbrunner *before* that of Janik bespeaks her "consideration" when judging the church of Passau in the Third Reich. Yet this consideration was not appreciated by her own people. Amid ridicule, threats, and lawsuits, the young author chose to leave her hometown for the United States, where, according to Henryk Broder, the Americans were only too happy to have finally found a "German who was good through and through."[68]

Rosmus-Wenninger's ordeal demonstrated how difficult it could be for the younger generations to **uncover the truth about their (grand)parents' Nazi past.** Yet they were not alone in their fight

---

64. Ibid., 108. He cited the "Arbeitsdienst"—a form of work provision for the youth by the Nazis—as something that "even today . . . would not be completely superfluous." Cf. Meinecke's *Deutsche Katastrophe* in **P8**.

65. Rosmus-Wenninger, *Widerstand und Verfolgung*, 108.

66. "Rechter Arm zittert."

67. Rosmus-Wenninger, *Widerstand und Verfolgung*, 84–85.

68. Henryk M. Broder, "Eine Art Säulenheilige," *Der Spiegel*, no. 42 (1996).

against the resistance of the former generations. In 1987, four years after the Passauer exposé erupted, German-Jewish writer Ralph Giordano published *Die zweite Schuld oder Von der Last Deutscher zu sein* (The Second Guilt or On the Burden of Being German), which sparked an intense German-Jewish intergenerational discussion in the late 1980s.[69] At first sight, one might have the impression that the author was affirming the guilt of the children, which they have "inherited" from their fathers—that is, second guilt as the guilt of the second generation of Germans. Nothing is farther from the message of *The Second Guilt*, which the author dedicated to "the innocently burdened (*schuldlos beladenen*) sons, daughters, and grandsons."[70] The "second guilt" in question was in fact repeatedly stressed and defined as the post-1945 "repression and denial of the first [guilt]," which was "the guilt of the Germans under Hitler."[71] Giordano's accused were primarily *not* the younger generations but the *older ones*, the "Hitlerian generations": "When will the generations of the parents and grandparents finally stop burdening their own sons, daughters, and grandsons with their compulsive justifications?"[72] He complained of the "Hitler" who was "militarily defeated, but not ideologically."[73] "The womb from which it crept is still fruitful."[74] That womb, though, was not biological, but social: the German society in which lies about the Nazi past and "peace" with the perpetrators reigned. He demanded "honesty" instead of "masks" from these "bearers of the second guilt," in order to overcome what he called "organized impenitence" (*organisierte Unbußfertigkeit*).[75]

Drawing extensively from the Mitscherlichs' *Inability to Mourn*, Giordano expanded the thesis with a theological vocabulary, hence transforming it from a by and large sociopsychoanalytical

---

69. Ralph Giordano, *Die zweite Schuld oder Von der Last Deutscher zu sein* (Cologne: Kiepenheuer & Witsch, 2000).

70. Ibid., 13.

71. Ibid., 17.

72. Ibid., 18.

73. Ibid., 17.

74. Ibid., 20.

75. Ibid., 19–22.

argument to an intergenerational one.[76] This specific intergenerational guilt, the **"broken generational contract,"**[77] the continual existence of sociopsychological "contaminants," the transferred "sign of Cain of the first guilt,"[78] and the transmitted "powers and ways of thinking"[79] were the main concerns of Giordano's *Second Guilt*:

> The discussion of the second guilt is not about the question of whether the Federal Republic is threatened by a second 30 January 1933 or a second establishment of National Socialism. Rather, it is about a serious offense committed by the guilty older generations against the innocently burdened sons, daughters, and grandsons—they are the actual victims of the second guilt (*eigentliche Opfer der zweiten Schuld*), *for what the grandparents and parents have not paid off* (abtragen) *is transferred onto them.*[80]

Like other turners, Giordano did not speak to his accused as a "pure victim" of National Socialism—in fact, he was speaking *for* the victims (of the second guilt, not the first), the younger generations of Germans. Furthermore, he also "invented" ways to connect himself to the accused, using the Mitscherlichs' concept of the "super-father." He spoke of "parallels" between the Nazi past and *his* Communist faith, that is, his "uncritical faith in a super-father (*Übervater*)": "I was bound with devotion to a political god (*Polit-Gott*), who in my case bore the name Stalin. . . . I know only too well, therefore, from my own experience, the blindness of ideologies and their mechanism of de-realizing (*entwirklichen*) reality according to need."[81]

---

76. Ibid., 25.

77. Ibid., 344. It is interesting to note how Giordano turned the German concept of *Generationenvertrag* around, that is, from a pension liability by which the younger generation "promises" to support the older generation, to an intergenerational guilt in which the older generation "owes" the younger generation something.

78. Giordano, *Zweite Schuld*, 344.

79. Ibid., 32.

80. Ibid., 27 (emphasis added).

81. Ibid., 28–29.

Yet if any of the German youth takes Giordano's self-condemnation and his "acquittal" of the younger generations for granted, they are missing his message entirely. For although he did not say it out loud, any could see that what constitutes the "second guilt," the guilt of repression and denial of the first, is something that even the younger ones—or, for that matter, the generations that are yet to come—can beget. As one of Sichrovsky's interviewees, "Stefanie," reminds us, the youth were in no way immunized against the "sin of the fathers" simply by virtue of being born later.[82] Following the Mitscherlichs, Giordano warned his readers that "the hope that the postwar period is now over, which is repeatedly expressed by leading German politicians, must be judged as false."[83] The *Second Guilt* was thus simultaneously a liberating and a challenging message for postwar German youth.

Where Giordano, who was born to a Jewish mother in Hamburg in 1923, saw the unjust burdening of German youth by their "second-guilty" (grand)parents, the German philosopher Jürgen Habermas, born in Düsseldorf in 1929, saw a legitimate, or even *necessary*, **cross-generational liability**. From the mid-1980s to the 1990s, a period that saw the Historikerstreit, the reunification of the two Germanys, and the Berlin memorial debates, Habermas repeatedly stepped into the public sphere to contribute to a particular understanding of generational guilt in the struggle against the "apologetic tendencies," the relativistic impulses, the "close-the-file" attitudes of his time. Already in 1985, when the Kohl administration was engaging in a series of activities stressing or purportedly stressing the ideas of a "new," "guiltless," and "reconciled" Germany, Habermas was unimpressed by what he considered to be a "staged" return to "normality," an "arrangement of extorted reconciliation" (*Arrangement erpreßter Versöhnung*).[84] In a stark reading of Kohl's 1984 speech before the Knesset (**P8**), Habermas argued against the idea of "innocence because of late

---

82. Sichrovsky, "Ich war's nicht I."
83. Giordano, *Zweite Schuld*, 32.
84. See Jürgen Habermas, "Die Entsorgung der Vergangenheit: Ein kulturpolitisches Pamphlet," *Die Zeit*, 17 May 1985.

birth" in favor of Karl Jaspers's differentiated personal/collective guilt thesis.[85] Those who contested the claim of collective guilt—its complexities notwithstanding—indicated their "false assumption," as if the "irresolvable link" between identity, tradition, and history could be evaded.[86] The philosopher had only contempt for those who "pick up their own past with their fingertips and make it the past of the others," such as those historians who tried to consign the guilt to Hitler or the Hitlerian clique alone.[87]

But then, even if the "common liability" arising from the "collective silence" did make some sense in Jaspers's time, what about those Germans who were not even born then, who could not even have "participated" in the liability-generating nonaction, who were Habermas's main audience *now*? Can "irresolvable identity" alone answer for this? In 1986, the philosopher would once again take up his forerunner's argument to lay down a new affirmation of collective liability for the Nazi past—applicable even to subsequent generations of Germans: "[Jaspers's differentiation between the personal guilt of commission and the collective guilt of omission] is no longer sufficient for the problem of the later generations (*Nachgeborenen*), to whom the act of omission (*Unterlassungshandeln*) of their parents and grandparents cannot be made a burden."[88] To answer the question of continual "co-liability" (*Mithaftung*), the philosopher referred to connections between then and now that were not "something of the past" but a living presence:

> As always, there is the simple fact that the later generations, too, have grown up in a way of life (*Lebensform*) in which *that* was possible. Our own life is tied with that context of life (*Lebenszusammenhang*) in which Auschwitz was possible. . . . Our way of life is bound with that of our parents and grandparents through a tightly entangled nexus of familial, local, political, as well as intellectual traditions—that is, through a historical milieu, which has made us what and who we are today.

---

85. Ibid.

86. Ibid.

87. Ibid. See similar guilt-shoveling tendencies in the immediate postwar period in **P2** and **P8**.

88. Jürgen Habermas, "Vom öffentlichen Gebrauch der Historie," *Die Zeit*, 7 Nov. 1986.

None of us can sneak out of this milieu, because our identity, whether as individuals or as Germans, is irresolvably interwoven (*unauflöslich verwoben*) with it. . . . We must own up to our traditions if we are not to disown ourselves.[89]

But unlike his opponents, who also invoked ideas such as "identity" and "self-esteem," "culture" and "tradition," to support the construction of a more "positive"—that is, more approving, less denigrating—national attitude, Habermas saw in these the precise reasons for affirming cross-generational liability. Where the first saw breaks, he saw links, and vice versa: "Can one continue the traditions of German culture without taking over the historical liability for the way of life in which Auschwitz was possible?" Historical comparison should not serve as a stratagem to "sneak out of the liability for the risk pool of the Germans (*Risikogemeinschaft der Deutschen*)."[90] Later on, Habermas also challenged his fellow citizens of the reunified Germany to "take over the liability for the consequences" of the deeds of the "perpetrators' generation" (*Tätergeneration*), and to "accept the unsettling political responsibility" arising from the "civilizational collapse (*Zivilisationsbruch*) committed, supported, and tolerated by Germans and which now falls on the shoulders of those born late, as an element of a broken national identity (*gebrochene nationale Identität*)."[91] This "brokenness" is to be understood as "the will to the discontinuation of misguiding ways of thinking in the continuation of one's own traditions. . . . The break in the continuation of our supporting traditions is the condition for regained self-respect."[92]

For the philosopher, the answers to these questions were of immense importance to Germans themselves not only in relation to their own traditions, but also in view of the victims. Collective coliability was applicable to the later generations because of the "obligation (*Verpflichtung*) that we in Germany . . . have to keep awake

---

89. Ibid (emphasis in the original).

90. Ibid.

91. Jürgen Habermas, "Der Zeigefinger: Die Deutschen und ihr Denkmal," *Die Zeit*, 31 Mar. 1999.

92. Ibid.

the remembrance of the suffering of those murdered by German hands."[93] Such remembrance is the expression of solidarity with the deceased. Failing this, Habermas warned, it would be impossible for "fellow Jewish citizens . . . , the sons, the daughters, and the grandsons of the murdered victims to breathe in our country."[94]

In fact, not only the victims and their later generations but also German youths themselves could "find it hard to breathe" in a country where cross-generational solidarity with the victims was missing. A letter writer in her early twenties writing to Giordano in response to the problem of second guilt exclaimed with bewilderment and despair over the lingering Nazi presence in the postwar German judicial system: "How can this generation still breathe actually?" "Melissa R." lamented.[95] The electoral success of Franz Schönhuber's Republican Party in 1989 was for her living proof of the presentness of the past: "Are the roots of poisonous plants finding nourishment again even on rotten soil . . . ? It shows once again that the roots were never torn out, only concealed. . . . The first and second guilt has accumulated to an infinite sum. And the third guilt will soon arrive."[96]

The children's exploration of their family roots in connection with the Nazi past sometimes went beyond the immediate Nazi generation of their parents, as in the case of Dörte von Westernhagen, daughter of SS officer Heinz von Westernhagen. Sichrovsky complained in the postscript of the 1988 English translation of his book, *Born Guilty,* that "up to now nothing has been written about the children of the perpetrators," that it was left to a Jew "not burdened by past guilt" to explore "how these descendants of the perpetrators come to terms with the problem."[97] He was mis-

---

93. Habermas, "Gebrauch der Historie."

94. Ibid.

95. Ralph Giordano, ed., *'Wie kann diese Generation eigentlich noch atmen?' Briefe zu dem Buch: Die zweite Schuld oder Von der Last Deutscher zu sein* (Hamburg: Rasch und Röhring, 1990), 15.

96. Ibid. Cf. the similar expression of another German youth in Peter Sichrovsky, ed., *Born Guilty: Children of Nazi Families* (New York: Basic Books, 1988), 168.

97. Sichrovsky, *Born Guilty,* 172.

taken. For already in 1986, Dörte von Westernhagen had published a lengthy article in *Die Zeit* about four cases of the "children of the perpetrators" (*Kinder der Täter*), whom she had interviewed and who had in some way attempted the "unmasking of the parents" (*Entlarvung der Eltern*).[98] She expanded the article—with more cases and tracing her own family roots back to her grandfather—to a book with the same title soon after Sichrovsky published his in 1987.[99]

Empowered by Günther Anders's *chosen* identification with the children of Nazis, Westernhagen's exploration of her own family and her fellow German "second generation" members revealed painful intergenerational confrontations as well as hidden dangers.[100] Since she did not have any personal memories of her own father—whose death occurred in 1945, when she was barely two—she expanded Anders's call of "moving away from your father" to include **Nazi mothers**, who had been, according to Westernhagen, "perversely glorified by the Hitler regime."[101] Westernhagen did this in order to analyze Nazi influences (such as the glorification of harshness and the disdain for weakness) passing through the mothers to the children, including through her own mother to herself. In lieu of personal memories of encounters with her father, she used his wartime letters to the family and, more extensively, her grandfather Max's diary as her sources.[102] Painstakingly extracting details from the diary entries, the granddaughter reconstructed how her grandfather, who was born in 1863 in Hamburg and suffered through the turbulent economic downturns in the interwar years, had equated every possible enemy—whether the Social Democrats, the "traitors," the Communists, Russia, England, or France—with

---

98. Dörte von Westernhagen, "Die Kinder der Täter," *Die Zeit*, 28 Mar. 1986.

99. Dörte von Westernhagen, *Die Kinder der Täter: Das Dritte Reich und die Generation danach* (Munich: Kösel-Verlag, 1987).

100. It was not the only time that Westernhagen used Anders's work as the starting point of hers. See also, for example, Westernhagen, "Wider den Schlaf des Gewissens," *Die Zeit*, 21 Nov. 1986.

101. Westernhagen, *Kinder der Täter*, 172.

102. Ibid., 10–11.

the Jews.[103] She noted that it was odd that, with just one incon-
sequential exception in the entire 230-page diary, which covered
over forty years of his life (between 1899 and 1943), self-doubt
and self-accusation were altogether missing: "Since Max could
bring the pain and the pressure . . . neither to himself nor to his
Christianity, they became a breeding ground (*Nährboden*) for the
burgeoning hostile fantasies and for the corresponding myths of
salvation."[104] For the younger Westernhagen, dumping all the guilt
on Hitler while "saving" one's own forefather as "being misled"
wasn't doing justice at all, for the salvific fantasies and extermina-
tory hostility against "the world enemy" "already appeared in the
diary before Hitler was mentioned at all. . . . The diary allowed me
to see to what extent Hitler and his follower could be 'a pair.'"[105]
But this knowledge of parental guilt is only part of the task facing the "second generation," for if they are unable to connect this
guilt to themselves as the succeeding generation, they run the risk
of continuing with the **"unrecognized identification" with their
parents**—even in the revolt against them.

Belonging to the 1968 generation, Dörte von Westernhagen
had once been at the forefront of protests against the Nazi generations.[106] But being witness to the violence of the time, she also
became aware of the problem of punishing Nazi parents with quasi-
Nazi methods, or what she called the "return of the persecutor."[107]
Specifically referring to the students movement, she criticized the
"radicalism and mercilessness" of the younger generation, which
proved that "the children themselves were likewise in danger of
succumbing to a new influence of the masses (*Massensuggestion*),"
thus revealing the "not-recognized identification (*nichterkannte*

---

103. Ibid., 35.

104. Ibid., 36. That exception was when Max, a dentist, questioned whether
it was his old age or the effects of war reparation that was to blame for the paucity of patients.

105. Westernhagen, *Kinder der Täter*, 39.

106. See "Gestörte Identität, stolpernder Gang," *Der Spiegel*, no. 6 (1987).

107. Westernhagen, *Kinder der Täter*, 102. Cf. Fritz Bauer's concern about "reforming German justice," not just bringing Nazis to "Nazi justice" in **P4**.

Identifizierung) with the parents."[108] Already in 1982, Westernhagen expressed concern about this hidden identification among the members of her protest-generation: "The wrath of the children was exhausted in the fight against the institutions; the unconscious *(unbewußt)* identification with the parents, however, was not detached."[109] One reason for the survival of this unrecognized/unconscious identification with the parents was for Westernhagen, who also borrowed heavily from the Mitscherlichs in her work, the convenient psychological projection that she herself used to employ for her father:

> The projection made everything of that era [of the parents] reprehensible and evil, while freeing me at the same time from having to see my secret *(geheim)* identification with him or even myself in the perpetrator's situation. I sided with the victims and let the perpetrators live behind my back.[110]

In contrast to this "widening-gap" attitude,[111] Westernhagen sought to affirm the link of generational guilt by extending Jaspers's concept of metaphysical guilt (P2): "Here begins the tradition, the non-release *(Nicht-Entbindung)*. For 'it lays inerasable guilt on me, that I'm still living, when such [atrocity] has happened.' *We take over* (übernehmen) *the guilt of the fathers*."[112] This **"takeover" of guilt** was furthermore legitimized by the unrecognized identification already mentioned: "Only in the failure of the seventies . . . [did] the realization begin to dawn on us: *We are children of these parents.* . . . Whether we like it or not, we are identified with them, even in the negation, in the furious onslaught against them. 'Debt assumption' *(Schuldübernahme)* is obviously not only a juridical construction of civil law."[113]

---

108. Westernhagen, "Kinder der Täter."
109. Dörte von Westernhagen, "Der Januskopf—Ergebnisse einer Grabung," *Familiendynamik* 7 (1982); reprinted in Westernhagen, *Kinder der Täter*, 213–16.
110. Westernhagen, *Kinder der Täter*, 90.
111. See Goldhagen's distancing of the world of "theirs" and the world of "ours" in **P8**.
112. Westernhagen, *Kinder der Täter*, 68 (emphasis added).
113. Ibid., 224 (emphasis added).

Westernhagen saw in the postwar German administration a mirror image of her entangled self: the former being staffed with those compromised by their Nazi past, and herself being influenced by the "unrecognized and concealed" contradictory image of the father.[114] Employing further theological terminology of her own, she asserted that even those born late were not spared of this "context":

> The happenings in the Third Reich stand for the historically developed—i.e., realized on earth and not yet past (*nicht vergangen*)—incarnation of evil. Those who have lived in this time have somehow come in contact with the horror and fascination that belong to this time; no one is exempted, no one is spared. Also those born late are not.[115]

The solemn admission of cross-generational guilt, Westernhagen's sober vision, which sometimes bordered on despair if not for the hope offered by fore-turners like Jaspers, Anders, and the Mitscherlichs, was not something that her fellow members of the "second generation" could easily share. Some of her interviewees sought alternative ways out—but only to betray a deeper enmeshment in their Nazi parents' unpaid debts.

The interview with "Herbert D." was for Westernhagen the "most depressing of all."[116] Like his interviewer, Herbert grew up without the father, who had taken part in the Nazi euthanasia atrocities and committed suicide during investigation in 1949, when Herbert was still an infant. But unlike Westernhagen, he refused to learn more about his own father aside from what he could get from a more or less "intellectual" angle. He had his reason, an altogether *reasonable* one:

> There is a book about this extermination camp, in which my father can be found, but I have never read it. . . . I say, that's it, enough. You can't change anything there after all. It burdens you some more and damages your. As such, it is an indirect tribal liability (*Sippenhaftung*), and we reproach the Nazis exactly for that. If I put myself intellectually in the cage (*sich selber geistig in den Käfig setzen*), then I commit tribal

---

114. Ibid., 219.
115. Ibid., 91.
116. Ibid., 145.

liability myself. That's why I have to fight back and say, Here is the separation between generations.[117]

Günther Anders, as we have seen above, had also explicitly spoken out against tribal liability when speaking to Klaus Eichmann. But the distinction in spirit cannot be more conspicuous: whereas the original expression was made to enable, to empower, and to encourage the difficult path-taking toward the truth about one's own father (and hence his *real* connections to oneself), the application here was to stall the gaining of insight and to block further invitation to go deeper than superficial knowledge. Instead, that state of unknowing was clung onto like some kind of float. "It's enough for me, what I already know," Herbert repeatedly defended his refusal to know more about his father.[118]

What was "depressing" about Herbert's story was not so much his unwillingness to gain insight, but more his failure to see altogether how he had actually been suffering from that mind-set of tribal liability, from which he was apparently intellectually "emancipated." He recalled his childhood experience of being bullied by his classmates, and not being allowed to fight back: "I was absolutely forbidden by my mother to fight, so that none can say, 'Like father, like son.'"[119] He also told Westernhagen about an adolescent idea about becoming a priest, so he could give up having children: "Not because I wanted to enter a religious order. . . . The problem is, there is perhaps a criminal heritage (*verbrecherisches Erbe*), which one passes on to one's children."[120] He recounted also how he argued with his mother, who had wanted him to become a medical doctor. "Then I said [to her]: 'If one has broken the oath of Hippocrates before, then I as the son of my father cannot become a physician. Imagine, I am called to the sickbed of a psychologically handicapped person, and he dies at my hands. People will immediately say, Alright, no surprise.'"[121] Astoundingly, that

---

117. Ibid., 153.
118. Ibid.
119. Ibid., 147.
120. Ibid., 150.
121. Ibid., 148.

mindfulness of how one is being seen and judged by the others in society suffused the twelve or so odd pages dedicated to Herbert's interview by Westernhagen. That gate of "escape" (**R6**) looked like the gate to a cage for Herbert, and was rejected. Hence the perpetrator's child remained in that real prison of tribal-liability constellation, which continued to exert its debilitating influence on his life, "unrecognized and concealed." Giordano was right: "Only he can be uninhibited (*unbefangen*) who has. . . *first* declared himself inhibited."[122]

So although Herbert was unlike Sichrovsky's "Rudolf," who firmly believed in the inevitability of cross-generational punishment, neither was he freed from it by his "intellectual knowledge" that something like that *should not* be allowed to exist. The narrow exit of "tradition-breaking" (Habermas) and "identity-persevering" (Buber),[123] as taken by Westernhagen and some other brave individuals of the "second generation" interviewed by her and by Sichrovsky, proved elusive for many and, in any case, was also fraught with its own dangers.[124] In these, and especially these difficult, moments, the generous initiatives and support offered by Anders, Giordano, and others from the *other side* proved indispensable.

---

122. Giordano, *Zweite Schuld*, 344 (emphasis added).

123. See **P6**.

124. Aside from the dangers of "unrecognized identification" with the parents and of the false identification *as* the victims in the rebelling children, as highlighted by Westernhagen, some critics of her work also rightly pointed to an "excess" of hers in that she wrote: "Every living individual then appears to be somehow bound (*verwoben*), responsible (*verantwortlich*), or entangled (*verstrickt*), also the resistance fighters and victims of persecution." Westernhagen, *Kinder der Täter*, 91. As we've seen in **P8**, the tendency to neutralize guilts by pointing to the guilt of the others—especially the supposed guilt of the suffering victims—was something that Westernhagen could have avoided. Yet, any reader of her entire work would not find it difficult to conclude that this was likely an aberration rather than the kernel of her endeavors, an honest mistake of a courageous path-breaker rather than the definitive statement of her work. This mistake could be rendered more understandable if the further complication of Westernhagen being a self-critical '68er is taken into account. The overlapping of the two historical periods (i.e., 1933–45 and 1968) in her one narrative might have lent her the (unjustified) license to speak of the guilt of the Nazi resisters as a resister herself in the 1960s. See a contemporary review of her book by Volker Ullrich, "Mit den Untaten der Eltern leben," *Die Zeit*, 12 Aug. 1988.

To end his attempted dialogue with Klaus Eichmann that spanned almost a quarter of a century, the then octogenarian Anders reiterated his position on generational guilt: "That I do not consider you guilty just because you are born to be your father's son, and that I would only consider you guilty if you . . . would remain your father's son."[125] Had Anders, who passed away in 1992, lived to listen to a song by a pop German youth band in 2003, he could at least have had the consolation that somehow his message was not entirely lost.

Believe him not who says you can change nothing.
Those who make these claims have only fear before change. . . .
It is not your guilt that the world is as it is.
It would only be your guilt if it remains so.[126]

---

125. Anders, "Zweiter Brief," 97.

126. The song by Die Ärzte is titled "Deine Schuld" and was included in their 2003 album *Geräusch*. When asked about the surprisingly serious content of the song, band member Bela B. blithely answered: "People like us who stand in the public sphere bear a certain responsibility." See "Popband Die Ärzte: 'Wir galten als Teufelszeug,'" *Spiegel Online*, 16 Oct. 2003.

15

"REMEMBER THE EVIL, BUT DO NOT FORGET THE GOOD" (P13)

On 25 June 1950, a rabbi returned to Kassel, Germany, where he used to minister a Jewish community, who were now no more. He had come to the Jewish cemetery there to officiate at the consecration ceremony of a memorial for the Jewish victims of Nazi Germany. "We gather here for a moment of remembrance," he began, "but do *we* need this moment? Our life is marked by gruesome memories in every moment. And if we could give expression to our pain at all, not the word but the scream, the piercing scream alone would be the expression for our suffering."[1] Indeed, what more could have been said then and there when the memories were still so fresh?

---

1. Robert Raphael Geis, "Gib, o Gott, daß in keines Menschen Herz Haß aufsteige!," *Freiburger Rundbrief* 3/4, no. 12/15 (1951/1952): 5 (emphasis in the original).

But Rabbi Robert Raphael Geis did have a word for his audience on that day, a word that puts memories of suffering and the hatred that it naturally engenders in some perspective. He remembered and reminded his listeners of the "memories upon memories" of suffering and humiliation.[2] He also remembered the love of the Jews for Germany that ended in catastrophe. But he was quick to remind his audience: "We were not alone in having made sacrifices (*Opfer gebracht haben*); the followers of democracy, the truly faithful Christians, they all belong to the victims (*zu den Opfern gehören*), whom we mourn."[3] Turning inward, he quoted Max Picard and warned his audience against forgetting the "sickness of Europe" that had made the atrocities possible, the healing of which required triumph over the "Hitler in ourselves" (**P9**). In the end he returned to the theme of memory:

> We commemorate our dead, who had to die as creatures of God. If we want to keep them in living remembrance, then . . . we must learn to recognize and love the human being as creature of God. Let me close with a prayer that is passed down to us in the Talmudic tractate of blessings: "The Eternal One, my God and God of my fathers, please grant that in no human heart shall hatred arise against us, and that **no hatred in our heart** shall arise against any one."[4]

Indeed, the memory of persecution and extermination can all too easily arouse antipathy—which is completely understandable—toward the perpetrators and their "willing executioners." But can one simply wish it away like that? Yes, there was a minority of German opponents and victims of Nazism, as Victor Gollancz has already reminded us (**P1**), and that minority was not necessarily "less" in value than the majority (**P10**). And granted, too, that there is also a "Hitler" within each of us, that the call of turning should begin from within, a turning that begins with inward finger-pointing (**P9**). But are these stereotype-shattering memories and turning-the-table

---

2. Ibid.
3. Ibid.
4. Ibid. (emphasis added).

insights enough to fight the strong currents of ill will that swell from the remembering heart? Is not "forgive and forget" a more direct remedy?

Rabbi Geis would be the last to prescribe forgetfulness as a cure for hatred, for he also saw danger on the other side: that Jews would neglect their duty of remembrance just because they were too busy participating in the postwar German economic "miracle," thus failing at their vocation of serving as a forewarning to other peoples. "To remember (*erinnern*), to truthfully, honestly remember, is no sentimental feeling of pain. To remember means always the expulsion of that which is untrue from the inner home. . . . May those who are kindhearted to us join us in keeping this in memory (*Gedächtnis*), what kind of storm warning it is when Jews are being attacked, that it is always a sign of the coming of dark powers, which almost never stop at [just attacking] the Jews. We as Jews, however, should know that we are the sign among peoples."[5]

If forgetting leads nowhere, and only leaves what is false in oneself and one's society unexamined, then the question remains: How can remembrance lead—or more precisely, which *configuration* of remembrance can lead—to the desired expulsion of the wrong without at the same time succumbing to hatred? A few months after Rabbi Geis's sermon in 1950, another German Jew found a possible answer to this question. In January 1951 Kurt R. Grossmann, one of the first German citizens to be deprived of Germany citizenship (*Ausbürgerung*) in 1933 for "violating the duty and loyalty to Reich and people,"[6] began to publish a series of short articles about non-Jewish rescuers of Jews, the **"unsung heroes"** (*unbesungen Helden*), in *Aufbau*.[7] The objective was, as the author later explained, to pay the "debt of thanks" (*Dankesschuld*) and the "debt

---

5. "Gedenkrede anläßlich des 15. Jahrestages der Deportation nach Gurs und der Synagogenzerstörungen des Jahres 1938," 1953, AR7263, Series II/1, Box 1, Folder 27, Papers of Robert Raphael Geis, Leo Baeck Institute, New York.

6. For a biography of Kurt R. Grossmann, see Lothar Mertens, *Unermüdlicher Kämpfer für Frieden und Menschenrechte: Leben und Wirken von Kurt R. Grossmann* (Berlin: Duncker & Humblot, 1997).

7. The concept was still unstable at this early stage. One of the "heroes" Grossmann hailed was an American telephone technician who had saved a handicapped

of honor" (*Ehrenschuld*) that he and the rescued Jews thought they owed their rescuers.[8] One of those praised by Grossmann was the German scavenger "Mieze," who, despite her poverty, had provided shelter and nourishment for two Jews in hiding in Berlin.[9] In speaking of another rescuer, a Polish maid who had smuggled Jewish children out of a ghetto, taken care of them, and returned them to their surviving relatives, Grossmann wondered whether "it was the godly spirit who lived in this pious Catholic woman, or instinct" that was behind the life-threatening rescue mission.[10] The remembrance of these heroes was at times also tinged with a sense of pity that they were not able to live a dignified life after the war as they well deserved. The report on Mieze, for example, ended with a reference to the squalid conditions in which the heroine lived in Berlin. Speaking of another German rescuer, Franz W. Fritsch, Grossmann was indignant that the hero was not recognized because he had "merely" saved Jews instead of "actively fighting" the Nazis, while the guilty were rewarded with "handsome pensions." "It is a travesty of justice—for when someone thwarted the plans of the Nazis to murder the Jews or to exploit them until complete exhaustion, he was in fact combating National Socialism. Such acts should be rewarded and praised!"[11] Grossmann's broadening of the concepts of resistance and heroism, together with his persistent efforts to arouse public remembrance for his heroes, would eventually lead to the first collective recognition of the German rescuers of Jews in postwar Germany (see below).

While Grossmann was in the process of collecting these stories of rescue (and meeting the rescued and the rescuers, like Gertrud

---

woman from a burning house. Kurt R. Grossmann, "Unbesungene Helden IV," *Aufbau*, 16 Mar. 1951.

8. Kurt R. Grossmann, *Die unbesungenen Helden: Menschen in Deutschlands dunklen Tagen* (Berlin-Grunewald: arani Verlag, 1961), 120. See also Dennis Riffel, *Unbesungene Helden: Die Ehrungsinitiative des Berliner Senats 1958 bis 1966* (Berlin: Metropol, 2007), 105–6.

9. Kurt R. Grossmann, "Unbesungene Helden II & III," *Aufbau*, 16 Feb. 1951.

10. Kurt R. Grossmann, "Unbesungene Helden I," *Aufbau*, 26 Jan. 1951.

11. Grossmann, *Menschen in Deutschlands dunklen Tagen*, 173. See also Thomas Kleine-Brockhoff and Dirk Kurbjuweit, "Die anderen Schindlers," *Die Zeit*, 1 Apr. 1994.

Luckner),[12] a law was passed in the newly established State of Israel to commemorate—among the Jewish victims and opponents of Nazism—the "high-minded Gentiles who jeopardized their lives to save Jews."[13] The "Martyrs' and Heroes' Commemoration (Yad Va-Shem) Law" was passed by the Knesset on 19 August 1953. The institution ("Remembrance Authority") established by the 1953 law (Art. 1) would in time be realized in the Yad Vashem commemorative and educational complex existing in Jerusalem today, and would include the **"Righteous Among The Nations"** commemoration (Art. 1.9). While why a nation would want to remember its *own* victims of foreign oppression is understandable, the reasons for writing a law to remember the *foreign* rescuers as well are not exactly obvious.[14] As it turns out, the inclusion of the "righteous (gentiles)" in the state commemorative project had to do with the formation of the Yad Vashem idea itself.

According to the Israeli historian Mooli Brog, the idea of erecting a "monument of testimony" for the commemoration of Holocaust victims predated the end of the war: in 1942 a kibbutznik, Mordechai Shenhavi, first proposed the "national project" to the Jewish National Fund (JNF).[15] Already at this time, Rabbi Moshe Burstyn of the JNF had suggested the use of the name Yad Vashem—literally, memorial and name—for this purpose, a term from the book of Isaiah (56:5).[16] Though Shenhavi initially refrained from using

---

12. He met Luckner in Freiburg in 1952, a German Catholic who had help Jews escape Nazi Germany and suffered eighteen months in the Ravensbrück concentration camp. Kurt R. Grossmann, "Bei Gertrud Luckner," *Aufbau*, 26 Sept. 1952; and Grossmann, "Gertrud Luckner—70 Jahre," *Aufbau*, 25 Sept. 1970.

13. Article 1.9 of the Martyrs' and Heroes' Commemoration (Yad Vashem) Law.

14. In fact, it remains contentious to this day that Jewish rescuers of Jews are not honored by Yad Vashem as among the Righteous. See Arno Lustiger, *Rettungswiderstand: Über die Judenretter in Europa während der NS-Zeit* (Göttingen: Wallstein, 2011), 414.

15. Mooli Brog, "In Blessed Memory of a Dream: Mordechai Shenhavi and Initial Holocaust Commemoration Ideas in Palestine, 1942–1945," *Yad Vashem Studies* 30 (2002): 297–336.

16. Brog also identified as the source the preexisting and "widespread custom in the new neighborhoods of Jerusalem" of using Isaiah 56:5 on dedication plaques for donated buildings for charity.

the name, he finally adopted it in 1945 when he publicized his idea amid a series of contentious discussions, lethargic responses, competing proposals, and public initiatives that saw the project of commemoration increasingly shaped by religious notions. It appears that the idea of establishing a "special room with the names of non-Jews who rescued Jews" was gleaned from another proposal and incorporated in the final "plan" Shenhavi presented to the public.[17] Given the non-Jewish-specific context of Isaiah 56, the inclusion of the foreign rescuers in the commemoration of Jewish victims was unproblematic, if not "natural." What emerged as a problem, however, was **how to name the perpetrator**: some in the Knesset called for the use of the name "German" instead of "Nazi," the "German" instead of the "Nazi" oppressor, the "German" instead of the "Nazi" enemy. The proposed revisions were rejected on the grounds that remembrance of the victims should not serve the incitement of "racial hatred."[18] The law was passed in its present form, without naming the "Germans" or "Germany" at all.

It would be almost a decade before the first non-Jewish rescuers of Jews would actually be recognized by Yad Vashem. In the meantime, the "debt" of remembering the righteous, or sustaining gratefulness instead of hatred in the heart, had to be shouldered by private initiatives. Rabbi Geis continued to promote the memory

---

17. The earliest proposal for remembering the righteous gentiles cited by Brog was presented by Baruch Zuckerman and Jacob Helman to the World Jewish Congress on 3 Feb. 1945, which was subsequently discussed by the JNF National Committee before Shenhavi's "Yad Vashem Plan" was published for the first time in *Davar* on 25 May 1945. This point was confirmed by Brog's correspondence with the author dated 9 Jan. 2013.

18. According to a report in the *Freiburger Rundbrief*, the right-wing opposition in the Knesset at the time proposed changing the wording of the legal text so that the word "German" would replace the word "Nazi." This proposal was rejected by the then foreign minister Moshe Sharett, who said: "We would not be honoring the memory of the victims but desecrating it, if we abuse it to kindle racial hatred in the land of Israel." See M. Y. Ben-Gavriêl, "Gesetz zur Verewigung des Andenkens an die vom Nationalsozialismus ermordeten Juden gebilligt," *Freiburger Rundbrief* 6, no. 21/24 (1953/54): 40–41. See also Tom Segev, *The Seventh Million: The Israelis and the Holocaust*, trans. Haim Watzman (New York: Hill and Wang, 1993), 436, 439.

of the "noble German human beings," the "good-doers," and "the other Germany" in his sermons and writings in the 1950s.[19] And in 1957, two of the earliest collections of rescue stories during the Holocaust in honor of the righteous were published—one in German by Kurt R. Grossmann, and the other in English by Philip Friedman[20]—thus complementing Geis's religious claims with historical evidence. Of the two, the work by Grossmann, *Die unbesungenen Helden: Menschen in Deutschlands dunklen Tagen* (The Unsung Heroes: Humans in Germany's Dark Days), is still of primary relevance to our analysis, not only because it was published in Germany, but also because of its (over)emphasis on German rescuers and—consequently perhaps—the responses it generated in German society.

Overcoming his earlier disappointment with postwar Germany, Grossmann advanced his project of remembering his "heroes" within Germany itself. He was encouraged by a publisher in Berlin, arani Verlag, to collect more testimonies and make them known to the wider German reading public.[21] Hence in early 1956, he made a public call (through the German dailies *Telegraf* and *Süddeutsche Zeitung*) for both the rescued and the rescuers to submit their testimonies, and received more than a hundred written responses.[22] When the collection was published in the autumn of 1957, about half of the 350-page volume was devoted to Germany and Austria, and included the stories of "Germans at home" and "Germans in occupied territories." Grossmann characterized his efforts to publish about the "unsung heroes" as a **Jewish duty to remember the gentile rescuers:**

---

19. "Yom Kippur Sermons," 1954–60, AR7263, Series II/3, Box 1, Folder 73, Papers of Robert Raphael Geis, Leo Baeck Institute, New York. See also Geis, "Es gibt keine Entschuldigung," *Allgemeine Wochenzeitung der Juden in Deutschland*, 25 Jul. 1952; Geis, "Es mahnen die Toten 1933–1945," *Mannheimer Hefte*, no. 3 (1952).

20. Philip Friedman, *Their Brothers' Keepers* (New York: Crown Publishers, 1957).

21. Mertens, *Grossmann*, 207. See also Riffel, *Ehrungsinitiative des Berliner Senats*, 38.

22. Mertens, *Grossmann*, 269.

These selfless individuals, who acted as the unorganized determined executioners (*Willensvollstrecker*) of the eternal law of humanity, arose when they helped the crushed creature—the Jews . . . with the risk of their own life. . . . I feel as a Jew the duty to tell the story of the brave non-Jewish men and women.[23]

One of the brave Germans remembered by Grossmann was Oskar Schindler. The account of Schindler's work was not only the longest in the volume, but probably also the most substantial report of his rescue mission published in German until then—a mission that has become world-famous thanks to Steven Spielberg's film *Schindler's List* (1993). Indeed, Schindler's story was apparently so important for Grossmann that he published a portrait of him, "Retter von 1100 Juden" (Rescuer of 1,100 Jews), in *Aufbau* even before his book appeared.[24] In this account we can perhaps trace Grossmann's passion for remembering the righteous back to the urgings of Jews rescued by Schindler, the *Schindlerjuden*: "In the year 1947, a group of Jewish women appeared at the Jewish World Congress and appealed to its members to send basic necessities to the *non-Jew Oskar Schindler*. 'Why should we send packets to a German?' I asked. 'What? Don't you know the story of Oskar Schindler, our rescuer?' The speaker of the group was incredulous."[25] Though Schindler was for a long time neglected by his fellow nationals, his beneficiaries remembered him, gave him financial support, and brought him to Israel to be honored by Yad Vashem, as among the first to plant a tree in the garden of the Righteous Among The Nations.[26] Gratitude toward Schindler was so great that Leopold "Poldek" Pfefferberg, one of the Schindlerjuden, would prove instrumental in making the German righteous a household name, as we shall see below.

---

23. Grossmann, *Menschen in Deutschlands dunklen Tagen*, 12.

24. "Retter von 1100 Juden: Begegnung mit Oskar Schindler," *Aufbau*, 12 Jul. 1957.

25. Ibid. (emphasis in the original).

26. See the honoring efforts of the Schindlerjuden and the relevant controversies in David M. Crowe, *Oskar Schindler: The Untold Account of His Life, Wartime Activities, and the True Story behind the List* (Boulder, CO: Westview Press, 2004), 493.

For Grossmann, the remembrance of rescuers like Schindler and Luckner was important for both the Germans and the relationship between them and the Jews: "It seems to me to be decisive for the relationship between Jews and Germans that what is humane is not suffocated in that cruel happening . . . for the few examples (of hundreds) prove that there is a weapon against hysteria of the masses, and that nonconformism is neither antistate nor antisociety; the masses can learn from the courageous deeds of individuals, to orient themselves anew and **to overcome the abject state of national shame.**"[27]

Grossmann's endeavor to bring recognition to these unsung heroes found an enthusiastic response in the Jewish community in Berlin, which decided in 1958 to set up a fund to support the livelihood of recognized rescuers who were in need. The same year, at the instigation of Senator Joachim Lipschitz, the Berlin Senate joined this private initiative to bring honor and support to more "Unsung Heroes" (U.H.), which was now the official term for the rescuers.[28] Senator Lipschitz, who had suffered Nazi persecution himself as a "half Jew," concurred with Grossmann in that he saw in the "existence of these human beings . . . the proof that even the harshest dictatorship is not able to wipe out all seeds of humanity."[29] Through the groundwork laid by Lipschitz and Grossmann, the rescued Jews and their relatives sought to pay, in their own words, the (inherited) "debt of thanks" and "debt of honor" they deemed they owed their benefactors.[30]

Between 1958 and 1966, the U.H. initiative gave recognition and financial support to 760 rescuers.[31] But more than just honoring the honorable, the initiators also wanted to turn Germans away from a **concept of heroism** that glorified only "patriots" like soldiers and generals, while "mere" citizens who followed their conscience were not considered. Grossmann was categorically against

---

27. Grossmann, *Menschen in Deutschlands dunklen Tagen*, 21 (emphasis added).
28. Ibid., 27.
29. Ibid., 28.
30. Riffel, *Ehrungsinitiative des Berliner Senats*, 105–6.
31. Ibid.

the all-excusing principle "My country, right or wrong"; rather he advocated the "eternal ethical law of humanity." For him, heroes are "those few who, remaining clear-headed even as waves of mass hysteria swept by, . . . have helped oppressed people despite the collateral dangers."[32] They are "human beings who risk their lives and freedom for the sake of truth. . . . They act with no reward other than the satisfaction that they have done in the time given them what seemed to them to be the self-evident commandment of humanity."[33]

Coincidentally, there was no better time to debate what true heroism means than the early 1960s, when the Eichmann trial in Jerusalem laid bare how even a very ordinary *paterfamilias* could commit monstrous crimes. The much-observed trial of Eichmann made it all the more urgent to cultivate a remembering of evil that does not slip into convenient hatred against a single perpetrator or the one "perpetrator-nation." We have already seen how Hannah Arendt's report on the trial sought to bring attention to the non-German-specificity of the Eichmann phenomenon, in conformity with her earlier work "Organisierte Schuld" (Organized Guilt) (P1). We shall now look at how a rabbi in California was so moved by certain materials coming out of the trial that he acted immediately to bring Jewish attention to the neglected rescuers, which later—without any obvious plan at work—helped support German remembrance of the Shoah victims *and* their German helpers through the American TV series *Holocaust*, which was broadcast in (West) Germany in January 1979.

Rabbi Harold M. Schulweis, born in New York in 1925 to Polish Jews from Warsaw, was listening to the Eichmann trial in Jerusalem when he heard for the first time the testimony of Hermann Friedrich Gräbe,[34] a German civil engineer who had saved Jews

---

32. Grossmann, *Menschen in Deutschlands dunklen Tagen*, 11.

33. Grossmann, "Unbesungene Helden I."

34. See a description of Gräbe's activities in Christian Habbe, "Einer gegen die SS," *Spiegel Special*, no. 1 (2001): 149–51; and Wolfram Wette, "Verleugnete Helden," *Die Zeit*, 8 Nov. 2007; and also Yad Vashem, "Der Zeuge, der beschloss zu handeln: Hermann Friedrich Graebe. Deutschland," accessed 14 Jun. 2012, www1.yadvashem.org/yv/de/righteous/stories/graebe.asp.

from mass killings in Ukraine and who later became the only German to testify for the prosecution in the Nuremberg trials.[35] He returned to his community in California and established the Institute for the Righteous Acts (later changed to the Jewish Foundation for the Righteous) in order to search for, make known, and take care of the rescuers wherever they could be found. Through ceaseless sermons and writings on these righteous gentiles, a Jewish-American writer and TV producer, Gerald Green, came to know these hitherto little-known stories of heroism during the Holocaust. Apparently touched by these stories and also by Schulweis's enthusiasm about their discovery, Green began to incorporate the "righteous Christian" in his own literary and media projects, culminating in the *Holocaust* TV series, in which Hermann Gräbe was remembered as "Kurt Dorf"—the good German civil engineer who had listened to his conscience and testified. In its novelized form, *Holocaust* was presented as a work of fiction that "will restore your faith [in humankind], despite its chronicle of monstrous deeds unparalleled."[36]

Yet, how can this be? How can the representation—even in fiction—of "monstrous deeds" in the Holocaust be anything but an antithesis to "faith in humankind"? For Rabbi Schulweis, the key lay in a particular kind of remembrance—**remembrance for "constructive repentance."** In May 1963, he gave a lecture at the University of Judaism in Los Angeles, in which he, like Rabbi Geis before him, broached the question of how to remember the Shoah. "Memory is an ambiguous energy," he said. "It can liberate or enslave, heal or destroy. . . . How we interpret the Holocaust holds serious consequences for the character and morale of our children, not only for the Jewish child but for the non-Jewish child as well."[37]

---

35. See Lustiger, *Rettungswiderstand*, 26–27; Peter Krahulec, "'The Road Not Taken. . .': Grundzüge einer Didaktik der Erinnerung," in *Erinnerungsarbeit: Grundlage einer Kultur des Friedens*, ed. Berhard Nolz and Wolfgang Popp (Münster: Lit Verlag, 2000), 55–64; and Eva Fogelman, *Conscience and Courage: Rescuers of Jews during the Holocaust* (London: Cassell, 1995), 11.

36. Gerald Green, *Holocaust* (London: Corgi Books, 1978).

37. The speech was reproduced in Harold Schulweis, "The Bias against Man," *Journal of Jewish Education* 34, no. 1 (1963): 6–14.

Schulweis, who had been a pupil of Abraham Joshua Heschel, was deeply concerned about a remembering that unwittingly solidifies the self-identification of Jews as "the world's eternal victim." As a father and educator, he wondered what Holocaust remembrance might do to the morale and moral strength of his children and students: "We dare not feign amnesia, but how are we to remember without destroying hope?"[38]

For some other Jewish thinkers, the solution was to highlight Jewish resistance by remembering also the Jews who had actively fought back—physically as well as spiritually, so as not to succumb to the pessimism of powerlessness.[39] Rabbi Schulweis took another route, one that looks outward for confidence, in the world *out there*, in the *hasidai umot ha-olam*, the righteous non-Jews:

> In Jewish tradition, belittling man does not raise the dignity of God. We do not turn toward God by turning our backs upon man. . . . It is not easy these days to speak for man. It is easier to believe in God than to believe that man is in His image. . . . How are we, as moral educators, to make memory the father of conscience and of constructive repentance? . . . Morality needs evidence, hard data, facts in our time and in our place to nourish our faith in man's capacity for decency. . . . While yet in its embryonic stages, the evidence steadily mounts of an unknown number of silent heroes who risked their lives and jeopardized the lives of their families to save our people.[40]

Schulweis cited Grossmann's and Friedman's pioneering studies as examples of this growing evidence. He also referred to the story of Hermann Gräbe—though neither *Their Brothers' Keepers* nor *Die unbesungenen Helden* had mentioned him. For Schulweis, these "acts of righteousness" were "events of godliness"; the righteous were the "face of God," the proof that God did not turn away from the victims, and the "evidence of the divine viability in our lives."[41] As such, Jews and Germans alike should endeavor to

---

38. Ibid.

39. See, for example, Yehuda Bauer, *The Jewish Emergence from Powerlessness* (London: Macmillan, 1980).

40. Schulweis, "Bias against Man," 9.

41. Ibid.

discover these valuable individuals: "We need Beate Klarsfelds and Simon Wiesenthals[42] to search out the rescuers of our people with the same zeal and energy with which the murderers of our people are properly hunted down and brought to justice."[43]

Like Gollancz before him, when speaking up for the German opponents of Nazism (**P11**), Schulweis was unimpressed by the argument that these good people were too few to be "representative" or "representable." "Which perverse logic holds that we obliterate the memory of man's nobility so as to preserve the memory of his degeneracy?" he argued.[44] And he resented that names like Göring and Goebbels should become remembered but not (Hermann) Gräbe and (Heinrich) Grüber.[45] Turning to Talmudic teachings, he noted:

> For the sake of thirty-six righteous the world is sustained; for the sake of thirty righteous non-Jews, the Talmud declares, the nations of the world continue to exist; for the sake of ten good men, Sodom and Gomorrah would be spared; for the sake of two righteous women—Naomi and Ruth—the Rabbis say the nations of Moab and Ammon were spared. Who measures righteousness by number?[46]

It is this willful—that is, unnatural, counternatural—tenacity in remembering the *righteous others* that contributes to moral remembrance, or remembrance for constructive repentance. "Memory can be a healing art but it requires skillful uses of materials at hand," observed Schulweis.[47] It is not only the spiritual health

---

42. Beate Klarsfeld, a German journalist, and Simon Wiesenthal, a Jewish survivor of the Holocaust, are both known for their engagement in bringing Nazis to justice.

43. Harold Schulweis, "Post-Holocaust Recovery: An Appeal for Moral Education," accessed 18 Dec. 2012, http://www.vbs.org/page.cfm?p=746.

44. Schulweis, "Bias against Man," 12.

45. Heinrich Grüber was a Nazi opponent and a rescuer recognized by Yad Vashem as a Righteous Among The Nations. Schulweis interviewed him in April 1962 and their conversation is recorded in Schulweis's book *Conscience: The Duty to Obey and the Duty to Disobey* (Woodstock, VT: Jewish Lights Publishing, 2008), 87.

46. Schulweis, "Bias against Man," 12 (emphasis added).

47. Ibid., 11.

of the victims' later generations that is at stake, but also that of the perpetrators, for "fingers of insistent accusation" may simply lead to resignation and "brooding guilt" rather than "constructive repentance."[48] Schulweis proposed instead that it is the duty of the Jews to help humanity regain a foothold after Auschwitz: "We are today called upon to tap the moral energy of Judaism for the sake of the world. We, who know man's capacity to destroy, bear witness to his capacity to save."[49]

Many of these exhortations from this early lecture by Schulweis would be reiterated and expanded in the ensuing decades of his career as a Conservative rabbi, culminating in his dictum, "Remember the evil, but do not forget the good."[50] His persistent message about **disproportionate remembrance of the righteous others** generated a broad range of responses: in academia, the nascent research on the "bystanders" and the "altruistic personality" in the United States was credited to Schulweis's initiative and encouragement.[51] In addition, before he delivered his lecture on the righteous, the rabbi had already contributed to the popularization of the righteous through Gerald Green, who was also born in New York. The result of this early intervention was a thirty-minute feature, "The Righteous," with six rescuers who had saved Jews from the Nazis recounting their stories, aired on Channel 11 (WIIC-TV, Pittsburgh) the evening of 24 December 1962.[52] This early encounter with the rescuers was apparently so captivating that Green would continue to work on this theme in his subsequent works.

---

48. Ibid., 8.

49. Ibid., 14.

50. Harold Schulweis, *Letting Go/Holding On: Jewish Consciousness in a Post-Holocaust World* (New York: The American Jewish Committee, 1988), 21. See also his "Aren't the Righteous Always a Minority?," *Sh'ma: A Journal of Jewish Responsibility* 11, no. 203 (Dec. 1980), 23–24; and "An Appeal to Jewish Holocaust Survivors," ibid. 16, no. 319 (Oct. 1986), 149–50.

51. See Gunnar Heinsohn, "Die Ermutigung des Rabbi Schulweis: Zum Phänomen des 'Bystander'-Verhaltens," *Universitas*, no. 5 (1993): 444–53.

52. Ibid. See also "TV Tonight," *Indiana Evening Gazette*, 24 Dec. 1962. According to this short description of the program, "the story [of rescue] came to the attention of producer Gerald Green through the writings of Rabbi Harold Schulweis."

In 1965 Green published a novel, *The Legion of Noble Christians*, about a reluctant Irish Catholic, "Buck Sweeney," commissioned by a Jew in America, "Sherman Wettlaufer," to seek out and reward those "righteous Christians" in Europe who had rescued Jews during the Holocaust. The story of Sweeney and Wettlaufer, both from New York, and the European "nobles" they tried to reach out to, became not only a tool for recounting the heroic deeds of rescue amid human horror, but also an arena for debate about how and why the righteous should be remembered, in spite of the (European) cynicism against their remembrance. Among the noble Christians interviewed by Sweeney was "Dr. Ludwig Helms," a German civil engineer who had testified in the war crimes trials.[53] The tribute to the real Hermann Gräbe, who was the only German witness for the prosecution in the trials, was conspicuous: like Gräbe, "Dr. Helms" testified about the massacres of Jews in Ukraine in 1942 and for that became a social outcast because of his "traitorous" act.[54] The testimonies of the two were almost identical.[55]

If Grossmann's *Helden* and Friedman's *Keepers* were the first historical accounts of the righteous as a group, then Green's *Legion* could be the first, if not the only, fictionalized account of

---

53. Gerald Green, *The Legion of Noble Christians or The Sweeney Survey* (New York: Trident Press, 1965), 64.

54. Ibid., 76. See also Habbe, "Einer gegen die SS."

55. Cf. Green, *Legion of Noble Christians*, 87–89. And affidavits of Hermann Gräbe made on 10 Nov. 1945; "Translation of Document 2992-PS," in *Nazi Conspiracy and Aggression*, ed. Office of United States Chief of Counsel for Prosecution of Axis Criminality (Washington, DC: United States Government Printing Office, 1946), 697. Aside from Gräbe's voice, other real-life righteous have also found expression in Green's *Legion of Noble Christians*. For example, Ona Simaite, a Lithuanian librarian, had saved and aided Jews and suffered torture for that. Her astonishing statement "I was ashamed that I was not Jewish myself" was recorded by Friedman, promoted by Schulweis, and resounded in Green's novel, though from the mouth of a fictional French priest. See Friedman, *Their Brothers' Keepers*, 21–25; Harold Schulweis, "Memory and Anger," accessed 18 Dec. 2012, http://www.vbs.org/page.cfm?p=724; and Green, *Legion of Noble Christians*, 26. Above all, the spirit of Schulweis himself is represented in the figure of Wettlaufer. Cf. Schulweis, *Letting Go/Holding On*, 15; Green, *Legion of Noble Christians*, 288–89.

remembering the righteous—as in searching for them and recognizing them—and the internal, psychological struggles involved in the enterprise.[56] When Green wrote this work, he could not have foreseen that the Jewish-Catholic collaboration—or more precisely, the Jewish-initiated joint effort—of remembering the righteous Christians would be replayed in real life in the 1980s, as we shall see later when a Polish Jew saved by a German Catholic insistently persuaded an Australian Catholic to write down the rescuer's story and to make his name known, while at the same time—albeit unwittingly—bringing world renown to a Talmudic saying concerning the rescuer.

It is a pity that *Legion* was never translated into German, as it could have added a timely canto for the unsung heroes to Peter Weiss's *Ermittlung.*[57] Nevertheless, another chance came more than a decade later when Gerald Green was tasked to write the teleplay for the *Holocaust* TV series, which, unlike *Legion,* had a profound impact on the collective memory of the victims of Nazism in Germany.[58] *Holocaust* was aired in the United States in 1978, and the novel in English came out the same year. Both were brought to German viewers and readers in 1979. The TV series itself was watched by millions of Germans, registering record ratings in postwar German TV history.[59] In this creation of Green's, Hermann Gräbe, the quintessential German righteous for Schulweis and Green—before Oskar Schindler's name came to the fore a few years later—once again appeared as the German civil engineer who had seen the atrocities committed in the German name and bore

56. Green, *Legion of Noble Christians,* 47, 292.

57. This drama by the German writer Peter Weiss was published and staged in 1965. It is a somber piece—divided into eleven cantos—that takes materials from the contemporaneous Auschwitz trials. Peter Weiss, *Die Ermittlung: Oratorium in 11 Gesängen* (Frankfurt a.M.: Suhrkamp, 1965).

58. For a concise assessment of the general influence of the TV series *Holocaust* in Germany, see Torben Fischer and Matthias N. Lorenz, eds., *Lexikon der 'Vergangenheitsbewältigung' in Deutschland: Debatten- und Diskursgeschichte des Nationalsozialismus nach 1945* (Bielefeld: transcript, 2007), 243.

59. See "'Holocaust': Die Vergangenheit kommt zurück," *Der Spiegel,* no. 5 (1979).

witness. "Kurt Dorf" was his name this time. And in addition to his role of being the only German who testified in the war crimes trials, Dorf also assumed the position of **German conscience**—the voice that kept speaking to closed German ears as the crimes unfolded. "Uncle Kurt" was portrayed by Green as attempting repeatedly to challenge the false moral certitude of his nephew, "Erik Dorf," the German youth who gradually lost all his bearings as he ascended in the Nazi hierarchy.

On his first appearance in Erik's diary, Kurt shocked his nephew by calling Reinhard Heydrich, Erik's boss, the "Blond Beast."[60] When Erik was participating in the Babi Yar massacre, in 1941, having "developed a crust, an armor around any pity or compassion that might have remained" in himself, Kurt was there as the still small voice asking, disconcertingly: "Who were the . . . victims? . . . so many civilians? Is it really necessary . . . ?"[61] When Erik's family was happily playing *Stille Nacht* with the piano "offered" to them (in reality stolen from the Jewish doctor, Josef Weiss), Kurt would not relent from inquiring about the real owner and the fate of his family.[62] When Erik wanted to discourage Kurt from employing Jews, who were "marked for special handling," Kurt bluntly told him: "Say what you mean, Erik, say the word. Murder."[63] And finally, when the defeat of Germany was imminent and Erik was frenetically burning the Auschwitz files, Kurt was there, too, admonishing him: "Do you honestly think you can now hide the murder of six million people? . . . You may just manage to cheat the hangman with that kind of logic [that one was just obeying orders, not doing something wrong]. But I hope to God you don't."[64] But Erik was already beyond admonishment at that point. "I should have had you shot long ago," he told his uncle.

---

60. Green, *Holocaust*, 95.
61. Ibid., 196–200.
62. Ibid., 208–11.
63. Ibid., 355.
64. Ibid., 392. It was also here that Green gave Kurt a chance to confess, to rid himself of self-righteousness.

Hence rather than just a footnote to the larger story, the German righteous was a thread throughout *Holocaust*.[65] In Green's execution, then, the vision of Rabbi Schulweis of **harnessing memory—the memory of the righteous—for cultivating conscience** was implemented. Whether it actually succeeded in this task, though, belongs to another inquiry. Furthermore, whether the Germans watching *Holocaust* actually recognized Hermann Gräbe in Kurt Dorf is another question, for the real righteous himself had received hitherto only scant recognition in his native land.[66] Gräbe himself was sure that Kurt Dorf was modeled after him.[67] But this connection was most probably beyond the average German TV viewer of 1979, not to mention Green's encounter with Gräbe's story through Schulweis, and the rabbi's clarion call to remember the righteous in the aftermath of the Eichmann trial. Nevertheless, it is presumptuous to conclude that the unknown or little-known existence of real heroes behind their fictional adaptions "does not count." For if and when a desperate German youth rejects Green's message of "faith in humankind" in his *Holocaust,* because such "good Germans" could only exist in fiction, he can be comforted by the "hard evidence" that the German righteous exist, that there is a choice to do good even in "impossible" moral situations. It is little wonder then that a contemporary German commentator, who had a Nazi father, found Green's *Holocaust* "merciful" (*barmherzig*),[68] for not only were the German viewers spared the even more unpalatable

---

65. In contrast to the novelized form, the original TV series had dedicated the first appearance of righteous Germans not to Hermann Gräbe, a.k.a. Kurt Dorf, but Fr. (Bernhard) Lichtenberg, whose actual words about the church praying *also* for the Jews were repeated almost verbatim in the artistic representation (see the first part of the four-part TV series).

66. The first full-length biography of Gräbe, published in English by Douglas Huneke in 1985, was only translated into German in 2002. See Douglas Huneke, *In Deutschland unerwünscht: Hermann Gräbe*, trans. Adrian Seifert and Robert Lasser (Lüneburg: Dietrich zu Klampen Verlag, 2002). See also Gräbe's belated recognition in his own birthplace, Solingen, in Wette, "Verleugnete Helden."

67. "Real 'Holocaust' Figure Talks Up," *Merced Sun-Star*, 10 May 1978.

68. See Gerhard Mauz, "Das wird mit keinem Wind verwehen," *Der Spiegel*, no. 5 (1979).

brutality and bestiality committed in the German name in historical reality, which had been brought to light in previous court proceedings but had not been shown on TV, but there was also the
remembrance of the German righteous, the light to look to in times
of almost complete darkness and moral despair.[69]

Between *Legion* and *Holocaust*, (West) Germany was in an
eventful phase of *Vergangenheitsbewältigung*: in the courts were
the Auschwitz trials, in theaters dramatized scenes of the trials
were presented through Weiss's *Ermittlung*, and soon the streets
and campuses would be swamped by German youth yearning for
change. But also in the Bundestag, politicians were debating about
Verjährungsfrist, or the period of limitation for prosecuting Nazi
murders. It was a time of intense remembering; some two decades
after the downfall of Nazi Germany, the past was never quite as
present as in this period.

For our present analysis of remembrance, a small detail in the
Verjährung debates deserves mention, for quite unexpectedly, even
in these ostensibly legal-political processes, Jewish conceptions of
remembrance were injected into the German public sphere, thereby
introducing **the link between remembrance and atonement/reconcilia-
tion** to German political culture. On 10 March 1965, a young German
politician made his name with a speech before his fellow members of
parliament. The subject of the debate was whether it made sense to
give special treatment to murder, thus making Nazi murderers prose-
cutable even *beyond* the standing period of limitation of twenty years.
Affirming such special treatment, the speaker argued that for those
who were supporting the motion of extending the limit "a single consideration stands above all considerations of juridical nature, namely,
that the sense of justice (*Rechtsgefühl*) of a people would be unbear-
ably corrupted if murders have to remain unatoned for (*ungesühnt*)

---

69. It is interesting to note that, typical of "repentant disagreement" (P8), it
was a Jewish survivor, Elie Wiesel, who had in fact complained about the "exaggerated emphasis" on brutality and stereotyping in Green's *Holocaust*. See his
"Trivializing the Holocaust: Semi-Fact and Semi-Fiction," *New York Times*, 16
Apr. 1978.

when they can be atoned for."[70] For him, the argument that the issue must be brought to a close for the sake of national honor should be rejected, because "the honor of the nation is for me in making the honest attempt to do it [make atonement], although the attempt will, I know, remain incomplete, so that one can say, That which is possible has been done."[71] The speech itself was brilliant (and the motion succeeded, to a certain extent),[72] but it was a single quotation in the speech that ensured that it would be remembered:

> Finally I would like to close my speech with a saying. There is this saying in the memorial in Jerusalem for the six million murdered Jews. . . . The saying is from a Jewish mystic of the early eighteenth century—. . . **Forgetfulness extends (*verlängert*) the exile, the secret of redemption is remembrance.**[73]

The extension of "exile" for Germany (i.e., its being left outside of the community of nations) would thus result if the Germans failed to remember their "unatoned" wrongdoings through the "extension" (*Verlängerung*) of the period of limitation. This paradox was noted by a contemporary observer of the parliamentary debate: "[The Parliament] has faced up to the German past without hiding and dodging, it has conjured up painful memories, but precisely by doing this, it has pointed to a way out of the exile, the way that the Jewish mystic has spoken about."[74]

The speaker on that day was Ernst Benda, a Christian Democrat who led a minor dissenting faction in his own party to join ranks with the Social Democrats on this issue. He had just visited Israel

---

70. Speech of Ernst Benda, quoted in Peter Borowsky, "Das Ende der 'Ära Adenauer,'" *Informationen zur politischen Bildung*, no. 258 (1998), accessed 20 Jan. 2017, http://www.bpb.de/izpb/10093/das-ende-der-aera-adenauer; also in "Das Gewissen entscheidet," *Union in Deutschland* 19, no. 11 (1965).

71. Borowsky, "Ende der 'Ära Adenauer.'"

72. The beginning of the counting of twenty years was changed from 1945 to 1949, hence the decision on extension was postponed to 1969, when it was decided to extend the period to thirty years. Only in 1979 was it decided to definitively abolish the period of limitation for murder and genocide.

73. Borowsky, "Ende der 'Ära Adenauer'" (emphasis added).

74. Rolf Zundel, "Strich unter die Vergangenheit?," *Die Zeit*, 19 Mar. 1965.

in 1964, where he paid tribute to Yad Vashem. Benda's grandfather was Jewish, and his grandmother was among the "wives of Rosenstrasse" who had protested in Berlin for their imprisoned Jewish husbands.[75] Benda's translation of this Jewish saying attributed to the Baal Shem Tov became the standard German translation that would illuminate the meaning of remembrance, of painful but recuperative remembrance, for later generations of Germans up to the present.[76]

While Benda, who would later become the president of Germany's Federal Constitutional Court, was to be credited for introducing this Jewish redemptive meaning of remembrance to German public debates about a topic of the Nazi past, it was another German politician who would popularize it—also in the Bundestag—two decades later. Richard von Weizsäcker, the sixth president of the Federal Republic, gave a speech on 8 May 1985 to commemorate the fortieth anniversary of German capitulation. He called the day a "day of remembrance" (*Tag der Erinnerung*), "especially of the six million Jews who were murdered in German concentration camps."[77] Like Geis, he made use of the peculiarity of the German word for "remembering" to call for the internalization of history; but unlike Geis, who emphasized (to his Jewish audience) the task of "expulsion of that which is untrue," including ethnic hatred, Weizsäcker emphasized (to his German listeners) the inclusion of

---

75. See Dietrich Strothmann, "Kärrner der Gerechtigkeit," *Die Zeit*, 19 Mar. 1965. On the history of the Rosenstrasse protest, see Nathan Stoltzfus, "Jemand war für mich da," *Die Zeit*, 21 Jul. 1989; and Stoltzfus, *Resistance of the Heart: Intermarriage and the Rosenstrasse Protest in Nazi Germany* (New York: W.W. Norton, 1996). A film based on this history and directed by Margarethe von Trotta was produced in 2003.

76. "Das Vergessenwollen verlängert das Exil, und das Geheimnis der Erlösung heißt Erinnerung." See Borowsky, "Ende der 'Ära Adenauer.'" Its standard English rendering can be found in Elie Wiesel, *Souls on Fire: Portraits and Legends of Hasidic Masters* (New York: Simon & Schuster, 1993), 227: "Oblivion is at the root of exile the way memory is at the root of redemption."

77. Richard von Weizsäcker, *Zum 40. Jahrestag der Beendigung des Krieges in Europa und der nationalsozialistischen Gewaltherrschaft: Ansprache am 8. Mai 1985 in der Gedenkstunde im Plenarsaal des Deutschen Bundestages*, pp. 1–2, accessed 20 Jan. 2017, http://www.bundespraesident.de/SharedDocs/Downloads/DE/Reden/2015/02/150202-RvW-Rede-8-Mai-1985.pdf?__blob=publicationFile.

the victims, the survivors, and their values system in one's deepest concerns: "To remember (*erinnern*) means to commemorate (*gedenken*) an event so honestly and plainly that it becomes part of one's own interior (*Teil des eigenen Innern*)."[78] Remembrance is akin to erecting a "memorial (*Mahnmal*) of thoughts and feelings in our own interior."[79] For Weizsäcker, the task of keeping remembrance awake is vital to Germans old and young, guilty or not, because he "who does not want to remember inhumanity is again susceptible to new dangers of infection." Furthermore, remembrance on the part of the Germans is the precondition for any talk about reconciliation with the Jews:

> The Jewish people remember and will always remember. We seek as human beings reconciliation (*Versöhnung*). Precisely because of that, we must understand that there can be no reconciliation without remembrance. . . . *Forgetfulness extends the exile, the secret of redemption is remembrance.* What this oft-cited Jewish wisdom probably wants to say is that faith in God is faith in his works in history. If we on our side are willful in forgetting . . . we would then offend the faith of the surviving Jews and ruin the sprouts of reconciliation.[80]

This gradual migration of emphasis from "redemption" (*Erlösung*)— an originally religious, divine-human concept—to "reconciliation" (*Versöhnung*), *interhuman* reconciliation, would spread after Weizsäcker's landmark speech as the secularized interpretation of

---

78. Ibid.

79. The German words for memorial, such as *Mahnmal* and *Denkmal*, of course carry different connotations. A *Mahnmal* is not only a memorial per se but a memorial as admonishment (*Mahnung*), so that the event remembered may not take place again.

80. Weizsäcker, *Ansprache am 8. Mai 1985*, 5. The wording of the Jewish saying used by Weizsäcker was exactly the same as Benda's. According to Weizsäcker's biographer, the preparation of the speech involved teamwork that lasted for months. See Harald Steffahn, *Richard von Weizsäcker mit Selbstzeugnissen und Bilddokumenten* (Reinbek bei Hamburg: Rowohlt Taschenbuch Verlag, 1991), 107–9. At any rate, Weizsäcker wouldn't have to look far for advice, for the saying, as he said, was already "oft-cited" by the German press around the time of the preparation of his speech. See, for example, the essay by Saul Friedländer, "Bewältigung—oder nur Verdrängung?," *Die Zeit*, 8 Feb. 1985; and also "Eine eigenartige geistige Gymnastik," *Der Spiegel*, no. 17 (1985).

the Jewish precept.[81] The "exile" was interpreted to mean, among other things, also the division of Germany and the loss of former German territories. Quoting a sermon by Cardinal Meisner in East Berlin, Weizsäcker said, "The disconsolate result of sin is always separation (*Trennung*)."[82] As such, he called for the strengthening of the "ability to make peace and the readiness for reconciliation within and without," and commended Aktion Sühnezeichen for its "works of understanding and reconciliation" in Poland and Israel.[83] Likewise, the meaning of forty years was also borrowed from the "Old Testament"—which, according to Weizsäcker, "holds deep insights for everyone regardless of his faith"—to signify a full generational shift from the "responsible fathers' generation," and to serve as a warning of the "danger of forgetting" and its consequences. Citing the book of Judges, he warned his fellow Germans that "often the remembrance of help and rescue . . . lasted only forty years. When remembrance broke down, peace ended."[84]

Postwar Germans did not only borrow this idea of remembrance in the service of redemption/reconciliation from the Jewish culture of remembrance. Another Jewish idea, which justifies the disproportionate remembrance of the rescuers because of the moral weight assigned to them, also figures prominently in the German culture of remembrance: **"He who saves a single life saves the entire world."**[85]

---

81. See, for example, Klaus-Dieter Gernert and Helmut Wolff, *Das Geheimnis der Versöhnung heißt Erinnerung: Zur Situation von Kriegsgefangenen und Fremdarbeitern während des Zweiten Weltkrieges in Rösrath und andere zeitgeschichtliche Beiträge* (Rösrath: Geschichtsverein für die Gemeinde Rösrath und Umgebung, 1991).

82. Weizsäcker, *Ansprache am 8. Mai 1985*, 7.

83. Ibid., 9.

84. Ibid., 13. In the book of Judges, one reads about the "peace that lasted in the land for forty years" under the leadership of Othniel, an interregnum between periods of subjugation caused by sin (3:9–12).

85. Contrary to Benda's translation of the "secret of redemption," there doesn't seem to be a standard German rendering of this Talmudic saying. The commemorative stamp (2008) of Oskar Schindler, for example, reads, "Der Bewahrer eines einzigen Lebens hat eine ganze Welt bewahrt." The German translation of Thomas Keneally's *Schindler's List*, however, reads, "Wer ein einziges Leben rettet, der rettet die ganze Welt." See "Der gerechte Goi und die Schindlerjuden," *Der Spiegel*, no. 7 (1983).

This quote from the Talmud has been used to commemorate individual German rescuers—even rescuers of non-Jews—from Oskar Schindler to John Rabe.[86] The origins of its importation to postwar German discourse on the "good Nazi" were in fact to be found in Schindler's rescue mission, which earned him a gold ring engraved with this saying made by the Jews he had rescued.[87] Yet, if it were not for the persistent efforts of some Schindlerjuden to help spread the story of Schindler, this Jewish saying would probably have remained in the sphere of private memory, that is, between the rescued and the rescuer himself.

The Jewish-Catholic collaboration in making the righteous known that was prefigured in Green's *Legion* took place in real life in the early 1980s, when Thomas Keneally, an Australian-Catholic writer of Irish ancestry, chanced upon Leopold Pfefferberg (a.k.a. Paul Page), a Schindlerjude in America, who insisted that the novelist write about the life of Schindler. Keneally initially declined Pfefferberg's request, after listening to the story and seeing the documents. "I'm a Catholic and I do not know much about what happened to Jews during the Holocaust," he said. "I will tell you all I know," Pfefferberg insisted, and then added, "As a Catholic of Irish origin and a famous writer, you will be more reliable. . . . Human suffering, either Jewish or Irish, is the same."[88] What transpired was that the two flew around the United States and Europe together, interviewing people and fact finding, and eventually a novel was published that immortalized the name of Schindler.

Keneally's *Schindler's Ark* appeared in 1982 and became the blueprint for Steven Spielberg's film *Schindler's List,* which debuted a decade later. A contemporary review of the book in *Der Spiegel*

---

86. See the German poster of Florian Gallenberger's film *John Rabe* (2009), which reads, "Wer ein Leben rettet, rettet die ganze Welt."

87. See Crowe, *Oskar Schindler,* 454. See also Thomas Keneally, *Schindler's Ark* (London: Hodder and Stoughton, 1982), 399.

88. This is Pfefferberg's account of what happened when he first met Thomas Keneally, the future author of *Schindler's Ark/List.* See Aleksander B. Skotnicki, ed., *Oskar Schindler in the Eyes of Cracovian Jews Rescued by Him* (Kraków: Wydawnictwo, 2007), 239–42. See also Keneally's own account in his *Searching for Schindler* (London: Septre, 2008), 33.

carried a photo of the Kraków-Plaszów concentration camp with the quote "He who saves a single life saves the entire world."[89] This Talmudic saying is originally expressed in two parts: He who destroys a single soul (of Israel), destroys the entire world. He who saves a single soul (of Israel), saves the entire world (Sanhedrin 4:5; 23a-b). In its original context, it is about warning people of the severity of giving witness to cases concerning life and death in court, hence the twofold structure. It is an interpretation of the "bloods of your brother" in Genesis 4:10 and the guilt of the silent witness in Leviticus 5:1. In Keneally's *Ark*, this saying marked the inception and completion of Schindler's rescue mission, as Itzhak Stern, a persecuted Polish Jew, is portrayed as instilling this "crucial dictum" in the mind of his future rescuer, when they first met in late 1939, in whom he saw a possible "safe house, a zone of potential shelter."[90]

What is significant about this dictum is that it not only emphasizes to the potential rescuer the importance of the rescue mission. It also points out to later generations the great claim the rescuer has to their memory, even if she or he has saved only a single soul amid the murder of millions. As Rabbi Schulweis put it, the quantity of the rescuers has nothing to do with their quality. "We're not dealing with a sack of potatoes. . . . He who saves a single life saves the entire world. These rescuers have saved many worlds."[91] The same sentiment was expressed by Philip Friedman, whose wife and daughter were murdered by the Nazis: "We are willing to call them heroes if they saved even one human life."[92] In other words, this dictum legitimates the supposedly "disproportionate" remembrance of the righteous, which can all too easily be dismissed on "statistical" grounds.[93]

---

89. "Der gerechte Goi."

90. Keneally, *Schindler's Ark*, 51–54. Crowe's historical research has revealed a somewhat different account but with the essentials in agreement with Keneally's. See Crowe, *Oskar Schindler*, 99–102.

91. Schulweis, "Post-Holocaust Recovery."

92. Friedman, *Their Brothers' Keepers*, 179.

93. Needless to say, the potential to use the other half of the self-same Talmudic saying to "disproportionately" remember or even punish the murderer exists.

But for one relatively just man, Noah, the world would have been completely destroyed, according to the book of Genesis. For some Schindlerjuden, the experience of being rescued by one man (and his wife, Emilie) could find expression in this biblical symbol; the ark of rescue is thus also **the ark of memory**—the carrier and transmitter of transformative remembrance. A Polish newspaper ran an article in 1983 calling Oskar Schindler "the Noah in Kraków." "More than a thousand Jews found shelter in Enamel Dish and Munitions Factory in Kraków. It was a Noah's Ark in times of contempt, when each day was filled with fear of Auschwitz," a survivor was quoted as saying.[94] Friedman quoted Sholem Asch in the introduction of his documentation *Keepers:* "On the flood of sin, hatred and blood let loose by Hitler upon the world, there swam *a small ark* which preserved intact the common heritage of a Judeo-Christian outlook. . . . It was saved by the heroism of a handful of saints."[95] Schulweis, on the other hand, quoting Isaiah 32:2, described the rescuers as having made themselves "as hiding places from the wind and shelters from the tempest; as rivers of water in dry places; as shadows of a great rock in a weary land."[96] For Keneally, who had once studied in a seminary,[97] the multifarious symbol of the "ark" was also preferred to the "list": "I liked *Ark* better than *List*. It was not only the question of Noah's ark, but the Ark of the Covenant, a symbol of the contract between Yahweh and the tribe of Israel. A similar though very rough compact had existed between Schindler and his people. If they did their work properly . . . he would rescue them."[98] *List* was subsequently preferred by Keneally's American publisher in consideration of American-Jewish feelings (for the ark of Noah could have conveyed the unintended message of passivity during the Holocaust). It was at this point that the originally theologically rich but potentially offensive

---

It is all the more remarkable how rarely, if at all, this potential is realized in postwar German-Jewish discourse.

94. Translated and reproduced in Skotnicki, *Oskar Schindler*, 361.

95. Friedman, *Their Brothers' Keepers*, 13–14.

96. Schulweis, *Letting Go/Holding On*, 12.

97. Keneally, *Searching for Schindler*, 38.

98. Ibid., 188–91.

symbol of the "ark"—which points to both divine fidelity and the saving power of human righteousness—was dropped in favor of the nonreligious, inoffensive "list."

But can the remembrance of the righteous really be offensive? Even with religious symbols that are at once evocative and ambiguous? Our brief survey above of German-Jewish efforts and collaborations in remembering the righteous can at least point to a palpable tradition in this characteristic remembrance, and to those turners who rose to take up this potentially hazardous task. After all, as is the case with any act of turning, this determined remembrance is also not without danger of abuse. Isn't it a historical fact that both Schindler and Gräbe were Nazis?[99] Then what's wrong with statements like "Not all Nazis are bad" or "The Nazi era wasn't all that terrible"? Attention and care are therefore called for when dealing with the remembrance of the righteous, to guard against such manipulation of subtle changes in context and connotation.

Jewish historian Yehuda Bauer once made a bold statement in the Bundestag concerning "memory work" in Germany: "We, Germans and Jews, are dependent on one another in this undertaking. You cannot cope with the memory work without us. . . . Together, we have a very special responsibility vis-à-vis all of humanity."[100] In light of the difficulty for Germans in remembering German rescuers of Jews without falling into the trap—real or suspected—of "whitewashing German history," one has to concur with Bauer's conclusion. Indeed, in remembering their helpers, the surviving Jews and the proponents of Jewish memory of the righteous are also helping Germans to remember a past, *their* past, that could otherwise be demoralizing to the point of paralyzing. On the constructed common ground of remembrance of the righteous, Jews lower themselves to the place of German bystanders and later generations where they

---

99. Both were for a time nominally registered members of the NSDAP.

100. Yehuda Bauer's speech given in the Bundestag on 27 Jan. 1998. Reprinted in his *Die dunkle Seite der Geschichte: Die Shoah in historischer Sicht; Interpretationen und Re-Interpretationen*, trans. Christian Wiese (Frankfurt a.M.: Jüdischer Verlag, 2001), 327.

can both turn to the righteous few in humility. As the Israeli poet Chaim Hefer wrote in 1987 in "The Righteous," "Would I have opened my family door / To a foreign child of men at my gate? . . . Remember the time of Sodom!"[101] Without a doubt, the cooperation in memory work that Bauer spoke about also entails the more unpleasant task of remembering and examining the darkness, not just the sparks of righteousness surrounded by it, or else constructive repentance cannot also occur. There is no guarantee of the acceptance of the offer of cooperation in remembrance; indeed, as Stephan Braese observed in the first decades of postwar West German literature, "competitive memory" can still dominate.[102]

---

101. Excerpted and translated from the German rendition by Arno Lustiger. See his *Rettungswiderstand*, 9–10.

102. Stephan Braese, *Die andere Erinnerung: Jüdische Autoren in der westdeutschen Nachkriegsliteratur* (Berlin: Philo, 2001), 7–10.

16

"We Are Not Authorized to Forgive" (P14)

When Erich Lüth, director of the state press office in Hamburg, traveled from Amsterdam to Tel Aviv on 8 April 1953, he was one of the first non-Jewish Germans to visit the State of Israel.[1] To hide his German identity, he had to use a couple of pseudonyms. His Israeli companions introduced him to Holocaust survivors in Israel as "Julius Bermann from Antwerp."[2] Lüth's journey was part of his ongoing personal quest for "peace with Israel," for "reconciliation with the Jews" as a member of the German nation, which had committed the crime of murdering six million Jews, and others.

---

1. See Jörg Thierfelder, "Hermann Maas—Retter und Brückenbauer," *Freiburger Rundbrief* 14, n.s., no. 3 (2007): 162–72.

2. Erich Lüth, ed., *Die Friedensbitte an Israel 1951: Eine Hamburger Initiative* (Hamburg: Hans Christians Verlag, 1976), 53. See also a series of essays by Lüth about what he had seen in Israel during the two-week visit: Lüth, "Flugreise ins Gelobte Land I-III," *Hamburger Abendblatt*, 9/10, 12, 19 May 1953; and Lüth, "Pioniere aus Deutschland," *Hamburger Abendblatt*, 27 May 1953.

Together with fellow publicist Rudolf Küstermeier, who had survived eleven years in concentration camps as a socialist, Lüth started
the "Friede mit Israel" (Peace with Israel) campaign in 1951, and
called on fellow Germans to donate olive trees to the newly established Jewish state. At home, he was also known for his engagement in ridding the German cultural scene of lingering or resurgent
Nazism and antisemitism.[3]

But what could a single German possibly do after millions of deaths
at German hands? Is reconciliation at all possible after the breach of
absolute evil? What made Lüth think that his "peace" initiative and his
incognito visit would have any chance of bridging the seemingly un-
bridgeable chasm separating the two peoples? Wasn't that a quixotic
quest at best or perhaps even betraying his own self-overestimation?
For Lüth, whether German-Jewish reconciliation was possible or not
was not a subject for philosophical speculation but an article of faith:
he simply believed that he had found the "bridge" to the Jews already
laid down by others. As he wrote in 1951,

> It would be wrong to say that there had never been these Germans
> who struggle for an effective reparation (*Wiedergutmachung*), or there
> would never be again. Many thousands of socialists, democrats, and
> Christians died the same death that their Jewish brothers suffered in
> Hitler's concentration camps, because of their resistance against the per-
> secution of Jews. . . . They have built with their own bodies the first
> bridge of reconciliation (*die erste Brücke der Versöhnung*) between Ger-
> mans and Jews, a bridge that spans the time before 1933 to the pres-
> ent. . . . Not Israel . . . not the individual Jew . . . can speak the first
> word. We are the ones who must begin. We must say: "We beg Israel for
> peace (*Wir bitten Israel um Frieden*)!"[4]

And so in his own mind, Lüth wasn't just taking a plane to Lydda
as a clandestine German tourist, but as a self-conscious member of

---

3. Lüth is remembered for his public call to boycott the films of Veit Harlan,
director of the notorious Nazi propaganda film *Jud Süß* (1940), for which he was
dragged into years of legal battle. See Peter Reichel, *Vergangenheitsbewältigung
in Deutschland: Die Auseinandersetzung mit der NS-Diktatur von 1945 bis heute*
(Munich: C. H. Beck, 2001), 134–37.

4. Lüth, *Friedensbitte*, 114. Lüth's and Küstermeier's petitions were publicized
on 31 Aug. and 1 Sept. 1951 and documented in Lüth, *Friedensbitte*, 112–18.

the German nation crossing the bridge of reconciliation, which had already been laid down by the German resisters. He later explained why he had accepted the invitation from the Israeli government to visit at a time when there were real, personal security concerns: "I considered a second step unavoidable after we had taken the first step."[5]

But, one must pause to ask, even if there were indeed such a "bridge," or a remaining ridge in the sunken relational landscape, who would be there on the other side to meet him? Or to put it another way, if only the Germans or some Germans like Lüth believed in this "theory" of reconciliation, wouldn't this be just another example of German wishful thinking, like the belief that successful Western integration or economic reconstruction means in effect "reconciliation" accomplished? Fortunately for Lüth, there were some *from the other side* of the relational gulf who crossed this bridge to meet him.

Lüth and Küstermeier's initiative generated a considerable response within the Federal Republic, paving the way for Konrad Adenauer's speech in the Bundestag on 27 September the same year, in which the German determination to make "moral and material reparation (*Wiedergutmachung*)" to Jewish individuals and Jewish communities was unequivocally expressed, which in turn paved the way for the Luxembourg Agreement between Israel and (West) Germany to be signed and ratified in 1952–53.[6] More critical to the success or failure of Lüth's endeavor, however, were of

---

5. Lüth, *Friedensbitte*, 51.

6. See supportive responses in Lüth, *Friedensbitte*, 118. Adenauer's speech was recorded in "Die Erklärungen Bundeskanzler Dr. Adenauers und der Parteien zur Wiedergutmachung," *Freiburger Rundbrief* 3/4, no. 12/15 (1951/1952): 9. Though this was not the first time that Adenauer expressed the intention of his administration to do *Wiedergutmachung* to Jewish victims, it was only after the 27 Sept. speech that concrete and substantial steps were taken to realize that intention, when Lüth's initiative was an "exception" in the general apathy in civil society concerning the question of restitution. See Constantin Goschler, *Wiedergutmachung: Westdeutschland und die Verfolgten des Nationalsozialismus 1945–1954* (Munich: R. Oldenbourg, 1992, 199–201; Goschler, *Schuld und Schulden: Die Politik der Wiedergutmachung für NS-Verfolgte seit 1945* (Göttingen: Wallstein, 2005), 136.

course the Jewish responses, from which the presence or absence of the Jewish will to *restoration*—that is, the willingness on the Jewish side to take part in repairing the damaged German-Jewish relationship—could be gleaned. In this regard, it was not surprising that the early Jewish responses were mixed: some expressed doubt; others warmly welcomed the initiative of Lüth.[7] The key point, though, is that it was neither rejected outright as a hopeless attempt, nor, what would be even worse, ignored altogether as irrelevant. An official letter from the Israeli government to Lüth dated 24 September 1951 served as a personal encouragement, stating with reservation that "if your call be taken up by the entire German people, **our ears will not be deaf**," while holding the "possibility of reconciliation" open.[8]

This willingness to "incline one's ear" was accompanied by the willingness to "answer the other's call." Israel Gelber, a Jewish survivor of the Buchenwald concentration camp, wrote from Jerusalem in an open letter to Küstermeier and Lüth published on 18 October 1951: "I may not speak for Israel or for one of the millions who suffered, just as I may not remain silent for myself."[9] The former "Häftling" then went on to recount the many German helpers who had made his survival of seven years of imprisonment possible. He adopted approvingly Lüth's idea of the German righteous as a "bridge of reconciliation": "Such human beings alone could form a bridge between Jews and Germans. With my rescuers, I don't find myself in a state of war."[10] Gelber called these righteous the "rescuers of the German human dignity" (*Retter der deutschen Menschenwürde*) and, without reservation, sent peace to Germany: "Ich schenke Deutschland den Frieden."[11]

Encouraging and magnanimous as it was as a personal statement of goodwill from a Jewish survivor, wouldn't this response be "premature"—in the sense that at this point in the history of

---

7. See, for example, "Ölzweig und Amalek," in Lüth, *Friedensbitte*, 141.
8. Lüth, *Friedensbitte*, 22–23.
9. See Israel Gelber, "Ich schenke Deutschland den Frieden," *Freiburger Rundbrief* 3/4, no. 12/15 (1951/1952): 13–14.
10. Ibid.
11. Ibid.

(West) Germany's "policy of the past," the process of denazification was hardly complete if not on reverse course,[12] wouldn't this
"peace to Germany" be counterproductive? We will return to this
question later when we explore the response of another Jewish
survivor—Jean Améry.

More cautious Jewish voices indicated the directions that Lüth's
initiative should take if this "peace" were to attain a deeper significance than a mere interstate détente. For instance, Wolf Wester,
a German Jew living in Israel, wrote an essay in *Die Zeit* advis-
ing Germans on the **difference between international peace and
reconciliation between peoples**: " 'Reconciliation with the Jews'
(*Aussöhnung mit den Juden*) is an affair that concerns the entire
Jewry (*Judentum*) directly and the State of Israel only indirectly; it
is also an action of purely moral nature between the German and
the Jewish peoples. 'Peace with Israel' by contrast means a state
action (*Staatsaktion*) of a political and not least material character,
which concerns the Federal Republic of Germany and the State of
Israel directly, and the world Jewry only indirectly."[13] Wester was
worried that interpeople reconciliation would be neglected by the
sole consideration of interstate peace, and concluded that "only
when the message comes from the Jews living in Germany to world
Jewry that they experience true restitution and are treated by the
Germans as equal citizens in value and in footing, can one hope
that real reconciliation between both peoples develops."[14] This was
not the first time that the crucial role of German Jews and other
victims of Nazi persecution in the reconciliation between Germany
and Israel and the world at large was emphasized, as we shall see
in Eugen Kogon's contribution below.

---

12. See Frei's chapter 2, "Die 'Liquidation' der Entnazifizierung," in Norbert
Frei, *Vergangenheitspolitik: Die Anfänge der Bundesrepublik und die NS-Vergangenheit* (Munich: Deutscher Taschenbuch, 2003), 29.

13. Wolf Wester, "Versöhnung mit den Juden," *Die Zeit*, 4 Oct. 1951.

14. Ibid. Lüth apparently took this advice seriously and produced a second
document under the "Peace with Israel" initiative with the title "Reconciliation
with the Jews" (Versöhnung mit den Juden) in December 1951. Lüth, *Friedensbitte*, 152.

All in all, there was no objection whatsoever that postwar Germans *could not use* the "bridge" built by the German righteous to reach the destination of reconciliation with the surviving Jewish victims and their descendants. Rather, encouragement and advice on how Germans *should use* that infrastructure in a broader and deeper way were offered from the Jewish side. This readiness to accept such a striking proposal was not to be taken for granted. After all, although the German righteous deserve the honor of remembrance in their own right (**P13**), why should they become some kind of moral asset for other Germans? On this point, there seems to be once again **preexisting agreement** beyond, before, and after the twelve years of Nazi terror. As Henning von Tresckow, one of those behind the 20 July attempted assassination of Hitler, said after learning about the plot's failure,

> Now they will all fall upon us. . . . But I am convinced, now as much as ever, that we have done the right thing. . . . In a few hours' time, I shall stand before God and answer for both my actions and the things I neglected to do. I think I can with a clear conscience stand by all I have done in the battle against Hitler. Just as God once promised Abraham that He would spare Sodom if only ten just men could be found in the city, I also have reason to hope that, for our sake, He will not destroy Germany.[15]

The same thought was a bridge between Tresckow and Gelber, who made use of the same scripture to justify his own open attitude toward reconciliation with the Germans: "Since God would have been willing to spare Sodom and Gomorrah if only ten righteous could be found within their walls, Israel can in no way demand a three-digit number [of German rescuers of Jewish lives]."[16]

---

15. Fabian von Schlabrendorff, *The Secret War against Hitler*, trans. H. Simon (Boulder, CO: Westview Press, 1994), 294–95. I would like to thank Simon Goldberg, former director of education of the Hong Kong Holocaust and Tolerance Centre, for directing me to this quotation.

16. Gelber, "Ich schenke Deutschland den Frieden," 13–14. See related interpretations of the same scripture by Gollancz (**P10**) and Schulweis (**P13**). Gelber's specific reference to the "three-digit number" (*dreistellige Zahl*) can be read as a mild criticism of Lüth's claim that there were "many thousands" of German righteous, as Gelber directly addressed him and Küstermeier in the same paragraph:

This deliberate construction of the connection between the divine and the mundane was also employed in other spheres to advance the message of German-Jewish reconciliation. Rabbi Robert Raphael Geis, for example, utilized Yom Kippur to urge fellow Jews to consider the **relationship between divine-human reconciliation and interhuman reconciliation.** On the annual Versöhnungstag, as Yom Kippur—the Jewish day of atonement—is called in German,[17] Rabbi Geis repeatedly reminded his fellow Jews in Germany of the "noble German individuals" (*edle, deutsche Menschen*)—no matter how weak their political voice was—the "good-doers (*Wohltäter*) among us, who . . . taught us again and again to believe in the good in man through their selflessness," to guard against "boundless self-pity and self-importance," and to be ready instead to "come to reconciliation even in the most terrifying suffering."[18] In the sermon marked "Versöhnungsfest 1960," Rabbi Geis pointed to the fact that the book of Jonah—the unwilling Jewish prophet who was sent according to tradition by Yahweh to the pagan city of Ninive to preach the message of repentance—is part of the liturgical readings for Yom Kippur. He called Jonah the one who "would only be too eager to see God as an enraged and punishing God," and concluded that both God and the Jewish sages have a distinct understanding of history that "is not plainly comprehensible like our history books." He challenged his Jewish listeners to ponder their own Jonah-like resistance toward God's granting the chance of repentance and reconciliation to the pagan wrongdoers: "It still counts for us Jews, even as we are very much against it. Yes, should it not perhaps also count for the German people, if they understand correctly their present moment, an hour of powerlessness?"[19] Hence through theological argumentation,

---

"As men of the press, you must therefore first and foremost ask the few women and men who had selflessly saved Jewish lives to speak. One shouldn't artificially enlarge their numbers" (14).

17. See chapter 2.

18. These references are found in Robert Raphael Geis, "Yom Kippur Sermons," 1954–60, AR7263, Series II/3, Box 1, Folder 73, Papers of Robert Raphael Geis, Leo Baeck Institute, New York.

19. Ibid.

the mirroring of the divine initiative in reconciling Israel with God himself, and the Jewish readiness for reconciling with the Germans, was complete.

Rabbi Geis's efforts with regard to German-Jewish reconciliation were not confined to religious ritual and the public podium. He also interceded in 1953, for example, for an "immaculate and decent" German youth who could no longer afford his studies as a consequence of the restitution law (*Rückerstattungsgesetz*) in the British zone, and asked his fellow Jew in Tel Aviv to "stretch out the hand of reconciliation" instead of demanding full restitution.[20] Though the intercession was apparently in vain,[21] this attempt made a lasting impression on the young German theologian, who recalled fondly his encounter with the rabbi and remained immensely thankful for his personal intervention.[22]

Whereas Geis used his podium and personal weight as a rabbi to expand the readiness of Jews to reconcile with the Germans, Victor Gollancz deployed his publishing house and personal fame to broadcast to the wider world in the early days of the postwar period a peculiar message of reconciliation that **challenges the popular understanding of repentance and forgiveness.** In his *Our Threatened Values*, Gollancz boldly countered his British (Christian) readers who held—reasonably enough—that they would only consider forgiving the Germans *after* they had repented: "People who talk like that confuse the prerogative of God with the duty of man. . . . For a man to set himself up and say 'I will forgive you, if you repent' is to break the third commandment, and to take the name of the Lord our God in vain."[23]

How is that so? Like Hannah Arendt, whose argument concerning "pardon" we shall examine later in this chapter, Gollancz

---

20. "Robert Raphael Geis to Max Israel," 25 May 1953, AR7263, Series III/1, Box 2, Folder 23, Papers of Robert Raphael Geis, Leo Baeck Institute, New York.

21. "Ulrich Wilckens to Dietrich Goldschmidt," 11 Jan. 1977, AR7263, Series III/1, Box 3, Papers of Robert Raphael Geis, Leo Baeck Institute, New York.

22. "Ulrich Wilckens to Robert Raphael Geis," 21 May 1953, AR7263, Series III/1, Box 3, Papers of Robert Raphael Geis, Leo Baeck Institute, New York.

23. Victor Gollancz, *Our Threatened Values* (London: Victor Gollancz, 1946), 84.

considered it blasphemous for humans to assume that they were capable of issuing "forgiveness" as if they were God or the victim himself. Rather, "forgiveness simply means, as between man and man, wishing the other well."[24] Hence, for the world to wish Germany well in this hour could only mean extending a helping hand in German repentance, rather than just sitting there and waiting for it to happen. It is a human duty, not a divine prerogative. "Most of all in need of healing are those who ordered or committed abominations, or approved of their commission, and are unrepentant; they are most in need of healing because they are unrepentant."[25] The victors and the victims were duty-bound to help Germans in their repentance, Gollancz asserted, and he was sure about their success in generating the change in the "spiritual atmosphere," the "accustomed habits of thought," and the "dominant features" of the German character. "Can we effect the psychological transformation? . . . I am sure that we can bring this change. It is the one thing, in the political world of today, of which I am completely sure."[26] If Gollancz at times sounded excessively ebullient, he might be excused for attempting to turn his largely Christian audience from the **arrogance of "forgiveness-keepers"** (see below) toward the **humbler path of repentance-helpers** and to the hope in the co-repentability, or mutual-turning, of human beings. "If we treat these Germans kindly, kindness will stir in them. . . . And if we respect them— . . . respect, by some process of mutuality, will be born in them."[27]

Indeed, even before Lüth urged fellow Germans to take "the first step" in reconciling with the Jews, some Jews and Germans had already taken tentative steps to reach out to each other. Aside from Gollancz, Kogon also broached the question of reconciliation between Germans and the victims of German crimes under Nazism, and of the function German Jews and other persecuted Germans could perform in this process. In 1948, he penned a

---

24. Ibid.
25. Ibid.
26. Ibid., 87.
27. Ibid., 87–88.

critique, "**The Policy of Reconciliation**," concerning the few cases where attempts by German youths to rebuild European towns destroyed by the Nazis had been rejected by the survivors.[28] He expressed understanding for the foreign victims' refusal but called on his fellow German victims of Nazi persecution, the *Vereinigung der Verfolgten des Naziregimes* (Association of Persecutees of the Nazi Regime), "*to begin with ourselves, in our own country*" the "policy of understanding among Germans," which would "convince the outside world."[29] He cited the tragedy of a repentant Nazi, "a high German officer from the former Ministry of Food (*Ernährungsministerium*)," who had confessed to him in writing just before committing suicide. "I see in you the former concentration camp inmate, to whom I may say the following with effect for all concentration camp victims and their relatives," Kogon quoted the German officer's letter to him. "The anguish of my soul and my self-accusation are immeasurably great. . . . Only one thing now remains for me in front of my victims and their relatives: **the plea for pardon** (*die Bitte um Verzeihung*). Pardon me my inadequacy (*Unzulänglichkeit*), my lack of care (*Sorgfalt*) . . . ; my trust in the correctness of the proposals presented to me . . . , I know that many will not pardon me. But that shall not be a reason for me to fail to plead for pardon. May God be a merciful judge for me."[30] Kogon, like Geis, urged his fellow surviving victims to be ready to reconcile with their former perpetrators who had turned to them for help, so that suicide would not remain their only "atonement" option: "This man was not guiltier than most of us. . . . he sought, in his own way, to atone (*sühnen*) for [his guilt]. We must extend the hand of reconciliation (*die Hand der Versöhnung reichen*) to all those who are still alive and of his spirit. Then it will once again be well for Germany; sustainable (*nachhaltig*), and perhaps even soon."[31]

---

28. Eugen Kogon, "Politik der Versöhnung," *Frankfurter Hefte* 3, no. 4 (1948): 317–24.

29. Ibid., 319 (emphasis in the original).

30. Ibid., 324.

31. Ibid.

As Kogon rightly saw, without the readiness on the part of the victims to reconcile (which is not to be automatically equated with "to forgive," as we shall see further below), the perpetrators' or their representatives' repentance efforts would have no hope of restoring the damaged relationship. This simple truth was perhaps best reflected in the early history of the ASF, which depended on the goodwill of the receiving communities at every step to complete their "atonement work" there.[32] Yet in offering their readiness to reconcile, the survivors and the bereaved were also taking great risks: wouldn't this "reconciliation" be misconstrued as "foreclosure" of the past, which was in reality not even "past"—that is, the unresolved issues of justice, restitution, cultural transformation, and so on? Wouldn't this turning—like any other genuine turning—be abused by those who seek to cover up with cosmetics the still festering wounds, rather than to reveal and to heal them?

In this regard, Lothar Kreyssig, founder of the ASF, exhibited a keen awareness of this dilemma of the victims. For, in fact, the organization was in the beginning called Aktion Versöhnungszeichen—that is, "symbol of reconciliation" instead of "atonement"—expressing the goal of the German founders and volunteers to achieve reconciliation with the victims.[33] But soon enough, Kreyssig was advised to change its name from "reconciliation" to "atonement" because of the **hidden arrogance in the perpetrator's claim of reconciliation,** which could be counterproductive. Kreyssig wrote: "[Erich Müller-Gangloff] suggests that we gradually rename the Aktion as Sühnezeichen, with the convincing justification that atonement comes from the guilty, whereas reconciliation is essentially mutual and unthinkable as a symbol without

---

32. See Karl-Klaus Rabe, *Umkehr in die Zukunft: Die Arbeit der Aktion Sühnezeichen/Friedensdienste* (Bornheim-Merten: Lamuv Verlag, 1983); and Gabriele Kammerer, *Aktion Sühnezeichen Friedensdienste: Aber man kann es einfach tun* (Göttingen: Lamuv Verlag, 2008).

33. In the original "call" for the creation of the organization, "Wir bitten um Frieden," published on 30 Apr. 1958, the "good works" to be accomplished were conceived as "symbols of reconciliation," and the name Aktion Versöhnungszeichen already appeared. See Rabe, *Umkehr in die Zukunft,* 14–15.

the consent of the wounded."[34] Futhermore, for Kreyssig, even this atonement is only possible when enabled by the victim; it is not something that the guilty can "achieve" on their own: "Atonement (*Sühne*) happens when the wounded considers the regret (*Reue*) shown to him and grants forgiveness (*Vergebung*). It can only be asked for (*erbitten*), but not proclaimed (*proklamieren*)."[35]

In this way, the "atoning Germans" tried to make it lighter for the surviving victims and their communities to accept their volunteer work—just as these made their burden lighter by accepting it—through removing the implicit requirement or unilateral declaration of reconciliation and all the collateral connotations. The naming of the initiative as Sühnezeichen was in a way not to take the victims' reconciliation-readiness for granted, while at the same time expressing the founders' and volunteers' perseverance with the identity of the guilty (**P6**), even as they themselves might not be guilty in any direct sense. This makes the ASF unique among the "peace" volunteer organizations in postwar Germany (e.g., Pax Christi), whose names do not embed this *assumption* of guilt—in both senses of the word—thus conflating "doing good" with "repairing wrong," one's *own* wrong.[36] This uniqueness is based on the insight of the ASF concerning the contribution of guilt consciousness to interpeople reconciliation. As Kreyssig explained, "In the relationship between people and people, such an entreaty [of atonement] is only realistic when the wounded is informed about who is sponsoring the entreaty with his willingness to bring symbolic, personal sacrifice; otherwise it becomes cheap and noncommittal."[37] The fruitful and sustainable collaboration

---

34. Note by Lothar Kreyssig dated 7 Jul. 1958, quoted in Kammerer, *Aktion Sühnezeichen*, 14–15. Erich Müller-Gangloff was the director of the Evangelical Academy in Berlin.

35. Quoted in Rabe, *Umkehr in die Zukunft*, 19–20.

36. The addition of Friedensdienste (Peace Services) to the name in 1968 thus reflects, in my view, this resurgent ambivalence, which Kreyssig had overcome at the beginning. Ibid., 80.

37. Quoted in Rabe, *Umkehr in die Zukunft*, 19–20.

between ASF volunteers and the victim communities of Nazi Germany attests to this.[38]

For his engagement with Israel, Lüth also received a new name, "Israelüth," which the Israeli press favorably spread.[39] And this name was cited within intra-Jewish dialogue as that of the one German who had publicly confessed to the Jews, thus making German atonement in the form of *Wiedergutmachung* less unacceptable.[40] Though certainly not the first to confess German guilt in public, as we have seen previously (**P2**), the initiative of Lüth is to be credited for *directly* generating further **public confessions in (West) Germany.** Take the "confession of Freiburg students" in 1952, who protested against the screening of a new production by Harlan. In one of these protests, in which about 800 students were reported to have taken part, a student representative said: "It is a gross distortion of the facts that since we did not want to forget, we are accused of being unpeaceable (*Unfriedfertigkeit*). We want peace! But peace with Israel is more important for us than peace with Mr. Harlan!"[41]

The Freiburg students' declaration could count as one of those public confessions by German groups that specifically targeted the Jewish audience. These included Christian (both Protestant and Catholic) statements concerning the so-called Jewish question (*Judenfrage*) issued in the early postwar period. The "Message Concerning the Jewish Question" was issued in 1948 by the leaders of the Confessing Church.[42] In the same year, German Catholics

---

38. Bernhard Krane et al., eds., *Aktion Sühnezeichen Friedensdienste in Israel: 1961–2011; Geschichte(n) erleben* (Berlin/Jerusalem: Aktion Sühnezeichen Friedensdienste, 2011).

39. M. Y. Ben-Gavriêl, "Der Jisraelüth," in Lüth, *Friedensbitte*, 61.

40. Walter A. Berendsohn, a German Jew in Hamburg, was once challenged by an Israeli politician who was against the acceptance of the "blood money" from Germany: "Give me one single German name who has confessed to the guilt against the Jews." Berendsohn sent him Lüth's petition. Lüth, *Friedensbitte*, 146–47.

41. Remark by Manfred Hättich, quoted in "Die Freiburger Veit-Harlan-Demonstrationen und ihre Folgen," *Freiburger Rundbrief* 5, no. 17/18 (1952/1953): 39. See also "Veit Harlan als Symptom," *Freiburger Rundbrief* 4, no. 16 (1951/1952): 20–21; "Das Bekenntnis der Freiburger Studenten," a report dated 18 Jun. 1952 in the *Badische Zeitung*, excerpted in Lüth, *Friedensbitte*, 139–40.

42. Original in German documented in "Die Botschaft des Bruderrats der Bekennenden Kirche von 1948," *Freiburger Rundbrief* 1, no. 1 (1948): 6–8. See P2.

issued their own "resolution" on the "Jewish question" during the *Katholikentag*.[43] And in 1950, the EKD Synod issued the Berlin-Weißensee "declaration" clarifying the status of Judaism in Evangelical thought.[44] Comparing these statements, we can see the relative emphases of the different Christian groups, as well as similar **pitfalls and subsequent rectification in these confessions.**

The earliest of these, the "message" of 1948, was also the most controversial because of its ambiguous attitude toward the Jews. While on the one hand, it confessed Christian guilt vis-à-vis Israel (see **P2**)—as a correction to the 1947 Darmstadt statement in which no specific word was dedicated to turning to the victims although it aimed at "reconciliation," as if absolution through faith alone were enough—it remained mired in the lingering anti-Judaism in its theology, which was at the very least one contributor to modern antisemitism. Aside from upholding the traditional theological view that the election of Israel had, since Christ, been "transferred" (*übergegangen*) to the church, the 1948 "message" also seemed to entertain the view that Jewish suffering was the result of their own failure to "convert" (*bekehren*).[45]

The Catholic confession issued in the same year had similar shortcomings. When it urged all Christians to shun the "resurgent antisemitism," it simultaneously argued that only as "loving ones" could they draw home the entire Jewish people, in effect upholding the continual negation of Judaism.[46] The Catholic confession differed from the Protestant statement in its emphasis on reparation (*Wiedergutmachung*), the return of ill-gotten properties to their original Jewish owners. As a participant in the Catholic discussion of the "Jewish question" put it, "The Jews have a valid claim against us for indemnification."[47]

---

43. See "Die Judenfrage auf dem Katholikentag," *Freiburger Rundbrief* 1, no. 2/3 (1949): 2–5.

44. See "Erklärung zur Judenfrage in Berlin-Weißensee," *Freiburger Rundbrief* 2, no. 8/9 (1949/1950): 18–19.

45. See sections 3 and 5 of the 1948 "Botschaft."

46. See sections b and c of the Catholic "resolution."

47. Remarks by Hans Lukaschek, quoted in "Die Judenfrage auf dem Katholikentag," 3–4.

Thus anti-Judaic streams of thought continued even as Christian communities attempted to confess their guilt toward the Jews. Hence concern on the part of the Jews about uttering the words "reconciliation" or "peace" prematurely was not without reason. In this regard, the 1950 Berlin-Weißensee "Erklärung" was a much-needed clarification indeed, for it challenged head-on a long-standing pillar of Christian anti-Judaism: the unequal standing of the "old" and the "new" peoples of God. In contradistinction to the 1948 "message," the "declaration" began by *affirming* the continual validity of Judaism:

> We believe that God's promise for his chosen people of Israel remains in force (*in Kraft geblieben ist*) even after the crucifixion of Jesus Christ.[48]

And instead of holding up "Jewish fate" and "Israel under judgment" as a warning to Christians, as the 1948 "message" had, the "declaration" turned to the German catastrophe as a caution:

> We warn all Christians not to set off (*aufrechnen*) what we have done to the Jews against what has come upon us Germans as God's judgment; for in judgment, God's hand seeks the repentant (*Bußfertigen*).[49]

During the discussion on the text of the 1950 Protestant declaration, some participants doubted whether confessing before the world, and especially before those who had collaborated with the Nazis, was appropriate. Martin Niemöller, who was also present, argued vehemently against this attitude of comparing and scaling guilt: "I confess to be guiltier than many an SS," the pastor said.[50] In other words, if a resister from the Confessing Church could consider himself no less guilty than an active perpetrator of Nazi crimes, what justified objection could a German bystander have to confessing before Nazi collaborators? Kreyssig, who would found the Aktion Sühnezeichen eight years later, concurred and supported Niemöller: "Brothers! None of us attempted to join the

---

48. "Erklärung zur Judenfrage in Berlin-Weißensee."
49. Ibid.
50. Quoted in "Erklärung zur Judenfrage in Berlin-Weißensee."

ride to the gas camps. God has once shown me this way to the east; in the evening, I was willing; the next morning, I became a coward. Hence repentance! Let us **confess our guilt before God and before man!**"[51]

Such expression of guilt-consciousness—even when real guilt wasn't conspicuous—never failed to gain an appreciative hearing from the victims. In his book, *Jenseits von Schuld und Sühne* (Beyond Guilt and Atonement),[52] Jean Améry recalled approvingly Thomas Mann's public confession, "Germany and the Germans," which he had made in the United States right after the end of the war.[53] After citing the letter of a German youth who was "fed up" with accusations of the "guilt of the fathers" (**P12**), who sought to find escape instead in the "guilt of the others" (**P8**), Améry affirmed his factual innocence but wished he had a bit of Thomas Mann's guilt-consciousness based on a responsible (and realistic) attitude toward his own national tradition:

> Thomas Mann knew that, as he wrote in his essay "Germany and the Germans," "it is quite impossible for one born there (*deutschgeborener Geist*) simply to . . . declare: 'I am the good, the noble, the just Germany in the white robe.' . . . Not a word of all that I have just told you about Germany . . . came out of alien, cool, objective knowledge, it is all within me, I have been through it all." . . . I can only hope that German youths do not find it too difficult to connect themselves with Thomas Mann.[54]

While attentive to and appreciative of German confessions like Mann's, Améry was not the typical turner we have seen so far: on the one hand, his unique voice demonstrated the strength of the Jewish victim's willingness to speak to the perpetrators and bystanders—even self-admittedly without any religious

---

51. Quoted in "Erklärung zur Judenfrage in Berlin-Weißensee."

52. Jean Améry, *Jenseits von Schuld und Sühne: Bewältigungsversuche eines Überwältigten* (Munich: Szczesny Verlag, 1966).

53. Thomas Mann, *Deutschland und die Deutschen 1945, mit einem Essay von Hans Mayer* (Hamburg: Europäische Verlagsanstalt, 1992).

54. Améry, *Jenseits von Schuld und Sühne*, 122–23. The quoted text by Mann is taken from his "Germany and the Germans," 64–65.

inspiration;[55] but on the other hand, it also laid bare some of the limits of the non-three-dimensional view of the victim-perpetrator relationship (R2).

Unlike other Jewish turners, Améry was against not only the idea of forgiveness, but also reconciliation itself. He lambasted those Jewish turners who were not themselves—strictly speaking—victims. In explaining why "resentment" had become his "existential dominant," he said: "The Jews who were at the moment shaking before the forgiveness- and reconciliation-pathos, whether a Victor Gollancz or Martin Buber, were almost as unpleasant (*unangenehm*) to me as those others . . . hurrying from the US, from England or France to Germany, West or East, in order to play the role of the so-called reeducator (*Umerzieher*)."[56] "Hence my least inclination toward reconcilability (*Versöhnlichkeit*), more precisely: the conviction that the loudly demonstrated reconciliation-readiness (*Versöhnungsbereitschaft*) of victims of Nazism can only be either dullness in feeling (*Stumpffühligkeit*) and indifference to life (*Lebensindifferenz*) or masochistic conversion of suppressed, genuine demand for revenge (*Racheforderung*). . . . Indeed, the dull-feeling and indifferent one forgives. He lets the past (*Geschehene*) be, just as it was."[57]

Repeatedly, Améry referred to himself as "unreconcilable," and to his "nasty unreconcilability."[58] His work was to explain to the Germans his resentments against them: "I speak as a victim and examine my resentments (*Ressentiments*)."[59] "I bore Germany a grudge for the twelve years of Hitler . . . , I harbored my

---

55. Améry, *Jenseits von Schuld und Sühne*, 9.

56. Ibid., 106. Elsewhere he also disparaged Hannah Arendt (48), and "men born Jewish like Gabriel Marcel" (108), whom he accused of having either underestimated human evil or presented the Holocaust as if it were an "industrial accident" (*Betriebsunfall*).

57. Améry, *Jenseits von Schuld und Sühne*, 114.

58. Ibid., 115.

59. Ibid., 102. Améry's use of *Ressentiments* is essentially different from the usual understanding of resentment. See below and Melanie Steiner Sherwood, "Jean Améry and Wolfgang Hildesheimer: Ressentiments, Melancholia, and the West German Public Sphere in the 1960s and 1970s" (PhD diss., Cornell University, 2011).

resentments. And since I neither can nor want to let go of them, I have to live with them and am duty-bound to illuminate them to those whom they are directed against."[60]

For a human being who has undergone extreme torture to be commanded (whether by himself or by others) to bow down to the social pressure of forgiveness and reconciliation is tantamount to his suffering a new injury. For Améry, who had experienced just that, the experience in the camps had utterly shattered the foundation of his self-understanding as an intellectual. In Auschwitz, he said, unless one was sheltered by "religious or political faith," which he as an agnostic was not, "the intellect (*Geist*) was useless, or as useful as nothing."[61] "With the first blow, this confidence in the world (*Weltvertrauen*) collapses. The other . . . forces his own physicality upon me with the first blow. He is at me and exterminates (*vernichten*) me through it. It is like rape (*Vergewaltigung*)."[62]

Nevertheless, Améry's *Ressentiments* were not conceived as a kind of perpetual punishment for its own sake. Rather, they were presented as a Jewish contribution to German turning, and to his own envisioned German-Jewish "cooperation." Referring to the early postwar years when German self-pity was a widespread malaise, Améry said: "The Germans, who understood themselves as a people of victims (*Opfervolk*) and nothing else . . . were all too understandably not inclined to do more than—what was called at that time—coming to terms (*bewältigen*) with the past of the Third Reich in their own way. In those days, when the Germans simultaneously conquered the world markets with their industrial products and were, not without a certain sense of being compensated (*Ausgeglichenheit*), busy with coming to terms (*Bewältigung*) at home, our—or perhaps more reservedly said, my—resentments surged."[63] And the way toward a "co-human" future was prescribed in a German-Jewish mutuality. "Settlement could be had when resentment continues to exist in one camp, and, as aroused

---

60. Améry, *Jenseits von Schuld und Sühne*, 109.
61. Ibid., 31.
62. Ibid., 52.
63. Ibid., 107.

by it, self-mistrust (*Selbstmißtrauen*) in the other. Alone through the prick of the spurs of our resentments—and not in the least through a subjectively almost always dubious reconcilability, which is also objectively hostile to history (*geschichtsfeindlich*)—the German people would remain sensitive to the fact that a piece of their national history may not be neutralized by time, that it has to be integrated."[64]

In this broader perspective, Améry was similar to other Jewish turners, who sought to offer a viable way out of the "German problem," in which German-Jewish cooperation was deemed necessary (**P6**).[65] His recipe of mutual-turning might sound comparatively "harsh"—not only to the Germans he was speaking to, but also to the victims like himself, for resentment, as he frankly conceded, "is not only an anti-natural, but also a logically contradictory condition. It nails each of us firmly to the cross of his shattered past. Absurdly it demands that the irreversible be reversed, the occurrence be unoccurred. Resentment blocks the exit to what is really the human dimension, the future."[66] The worse condition, however, is to say "Peace! Peace!" when there is no peace. "The man of resentment cannot . . . join in the monotonous, ubiquitous peace choir, which cheerfully proposes: Let us not look backward, but forward to a better, common future!"[67] Hence Améry's resentment was in no way expressed as a complete and irreversible severance of relationship.[68] For if that were the case, then the path toward the "wiping out of shame" (*Auslöschung der Schande*) through

---

64. Ibid., 124. "Settlement" (*Austragung*) was the word used repeatedly by Améry in place of "reconciliation" or "forgiveness."

65. He also shared what is characteristic of Jewish memory: remembering the righteous (**P13**). He recalled those Germans who had shown him even the least gesture of kindness, such as the Wehrmacht soldier who had given him a cigarette after his torture, for instance. These gestures were too few, however, to counter the victim's belief that "Hitler was the German people." Améry, *Jenseits von Schuld und Sühne*, 118–19.

66. Améry, *Jenseits von Schuld und Sühne*, 110–11.

67. Ibid.

68. This stance of Améry's is clearly shown in Sherwood's work, "Jean Améry and Wolfgang Hildesheimer."

"laying claim to one's own negative property"[69] that he was offering to the Germans would have been superfluous, and there would have been no dialogue to begin with. To the contrary, he referred once again to Thomas Mann as a prototypical German intellectual demonstrating what he meant by "self-mistrust":

> Remaining in his exclusively literary reference system, Thomas Mann has spoken about this in a letter: "It is perhaps superstitious . . . but in my eyes, the books that could be printed at all in Germany between 1933 and 1945 are less than worthless. . . . An odor of blood and shame clings to them; they should all be pulverized." The intellectual pulverization (*geistige Einstampfung*) through the German people, not just books, but everything that was performed in the twelve years, would be the negation of negation: a highly positive, saving act. Only then would the resentment become subjectively satisfied and objectively unnecessary.[70]

What really sets Améry apart from other Jewish turners—at least those he himself has identified—is their **different ways of perceiving the victim-perpetrator relationship.** The three-dimensional way of seeing divine-human and interhuman relationships that comes with the biblical paradigm of repentance has allowed other turners to perceive the victim-perpetrator relationship in ways that are otherwise inconceivable. Rabbi Geis, for example, could say matter-of-factly that "because we were the beaten ones and not the ones beating, the persecuted and not the persecutors, we can say thanks."[71] In other words, the downtrodden are not—by way of persecution—"lowered" in any essential, fundamental sense; rather, it is the wrongdoers who have lowered themselves through their own wrongdoing. This only makes sense when a *divine* order of relationships centering around a just God who takes sides with the persecuted is perceived to be present beside the purely *social* one

---

69. Améry, *Jenseits von Schuld und Sühne*, 125.

70. Ibid., 125–26.

71. Robert Raphael Geis, "Gedenkrede anläßlich des 15. Jahrestages der Deportation nach Gurs und der Synagogenzerstörungen des Jahres 1938," 1953, AR7263, Series II/1, Box 1, Folder 27, Papers of Robert Raphael Geis, Leo Baeck Institute, New York.

and takes precedence over it. This doesn't make sense when what is seen and felt as social, interpersonal humiliation is reckoned as humiliation and nothing else—that is, what is "lost" as human dignity by the victims is "gained" by the perpetrators, and there is no "god" whatsoever to even this inequality out on the victims' behalf.

This seems to be the case with Améry, who, though showing an acute awareness and appreciation of the religious paradigm of his fellow persecuted Jews, chose not to adopt it for himself.[72] He spoke about "settling" (*austragen*) with the perpetrators, not through revenge, but through encountering the victims in their state of helplessness and hopelessness. "[The torturer] is lord over flesh and spirit, life and death. . . . There were moments when I had a kind of shameful reverence (*schmähliche Verehrung*) for the sovereignty of the torturers, which they exercised over me. For is he not God or at least a half god, who can turn a man so totally to mere body and whimpering death-prey?"[73] "It is not about revenge, nor atonement. . . . The experience of torture was in the final analysis the extreme *loneliness* (*Einsamkeit*). For me, it is about the release (*Erlösung*) from this still perpetuating abandonment (*Verlassensein*). . . . [The perpetrator being led to his execution] was in this moment with *me*—and I was not alone anymore."[74] "The mastering one and the mastered one . . . would encounter each other at the meeting point of the wish for time-reversal (*Zeitumkehrung*) and for the moralizing of history."[75]

This perpetrator-above-victim paradigm, though corresponding to fact as actually seen and experienced, is markedly different from that founded on the three-dimensional way of seeing relationships. Arendt, for instance, sketched in her *Denktagebuch* in 1950 the broad outlines of the triangular relationship burdened by human wrongdoing:

> Injustice done is the burden on one's shoulders, which one carries because he has loaded it upon himself. . . . The burden, which he has loaded upon his shoulders, can only be removed (*abnehmen*) by God. . . . The

---

72. Améry, *Jenseits von Schuld und Sühne*, 29.
73. Ibid., 63–64.
74. Ibid., 113 (emphasis in the original).
75. Ibid., 125.

man who reconciles simply co-loads (*sich mitladen*) the burden upon the shoulders voluntarily, which the other carries in any case. That is, he reestablishes equality (*Gleichheit*).[76]

In other words, the perpetrator did not "elevate" himself in any sense by his wrongdoing, just as the victim was not "lowered" by it. Quite the contrary: guilt as burden drags down the wrongdoer.

The two paradigms are so diametrically different that there doesn't seem to be any easy way to bridge the two through rational argument; rather, the very assumption of the most fundamental issues seems to be at stake—on which no outsider of a particular relationship is warranted to make judgment. What is relevant to us as social observers and participants is the question of *substitute*: for those victims who are unable or unwilling to adopt the three-dimensional paradigm, what can society do to help "elevate" their self-perception after abject dehumanization? Améry himself had hinted at **social recognition as a possible alternative**, though it was probably nowhere near enough as a full substitute for the faith-oriented restitution: "What can people like us still demand, more than that German newspapers and radio stations grant us the possibility to be coarse and tactless toward the German people and still get paid for that? I know, even the most well-meaning ones will become at the end impatient with us. . . . We victims must 'get done with' (*fertigwerden*) the reactive grudge. . . . We must and will soon be done with that. Until then, we ask for patience from those whose peace is disturbed by our grudge-bearing (*Nachträgerei*)."[77]

Yet despite the differences of the two paradigms, the example of Améry's *Ressentiments* shows that it would be erroneous to assume that only from the religious viewpoint or by adopting an overtly religious language can one contribute to the process of three-dimensional turning of the other. Indeed, the kind of superficial and premature "reconcilability" that he was really criticizing could be counter-turning, that is, when "reconciliation" takes

---

76. Hannah Arendt, *Denktagebuch: 1950 bis 1973*, ed. Ursula Ludz and Ingeborg Nordmann (Munich: Piper, 2002), 3–4.

77. Améry, *Jenseits von Schuld und Sühne*, 129–30.

place at the cost of—instead of *through*—thoroughgoing repentance. While one may argue that his pronounced "unreconcilability" was just as counter-turning (for if taken out of context, it could be read as *indifference* to German repentance), his offer of self-disclosure and insights to the "resented" did provide a viable answer to German youths struggling with the German question of coming to terms with the past. Such answers would not have come about either in "forgiveness" without turning or in definitive separation in the form of noncommunication, both of which can be derived from religious or nonreligious perspectives.[78]

As also brought out by Améry's *Ressentiments*, the question of forgiveness is indeed unavoidable in any discussion of reconciliation, especially when there is so much social expectation—or even *demand*—for it, that the victims risk being blamed if they don't forgive.[79] In closing this chapter, we will examine some Jewish critiques of "forgiving," as well as some contemporary German adaptions that have distorted their original message.

As already mentioned above, Gollancz considered those who demanded repentance before they would grant forgiveness "blasphemous," for in the human sphere, forgiveness can only mean "wishing well," and one's task in facing a sinner (or a nation of sinners) is to help them repent—not to consider when or whether one would "issue" forgiveness.[80] Arendt's understanding of "pardon" (*Verzeihung*) and "reconciliation" (*Versöhnung*) as revealed in her *Denktagebuch*—which gives important insights into her contributions in German-Jewish turning from "Organisierte Schuld" to *Eichmann in Jerusalem* (**P1**)—concurred with Gollancz's skepticism

---

78. Economic interests, the assessment of post-Holocaust German-Jewish relations based on an alternative interpretation of the biblical passages concerning the Amalekites (see **R13**), as well as Confucius's dictum "not to live under the same heaven" with the murderers of one's own parents (Liji, Tan Gong I), are just some of the possible sources.

79. "*I* am burdened with collective guilt, I say I: not they. The world that forgives and forgets has condemned me instead of those who murdered or let murder happen." Améry, *Jenseits von Schuld und Sühne*, 120 (emphasis in the original).

80. Gollancz, *Our Threatened Values*, 84.

concerning "forgiving," or more precisely, **the condescension of those who deem themselves fit to forgive.** For Arendt,

> there is *pardon* only between those who are in principle qualitatively separated from one another: the parents can pardon the children, so long as they are children, because of the absolute superiority (*Überlegenheit*). The gesture of pardon destroys equality (*Gleichheit*)—and thus the foundation of human relationships—so radically that actually after such an act no relationship is possible anymore. . . . Pardon, or what is commonly called as such, is in truth only a hypocritical process (*Scheinvorgang*), in which one behaves superciliously (*überlegen*) while the other demands what human beings can neither give nor remove (*abnehmen*). The fake process exists in that the burden on one's shoulders is ostensibly taken away by the other, who presents himself as unburdened (*unbelastet*). . . . Pardon is perhaps possible, insofar as it is only the explicit recognition of "we are all sinners," that is, it claims that everyone could have done that, and in this way it establishes an equality—not of rights, but of nature. Pharisaism is then the arrogance (*Anmassung*) of not being willing to recognize the equality of human beings.[81]

Juxtaposed to this "pardon," "reconciliation" was championed by Arendt—though with reservation on its effect—as the more humanly appropriate attitude toward addressing the aftermath of human injustice: "Reconciliation with the other is . . . not a hypocritical process, for it does not pretend to accomplish what is impossible to do—it does not promise the exoneration (*Entlastung*) of the other, and does not act in one's own unburdenedness (*Unbelastetheit*). . . . Reconciliation is the exact opposite of pardon, which generates *inequality*."[82]

This attitude of humility before God—that is, challenging human "superiority" to grant each other forgiveness on unequal footings—is matched by another Jewish attitude that is equally critical about such arrogance but is expressed in a slightly different form and is ultimately based on humility before the real, individual victims. This second attitude is at present articulated most

---

81. Arendt, *Denktagebuch*, 3–4 (emphasis in the original). I would like to thank the late Thomas Hollweck for directing me to this text.
82. Arendt, *Denktagebuch*, 3–4 (emphasis in the original).

succinctly and persistently by someone who had left Buchenwald as a child and ended up as the chief rabbi of Israel—Rabbi Israel Meir Lau.[83] On 11 April 1995, the fiftieth anniversary commemoration of the liberation of the Buchenwald concentration camp, Rabbi Lau spoke as one of the invited speakers. "I'm not coming here to forgive," he told the audience, probably shocking those who had expected nothing but benevolent (and somnolent) words from world religious leaders. "My murdered family and the six million dead have given me no mandate for that."[84] On another occasion of commemoration, the rabbi reiterated his message in conjunction with the Jewish duty to remember (**P13**): "We cannot forget, it's impossible to forget, and we are not authorized to forgive."[85]

If Lau was out to attract sympathy for the Jewish victims and the surviving Jews, he would probably have done no better by donning a conciliatory and all-forgiving tone. Yet it was apparently not his primary concern when speaking to the world. Rather, his message was a challenge to **unwarranted representative forgiveness** and its detrimental effects. He was consistent in his refusal to grant forgiveness—or rather, to pretend he had the representative authority to do so—on the same moral ground. In his autobiography, he recalled a delegation of 500 members of Christian denominations coming to see him in Jerusalem in 1999 to seek forgiveness for the "Christian" crusades: "I replied that I had neither the mandate to grant pardon nor the power to forgive. I did express my honest appreciation for the fact that they had come to Jerusalem. . . . But, I clarified, in no way did the presentation of [the request for forgiveness] to me erase the past or forgive its despicable sins."[86] In another instance, a Japanese Buddhist leader, Etai Yamada, also

---

83. Rabbi Lau was the Ashkenazi chief rabbi of Israel for ten years until 2003.

84. Cited in Klaus Hartung, "Ein deutscher Sonntag," *Die Zeit*, 14 Apr. 1995.

85. "Statement by Rabbi Yisrael Meir Lau during the Holocaust Memorial Ceremony at the Trusteeship Council Chamber on 27 January 2009," accessed 18 May 2012, http://www.un.org/en/holocaustremembrance/2009/statements09_lau.shtml.

86. Israel Meir Lau, *Out of the Depths: The Story of a Child of Buchenwald Who Returned Home at Last*, trans. Jessica Setbon and Shira Leibowitz Schmidt (New York: Sterling, 2011), 302.

approached Lau for forgiveness. "As a member of the nation that aided the killers, I am guilty of the murder of your parents," the venerable monk said. The rabbi once again declined to act as he was bidden: "I explained to the Japanese leader, I did not know if I had the mandate to forgive him in the name of the victims. As for myself, I had one mission to fulfill: to remember, and not permit the world to forget. Still I emphasized my great appreciation for his honest statement."[87]

In understanding these Jewish voices—Lau's, Arendt's, Gollancz's, and also Buber's (**P10**)—which express doubt concerning human "forgiving," especially *on behalf* of the victims who had perished, it is important to distinguish this attitude from the unwillingness to forgive. The first does not presume oneself to have the authority to issue forgiveness (whether on God's or the victims' behalf); the second takes it for granted but refuses—for whatever reasons—to grant it. In fact, one is hard pressed to find a single instance in which the second attitude (i.e., "I will not forgive you—although I'm qualified to do so!") was demonstrated by these turners. Rather, it has been expressed—in an ironic twist—during some recent protests in Germany against neo-Nazis. "Kein Vergeben! Kein Vergessen!" (No forgiving! No forgetting!) or "Nichts vergeben! Nichts vergessen! (Forgive nothing! Forget nothing!) was their mantra.[88] Though the general opposition of the German populace to the ebbs and flows of neo-Nazism within their neighborhood and to old Nazis at large is to be appreciated, it is certainly not within a protester's "mandate" to grant *and* to deny forgiveness.[89] As Abraham Heschel has said in different contexts, "Even God Himself can only

---

87. Ibid., 310–11.

88. See, for example, "Familie von NSU-Opfer schlägt Gaucks Einladung aus," *Zeit Online*, 16 Feb. 2013. A simple search on the Internet reveals numerous images of the use of "Kein Vergeben! Kein Vergessen!" and similar phrases used as protest slogans by anti-Nazi and neo-Nazi demonstrators alike.

89. It is most probably not, to be fair, the anti-Nazi protesters' intention to claim the victims' privilege to deny forgiveness, for there can always be qualifications attached to the "no forgiving" clause. But this is precisely the problem of reducing a complex and theologically rich insight (i.e., unwarranted representative forgiveness) to a catchy banner slogan, which carries certain resemblance to its original source but generates misleading implications of its own, which can in turn

forgive sins committed against Himself, not against man."[90] The same goes, of course, also for the preclusion of forgiveness.

Despite the lack of "forgiving"—or because of the perpetual drive toward repentance due precisely to this "empty chair" of forgiveness?—there is little cause today for Germans traveling to Israel to take the kind of precautions necessary in Lüth's time.[91] Furthermore, since 1993 the "atoning Germans" of the ASF have been bringing Israeli volunteers to Germany (certainly not to make *Sühnezeichen* but perhaps *Versöhnungszeichen*), and that is not to mention the growing and thriving Jewish communities in the Federal Republic after 1989.[92] None of these developments, to be sure, means "reconciliation achieved" or the "end of repentance," which are dubious goals in themselves. They do mean, however, that the German-Jewish relationship, damaged and burdened as it is by the crimes of Nazi Germany, is not dilapidated beyond resuscitation. In fact, one might even ask: When in the history of German-Jewish interaction has such a state of relationship occurred? Or are we not witnessing something *new* altogether?

At the end of "Israelüth's" first visit to the promised land, he couldn't help being envious of another German who had found

---

overshadow the original insight. The fact that neo-Nazis are now also using this slogan to commemorate *their* "victims" should be an occasion for clarification.

90. See Heschel's contribution in Simon Wiesenthal, *The Sunflower: On the Possibilities and Limits of Forgiveness*, revised and expanded ed. (New York: Schocken Books, 1998), 164–66. Previously, Heschel had expressed the same idea in a 1963 speech, "Religion and Race," addressing the problem of racism in the United States. In this earlier context, Heschel was speaking as a white person to whites, pointing to the necessity of turning to the black victims, not just seeking forgiveness through religious services among whites. Hence the nuanced formulation: "It is not within the power of God to forgive the sins committed toward men. We must first ask for forgiveness of those whom our society has wronged before asking for the forgiveness of God." See Abraham Joshua Heschel, *Insecurity of Freedom: Essays on Human Existence* (New York: Schocken Books, 1972), 89.

91. According to Katharina von Münster, former ASF representative in Israel, every German volunteer—and their parents—worried about Israeli hatred against the Germans before they came. Yet all returned surprised by its actual absence. Interview with Katharina von Münster, 15 Oct. 2010, Jerusalem.

92. See Thomas Heldt, "Die Israelis kommen!" in Krane et al., *Aktion Sühnezeichen*, 44–45.

the love of Israeli Jews—the German-Israeli actress Orna Porat.
"The young actress has already established the bridge of human
understanding," Lüth told his German readers, "which we all are
still seeking."[93] With the wealth of examples lived out by the pioneering turners before them, Germans and Jews of today facing old
and new challenges to their renewed relationship are well equipped
to find that "way" of mutual-turning to each other—which some
other peoples torn by wrongdoings in the past are still seeking.

---

93. Lüth, "Pioniere aus Deutschland." Porat's own life was nothing less than extraordinary. See Gisela Dachs, "Das Geheimnis einer Ehe," *Die Zeit*, 3 Jan. 2002.

CONCLUSION

It would not have been even remotely decent for a non-Jewish person to have suggested to Jews that they ought to become reconciled to the Germans immediately after World War II.[1]

DUTCH VISITOR TO SOUTH AFRICA'S TRUTH AND RECONCILIATION COMMISSION (TRC)

The event that is called repentance from the world's side is called redemption from God's side.[2]

MARTIN BUBER

I

The preceding chapters of this book have sought to demonstrate the contributions of the Jewish instrument of repentance to the German process of coming to terms with the Nazi past. In this process, both Jewish and German individuals as well as some other

---

1. Truth and Reconciliation Commission, *Truth and Reconciliation Commission of South Africa Report*, vol. 1, chap. 5, para. 48, http://www.justice.gov.za/trc/report/.

2. Martin Buber, *Ich und Du* (Heidelberg: Lambert Schneider, 1979), 141.

relational partners have made use of the Jewish resource of repentance (*tshuvah*)—defined as asymmetric mutual-turning in the first part of this study—to reach out to each other, to perceive and analyze the German problem, and to propose viable solutions to it. Hence not only "reconciliation" is a joint venture, as is popularly perceived, but "repentance" itself is shown to be a collaborative effort. Though the samples collected here are in no way "representative," statistically speaking, their spheric diversity—from philosophical treatise to political-juridical debate, from theological reflection to civil initiatives, from literature to historiography and mass media—does show that such collaboration is also in no way a "niche" phenomenon, negligible and insignificant.

This has not always been the case. In the aftermath of World War I, the German-Jewish philosopher Max Scheler[3] repeated his call for the "act of repentance" (*der Akt der Reue*)[4] as the path to rebirth from the "collective guilt of Europe," but apparently in vain, for "modern philosophy tends to regard repentance as an almost only negative and also most uneconomical act."[5] If Scheler's assessment is any indicator of the intellectual climate of the interwar period, or of modernity in general, it is but a stark reminder of how even a shared intellectual resource such as biblical repentance can "fail" if nobody is paying heed. "And so the oppression of guilt (*Schulddruck*) is allowed to amass into an avalanche."[6]

To Scheler, repentance empowers the guilt-laden to break away from that "determining power of their past," or to use a

---

3. Born to a Jewish family in Munich in 1874, Scheler later became a noted Catholic thinker of his time. Zachary Davis and Anthony Steinbock, "Max Scheler," in *The Stanford Encyclopedia of Philosophy* (2014), http://plato.stanford.edu/archives/sum2014/entries/scheler/.

4. *Reue* is usually translated as "regret" in English. However, it is clear in the context that by *Reue*, Scheler was in fact referring to repentance in its fullest sense, i.e., an ability "God lent to the soul" to "return to him." Max Scheler, "Reue und Wiedergeburt," in *Vom Ewigen im Menschen* (Leipzig: Der Neue Geist, 1921), 1:12. This essay was first published in 1917. See its English translation as "Repentance and Rebirth," in *On the Eternal in Man*, trans. Bernard Noble (Hamden, CT: Archon Books, 1972), 33–65.

5. Schele, "Reue und Wiedergeburt," 6, 48.

6. Ibid., 17.

prophetic expression, the uncovering of guilt is a fate-changing event.[7] Though one may not share his optimism that the language of repentance bespeaks true repentance as spiritual reality,[8] the preceding chapters have nonetheless shown that repentance according to Jewish thought is a source of answers to the myriad of conundrums besetting postwar Germans—from the dilemma of condoning and scapegoating to cross-generational guilt and responsibility to the possibility of reconciliation itself. One may of course further disagree with these answers, or propose better ones based on alternative intellectual resources and measured by alternative standards. In any case, it is no longer possible to overlook the correspondence between biblical repentance and the history of *Vergangenheitsbewältigung*, if the latter is not to be preconceived as a purely "secularized" domain (see the introduction).

II

The desecularization of the study of German coming to terms with the Nazi past will hopefully create a new space for debates and dialogues in connection with other regional experiences of dealing with past atrocities. In overcoming the legacies of apartheid in South Africa and other gross human rights violations in Latin America, it has long been observed that religious concepts such as "reconciliation" and "forgiveness" have played a significant role in these processes—for better (i.e., overcoming violence or civil war) or for worse (neglecting retributive justice).[9] The German example, however, has rarely been accorded such conceptual focus,[10] result-

---

7. Ibid., 18; Lamentations 2:14 (esp. the Einheitsübersetzung version).

8. Schele, "Reue und Wiedergeburt," 46–48.

9. See Desmond Tutu, *No Future without Forgiveness* (New York: Doubleday, 1999), 54–55; and John Borneman, *Settling Accounts: Violence, Justice, and Accountability in Postsocialist Europe* (Princeton, NJ: Princeton University Press, 1997).

10. One exception is Ralf K. Wüstenberg's theological study of dealing with guilt in transitional Germany and South Africa. But the handling of the "red past"

ing in the bizarre situation that even those who would like to learn from this experience—imperfect and incomplete as it is—often do not know where to begin.[11]

With the central argument of this book—that the Jewish idea of repentance has been at work in the German history of coming to terms with the past—it is now possible to engage in comparative case studies and debates about the relative merits and "blind spots" of a forgiveness-dominated discourse versus a repentance-centric one, and of the different visions or "levels" of reconciliation embedded in these discourses.[12] It would be a blatant oversimplification to attribute the relative emphases on repentance and forgiveness to Judaism and Christianity respectively, as if the two concepts and traditions were alien to each other. It would be meaningful, however, to compare the ramifications in terms of societal transformation in postatrocity settings with these relative preoccupations.

The repentance-perspective of German *Vergangenheitsbewältigung* also makes new contributions to the ongoing debates about the global effects of the "German culture of remembrance" (Confino). The globalization of Holocaust remembrance has been hailed as potentially boundary-transcending and sensitizing toward the suffering of others. Taking into account its historical development in Germany as well as Israel and the United States, Daniel Levy and Natan Sznaider argue that the shared "cosmopolitan memory" of the destruction of European Jewry by Nazi Germany is a

---

after 1989 rather than the "brown past" after 1945 is the object of its comparative analysis. See Ralf K. Wüstenberg, *Die politische Dimension der Versöhnung: Eine theologische Studie zum Umgang mit Schuld nach den Systemumbrüchen in Südafrika und Deutschland* (Gütersloh: Chr. Kaiser/Gütersloher Verlagshaus, 2004).

11. It is a telltale sign that, for example, in the TRC report, the German case can only offer "lessons" in material reparations and memorials, nothing more. *TRC Report*, 5:9:102; 6:2:3:24.

12. Erin Daly and Jeremy Sarkin suggest that the (post-1989) German focus on "bilateral and communal reconciliation" and the South African emphasis on "political or national reconciliation" are due to the different types of damage left by the preceding regimes, which also account for the relative ease in the former case. See Erin Daly and Jeremy Sarkin, *Reconciliation in Divided Societies: Finding Common Ground* (Philadelphia: University of Pennsylvania Press, 2007), 43, 70.

"memory that harbors the possibility of transcending ethnic and national boundaries."[13] Connecting Holocaust remembrance and the process of decolonization, Michael Rothberg contends that "multidirectional memory"—as against *competitive* memory of "our" versus "their" suffering—has the "potential to create new forms of solidarity and new visions of justice."[14] Both assertions are surprising: after all, isn't it more reasonable to expect that the memory of one's own suffering will *strengthen* rather than transcend ethnic and national boundaries?[15] And the dualistic nature of Holocaust remembrance, as Rothberg concedes, can serve as both "screen projection" (leading to "disturbing" memories of one's own) and "barrier to remembrance" (as diversion), with no telling in advance which will gain the upper hand.[16] How then can one get closer to realizing the better "potentials" of Holocaust remembrance, especially in non-European settings?

That memory of suffering is an "ambiguous energy," as we have seen (**P13**), has long been a problem in German VgB, which turners like Rabbi Harold Schulweis and Rabbi Robert Raphael Geis have attempted to tackle. Their strategy to steer this energy away from a pathos of self-pity or "brooding guilt" toward "constructive repentance" seems to be a promising solution to the problem we pose above. Its key elements of antidemonization of the perpetrator (**R1**), disproportionate remembrance of the righteous other (**R13**), and self-turning (**R9**) are crucial in harnessing this anamnestic energy for repentance. Is it possible that these are also among the determining factors in making Holocaust remembrance boundary-transcending and solidarity-creating?

---

13. Daniel Levy and Natan Sznaider, *The Holocaust and Memory in the Global Age*, trans. Assenka Oksiloff (Philadelphia: Temple University Press, 2006), 4.

14. Michael Rothberg, *Multidirectional Memory: Remembering the Holocaust in the Age of Decolonization* (Stanford, CA: Stanford University Press, 2009), 5.

15. As Chinese are used to reminding one another, "[We were] backward, hence [we were] beaten up." Ergo, we the victims need a "wealthy state and powerful army" to buttress our borders. The Great Wall is apparently not only a physical relic. See Wang Zheng, *Never Forget National Humiliation: Historical Memory in Chinese Politics and Foreign Relations* (New York: Columbia University Press, 2012).

16. Rothberg, *Multidirectional Memory*, 16.

To transfer this strategy to the non-European and postcolonial relational contexts, one needs to look into specific discourses to see whether, for example, the crimes of the colonizers or the Nanjing Massacre are sufficiently decoupled from the perpetrators and viewed from the "sin-perspective" (P2)—that is, atrocities are not primarily seen as acts of the "demon others," but sins of "ordinary people."[17] It is also relevant to determine whether there is a perceptible and persistent (or even institutionalized) remembrance of the counterstereotyping righteous others side by side with the remembrance of the suffering of one's own people; and whether the increased "articulation of other histories [of suffering]" (Rothberg),[18] brought about by the globalization of Holocaust memory, is geared toward "constructive repentance" rather than "brooding guilt." And finally, whether there are authentic and legitimate attempts to identify one's possible connections—no matter how improbable or objectionable by popular standards—to one's own suffering or that of one's own people. In other words, whether the globalization of Holocaust remembrance has in fact led to more instances of localized *Vergangenheitsbewältigung*. In this respect, it appears that a repentance-centric discourse can be more conducive to generating such unlikely responses to past atrocities than one predicated on forgiveness.

The problem with a forgiveness-dominant discourse is that it inadvertently predisposes a person to identify himself as victim—that is, one who is *in the position* to consider whether to forgive or not—or more precisely, to choose from among the possible identities available to him the one(s) that can allow him to imagine himself doing forgiveness. As an illustration: among those asked by Simon Wiesenthal about the possibility of forgiveness were one Tibetan and one Han. Whereas the Tibetan spoke about the dangers of self-righteousness and "losing compassion" as a reaction to decades-long Chinese atrocities against the Tibetan people,[19] the Chinese also spoke about

---

17. This is the observation of Leung Man-Tao, a noted essayist in Hong Kong. See his "為什麼日本不像德國?" [Why Is Japan unlike Germany? I & II], *Ming Pao*, 4 and 11 May 2005.

18. Rothberg, *Multidirectional Memory*, 6.

19. See the Dalai Lama's response in Simon Wiesenthal, *The Sunflower: On the Possibilities and Limits of Forgiveness*, revised and expanded ed. (New York: Schocken Books, 1998), 129–30.

victimhood under the Chinese government—his own. "During my nineteen years in prison, I often experienced harsh treatment at the hands of guards and prison officials. I was beaten and degraded," he recalled.[20] Of course, as a persecuted dissident, the Chinese intellectual's victim status vis-à-vis his own government is beyond doubt. The discursive environment of forgiveness, however, did not predispose him to see his own guilt and responsibility as a Han intellectual vis-à-vis the Tibetan people, that is, one in need of seeking forgiveness instead of granting it. Hence both the Tibetan and the Han spoke about the year 1959, when the Han Communists suppressed the Tibetan 10 March uprising,[21] but the turning movement (for compassion, against self-righteousness) from one side of the wounded relationship was not met—albeit only indirectly—with a commensurate response from the other side.[22]

This problem of victim-predisposal may have some legitimacy in the unusual situation where the victims and survivors are in fact in the position—in terms of postatrocity power relations[23]—to consider the option of retributive or restorative justice, and where the predisposer has genuine credibility in his claims to shared victimhood with the predisposed.[24] Where the victims and survivors are not in that position, the talk of forgiveness becomes either an unbearable self-absolution (e.g., Han democrats "forgiving" Han Communists after the eventual democratic transition) or, to borrow Jürgen

---

20. See Harry Wu's response in Wiesenthal, *Sunflower*, 271–74.

21. See Tubten Khétsun, *Memories of Life in Lhasa under Chinese Rule*, trans. Matthew Akester (New York: Columbia University Press, 2008); and Palden Gyatso and Tsering Shakya, *Fire under the Snow: Testimony of a Tibetan Prisoner* (London: Harvill, 1997).

22. It has to be stated, however, that Harry Wu has also been a longtime supporter of the Tibetan cause on other occasions. Some of these are documented on the official website of his Laogai Research Foundation based in Washington, DC (www.laogai.org).

23. See chapter 2.

24. Appealing to the examples of magnanimity of both Jesus on the cross and Nelson Mandela ravaged by incarceration, Tutu's response to Wiesenthal draws from the moral capital of these "ultimate victims" to effect a wider acceptance of forgiving as a response. The key question of "who is entitled to forgive what," however, is left unanswered. Wiesenthal, *Sunflower*, 266–68.

Habermas's phrase, "coerced reconciliation."[25] As a Han Chinese pondering the possible futures of post-Communist China, where the reversal of the ethnic majority-minority power relations seems most unlikely, I am inclined to think that the repentance-centric discourse is more instructive, if Chinese coming to terms with the past—one that is truly worthy of its name[26]—is to be realized, and if Han-Tibetan and Han-Uighur reconciliation—rather than mere "national unity" during transition[27]—is to be achieved at all.

III

In the final analysis, my decade-long engagement with the problems of coming to terms with the past in Europe and in East Asia has led me to the conclusion that the Jewish tradition of repentance belongs to what the TRC final report calls "healing and restorative truth." The report

> rejects the popular assumption that there are only two options to be considered when talking about truth—namely factual, objective information or subjective opinions. There is also "healing" truth, the kind of truth that places facts and what they mean *within the context* of human relationships. . . . This kind of truth was central to the Commission.[28]

Indeed, this kind of truth, which provides a context and a sense of purpose[29] for the other types of truth—factual, narrative and

---

25. Jürgen Habermas, "Die Entsorgung der Vergangenheit," *Die Zeit*, 17 May 1985.

26. For some initial steps in this direction, see, for example, Yu Jie, "向西藏懺悔—讀《雪山下的火焰 一個西藏良心犯的證言》" [Repent to Tibet: Reading 'Fire under the Snow'], *Open Magazine*, Jun. 2004; Cao Changqing, ed., 中國大陸知識分子論西藏 [Mainland Chinese Intellectuals on Tibet] (Taipei: China Times Publishing, 1996); Li Jianglin, *1959 Lhasa!* (Hong Kong: New Century Media & Consulting, 2010); and Wang Keming and Song Xiaoming, eds., 我們懺悔：未刪節全本 [We Repent—Uncut Full Version] (Hong Kong: Great Mountain Culture, 2014).

27. "National unity" was in fact a professed aim of reconciliation efforts in post-apartheid South Africa. Daly and Sarkin, *Reconciliation in Divided Societies*, 97–98.

28. *TRC Report*, 1:5:43 (emphasis added).

29. Ibid., 1:5:44.

social—[30] is beyond the subjective-objective dimension. It reminds one of what Abraham Heschel called the "three-dimensional" way of seeing—that is, not directly from the subject to the object ("2-D") but through the inculcated divine viewpoint.[31] From this vantage point, hitherto nonexistent or unnoticed possibilities emerge when one is dealing with otherwise intractable problems arising from interhuman atrocities—problems and questions not only about memory but also about justice, the comparison of guilt, the proper "apology," the responsibilities of future generations, and the desirability of reconciliation itself.

During the revision and completion of this book, I taught an introductory course in European studies at my university in Hong Kong for undergraduate students who are not specializing in the subject. In the few lectures I could spare on "European reconciliation," I introduced the Jewish concepts of repentance and reconciliation as an example of how shared ideational resources can have an impact on international relations. At one point I encouraged my students to think critically about these ideas, especially in view of the East Asian cultural context. Thereupon remarked a Hong Kong student: "I'm actually quite critical of the religious approach . . . but it seems to me that [the Jewish idea of repentance] provides the answer to the question, Why [should nations divided by past atrocities] strive for reconciliation at all?"

Without this basic commitment, taking the strenuous path of "coming to terms with the past" can seem pointless indeed. The findings of this study are perhaps only helpful to those who have

---

30. Ibid., 1:5:29–42.

31. Abraham Joshua Heschel, *The Prophets*, Perennial Classics (New York: HarperCollins, 2001), 29. Ostensibly, the TRC report refers only to the human relationships among citizens and between the state and its citizens (1:5:43), while leaving the divine dimension unspoken. The centrality of this dimension to the actual proceedings of the commission, however, can be seen from the insistence of Tutu, its chairperson, on opening prayers before the beginning of commission proceedings, that is, the reenactment of the three-dimensional paradigm. Jennifer J. Llewellyn and Daniel Philpott, eds., *Restorative Justice, Reconciliation, and Peacebuilding* (Oxford/New York: Oxford University Press, 2014), 2, 108–9.

already somehow found the will to this commitment in their own relational contexts, which this study cannot provide. I can also imagine the disappointment of those expecting to find policy advice, a new periodization of postwar German history, or new formulas of "contrition score"[32] in this book, which they won't. These are some of the limitations of the approach I've adopted in this work, which, above all, is dedicated to those who, despite the fact that they are not in any position to affect government policy or effect "institutionalized Vergangenheitsbewältigung,"[33] seek nonetheless to "restore the [wounded] order of being (*Seinsordnung*) . . . in the given historical and biographical situations" in which they find themselves.[34]

One cannot, even with the machinery of a prosperous and powerful state, undo the damages caused by the Nazis, Yasukuni-ists,[35] racists, and the like in the past. But by doing *tshuvah*, restoration is still possible, "for the wounds of the order of being can be healed in infinitely many places other than where they were inflicted."[36]

---

32. David Art, *The Politics of the Nazi Past in Germany and Austria* (New York: Cambridge University Press, 2006), 80, 215–18.

33. Wüstenberg, *Politische Versöhnung*, 65.

34. Martin Buber, *Schuld und Schuldgefühle* (Heidelberg: Lambert Schneider, 1958), 41.

35. On "Yasukuni-ism," see Yagyû Kunichika, "Der Yasukuni-Schrein im Japan der Nachkriegszeit: Zu den Nachwirkungen des Staatsshintô," in *Erinnerungskulturen: Deutschland, Italien und Japan seit 1945*, ed. Christoph Cornelißen, Lutz Klinkhammer, and Wolfgang Schwentker (Frankfurt a.M.: Fischer Taschenbuch, 2004), 246.

36. Buber, *Schuld und Schuldgefühle*, 41. See P6.

BIBLIOGRAPHY

Adler, H. G. *Theresienstadt 1941–1945: Das Antlitz einer Zwangsgemeinschaft.* Tübingen: J. C. B. Mohr (Paul Siebeck), 1955.

Aktion Sühnezeichen Friedensdienste. *Aktion Sühnezeichen Friedensdienste 1958–2008: Eine Chronik in Stichworten; 50 Jahre im Überblick.* Berlin: ASF, 2008.

Améry, Jean. *Jenseits von Schuld und Sühne: Bewältigungsversuche eines Überwältigten.* Munich: Szczesny Verlag, 1966.

"Amnon, die Katze." *Der Spiegel,* no. 24 (1988).

Anders, Günther. *Wir Eichmannsöhne: Offener Brief an Klaus Eichmann.* Munich: C. H. Beck, 1964.

——. "Zweiter Brief an Klaus Eichmann: Gegen die Gleichgültigkeit." In *Wir Eichmannsöhne: Offener Brief an Klaus Eichmann,* 76–100. Munich: C. H. Beck, 1988.

Anders, Günther, and Claude Eatherly. *Off limits für das Gewissen: Der Briefwechsel Claude Eatherly Günther Anders.* Reinbek bei Hamburg: Rowohlt, 1961.

"An unsere Leser!" *Frankfurter Hefte* 1, no. 1 (1946): 1–2.

Arendt, Hannah. *Denktagebuch: 1950 bis 1973.* Edited by Ursula Ludz and Ingeborg Nordmann. Munich: Piper, 2002.

———. *Eichmann in Jerusalem: A Report on the Banality of Evil.* London: Faber, 1963.

———. "Organisierte Schuld." *Die Wandlung* 1, no. 4 (1946): 333–44.

Arndt, Adolf. "Kein Sondergesetz! Kein Sonderschutz!" *Sozialdemokratischer Pressedienst*, 3 Feb. 1960, 1.

Art, David. *The Politics of the Nazi Past in Germany and Austria.* New York: Cambridge University Press, 2006.

Ashley, J. Matthew. Introduction to *Faith in History and Society: Toward a Practical Fundamental Theology*, by Johann Baptist Metz. New York: Crossroad Publishing, 2007.

———. "Johann Baptist Metz." In *The Blackwell Companion to Political Theology*, edited by Peter Schott and William T. Cavanaugh, 241–55. Malden, MA: Blackwell Publishing, 2003.

Assmann, Aleida. *Das neue Unbehagen an der Erinnerungskultur.* Munich: C. H. Beck, 2013.

Assmann, Aleida, and Ute Frevert. *Geschichtvergessenheit, Geschichtsversessenheit: Vom Umgang mit deutschen Vergangenheiten nach 1945.* Stuttgart: Deutsche Verlags-Anstalt, 1999.

Ausschuß für gesamtdeutsche Fragen. *Die völkerrechtlichen Irrtümer der evangelischen Ost-Denkschrift.* Bonn: Bund der Vertriebenen—Vereinigte Landsmannschaften und Landesverbände, 1966.

Baeck, Leo. "Gedenken zur jüdischen Situation." *Aufbau*, 30 Aug. 1946.

Baehr, Peter, ed. *The Portable Hannah Arendt.* New York: Penguin Books, 2000.

Bahr, Raimund. *Günther Anders: Leben und Denken im Wort.* Berlin: epubli GmbH, 2012.

Barkai, Avraham. "German Historians versus Goldhagen." *Yad Vashem Studies* 26 (1998): 295–328.

Barkan, Elazar. *The Guilt of Nations: Restitution and Negotiating Historical Injustices.* New York: Norton, 2000.

Barth, Karl. "Ein Wort an die Deutschen." In *Der Götze wackelt*, 87–97. Berlin: Käthe Vogt Verlag, 1961.

———. *Zur Genesung des deutschen Wesens: Ein Freundeswort von draußen.* Stuttgart: Verlag von Franz Mittelbach, 1945.

Bauer, Fritz. *Das Verbrechen und die Gesellschaft.* Munich/Basel: Ernst Reinhardt, 1957.

———. "Der Zweck im Strafrecht." In *Vom kommenden Strafrecht*, 17–41. Karlsruhe: C. F. Müller, 1969.

———. "Die Schuld im Strafrecht." In *Die Humanität der Rechtsordnung: Ausgewählte Schriften*, edited by Joachim Perels and Irmtrud Wojak, 249–78. Frankfurt/New York: Campus, 1998.

———. *Die Wurzeln faschistischen und nationalsozialistischen Handelns.* Frankfurt a.M.: Europäische Verlagsanstalt, 1965.

———. "Eine Grenze hat Tyrannenmacht: Plädoyer im Remer-Prozeß." In *Die Humanität der Rechtsordnung: Ausgewählte Schriften*, edited by Joachim Perels and Irmtrud Wojak, 169–80. Frankfurt/New York: Campus, 1998.

——. "Im Kampf um des Menschen Rechte." In *Die Humanität der Rechts-ordnung: Ausgewählte Schriften*, edited by Joachim Perels and Irmtrud Wojak, 37–49. Frankfurt/New York: Campus, 1998.

Bauer, Yehuda. *Die dunkle Seite der Geschichte: Die Shoah in historischer Sicht; Interpretationen und Re-Interpretationen*. Translated by Christian Wiese. Frankfurt a.M.: Jüdischer Verlag, 2001.

——. *The Jewish Emergence from Powerlessness*. London: Macmillan, 1980.

Bazyler, Michael J. "Holocaust Denial Laws and Other Legislation Criminalizing Promotion of Nazism." Accessed 31 Oct. 2012. http://www.yadvashem.org/yv/en/holocaust/insights/pdf/bazyler.pdf.

Bell, George K. A. "Die Ökumene und die innerdeutsche Opposition." *Vierteljahrshefte für Zeitgeschichte* 5, no. 4 (1957): 362–78.

Ben-Gavriêl, M. Y. "Der Jisraelüth." In *Die Friedensbitte an Israel 1951: Eine Hamburger Initiative*, edited by Erich Lüth, 61. Hamburg: Hans Christians Verlag, 1976.

——. "Gesetz zur Verewigung des Andenkens an die vom Nationalsozialismus ermordeten Juden gebilligt." *Freiburger Rundbrief* 6, no. 21/24 (1953/54): 40–41.

Bensberger Kreis. *Ein Memorandum deutscher Katholiken zu den polnisch-deutschen Fragen*. Mainz: Matthias-Grünewald-Verlag, 1968.

Bergengruen, Werner. *Dies Irae*. Munich: Verlag Kurt Desch, 1947.

Beutler-Lotz, Heinz-Günter, ed. *Die Bußpsalmen: Meditationen, Andachten, Entwürfe*. Göttingen: Vandenhoeck & Ruprecht, 1995.

Biller, Maxim. "Die Nachmann-Juden." In *Die Tempojahre*, 171–74. Munich: Deutscher Taschenbuch, 1991.

Blätter-Redaktion. "50 Jahre Blätter." *Blätter für deutsche und internationale Politik* 11 (2006): 1284–86.

Boda, Mark. "Renewal in Heart, Word, and Deed: Repentance in the Torah." In *Repentance in Christian Theology*, edited by Mark Boda and Gordon Smith, 3–24. Collegeville, MN: Liturgical Press, 2006.

Bodemann, Y. Michal. "Nachmann Scandal." *American Jewish Year Book*, 1990, 362–65.

Böll, Heinrich. "Nachwort." In *Aufbewahren für alle Zeit*, by Lev Kopelev, 595–605. Hamburg: Hoffmann und Campe, 1976.

Borneman, John. *Settling Accounts: Violence, Justice, and Accountability in Postsocialist Europe*. Princeton, NJ: Princeton University Press, 1997.

Borowsky, Peter. "Das Ende der 'Ära Adenauer.'" *Informationen zur politischen Bildung*, no. 258 (1998). http://www.bpb.de/izpb/10093/das-ende-der-aera-adenauer.

Boyens, Armin. "Das Stuttgarter Schuldbekenntnis vom 19. Oktober 1945: Entstehung und Bedeutung." *Vierteljahrshefte für Zeitgeschichte* 19, no. 4 (1971): 374–97.

Braese, Stephan. *Die andere Erinnerung: Jüdische Autoren in der west-deutschen Nachkriegsliteratur*. Berlin: Philo, 2001.

Brandt, Willy. *Begegnungen und Einsichten: Die Jahre 1960–1975*. Hamburg: Hoffmann und Campe, 1976.

——. *Mein Weg nach Berlin*. Munich: Kindler, 1960.

Briegleb, Klaus. *Mißachtung und Tabu: Eine Streitschrift zur Frage: 'Wie anti-semitisch war die Gruppe 47?'* Berlin/Vienna: Philo, 2003.

Broder, Henryk M. "Die Opfer der Opfer." *Die Zeit*, 14 Jul. 1989.

——. "Eine Art Säulenheilige." *Der Spiegel*, no. 42 (1996).

——. "Rehabilitiert Werner Nachmann." In *Aufbau nach dem Untergang: Deutsch-jüdische Geschichte nach 1945*, edited by Andreas Nachama and Julius H. Schoeps, 299–303. Berlin: Argon, 1992.

——. "Warum ich lieber kein Jude wäre; und wenn schon unbedingt—dann lieber nicht in Deutschland." In *Fremd im eigenen Land: Juden in der Bundesrepublik*, edited by Henryk M. Broder and Michel R. Lang, 82–102. Frankfurt a.M.: Fischer Taschenbuch Verlag, 1979.

Brog, Mooli. "In Blessed Memory of a Dream: Mordechai Shenhavi and Initial Holocaust Commemoration Ideas in Palestine, 1942–1945." *Yad Vashem Studies* 30 (2002): 297–336.

Browning, Christopher. *Ordinary Men: Reserve Police Battalion 101 and the Final Solution in Poland*. New York: HarperCollins, 1992.

Bruckner, Pascal. *The Tyranny of Guilt: An Essay on Western Masochism*. Translated by Steven Rendall. Princeton, NJ/Oxford: Princeton University Press, 2010. Original in French: *Tyrannie de la pénitence*.

Buber, Martin. "Brief aus Palästina." *Frankfurter Hefte* 5, no. 1 (1950): 29.

——. "Das echte Gespräch und die Möglichkeit des Friedens: Eine Dankes-rede." Accessed 18 Jul. 2013. http://www.friedenspreis-des-deutschen-buchhandels.de/.

——. "Die Forderung des Geistes und die geschichtliche Wirklichkeit." *Frankfurter Hefte* 3, no. 3 (1948): 209–16.

——. "Falsche Propheten." *Die Wandlung* 2, no. 4 (1947): 277–83.

——. *Ich und Du*. Heidelberg: Lambert Schneider, 1979. First published in 1923.

——. "'Pharisäertum.'" *Der Jude: Sonderheft; Antisemitismus und jüdisches Volkstum* 1 (1925–27): 123–31.

——. *Schuld und Schuldgefühle*. Heidelberg: Lambert Schneider, 1958.

Buber, Martin, and Franz Rosenzweig. *Die Schrift: Bücher der Kündung*. Stuttgart: Deutsche Bibelgesellschaft, 1992.

——. *Scripture and Translation*. Translated by Lawrence Rosenwald and Everett Fox. Bloomington: Indiana University Press, 1994.

Bubis, Ignatz. "Rede des Präsidenten des Zentralrates der Juden in Deutsch-land." In *Die Walser-Bubis-Debatte: Eine Dokumentation*, edited by Frank Schirrmacher, 106–13. Frankfurt a.M.: Suhrkamp, 1999.

Bund der Vertriebenen. "Zum Tode von Marion Gräfin Dönhoff." Accessed 15 Jul. 2013. http://www.bund-der-vertriebenen.de/presse/index.php3?id=13& druck=1.

Burg, Avraham. *The Holocaust Is Over; We Must Rise from Its Ashes*. Translated by Israel Amrani. New York: Palgrave Macmillan, 2008.

——. "Vorwort zur deutschen Ausgabe." Translated by Ulrike Bischoff. In *Hitler besiegen: Warum Israel sich endlich vom Holocaust lösen muss*, 9–20. Frankfurt/New York: Campus, 2009.

Cao Changqing, ed. 中國大陸知識分子論西藏 [Mainland Chinese Intellectuals on Tibet]. Taipei: China Times Publishing, 1996.

Casper, Bernhard. "Transzendentale Phänomenalität und ereignetes Ereignis: Der Sprung in ein hermeneutisches Denken im Leben und Werk Franz Rosenzweigs." In *Der Stern der Erlösung*, by Franz Rosenzweig, V–XVI. Freiburg im Breisgau: Universitätsbibliothek, 2002.

"Charta der deutschen Heimatvertriebenen." In *Die völkerrechtlichen Irrtümer der evangelischen Ost-Denkschrift*, by Ausschuß für gesamtdeutsche Fragen, 29–30. Bonn: Bund der Vertriebenen—Vereinigte Landsmannschaften und Landesverbände, 1966.

Confino, Alon. *Germany as a Culture of Remembrance: Promises and Limits of Writing History.* Chapel Hill: University of North Carolina Press, 2006.

Cornelißen, Christoph, Lutz Klinkhammer, and Wolfgang Schwentker, eds. *Erinnerungskulturen: Deutschland, Italien und Japan seit 1945.* Frankfurt a.M.: Fischer Taschenbuch, 2004.

Cornwell, John. *Hitler's Pope: The Secret History of Pius XII.* New York: Viking, 1999.

"Council Framework Decision 2008/913/JHA of 28 November 2008 on Combating Certain Forms and Expressions of Racism and Xenophobia by Means of Criminal Law." *Official Journal of the European Union* 51, no. L328 (6 Dec. 2008): 55–58.

Cristaudo, Wayne. *Power, Love, and Evil: Contribution to a Philosophy of the Damaged.* New York: Rodopi, 2008.

Crowe, David M. *Oskar Schindler: The Untold Account of His Life, Wartime Activities, and the True Story behind the List.* Boulder, CO: Westview Press, 2004.

Dachs, Gisela. "Das Geheimnis einer Ehe." *Die Zeit*, 3 Jan. 2002.

Dalin, David G. *The Myth of Hitler's Pope: How Pope Pius XII Rescued Jews from the Nazis.* Washington, DC: Regnery, 2005.

Daly, Erin, and Jeremy Sarkin. *Reconciliation in Divided Societies: Finding Common Ground.* Philadelphia: University of Pennsylvania Press, 2007.

"Das Gewissen entscheidet." *Union in Deutschland* 19, no. 11 (1965): 1–2.

Davis, Zachary, and Anthony Steinbock. "Max Scheler." In *The Stanford Encyclopedia of Philosophy* (2014). http://plato.stanford.edu/archives/sum2014/entries/scheler/.

"Der gerechte Goi und die Schindlerjuden." *Der Spiegel*, no. 7 (1983).

"Der Kremlchef muß am Rhein regieren." *Der Spiegel*, no. 24 (1989).

"Der Schießbefehl an der Ost-West-Grenze." *Der Standard*, 24 Apr. 2002.

"Die Antwort der deutschen Bischöfe an die polnischen Bischöfe vom 5. Dezember 1965." In *'Wir vergeben und bitten um Vergebung': Der Briefwechsel der polnischen und deutschen Bischöfe von 1965 und seine Wirkung*, edited by Basil Kerski, Tomasz Kycia, and Robert Zurek, 223–28. Osnabrück: Fibre, 2006.

"Die Botschaft des Bruderrats der Bekennenden Kirche von 1948." *Freiburger Rundbrief* 1, no. 1 (1948): 6–8.

"Die Erklärungen Bundeskanzler Dr. Adenauers und der Parteien zur Wiedergutmachung." *Freiburger Rundbrief* 3/4, no. 12/15 (1951/1952): 9–11.

"Die Freiburger Veit-Harlan-Demonstrationen und ihre Folgen." *Freiburger Rundbrief* 5, no. 17/18 (1952/1953): 38–40.

"Die große Schuld." *Freiburger Rundbrief* 15, no. 57/60 (1963/1964): 32.

"Die heimlichen Rädelsführer." *Der Spiegel*, no. 27 (1993).

"Die Judenfrage auf dem Katholikentag." *Freiburger Rundbrief* 1, no. 2/3 (1949): 2–5.

di Lorenzo, Giovanni. "Die intellektuelle Feuerwehr." *Der Spiegel*, no. 6 (1993).

Dirks, Walter. "Die geistige Aufgabe des deutschen Katholizismus." *Frankfurter Hefte* 1, no. 2 (1946): 38–52.

Dönhoff, Marion Gräfin. "Ein Kreuz auf Preußens Grab." *Die Zeit*, 20 Nov. 1970.

——. "Lobbyisten der Vernunft." *Die Zeit*, 2 Mar. 1962.

——. "Mitleid mit den Deutschen: Neun Jahre Gefängnis." *Die Zeit*, 6 Feb. 1976.

——. *Polen und Deutsche: Die schwierige Versöhnung; Betrachtungen aus drei Jahrzehnten.* Munich: Goldmann, 1991.

——. "Warum D. J. Goldhagens Buch in die Irre führt." *Die Zeit*, 6 Sept. 1996.

Dowe, Dieter, ed. *Die Deutschen—ein Volk von Tätern? Zur historisch-politischen Debatte um das Buch von Daniel Jonah Goldhagen 'Hitlers willige Vollstrecker: Ganz gewöhnliche Deutsche und der Holocaust.'* Bonn: Friedrich-Ebert-Stiftung, 1996.

Dudden, Alexis. *Troubled Apologies among Japan, Korea, and the United States.* New York: Columbia University Press, 2008.

Eckern, Christel. *Die Straße nach Jerusalem: Ein Mitglied der 'Aktion Sühnezeichen' berichtet über Leben und Arbeit in Israel.* Essen: Ludgerus-Verlag Hubert Wingen, 1962.

Edwards, Ruth Dudley. *Victor Gollancz: A Biography.* London: Victor Gollancz, 1987.

"Eine eigenartige geistige Gymnastik." *Der Spiegel*, no. 17 (1985).

"Eine wichtige Instanz—Politiker und Kirchen gratulieren dem Zentralrat der Juden zum Sechzigsten." *Jüdische Allgemeine Wochenzeitung*, 19 Jul. 2010.

Einstein, Albert. "Gottesreligion oder Religion des Guten?" *Aufbau*, 13 Sept. 1940.

"Ein Wort des Bruderrats der Evangelischen Kirche in Deutschland zum politischen Weg unseres Volkes." *Flugblätter der Bekennenden Kirche*, Darmstadt, 8 August 1947.

Eitz, Thorsten, and Georg Stötzel. *Wörterbuch der 'Vergangenheitsbewältigung': Die NS-Vergangenheit im öffentlichen Sprachgebrauch.* Vols. 1–2. Hildesheim: Georg Olms, 2007 and 2009.

"Erklärung der Evangelischen Synode in Berlin-Weißensee vom April 1950 zur Judenfrage." *Freiburger Rundbrief* 2, no. 8/9 (1949/1950): 18–19.

Etzioni, Amitai, and David E. Carney, eds. *Repentance: A Comparative Perspective.* Lanham, MD: Rowman & Littlefield, 1997.

Faierstein, Morris M. "Abraham Joshua Heschel and the Holocaust." *Modern Judaism* 19 (1999): 255–75.

"Familie von NSU-Opfer schlägt Gaucks Einladung aus." *Zeit Online*, 16 Feb. 2013.

Feldman, Louis H. *'Remember Amalek!'* Cincinnati: Hebrew Union College Press, 2004.

Fischer, Torben, and Matthias N. Lorenz, eds. *Lexikon der 'Vergangenheitsbewältigung' in Deutschland: Debatten- und Diskursgeschichte des Nationalsozialismus nach 1945.* Bielefeld: transcript, 2007.

Florin, Mario. *Ein haß uber den alten menschen und eyn suchen des lebens yn dem newen menschen: Luthers Auslegung der Sieben Bußpsalmen (1517 und 1525), mit einem Exkurs über Luther und die Theologia Deutsch.* Bern: Peter Lang, 1989.

Fogelman, Eva. *Conscience and Courage: Rescuers of Jews during the Holocaust.* London: Cassell, 1995.

Frank, Matthew. "The New Morality—Victor Gollancz, 'Save Europe Now' and the German Refugee Crisis, 1945–46." *Twentieth Century British History* 17, no. 2 (2006): 230–56.

Frei, Norbert. *1945 und Wir: Das Dritte Reich im Bewußtsein der Deutschen.* Munich: C. H. Beck, 2005.

———. *Vergangenheitspolitik: Die Anfänge der Bundesrepublik und die NS-Vergangenheit.* Munich: Deutscher Taschenbuch, 2003. First published in 1996.

Freimüller, Tobias. "Der versäumte Abschied von der 'Volksgemeinschaft': Psychoanalyse und Vergangenheitsbewältigung." In *50 Klassiker der Zeitgeschichte*, edited by Jürgen Danyel, Jan-Holger Kirsch, and Martin Sabrow, 102–5. Göttingen: Vandenhoeck & Ruprecht, 2007.

Fretheim, Terence. "Repentance in the Former Prophets." In *Repentance in Christian Theology*, edited by Mark Boda and Gordon Smith, 25–45. Collegeville, MN: Liturgical Press, 2006.

Freud, Sigmund. *Gesammelte Werke.* Vol. 10, *Werke aus den Jahren 1913–1917.* Frankfurt a.M.: S. Fischer, 1991.

———. *Unbehagen in der Kultur.* Vienna: Internationaler Psychoanalytischer Verlag, 1930.

Friedländer, Saul. "Bewältigung—oder nur Verdrängung?" *Die Zeit*, 8 Feb. 1985.

Friedman, Philip. *Their Brothers' Keepers.* New York: Crown Publishers, 1957.

Fuchs, Eckhardt. "Zusammenarbeit mit Ostasien." *Eckert—Das Bulletin*, Summer 2011, 45–47.

Galinski, Heinz. "Die Ehrung bedeutet vor allem Verpflichtung: Rede vor dem Berliner Abgeordnetenhaus am 26. November 1987." In *Aufbau nach dem Untergang: Deutsch-jüdische Geschichte nach 1945*, edited by Andreas Nachama and Julius H. Schoeps, 79–84. Berlin: Argon, 1992.

Ganzfried, Daniel. *Der Absender.* Zurich: Rotpunktverlag, 1995.

———. "Die geliehene Holocaust-Biographie." *Die Weltwoche*, 27 Aug. 1998.

Gardner Feldman, Lily. *Germany's Foreign Policy of Reconciliation: From Enmity to Amity.* Lanham, MD: Rowman & Littlefield, 2012.

Geertz, Clifford. *The Interpretation of Cultures*. New York: Basic Books, 1973.

Geis, Robert Raphael. "Es gibt keine Entschuldigung." *Allgemeine Wochenzeitung der Juden in Deutschland*, 25 Jul. 1952.

——. "Es mahnen die Toten 1933–1945." *Mannheimer Hefte*, no. 3 (1952).

——. "Gedenkrede anläßlich des 15. Jahrestages der Deportation nach Gurs und der Synagogenzerstörungen des Jahres 1938." 1953. Papers of Robert Raphael Geis, Leo Baeck Institute, New York.

——. "Gib, o Gott, daß in keines Menschen Herz Haß aufsteige!" *Freiburger Rundbrief* 3/4, no. 12/15 (1951/1952): 5–7.

——. "Robert Raphael Geis to Max Israel." 25 May 1953. Papers of Robert Raphael Geis, Leo Baeck Institute, New York.

——. "Yom Kippur Sermons." 1954–60. Papers of Robert Raphael Geis, Leo Baeck Institute, New York.

Gelber, Israel. "Ich schenke Deutschland den Frieden." *Freiburger Rundbrief* 3/4, no. 12/15 (1951/1952): 13–14.

Gernert, Klaus-Dieter, and Helmut Wolff. *Das Geheimnis der Versöhnung heißt Erinnerung: Zur Situation von Kriegsgefangenen und Fremdarbeitern während des Zweiten Weltkrieges in Rösrath und andere zeitgeschichtliche Beiträge*. Rösrath: Geschichtsverein für die Gemeinde Rösrath und Umgebung, 1991.

"Gespräch mit Avraham Burg am 26. Oktober 2009." Accessed 23 Jul. 2013. http://www.3sat.de/mediathek/mediathek.php?obj=15101&mode=play.

"Gestörte Identität, stolpernder Gang." *Der Spiegel*, no. 6 (1987).

Gilman, Sander L. *Jewish Self-Hatred: Anti-Semitism and the Hidden Language of the Jews*. Softshell Books. Baltimore/London: Johns Hopkins University Press, 1992.

Giordano, Ralph. *Die zweite Schuld oder Von der Last Deutscher zu sein*. Cologne: Kiepenheuer & Witsch, 2000. First published in 1987.

——. ed. *'Wie kann diese Generation eigentlich noch atmen?' Briefe zu dem Buch: Die zweite Schuld oder Von der Last Deutscher zu sein*. Hamburg: Rasch und Röhring, 1990.

Glucksmann, André. "Hitler bin ich." *Spiegel-Spezial*, no. 2 (1989): 73–75.

Goldhagen, Daniel Jonah. *Hitler's Willing Executioners: Ordinary Germans and the Holocaust*. New York: Alfred Knopf, 1996.

——. "Vorwort zur deutschen Ausgabe." Translated by Klaus Kochmann. In *Hitlers willige Vollstrecker: Ganz gewöhnliche Deutsche und der Holocaust*. Berlin: Siedler Verlag, 1996.

Gollancz, Victor. *The Case of Adolf Eichmann*. London: Victor Gollancz, 1961.

——. *Our Threatened Values*. London: Victor Gollancz, 1946.

——. *Unser bedrohtes Erbe*. Translated by Adolf Halfeld. Zurich: Atlantis-Verlag, 1947. Original in English: *Our Threatened Values*.

——. *What Buchenwald Really Means*. London: Victor Gollancz, 1945.

Görres, Ida Friederike. "Brief über die Kirche." *Frankfurter Hefte* 1, no. 8 (1946): 715–33.

Goschler, Constantin. *Schuld und Schulden: Die Politik der Wiedergutmachung für NS-Verfolgte seit 1945*. Göttingen: Wallstein, 2005.

——. *Wiedergutmachung: Westdeutschland und die Verfolgten des National-sozialismus 1945–1954.* Munich: R. Oldenbourg, 1992.

Gosewinkel, Dieter. *Adolf Arndt: Die Wiederbegründung des Rechtsstaats aus dem Geist der Sozialdemokratie (1945–1961).* Bonn: J. H. W. Dietz Nachf., 1991.

Green, Gerald. *Holocaust.* London: Corgi Books, 1978.

——. *The Legion of Noble Christians or The Sweeney Survey.* New York: Trident Press, 1965.

Grosser, Alfred. "Israels Politik fördert Antisemitismus." *Stern,* 12 Oct. 2007.

——. *Mit Deutschen streiten: Aufforderungen zur Wachsamkeit.* Munich/Vienna: Carl Hanser, 1987.

Grossmann, Kurt R. "Bei Gertrud Luckner." *Aufbau,* 26 Sept. 1952.

——. *Die unbesungenen Helden: Menschen in Deutschlands dunklen Tagen.* Berlin-Grunewald: arani Verlag, 1961. First published in 1957.

——. "Gertrud Luckner—70 Jahre." *Aufbau,* 25 Sept. 1970.

——. "Retter von 1100 Juden: Begegnung mit Oskar Schindler." *Aufbau,* 12 Jul. 1957.

——. "Unbesungene Helden I." *Aufbau,* 26 Jan. 1951.

——. "Unbesungene Helden II & III." *Aufbau,* 16 Feb. 1951.

——. "Unbesungene Helden IV." *Aufbau,* 16 Mar. 1951.

Habbe, Christian. "Einer gegen die SS." *Spiegel-Spezial,* no. 1 (2001): 149–51.

Habermas, Jürgen. "Der Zeigefinger: Die Deutschen und ihr Denkmal." *Die Zeit,* 31 Mar. 1999.

——. "Die Entsorgung der Vergangenheit: Ein kulturpolitisches Pamphlet." *Die Zeit,* 17 May 1985.

——. "Die zweite Lebenslüge der Bundesrepublik: Wir sind wieder 'normal' geworden." *Die Zeit,* 11 Dec. 1992.

——. "Vom öffentlichen Gebrauch der Historie." *Die Zeit,* 7 Nov. 1986.

——. "Warum ein 'Demokratiepreis' für Daniel J. Goldhagen? Eine Laudatio." *Die Zeit,* 14 Mar. 1997.

Hahn, Eva, and Hans Henning Hahn. *Die Vertreibung im deutschen Erinnern: Legenden, Mythos, Geschichte.* Paderborn: Ferdinand Schöningh, 2010.

Hansen, Sven. "Geschichte der Anderen: Chinas Blick auf deutsche Vergangenheitsbewältigung." Accessed 15 Oct. 2014. http://www.boell.de/en/node/275908.

Hartung, Klaus. "Ein deutscher Sonntag." *Die Zeit,* 14 Apr. 1995.

Heimrod, Ute, Günter Schlusche, and Horst Seferens, eds. *Der Denkmalstreit— Das Denkmal?* Berlin: Philo, 1999.

Heinsohn, Gunnar. "Die Ermutigung des Rabbi Schulweis: Zum Phänomen des 'Bystander'-Verhaltens." *Universitas,* no. 5 (1993): 444–53.

Heldt, Thomas. "Die Israelis kommen!" In *Aktion Sühnezeichen Friedensdienste in Israel: 1961–2011; Geschichte(n) erleben,* edited by Bernhard Krane, Heike Kleffner, Gabriele Kammerer, and Katharina von Münster, 44–45. Berlin/Jerusalem: Aktion Sühnezeichen Friedensdienste, 2011.

"Hermann Langbein an Andreas Maislinger, Wien, 20. Dezember 1980." Accessed 23 Jul. 2013. http://gd.auslandsdienst.at/deutsch/archives/letters/1980/2012.php4.

Heschel, Abraham Joshua. "Antwort an Einstein." *Aufbau*, 20 Sept. 1940.
———. *Die Prophetie*. Kraków: Verlag der polnischen Akademie der Wissenschaften, 1936.
———. *God in Search of Man: A Philosophy of Judaism*. New York: Farrar, Straus and Giroux, 1983.
———. *The Insecurity of Freedom: Essays on Human Existence*. New York: Schocken Books, 1972.
———. *Man's Quest for God: Studies in Prayer and Symbolism*. New York: Scribner, 1954.
———. "The Meaning of This War." *Hebrew Union College Bulletin*, Mar. 1943, 1–2, 18.
———. "The Meaning of This War." *Liberal Judaism* 11, no. 10 (1944): 18–21.
———. *The Prophets*. Perennial Classics. New York: HarperCollins, 2001. First published in 1962; based on *Die Prophetie*.
———. "Versuch einer Deutung." In *Begegnung mit dem Judentum: Ein Gedenkbuch*, edited by Margarethe Lachmund and Albert Stehen, 11–13. Berlin: L. Friedrich, 1962.
Heschel, Susannah. *The Aryan Jesus: Christian Theologians and the Bible in Nazi Germany*. Princeton, NJ/Oxford: Princeton University Press, 2008.
Hessen, Johannes. *Der geistige Wiederaufbau Deutschlands: Reden über die Erneuerung des deutschen Geisteslebens*. Stuttgart: August Schröder Verlag, 1946.
Hirsch, Martin. "Vorwort." In *Widerstand und Verfolgung: Am Beispiel Passaus 1933–1939*, by Anja Rosmus-Wenninger, 9–10. Passau: Andreas-Haller Verlag, 1983.
Hochhuth, Rolf. *Der Stellvertreter*. Reinbek bei Hamburg: Rowohlt, 1963.
Hockenos, Matthew. *A Church Divided: German Protestants Confront the Nazi Past*. Bloomington: Indiana University Press, 2004.
"'Holocaust': Die Vergangenheit kommt zurück." *Der Spiegel*, no. 5 (1979).
Huneke, Douglas. *In Deutschland unerwünscht: Hermann Gräbe*. Translated by Adrian Seifert and Robert Lasser. Lüneburg: Dietrich zu Klampen Verlag, 2002. Original in English: *The Moses of Rovno*.
"Im Bett des Führers." *Der Spiegel*, no. 23 (1988).
Jarausch, Konrad. *Die Umkehr: Deutsche Wandlungen 1945–1995*. Munich: Deutsche Verlags-Anstalt, 2004.
Jaspers, Karl. *Die Schuldfrage*. Heidelberg: Lambert Schneider, 1946.
———. *Einführung in die Philosophie: Zwölf Radiovorträge*. Munich/Zurich: Piper, 1989.
———. *The Origin and Goal of History*. Translated by Michael Bullock. London: Routledge & K. Paul, 1953.
———. *Wohin treibt die Bundesrepublik? Tatsachen, Gefahren, Chancen*. Munich: R. Piper, 1966.
Jureit, Ulrike, and Christian Schneider. *Gefühlte Opfer: Illusionen der Vergangenheitsbewältigung*. Bonn: Bundeszentrale für politische Bildung, 2010.
Jüttner, Julia. "Rostock-Lichtenhagen: Als der Mob die Herrschaft übernahm." *Spiegel Online*, 22 Aug. 2007.

Kammerer, Gabriele. *Aktion Sühnezeichen Friedensdienste: Aber man kann es einfach tun.* Göttingen: Lamuv Verlag, 2008.

Kaplan, Edward K. "Coming to America: Abraham Joshua Heschel, 1940–1941." *Modern Judaism* 27, no. 2 (2007): 129–45.

——. *Holiness in Words: Abraham Joshua Heschel's Poetics of Piety.* New York: State University of New York Press, 1996.

Katz, Steven, Shlomo Biderman, and Gershon Greenberg, eds. *Wrestling with God: Jewish Theological Responses during and after the Holocaust.* New York: Oxford University Press, 2007.

Keneally, Thomas. *Schindler's Ark.* London: Hodder and Stoughton, 1982.

——. *Searching for Schindler.* London: Septre, 2008.

Khétsun, Tubten. *Memories of Life in Lhasa under Chinese Rule.* Translated by Matthew Akester. New York: Columbia University Press, 2008.

Kimche, Jon, and David Kimche. *The Secret Roads: The 'Illegal' Migration of a People, 1938–1948.* London: Martin Secker and Warburg, 1954.

Kirchenkanzlei der Evangelischen Kirche in Deutschland. *Die Lage der Vertriebenen und das Verhältnis des deutschen Volkes zu seinen östlichen Nachbarn: Eine evangelische Denkschrift.* Hannover: Verlag des Amtsblattes der EKD, 1965.

Kirkbright, Suzanne. *Karl Jaspers, A Biography: Navigations in Truth.* New Haven, CT/London: Yale University Press, 2004.

Klee, Hans. *Wir Juden und die deutsche Schuld.* Lausanne: Granchamp, 1945.

Kleine-Brockhoff, Thomas, and Dirk Kurbjuweit. "Die anderen Schindlers." *Die Zeit*, 1 Apr. 1994.

"Kniefall angemessen oder übertrieben?" *Der Spiegel*, no. 51 (1970).

Koch, Werner. "Die evangelische Kirche und die zweite Reformation." *Frankfurter Hefte* 2, no. 6 (1947): 557–67.

Kogon, Eugen. "Das Porträt: Eugenio Pacelli—Papst Pius XII." *Frankfurter Hefte* 2, no. 2 (1947): 192–94.

——. *Der SS-Staat: Das System der deutschen Konzentrationslager.* Berlin: Druckhaus Tempelhof, 1947. First published in 1946.

——. "Die deutsche Revolution." *Frankfurter Hefte* 1, no. 4 (1946): 17–26.

——. "Gericht und Gewissen." *Frankfurter Hefte* 1, no. 1 (1946): 25–37.

——. "Juden und Nichtjuden in Deutschland." *Frankfurter Hefte* 4, no. 9 (1949): 726–29.

——. "Politik der Versöhnung." *Frankfurter Hefte* 3, no. 4 (1948): 317–24.

Köhler, Lotte, and Hans Saner, eds. *Hannah Arendt Karl Jaspers Briefwechsel 1926–1969.* Munich/Zurich: R. Piper, 1985.

König, Helmut, Michael Kohlstruck, and Andreas Wöll. "Einleitung." In *Vergangenheitsbewältigung am Ende des zwanzigsten Jahrhunderts*, edited by Helmut König, Michael Kohlstruck, and Andreas Wöll. Opladen/Wiesbaden: Westdeutscher Verlag, 1998.

Konitzer, Werner. "Opferorientierung und Opferidentifizierung: Überlegungen zu einer begrifflichen Unterscheidung." In *Das Unbehagen an der Erinnerung: Wandlungsprozesse im Gedenken an den Holocaust*, edited by Ulrike

Jureit, Christian Schneider, and Margrit Fröhlich, 119–27. Frankfurt a. M.: Brandes & Apsel, 2012.

Kopelev, Lev. *Aufbewahren für alle Zeit.* Translated by Heddy Pross-Weerth and Heinz-Dieter Mendel. Hamburg: Hoffmann und Campe, 1976.

———. "Bekenntnisse eines Sowjetbürgers." *Die Zeit*, 11 Feb. 1977.

———. *Ease My Sorrows: A Memoir.* Translated by Antonina W. Bouis. New York: Random House, 1983.

Kostede, Norbert. "Erleuchtung für die Politik." *Die Zeit*, 29 Jan. 1993.

"Kräfte der Finsternis." *Der Spiegel*, no. 5 (1993).

Krahulec, Peter. " 'The Road Not Taken. . .' Grundzüge einer Didaktik der Erinnerung." In *Erinnerungsarbeit: Grundlage einer Kultur des Friedens*, edited by Berhard Nolz and Wolfgang Popp, 55–64. Münster: Lit Verlag, 2000.

Krane, Bernhard, Heike Kleffner, Gabriele Kammerer, and Katharina von Münster, eds. *Aktion Sühnezeichen Friedensdienste in Israel: 1961–2011; Geschichte(n) erleben.* Berlin/Jerusalem: Aktion Sühnezeichen Friedensdienste, 2011.

Küng, Hans. "Introduction: From Anti-Semitism to Theological Dialogue." In *Christians and Jews*, edited by Hans Küng and Walter Kasper, 9–16. New York: Seabury Press, 1975.

Kycia, Tomasz, and Robert Zurek. " 'Die polnische Gesellschaft war auf einen solchen Schritt nicht vorbereitet': Gespräch mit Tadeusz Mazowiecki." In *'Wir vergeben und bitten um Vergebung': Der Briefwechsel der polnischen und deutschen Bischöfe von 1965 und seine Wirkung*, edited by Basil Kerski, Tomasz Kycia, and Robert Zurek, 97–109. Osnabrück: Fibre, 2006.

LaCapra, Dominick. *Representing the Holocaust: History, Theory, Trauma.* Ithaca, NY: Cornell University Press, 1994.

Lang, Michel R. "Fremd in einem fremden Land." In *Fremd im eigenen Land: Juden in der Bundesrepublik*, edited by Henryk M. Broder and Michel R. Lang. Frankfurt a.M.: Fischer Taschenbuch Verlag, 1979.

Langbein, Hermann. *Menschen in Auschwitz.* Vienna: Europaverlag, 1972.

———. *People in Auschwitz.* Translated by Harry Zohn. Chapel Hill: University of North Carolina Press, 2004. Original in German: *Menschen in Auschwitz*.

Lapide, Pinchas E. *Rom und die Juden.* Translated by Jutta Knust and Theodor Knust. Freiburg/Basel/Vienna: Herder, 1967. Original in English: *The Last Three Popes and the Jews*.

Lau, Israel Meir. *Out of the Depths: The Story of a Child of Buchenwald Who Returned Home at Last.* Translated by Jessica Setbon and Shira Leibowitz Schmidt. New York: Sterling, 2011.

Lauder, Ronald S. "Sonntagsreden und Montagstaten." *Süddeutsche Zeitung*, 25 Jan. 2008.

Lederach, John Paul. *Building Peace: Sustainable Reconciliation in Divided Societies.* Washington, DC: US Institute of Peace Press, 1997.

Legerer, Anton. *Tatort: Versöhnung; Aktion Sühnezeichen in der BRD und in der DDR und Gedenkdienst in Österreich.* Leipzig: Evangelische Verlagsanstalt, 2011.

Leibler, Isi. "Avraham Burg: The Ultimate Post-Zionist." *Jerusalem Post*, 24 Dec. 2008.

Lempkowicz, Yossi. "Germany Pushes for EU-wide Law on Holocaust Denial." *European Jewish Press*, 19 Jan. 2007.

Leung, Man-Tao. "為什麼日本不像德國?" [Why Is Japan unlike Germany? I & II]. *Ming Pao*, 4 and 11 May 2005.

Levene, D. S. "'You shall blot out the memory of Amalek': Roman Historians on Remembering to Forget." In *Historical and Religious Memory in the Ancient World*, edited by Beate Dignas and R. R. R. Smith, 217–39. New York: Oxford University Press, 2012.

Levy, Daniel, and Natan Sznaider. *The Holocaust and Memory in the Global Age*. Translated by Assenka Oksiloff. Philadelphia: Temple University Press, 2006.

Lieberman, Benjamin. *Terrible Fate: Ethnic Cleansing in the Making of Modern Europe*. Chicago: Ivan R. Dee, 2006.

Li Jianglin. *1959 Lhasa!* Hong Kong: New Century Media & Consulting, 2010.

Liu Zaifu, and Lin Gang. 罪與文學：關於文學懺悔意識與靈魂維度的考察 [Confession and Chinese Literature]. Hong Kong: Oxford University Press, 2002.

Llewellyn, Jennifer J., and Daniel Philpott, eds. *Restorative Justice, Reconciliation, and Peacebuilding*. Oxford/New York: Oxford University Press, 2014.

Ludwig, Heiner. "Politische Spiritualität statt katholischem Fundamentalismus: Zum 20. Todestag von Eugen Kogon." *Neue Gesellschaft Frankfurter Hefte*, no. 12 (2007).

Lustiger, Arno. *Rettungswiderstand: Über die Judenretter in Europa während der NS-Zeit*. Göttingen: Wallstein, 2011.

Lüth, Erich, ed. *Die Friedensbitte an Israel 1951: Eine Hamburger Initiative*. Hamburg: Hans Christians Verlag, 1976.

——. "Flugreise ins Gelobte Land I-III." *Hamburger Abendblatt*, 9/10, 12, 19 May 1953.

——. "Pioniere aus Deutschland." *Hamburger Abendblatt*, 27 May 1953.

Luther, Martin. "Auslegung der sieben Bußpsalmen." In *Dr. Martin Luthers Sämtliche Schriften*, vol. 4, *Auslegung des Alten Testaments: Auslegung über die Psalmen*, edited by Johann Georg Walch, 1654–1743. Groß-Oesingen: Verlag der Lutherischen Buchhandlung Heinrich Harms, 1987.

Mäding, Klaus. "Historische Bildung und Versöhnung." *Eckert—Das Bulletin*, Winter 2008, 12–15.

Maechler, Stefan. *The Wilkomirski Affair: A Study in Biographical Truth*. Translated by J. E. Woods. New York: Schocken, 2001.

Maier, Charles. *The Unmasterable Past: History, Holocaust, and German National Identity*. Cambridge, MA: Harvard University Press, 1988.

Maimonides, Moses. *Acht Capitel: Arabisch und Deutsch mit Anmerkungen von M. Wolff*. Leipzig: Commissions-Verlag von Heinrich Hunger, 1863.

——. "Die Lehre von der Buße." In *Mischne Tora—Das Buch der Erkenntnis*, edited by Eveline Goodman-Thau and Christoph Schulte, 408–509. Jüdische Quellen. Berlin: Akademie Verlag, 1994.

Mann, Thomas. *Deutschland und die Deutschen 1945, mit einem Essay von Hans Mayer.* Hamburg: Europäische Verlagsanstalt, 1992.

——. "Germany and the Germans." In *Thomas Mann's Addresses Delivered at the Library of Congress, 1942–1949,* 45–66. Rockville, MD: Wildside Press, 2008.

Mauz, Gerhard. "Das wird mit keinem Wind verwehen." *Der Spiegel,* no. 5 (1979).

Mayer, Reinhold, ed. *Der Talmud.* Munich: Orbis, 1999.

Mayer-Reifferscheidt, Friedrich. *Victor Gollancz' Ruf: Rettet Europa!* Munich: Verlag Kurt Desch, 1947.

Meinecke, Friedrich. *Die deutsche Katastrophe: Betrachtungen und Erinnerungen.* Wiesbaden: Eberhard Brockhaus, 1946.

"Mein Pius ist keine Karikatur." *Der Spiegel,* no. 17 (1963).

Mertens, Lothar. *Unermüdlicher Kämpfer für Frieden und Menschenrechte: Leben und Wirken von Kurt R. Grossmann.* Berlin: Duncker & Humblot, 1997.

Metz, Johann Baptist. *Faith in History and Society: Toward a Practical Fundamental Theology.* Translated by J. Matthew Ashley. New York: Crossroad Publishing, 2007. Original in German: *Glaube in Geschichte und Gesellschaft.*

Metzger, Hartmut. "Wie kann es Frieden geben für Israel und Palästina? Das Friedensrezept der 'Berliner Erklärung' stimmt schon im Ansatz nicht." *Rundbrief des Denkendorfer Kreises für christlich-jüdische Begegnung,* 5 Feb. 2007.

Meusch, Matthias. *Von der Diktatur zur Demokratie: Fritz Bauer und die Aufarbeitung der NS-Verbrechen in Hessen (1956–1968).* Wiesbaden: Historische Kommission für Nassau, 2001.

Michaelis, Rolf. "Die Kraft der Schwachen." *Die Zeit,* 10 June 1983.

Mitscherlich, Alexander, and Margarete Mitscherlich. *Die Unfähigkeit zu trauern: Grundlagen kollektiven Verhaltens.* Munich: R. Piper, 1967.

Mohler, Armin. *Der Nasenring: Im Dickicht der Vergangenheitsbewältigung.* Essen: Heitz & Höffkes, 1989.

——. *Vergangenheitsbewältigung: Von der Läuterung zur Manipulation.* Stuttgart-Degerloch: Seewald, 1968.

Naimark, Norman M. *Fires of Hatred.* Cambridge, MA: Harvard University Press, 2001.

——. *The Russians in Germany.* Cambridge, MA: Belknap Press of Harvard University Press, 1995.

Niemöller, Martin. *Reden, Predigten, Denkanstöße 1964–1976.* Cologne: Pahl-Rugenstein Verlag, 1977.

Nolan, Mary. "Air Wars, Memory Wars: Germans as Victims during the Second World War." *Central European History* 38, no. 1 (2005): 7–40.

"Overkill der guten Absichten." *Der Spiegel,* no. 5 (1993).

Pape, Matthias. "Mueller-Graaf, Carl-Hermann." *Neue Deutsche Biographie* 18 (1997): 497–98.

Peace Research Institute in the Middle East. *Learning Each Other's Historical Narrative: Palestinians and Israelis.* Preliminary draft of the English translation. Beit Jallah: PRIME, 2003.

Picard, Max. *Hitler in uns selbst.* Erlenbach-Zurich: Eugen Rentsch, 1946.

"Popband Die Ärzte: 'Wir galten als Teufelszeug.'" *Spiegel Online,* 16 Oct. 2003.

Proske, Rüdiger. "Ein Weg zur Verständigung." *Frankfurter Hefte* 2, no. 4 (1947): 324–26.

Prümm, Karl. *Walter Dirks und Eugen Kogon als katholische Publizisten der Weimarer Republik.* Heidelberg: Carl Winter Universitätsverlag, 1984.

Purdy, Daniel. *On the Ruins of Babel: Architectural Metaphor in German Thought.* Signale. Ithaca, NY: Cornell University Press and Cornell University Library, 2011.

Rabe, Karl-Klaus. *Umkehr in die Zukunft: Die Arbeit der Aktion Sühnezeichen/Friedensdienste.* Bornheim-Merten: Lamuv Verlag, 1983.

Radbruch, Gustav. "Die Erneuerung des Rechts." In *Rechtsphilosophie,* edited by Arthur Kaufmann, 107–14. Heidelberg: C. F. Müller Juristischer Verlag, 1990.

Raddatz, Fritz, ed. *Summa iniuria oder Durfte der Papst schweigen? Hochhuths 'Stellvertreter' in der öffentlichen Kritik.* Reinbek bei Hamburg: Rowohlt, 1963.

"Real 'Holocaust' Figure Talks Up." *Merced Sun-Star,* 10 May 1978.

"Rechter Arm zittert." *Der Spiegel,* no. 18 (1984).

Reichel, Peter. *Erfundene Erinnerung: Weltkrieg und Judenmord in Film und Theater.* Munich: Hanser, 2004.

——. *Vergangenheitsbewältigung in Deutschland: Die Auseinandersetzung mit der NS-Diktatur von 1945 bis heute.* Munich: C. H. Beck, 2001.

Riedl, Joachim. "Herrenloses Geld." *Die Zeit,* 27 May 1988.

Riemenschneider, Rainer. "Transnationale Konfliktbearbeitung: Das Beispiel der deutsch-französischen und der deutsch-polnischen Schulbuchgespräche im Vergleich, 1935–1998." In *Das Willy-Brandt-Bild in Deutschland und Polen,* edited by Carsten Tessmer, 121–31. Berlin: Bundeskanzler-Willy-Brandt-Stiftung, 2000.

Riffel, Dennis. *Unbesungene Helden: Die Ehrungsinitiative des Berliner Senats 1958 bis 1966.* Berlin: Metropol, 2007.

"Rock links, Rock rechts." *Die Zeit,* 18 Dec. 1992.

Röpke, Wilhelm. *Die deutsche Frage.* Erlenbach-Zurich: Eugen Rentsch, 1945.

Rosenzweig, Franz. *Der Stern der Erlösung.* Frankfurt a.M.: J. Kauffmann Verlag, 1921.

Rosmus-Wenninger, Anja. *Widerstand und Verfolgung: Am Beispiel Passaus 1933–1939.* Passau: Andreas-Haller Verlag, 1983.

Rothberg, Michael. *Multidirectional Memory: Remembering the Holocaust in the Age of Decolonization.* Stanford, CA: Stanford University Press, 2009.

Rovan, Joseph. *Erinnerungen eines Franzosen, der einmal ein Deutscher war.* Translated by Bernd Wilczek. Munich: Carl Hanser, 2000.

——. "L'Allemagne de nos mérites: Deutschland, wie wir es verdienen." In *Zwei Völker—eine Zukunft: Deutsche und Franzosen an der Schwelle des 21. Jahrhunderts*, 83–102. Munich/Zurich: Piper, 1986.

Rudolph, Hermann. "Der Fall Nachmann und die Deutschen." *Süddeutsche Zeitung*, 19 May 1988.

S., Th. "Gewissensgeld." *Die Zeit*, 20 May 1988.

Scharf, Inon. "Avraham Burg in München: Hitler besiegen." Accessed 15 Mar. 2012. http://www.hagalil.com/archiv/2009/11/04/burg-4/.

Scheler, Max. *On the Eternal in Man*. Translated by Bernard Noble. Hamden, CT: Archon Books, 1972.

——. "Reue und Wiedergeburt." In *Vom Ewigen im Menschen*, vol. 1, *Religiöse Erneuerung*, 5–58. Leipzig: Der Neue Geist, 1921.

Scherzberg, Lucia, ed. *Theologie und Vergangenheitsbewältigung: Eine kritische Bestandsaufnahme im interdisziplinären Vergleich*. Paderborn: Ferdinand Schöningh, 2005.

Schindler, Pesach. *Hasidic Responses to the Holocaust in the Light of Hasidic Thought*. Hoboken, NJ: Ktav, 1990.

Schlabrendorff, Fabian von. *The Secret War against Hitler*. Translated by H. Simon. Boulder, CO: Westview Press, 1994.

Schmemann, Serge. "Germans Are Wary of Jewish Scandal." *New York Times*, 26 May 1988.

Schmidt, Ludwig, ed. *Umkehr zu Gott: Themagottesdienste zu Passion, Karfreitag, Bußtag und zu den Bußpsalmen*. Göttingen: Klotz, 1982.

Schneider, Christoph. *Der Warschauer Kniefall: Ritual, Ereignis und Erzählung*. Konstanz: UVK Verlagsgesellschaft, 2006.

Schneider-Schelde, Rudolf. "Vorwort des Herausgebers." In *Victor Gollancz' Ruf: Rettet Europa!* by Friedrich Mayer-Reifferscheidt, 5–6. Munich: Verlag Kurt Desch, 1947.

Schoeps, Julius H., ed. *Ein Volk von Mördern? Die Dokumentation zur Goldhagen-Kontroverse um die Rolle der Deutschen im Holocaust*. Hamburg: Hoffmann und Campe, 1996.

Scholz, Heinrich. "Zur deutschen Kollektiv-Verantwortlichkeit." *Frankfurter Hefte* 2, no. 4 (1947): 357–73.

Schreiber, Hermann. "Ein Stück Heimkehr." *Der Spiegel*, no. 51 (1970).

Schueler, Hans. "Zu spät, zu viel." *Die Zeit*, 18 Dec. 1992.

Schulweis, Harold. "An Appeal to Jewish Holocaust Survivors." *Sh'ma: A Journal of Jewish Responsibility* 16, no. 319 (Oct. 1986): 149–50.

——. "Aren't the Righteous Always a Minority?" *Sh'ma: A Journal of Jewish Responsibility* 11, no. 203 (Dec. 1980): 23–24.

——. "The Bias against Man." *Journal of Jewish Education* 34, no. 1 (1963): 6–14.

——. *Conscience: The Duty to Obey and the Duty to Disobey*. Woodstock, VT: Jewish Lights Publishing, 2008.

——. *Letting Go/Holding On: Jewish Consciousness in a Post-Holocaust World*. New York: The American Jewish Committee, 1988.

——. "Memory and Anger." Accessed 18 Dec. 2012. http://www.vbs.org/page.cfm?p=724.

——. "Post-Holocaust Recovery: An Appeal for Moral Education." Accessed 18 Dec. 2012. http://www.vbs.org/page.cfm?p=746.

Schütt, Julian. "Wilkomirski: Alles vergisst." *Die Weltwoche*, 4 Apr. 2002.

Schwan, Heribert. *Die Frau an seiner Seite: Leben und Leiden der Hannelore Kohl*. Munich: Wilhelm Heyne Verlag, 2011.

Schweitzer, Albert. "Dankesrede." Accessed 31 Aug. 2012. http://www.friedenspreis-des-deutschen-buchhandels.de/sixcms/media.php/1290/1951_schweitzer.pdf.

Segev, Tom. *Die siebte Million: Der Holocaust und Israels Politik der Erinnerung*. Translated by Jürgen Peter Krause and Maja Ueberle-Pfaff. Reinbek bei Hamburg: Rowohlt, 1995.

——. *The Seventh Million: The Israelis and the Holocaust*. Translated by Haim Watzman. New York: Hill and Wang, 1993.

Seghers, Anna. "Die Umsiedlerin." In *Anna Seghers Gesammelte Werke in Einzelausgaben*, vol. 10: 272–79. Berlin: Aufbau-Verlag, 1977.

"Sehnsucht nach Entscheidungen: Interview mit André Glucksmann." *Der Standard*, 17 Apr. 2007.

Sherwin, Byron. *Abraham Joshua Heschel*. Atlanta: John Knox Press, 1979.

Sherwood, Melanie Steiner. "Jean Améry and Wolfgang Hildesheimer: Ressentiments, Melancholia, and the West German Public Sphere in the 1960s and 1970s." PhD diss., Cornell University, 2011.

Sichrovsky, Peter, ed. *Born Guilty: Children of Nazi Families*. Translated by J. Steinberg. New York: Basic Books, 1988.

——. " 'Ich war's nicht, verdammt noch mal' I." *Der Spiegel*, no. 6 (1987).

——. " 'Ich war's nicht, verdammt noch mal' II." *Der Spiegel*, no. 7 (1987).

——. " 'Ich war's nicht, verdammt noch mal' III." *Der Spiegel*, no. 8 (1987).

——. ed. *Schuldig geboren: Kinder aus Nazifamilien*. Cologne: Kiepenheuer & Witsch, 1987.

Siebrecht, Valentin. "Selbstbildnis der Leser: Zahlen und Tatsachen aus der Umfrage der *Frankfurter Hefte*." *Frankfurter Hefte* 2, no. 12 (1947): 1260–68.

Silens, Constantin. *Irrweg und Umkehr*. Basel: Birkhäuser, 1946.

Sirat, René-Samuel. "Judaism and Repentance." Paper presented at the Religions and Repentance Conference: Growth in Religious Traditions, Facing a New Era, Elijah Interfaith Institute, Jerusalem, 21 Mar. 2000.

Skotnicki, Aleksander B., ed. *Oskar Schindler in the Eyes of Cracovian Jews Rescued by Him*. Kraków: Wydawnictwo, 2007.

Staerk, Willy. *Sünde und Gnade nach der Vorstellung des älteren Judentums, besonders der Dichter der sog. Busspsalmen*. Tübingen: J.C.B. Mohr (Paul Siebeck), 1905.

"Statement by Rabbi Yisrael Meir Lau during the Holocaust Memorial Ceremony at the Trusteeship Council Chamber on 27 January 2009." Accessed 18 May 2012. http://www.un.org/en/holocaustremembrance/2009/statements09_lau.shtml.

Stauber, Roni. *The Holocaust in Israeli Public Debate in the 1950s: Ideology and Memory*. London: Vallentine Mitchell, 2007. First published in Hebrew in 2000.

Steffahn, Harald. *Richard von Weizsäcker mit Selbstzeugnissen und Bilddokumenten*. Reinbek bei Hamburg: Rowohlt Taschenbuch Verlag, 1991.

Stehle, Hansjakob. "Schlußpunkt unter die Vergangenheit." *Die Zeit*, 11 Dec. 1970.

Steinberger, Petra, ed. *Die Finkelstein-Debatte*. Munich: Piper, 2001.

Stern, Frank. *The Whitewashing of the Yellow Badge: Antisemitism and Philosemitism in Postwar Germany*. Translated by William Templer. Oxford/ New York/Seoul/Tokyo: Pergamon Press, 1992. Original in German: *Im Anfang war Auschwitz*.

Sternberger, Dolf. "Im dunkelsten Deutschland." *Die Wandlung* 2, no. 3 (1947): 196–201.

Stolleis, Michael. "Geleitwort." In *Fritz Bauer 1903–1968: Eine Biographie*, by Irmtrud Wojak, 7–9. Munich: C. H. Beck, 2009.

Stoltzfus, Nathan. "Jemand war für mich da." *Die Zeit*, 21 Jul. 1989.

———. *Resistance of the Heart: Intermarriage and the Rosenstrasse Protest in Nazi Germany*. New York: W.W. Norton, 1996.

Strickmann, Martin. *L'Allemagne nouvelle contre l'Allemagne éternelle: Die französischen Intellektuellen und die deutsch-französische Verständigung 1944–1950*. Frankfurt a.M.: Peter Lang, 2004.

Strothmann, Dietrich. "Eine Passauer Passion." *Die Zeit*, 14 Dec. 1984.

———. "Kärrner der Gerechtigkeit." *Die Zeit*, 19 Mar. 1965.

———. "Stirbt die Sünde mit den Menschen?" *Die Zeit*, 15 Jun. 1973.

"Stunde der Schwäche." *Der Spiegel*, no. 53 (1961).

"Suhrkamp zieht Bruchstücke zurück." *Berner Zeitung*, 13 Oct. 1999.

Thielicke, Helmut, and Hermann Diem. *Die Schuld der Anderen: Ein Briefwechsel*. Göttingen: Vandenhoeck & Ruprecht, 1948.

Thierfelder, Jörg. "Hermann Maas—Retter und Brückenbauer." *Freiburger Rundbrief*, n.s., 14 no. 3 (2007): 162–72.

"Translation of Document 2992-PS." In *Nazi Conspiracy and Aggression*, edited by Office of United States Chief of Counsel for Prosecution of Axis Criminality, 696–703. Washington, DC: United States Government Printing Office, 1946.

Truth and Reconciliation Commission. *Truth and Reconciliation Commission of South Africa Report*. http://www.justice.gov.za/trc/report/.

Tutu, Desmond. *No Future without Forgiveness*. New York: Doubleday, 1999.

"TV Tonight." *Indiana Evening Gazette*, 24 Dec. 1962.

Ullrich, Volker. "Mit den Untaten der Eltern leben." *Die Zeit*, 12 Aug. 1988.

van Dam, H. G. "Kein Naturschutzpark für Juden: Zum Gesetz gegen Volksverhetzung." *Die Zeit*, 19 Feb. 1960.

"Veit Harlan als Symptom." *Freiburger Rundbrief* 4, no. 16 (1951/1952): 20–21.

Verleger, Rolf. "Haben Opfer das Recht, Unrecht zu tun? Zur 'Außenansicht' vom 25.1.2008 ('Sonntagsreden und Montagstaten')." *Süddeutsche Zeitung*, 9 Feb. 2008.

——. *Israels Irrweg*. Cologne: PapyRossa-Verlag, 2008.

"Vertrag über gute Nachbarschaft, Partnerschaft und Zusammenarbeit zwischen der Bundesrepublik Deutschland und der Union der Sozialistischen Sowjetrepubliken vom 9. November 1990." *Bulletin des Presse- und Informationsamtes der Bundesregierung*, no. 133 (1990): 1379–82.

Visser't Hooft, Willem A. *Die Welt war meine Gemeinde: Autobiographie*. Translated by Heidi von Alten. Munich: Piper, 1972.

Walser, Martin. "Erfahrungen beim Verfassen einer Sonntagsrede." In *Die Walser-Bubis-Debatte: Eine Dokumentation*, edited by Frank Schirrmacher, 7–17. Frankfurt a.M.: Suhrkamp, 1999.

Wang Zheng. *Never Forget National Humiliation: Historical Memory in Chinese Politics and Foreign Relations*. New York: Columbia University Press, 2012.

Weber, Alfred. *Abschied von der bisherigen Geschichte: Überwindung des Nihilismus?* Hamburg: Claaßen und Goverts Verlag, 1946.

Weinke, Annette. *Die Verfolgung von NS-Tätern im geteilten Deutschland: Vergangenheitsbewältigungen 1949–1969 oder: Eine deutsch-deutsche Beziehungsgeschichte im Kalten Krieg*. Paderborn: Ferdinand Schöningh, 2002.

Weiss, Peter. *Die Ermittlung: Oratorium in 11 Gesängen*. Frankfurt a.M.: Suhrkamp, 1965.

Weizsäcker, Carl-Friedrich von, Hellmut Becker, Joachim Beckmann, Klaus von Bismarck, Werner Heisenberg, Günter Howe, Georg Picht, and Ludwig Raiser. "Das Memorandum der Acht." *Die Zeit*, 2 Mar. 1962.

Weizsäcker, Richard von. *Zum 40. Jahrestag der Beendigung des Krieges in Europa und der nationalsozialistischen Gewaltherrschaft: Ansprache am 8. Mai 1985 in der Gedenkstunde im Plenarsaal des Deutschen Bundestages*. Bonn: Bundeszentrale für politische Bildung, 1985.

Wertgen, Werner. *Vergangenheitsbewältigung: Interpretation und Verantwortung*. Paderborn: Ferdinand Schöningh, 2001.

Wester, Wolf. "Versöhnung mit den Juden." *Die Zeit*, 4 Oct. 1951.

Westernhagen, Dörte von. "Der Januskopf—Ergebnisse einer Grabung." *Familiendynamik* 7 (1982): 316–30.

——. "Die Kinder der Täter." *Die Zeit*, 28 Mar. 1986.

——. *Die Kinder der Täter: Das Dritte Reich und die Generation danach*. Munich: Kösel-Verlag, 1987.

——. "Wider den Schlaf des Gewissens." *Die Zeit*, 21 Nov. 1986.

Wette, Wolfram. "Verleugnete Helden." *Die Zeit*, 8 Nov. 2007.

Wiesel, Elie. *Souls on Fire: Portraits and Legends of Hasidic Masters*. New York: Simon & Schuster, 1993.

——. "Trivializing the Holocaust: Semi-Fact and Semi-Fiction." *New York Times*, 16 Apr. 1978.

Wiesenthal, Simon. *The Sunflower: On the Possibilities and Limits of Forgiveness*. Revised and expanded ed. New York: Schocken Books, 1998.

Wilckens, Ulrich. "Ulrich Wilckens to Dietrich Goldschmidt." 11 Jan. 1977. Papers of Robert R. Geis, Leo Baeck Institute, New York.

——. "Ulrich Wilckens to Robert Raphael Geis." 21 May 1953. Papers of Robert Raphael Geis, Leo Baeck Institute, New York.

Wilkomirski, Binjamin. *Bruchstücke: Aus einer Kindheit 1939–1948.* Frankfurt a.M.: Jüdischer Verlag, 1995.

———. *Fragments: Memories of a Wartime Childhood.* Translated by C.B. Janeway. New York: Schocken, 1996.

Wistrich, Robert S. "Jews against Zion." In *A Lethal Obsession: Anti-Semitism from Antiquity to the Global Jihad,* 515–42. New York: Random House, 2010.

Wojak, Irmtrud. *Fritz Bauer 1903–1968: Eine Biographie.* Munich: C.H. Beck, 2009.

Wolfschlag, Claus-M. "Das 'antifaschistische Milieu': Vom 'schwarzen Block' zur 'Lichterkette'—Die politische Repression gegen 'Rechtsextremismus' in der Bundesrepublik Deutschland." PhD diss., Rheinischen Friedrich-Wilhelms-Universität zu Bonn, 2001.

"Wort des Rates der Evangelischen Kirche Deutschlands zu den NS-Verbrecherprozessen anläßlich der Synode der EKD vom 13. März 1963." *Freiburger Rundbrief* 15, no. 57/60 (1963/1964): 37–38.

Wüstenberg, Ralf K. *Die politische Dimension der Versöhnung: Eine theologische Studie zum Umgang mit Schuld nach den Systemumbrüchen in Südafrika und Deutschland.* Gütersloh: Chr. Kaiser/Gütersloher Verlags haus, 2004.

Yad Vashem. "Der Zeuge, der beschloss zu handeln: Hermann Friedrich Graebe; Deutschland." Accessed 14 Jun. 2012. www1.yadvashem.org/yv/de/righteous/stories/graebe.asp.

Yagyû Kunichika. "Der Yasukuni-Schrein im Japan der Nachkriegszeit: Zu den Nachwirkungen des Staatsshintô." In *Erinnerungskulturen: Deutschland, Italien und Japan seit 1945,* edited by Christoph Cornelißen, Lutz Klinkhammer, and Wolfgang Schwentker, 243–53. Frankfurt a.M.: Fischer Taschenbuch, 2004.

Yonah, Rabbeinu. *The Gates of Repentance.* Translation and commentary by Yaakov Feldman. Northvale, NJ/Jerusalem: Jason Aronson, 1999.

Young, James E. "Die menschenmögliche Lösung der unlösbaren Aufgabe." *Der Tagesspiegel,* 25 Aug. 1998.

———. "Was keine andere Nation je versucht hat." *Berliner Zeitung,* 18 Dec. 1998.

Yu Jie. "向西藏懺悔—讀'雪山下的火焰 一個西藏良心犯的證言'" [Repent to Tibet: Reading 'Fire under the Snow']. *Open Magazine,* Jun. 2004, 78–80.

Zundel, Rolf. "Strich unter die Vergangenheit?" *Die Zeit,* 19 Mar. 1965.

Zurek, Robert, and Basil Kerski. "Der Briefwechsel zwischen den polnischen und deutschen Bischöfen von 1965: Entstehungsgeschichte, historischer Kontext und unmittelbare Wirkung." In *'Wir vergeben und bitten um Vergebung': Der Briefwechsel der polnischen und deutschen Bischöfe von 1965 und seine Wirkung,* edited by Basil Kerski, Tomasz Kycia, and Robert Zurek, 7–53. Osnabrück: Fibre, 2006.

INDEX

CPSIA information can be obtained
at www.ICGtesting.com
Printed in the USA
LVOW12s0136090817
544311LV00001B/143/P

9 781501 707629